CHILDREN AS 'RISK'

This book critically examines sociopolitical constructions of risk related to sexual offending behaviour by and among children and young people and charts the rise of harmful sexual or exploitative behaviour among peers, drawing on a range of theoretical frameworks and primary research. Discussion of these behaviours is exhibited against a backdrop of the premature cultural sexualisation of contemporary childhood, which challenges traditional conceptions of childhood, victimhood and gendered sexual identities more broadly.

The book examines the complexities of peer-based sexual behaviours in a range of settings, including within organisational contexts such as schools and care homes, within families and peer-based relationships, as well as online contexts, including sexting and cyberbullying.

It draws out the myriad legal, practical and policy challenges of negotiating the boundaries between normal/experimental, risky/problematic and harmful sexual behaviour, and in particular the demarcation between coercion and consent, for professionals as well as children and young people themselves.

ANNE-MARIE MCALINDEN is Professor of Law and Criminal Justice at Queen's University Belfast. She is an internationally recognised expert on sexual offending against children and the author/editor of more than 50 publications, including two previous sole-authored monographs, the first of which (*The Shaming of Sexual Offenders*) was awarded the British Society of Criminology Book Prize 2008. She has been Principal Investigator on a number of ESRC funded projects including a recently completed three-year study on 'Sex Offender Desistance'; and currently 'Apologies, Abuses and Dealing with the Past', where one of the case studies is institutional child abuse.

CAMBRIDGE STUDIES IN LAW AND SOCIETY

Founded in 1997, Cambridge Studies in Law and Society is a hub for leading scholarship in socio-legal studies. Located at the intersection of law, the humanities, and the social sciences, it publishes empirically innovative and theoretically sophisticated work on law's manifestations in everyday life: from discourses to practices, and from institutions to cultures. The series editors have longstanding expertise in the interdisciplinary study of law, and welcome contributions that place legal phenomena in national, comparative, or international perspective. Series authors come from a range of disciplines, including anthropology, history, law, literature, political science, and sociology.

A list of books in the series can be found at the back of this book.

CHILDREN AS 'RISK'

Sexual Exploitation and Abuse by Children and Young People

Anne-Marie McAlinden

Queen's University Belfast

CAMBRIDGE
UNIVERSITY PRESS

University Printing House, Cambridge CB2 8BS, United Kingdom

One Liberty Plaza, 20th Floor, New York, NY 10006, USA

477 Williamstown Road, Port Melbourne, VIC 3207, Australia

314–321, 3rd Floor, Plot 3, Splendor Forum, Jasola District Centre, New Delhi – 110025, India

79 Anson Road, #06–04/06, Singapore 079906

Cambridge University Press is part of the University of Cambridge.

It furthers the University's mission by disseminating knowledge in the pursuit of education, learning, and research at the highest international levels of excellence.

www.cambridge.org
Information on this title: www.cambridge.org/9781107144842
DOI: 10.1017/9781316534847

First published 2018

Printed and bound in Great Britain by Clays Ltd, Elcograf S.p.A.

A catalogue record for this publication is available from the British Library.

ISBN 978-1-107-14484-2 Hardback

CONTENTS

ACKNOWLEDGEMENTS

This book could not have been completed without the assistance and support of a number of people. I gratefully acknowledge the support of the National Organisation for the Treatment of Abusers (NOTA) and the award of a small research grant to allow me to complete the primary research. Thanks in particular are due to the professionals who gave so generously of their time and shared their invaluable knowledge and expertise with me during the interviews. Thanks also to my colleagues and friends at Queen's who offered support and encouragement as this book was being completed and in particular Professors Phil Scraton and Kieran McEvoy for providing constructive feedback on draft chapters. Finally, thanks above all to my family for their continued love and support: mum, dad, Trina, Stephen and Katie. To my parents-in-law, Mary and Brendan, for giving me peace of mind in working every day knowing that my children were being well cared for, and, above all, to my husband Stephen for keeping our home and family going in the final months of this book's completion. My greatest thanks are due to him and our two boys, Ben and Luke, for reminding me that there is a lot more to life.

PART I

THE THEORETICAL AND POLICY CONTEXT

1

CONCEPTUALISING CHILDREN AS 'RISK': AN INTRODUCTION

> This bill is part of a continuing fight against the *relentless predators* who target our children, the *most vulnerable members of our society*. I think that what people have to understand is . . . that *sexual offenders are different* . . . No matter what we do, the minute they get back on the street, many of them resume *their hunt for victims*, beginning *a restless and unrelenting prowl for children, innocent children to molest, abuse, and in the worst cases, to kill.*[1]

A key emergent issue for contemporary discourses on child protection and sex offender risk management is the commission of harmful sexual or exploitative behaviours by children and young people. While figures vary among studies, between one-quarter and one-half of all cases of child sexual abuse are committed by those under age 18 (Masson and Morrison, 1999; Taylor, 2003; Erooga and Masson, 2006; Vizard et al., 2007; Finkelhor et al., 2009; Barnardo's, 2011).[2] More recent studies demonstrate that the onset, prevalence and range of exploitative and abusive behaviours by children and young people among peers, particularly non-contact offences in the digital world, are areas of growing concern (Shariff, 2015).[3] In this respect, some of the most recent and contentious debates have

[1] Mr Schumer, US Congressional Record, Vol. 142, No. 6, Tuesday 7 May 1996, page H4453, cited in Lynch (2002: 554) [emphasis added].

[2] Other studies report higher percentages: see e.g. Radford et al. (2011), who found that 65.9 per cent of contact sexual abuse reported by children and young people is committed by those under age 18.

[3] See e.g. Finkelhor et al. (2000) who found that 48 per cent of online offenders in their study were under age 18.

centred on behaviours such as 'sexting'[4] and 'cyber bullying'.[5] These phenomena are also illustrative of what has been termed 'peer-to-peer grooming' (McAlinden, 2012a: 133–36, 182–84) and exploitative and abusive behaviours *by* and *among* as well as *of* young people. Despite the growing statistical prominence and significance of these behaviours, academic, official and public discourses have lagged someway behind.

Indeed, while peer-based sexual exploitation within age-appropriate relationships is among the fastest-growing forms of harm experienced by children (McAlinden, 2012a, 2014b), the complexity and nuances of such behaviour are insufficiently developed or understood in the relevant legal, sociological and criminological literature. Academic as well as professional understandings of sexually harmful or exploitative behaviours committed by children and young people are largely split between whether they represent innocent exploration and an experimental transitory phase and whether they are early indicators of the onset of something more prolonged and sinister (Craisatti et al., 2002; Taylor, 2003; Lussier and Davies, 2011; Van den Berg, Biljeveld and Hendriks, 2017).[6] The resulting social ambiguities surrounding what amounts to sexualised forms of risk to children also have implications for the formulation of policy and legal responses and the criminalisation of such behaviour.

Notwithstanding the recent prominence of terms such as 'sexting' or 'cyberbullying' in public consciousness, relatively little attention has been afforded to these issues at the public policy level. This is in large part due to the fact that they directly challenge traditional 'risk' paradigms and the culturally and institutionally entrenched notion that children and young people as sexual 'innocents' may be the victims but not the perpetrators of such offences (McAlinden, 2014b). Such puritanical conceptualisations of children and childhood are part of the broader process of social and cultural 'denial' (Cohen, 2001) concerning sexualised behaviour by children and young people and the deep-seated desire to avoid the rather uncomfortable reality that children may represent a source of harm to other children.

4 Findings from a range of studies have revealed rates of between 15 and 40 per cent among young people depending on age parameters and how sexting is defined and measured: see Ringrose et al. (2012) for an overview.

5 NSPCC figures, for example, show that 38 per cent of young people have been affected by cyberbullying (NSPCC, 2013).

6 There are few follow-up recidivism studies among children and young people displaying HSB, with most showing low reconviction rates for sexual crime of around 5–15 per cent: see e.g. Nisbet et al. (2004), Worling and Långström (2008).

The overall purpose of this book is to critically examine contemporary popular and state-led constructions of risk concerning children and young people who display harmful sexual or exploitative behaviour contextualised by an interdisciplinary perspective, drawing on the legal, sociolegal, criminological, sociological and psychological literature. Its four principal objectives are (i) to chart the emergence of the issue of sexual abuse or exploitation by children and young people as a distinct societal problem and critically examine why the notion of children as posing a 'risk' to others, as opposed to being 'at risk', has failed to capture the attention of legislators and policymakers; (ii) to highlight the nuances and complexities of harmful sexual or exploitative behaviours committed by children and young people, including new and emerging forms; (iii) to critically analyse social, legal and organisational responses to these behaviours and the related societal, policy and professional challenges they present; and (iv) to consider how we might reframe the current policy agenda to better capture the complexity of such risks and the evolving nature of contemporary childhood and adolescence.

As illustrated by the opening quotation, there is a range of socially constructed and entrenched assumptions concerning child sexual abuse or exploitation. These cultural constructs, which have also permeated policy, legal and organisational discourses, relate in particular to the respective identities of 'ideal' victims (Christie, 1986: 18) as pure and vulnerable and 'imagined offenders' (McAlinden, 2014b: 181) as 'predatory' and 'other' than us (Becker, 1963; Garland, 2001). This books unpacks and critically examines discourses on 'risk' related to harmful sexual or exploitative behaviour concerning children; challenges and confronts common misconceptions surrounding this behaviour within academic, official and public discourses; and highlights the highly complex processes of sexual exploitation and abuse by children and young people which occur in a range of contexts. The book also argues that because of the pragmatic difficulties of drawing clear boundaries between normative and harmful sexual behaviour between peers, current legal and policy frameworks are often limited in their response to peer-based sexual abuse and exploitation.

DEFINING TERMS

Given the ambiguities in popular discourse, it is important to define terms. A necessary starting point is what is meant by 'children and young people'. Although the age of majority by which children are legally regarded as adults is 18 throughout most of the United Kingdom, as it is within the European Union,[7] there are anomalies within the law in terms of how a child and the state of childhood are defined across a range of social activities and contexts. For example, age differentials vary widely from the age at which children are permitted to vote (16) or register to vote (16), drink (16)[8] or buy alcohol (18), drive a car (17), get married without parental consent (18), engage in consensual sexual activity (16),[9] be held criminally responsible (10)[10] or give unsworn evidence in court (14).[11] In particular, there is a fundamental disjuncture between the age of consent and the age of criminal responsibility and between legal and policy thresholds of victimhood (in itself based on the age of consent) across child sexual abuse (age 16) and indecent images of children (age 18). Viewed collectively, myriad ambiguities surround the precise legal demarcation of childhood/adulthood and the status of children as competent social actors. It will be argued that the relationship between sociocultural and legal constructions of children and childhood are circuitous and mutually reinforcing. That is, on the one hand, social constructions of childhood, and in particular a romanticised view of children, are reified by legal frameworks that, for the most part, are premised on the notions of children as victims rather than perpetrators. At the same time, such age-based legal definitions of victimhood, which may obfuscate contemporary social and cultural norms around sexual behaviour among children and young people, also have knock-on effects and potential deleterious consequences for identifying risk and protecting children.

Moreover, prescriptive age-based distinctions in assessment and intervention, which commonly distinguish between those under age 12 from those ages 12–18, can be determining factors in whether a child

[7] In Scotland, however, the age of majority is 16: see the Age of Legal Capacity (Scotland) Act 1991. See also the United Nations Convention on the Rights of the Child (1989), art 1, which defines a child in broad terms as 'every human being below the age of eighteen years unless under the law applicable to the child, majority is attained earlier'.

[8] Including wine, beer or cider, but excluding spirits.

[9] Note that children under age 16 may be given contraceptive advice or treatment by a healthcare professional if they are deemed *Gillick* 'competent': see *Gillick* v. *West Norfolk and Wisbech AHA* [1986] AC 112. See further Chapter 6.

[10] The age of criminal responsibility across the UK is one of the lowest in the world (where the median lies at 14): 10 in England and Wales and Northern Ireland, and 12 in Scotland where it was raised from the previous age of 8.

[11] See the Youth Justice and Criminal Evidence Act 1999, s 55(2) in the context of England and Wales, and its equivalent in Northern Ireland – the Criminal Evidence (NI) Order 1999, art 33(2).

displaying harmful sexual behaviour (HSB) enters the child protection or criminal justice system (Hackett, 2014; Ashurst, 2016). Indeed, much of the existing literature has tended to focus on adolescents rather than children with existing policy frameworks often lacking specific provision for preadolescent children in the age 10–12 bracket. For the purposes of this book, however, and while drawing out important age-based differences in behaviours, in tandem with the literature on HSB, the collective term 'children and young people' is adopted throughout reflecting the legal definition of 'child' – that is, those under age 18.

While a comprehensive discussion of the nature and extent of harmful sexual or exploitative behaviours by children and young people among peers is undertaken in Part II of the book, at this juncture it is also useful to broadly outline the nomenclature and scope of such behaviours. In relation to HSB, one much cited definition is that espoused by Palmer (1997: 11): 'Young people (under 18) who engage in any form of sexual activity with another individual, that they have powers over by virtue of age, emotional maturity, gender, physical strength, intellect and where the victim in this relationship has suffered a betrayal of trust.' This definition highlights the abuse and imbalance of power between the 'perpetrator' and the 'victim' which lies at the heart of peer forms of abuse. The broad term 'HSB', which focuses on the behaviour rather than the person, is widely accepted and adopted by contemporary policymakers and practitioners in preference to terms such as 'abuse' or 'abusive'; or 'offender' predicated terms such as 'abuser', 'perpetrator' or 'offending'.[12] This more neutral expression is assumed to help avoid the negative labelling and stigma associated with such terms, while also acknowledging the developmental context, stemming from biological or social influences, and the potential for change (see Calder, 2002; Hackett et al., 2006, 2014).[13] Indeed, this diverse term may include a range of behaviours encompassing both contact (such as touching, masturbation and penetration) and non-

[12] Earlier labels, for example, include 'children who molest' (Johnston, 1989), 'peer abusers' (Ambert, 1994), 'sexually aggressive children' (Burton et al., 1997), 'sexually abusive behaviour' (Skuse et al., 1998), 'young sexual abusers' (Masson and Morrison, 1999), 'children and young people who sexually abuse' (Erooga and Masson, 2006), 'juvenile sexual offenders' (Barbaree and Marshall, 2008; van den Berg et al., 2017), which are variously used to describe children and young people displaying HSB.

[13] A minority of scholars and practitioners use the alternative 'sexually harmful behaviour' (SHB) (see e.g. Griffin and Beech, 2004; McCrory et al., 2008; Potter and Reeves, 2015). This term, however, is generally set aside as being much narrower in focus, as it confines 'harm' to being of a sexual nature and the range of those affected by the behaviour to the immediate victim (see further Chapter 6).

contact behaviours (such as grooming, exhibitionism, voyeurism, and sexting or recording images of sexual acts via smart phones) (Ashurst, 2016).

'Peer-on-peer' abuse is an umbrella term that potentially captures a broad range of abusive behaviours. Research by Firmin and others (Firmin, 2013; Firmin and Curtis, 2015) has classified these into four main categories: (i) *abuse*, including sexual abuse, and control within intimate relationships; (ii) sexual abuse or exploitation within the context of exploitative *relationships or contexts*; (iii) sexual behaviour outside of the normative *parameters of development* (see e.g. Hackett, 2010); and (iv) within the context of serious violent *offences* (such as rape or assault). The majority of cases are not processed through the criminal justice system. However, since it is not possible to predict which children and young people displaying inappropriate or problematic sexual behaviours will develop into those who cause harm, it is important to identify and respond to inappropriate sexual behaviour at an early stage. In this vein, distilling this list further, the analysis in Part II of the book will situate peer-to-peer sexualised behaviours along a continuum of normal, problematic and harmful sexual behaviours by developing a typology of *harmful* sexual behaviour broadly premised on *peer-based relationships*, *peer-based recruitment* and *peer-based risk*.

The term 'sexting' is a portmanteau of 'sex' and 'texting' and is generally used to describe the act of sending or posting sexually suggestive or explicit messages and/or photographs via mobile phones or social networking sites (Ringrose et al., 2012: 9; Lee and Crofts, 2015: 454). As Lee and Crofts (2015: 454) note, citing the Law Reform Committee of Victoria (2013: 15), the term 'encompasses a wide range of practices, motivations and behaviours', from the sharing of images between a girlfriend and boyfriend, to the sharing of that image with someone else, to the recording of a sexual assault and even to the sending of an explicit image or text by an adult to a child for the purposes of sexual grooming. The police and courts distinguish between different levels of 'child pornography'[14] (Tate, 1990; Lanning, 1992; Taylor et al., 2001; O'Donnell and Milner, 2007) or 'indecent images of

[14] In the late 1990s, the COPINE scale was developed as an acronym from the project of the same name ('Combating Paedophile Information Networks in Europe') distinguishing 10 levels ranging from nudist or erotic images to those depicting sexually explicit activity and assault (Quayle, 2008). Subsequently, the Court of Appeal in *R* v. *Oliver, Hartrey and Baldwin* (2002) EWCA Crim 2766 further refined this classification of indecent images of children into five categories and produced sentencing guidelines based on these categories, ranging from images of erotic posing to penetrative sexual activity and sadism.

children' as the now often preferred term (Taylor and Quayle, 2003; Gillespie, 2005). The focus of this book is primarily on children sharing naked, often 'posed' erotic or suggestive images of themselves among peers, rather than sexually explicit activity, on both a consensual and non-consensual basis. Since not all indecent images of children are necessarily illegal (Taylor et al., 2001; Gillespie, 2010), it is argued that indecent images shared among children and young people may prove difficult for law enforcement to classify in terms of where victimisation is thought to crystallise. Cyberbullying, broadly defined, is the use of the Internet and other mobile technologies to harass, threaten or harm other people, usually in a deliberate and sustained manner (Kofoed and Ringrose, 2011). Although cyberbullying always has a harmful but not necessarily a sexual element, this book is concerned with sexualised forms of cyberbullying such as sexting.[15]

'Peer-to-peer grooming' – a term rarely featured in the existing literature – is an extension of the broader concept of 'grooming'. The latter has been used to describe the preparatory actions whereby the offender sets up opportunities to abuse by gaining the trust of the child or others to both facilitate abuse and subsequently prevent disclosure (Salter, 1995, 2003; McAlinden, 2006, 2012a). This study takes as its starting point, the definition employed previously in my earlier broader study on adult-child grooming:

> (1) the use of a variety of manipulative and controlling techniques (2) with a vulnerable subject (3) in a range of inter-personal and social settings (4) in order to establish trust or normalise sexually harmful behaviour (5) with the overall aim of facilitating exploitation and/or prohibiting exposure. (McAlinden, 2012a: 11)

In this vein, the analysis also sets out to explore whether the dynamics of victim selection and vulnerability and the processes of normalisation of HSB may be intrinsically different among peers; whether grooming can also be used to describe the actions of children in establishing trust with another child or young person to facilitate harmful sexual or

[15] Cyberbullying also includes a number of other behaviours such as 'flaming' (verbal exchanges between individuals such as in chat rooms), 'denigration' (spreading information that is untrue or derogatory), 'masquerading' (creating fake profiles or pretending to be someone else), 'outing and trickery' (sharing personal or embarrassing information about another individual with others), 'happy slapping' (the video recording and uploading of assaults) as well as online 'harassment' or stalking ('cyberstalking') or 'exclusion' from online groups or exchanges (see Kowalski et al., 2012: Ch. 3; Pyżalski, 2012).

exploitative behaviour either by themselves or others; or whether altogether different motivations and processes might apply.

Although there is some overlap in the scope of these behaviours, for example, sexting may be a form of cyber or online bullying between peers, important distinctions also emerge. Sexting and sexualised cyberbullying are focused on children's behaviour in the digital or virtual world, whereas peer-to-peer grooming can take place in both online as well as offline settings. Whereas the online context more often involves peers, the offline setting might also involve an older child grooming a younger sibling as a precursor to intra-familial abuse as well as extrafamilial abuse (e.g. Kaufman et al., 1996; Leclerc et al., 2008). Moreover, as noted earlier, while sexting may involve sending sexually explicit text as well as indecent images or videos, it is confined more typically to posed images rather than those relating to explicit sexual activity. Consequently, the book adopts a broad definition of 'child sexual abuse and exploitation' or 'harmful sexual or exploitative behaviour' in tandem with growing professional and academic recognition of emerging wider forms of sexualised harms to children beyond child sexual abuse (Chase and Statham, 2005; Pearce, 2009, 2013a; Melrose and Pearce, 2013; Firmin and Beckett, 2014).[16] That is, while HSB is more commonly associated with perpetrators and child sexual exploitation (CSE) with victims, the behaviours of children and young people may be part of a continuum which encompasses both categories (see Chapter 6).

As discussed further, there are complex challenges, both methodological and cultural, in accurately defining contemporary forms of child sexual exploitation and abuse (see generally Wyatt and Peters, 1986; Haugaard, 2000; Corby et al., 2012: Ch. 4). Such terms also vary across different research studies and policy and organisational contexts. As Melrose (2013: 166) contends, 'the vagueness of the term "sexual exploitation" and the different practices that might be deemed to constitute it add to this complexity.' Although the broader term of 'child sexual abuse' is often understood to involve forcing or enticing a child to take part in sexual activities (Sgori et al., 1982: 9; Finkelhor, 1991: 80; Alao and Molojwane, 2008: 10),[17] children may also be

[16] See also K Starmer QC (then director of public prosecutions), 'The Criminal Justice Response to Child Sexual Abuse: Time for a National Consensus', 6 March 2013, www.cps.gov.uk/news/articles/the_criminal_justice_response_to_child_sexual_abuse_-_time_for_a_national_consensus/.

[17] See also NSPCC: www.nspcc.org.uk/preventing-abuse/child-abuse-and-neglect/child-sexual-abuse/.

sexually exploited for a broader range of reasons other than sexual gratification including money, power or status. In relation to 'peer exploitation', Caroline Firmin (2013: 50), for example, has presented a useful definition which conveys the potentially wide-ranging scope of motivations and behavioural contexts: 'physical, sexual, emotional and financial abuse, and coercive control, exercised within young people's relationships, and influenced by power and gendered hierarchies within and external to their relationships'. Several participants in the study expressed concern that labels such as 'child pornography' and 'child sexual exploitation', which are enshrined in law and policy, are not entirely helpful as they tend to mask the complexities and dilute the very real harm that underlies the terminology, particularly where children and young people are concerned.

Indeed, recognised dangers are associated with such shorthand, pejorative terms, such as 'grooming' (Gallagher, 2000; Fernandez, 2006), 'sexting' and 'risky children', which tend to promote stereotypical and one-dimensional views of the problem, contributing to the 'moral panic' (Cohen, 1972) surrounding sexual offending against children and obscuring the complexities of such risks. Having acknowledged these limitations, however, such difficulties should not preclude critical academic discourse on these behaviours. For the purposes of this study, therefore, and to retain the integrity of the respective terms, they are used throughout the text, initially as they appear in the existing literature and subsequently as they emerge and become defined through the empirical research.

PUBLIC AND OFFICIAL DISCOURSES ON SEXUAL OFFENDING CONCERNING CHILDREN

Throughout the past few decades, the risk assessment and management of sexual offenders against children have become the structuring principle of regulatory discourses on sexual crime spawning a burgeoning amount of legislation and related policy frameworks (Parton et al., 1997; Kemshall and Maguire, 2001; McAlinden, 2006, 2010). Sexual offending encompasses a broad spectrum of offending behaviour, including contact and non-contact offences committed predominantly by men, but also by women[18] (Ashfield et al., 2010; Gannon and

[18] The number of female sexual offenders remains low, typically around 5–10 per cent (Cortoni and Hanson, 2005; Vandiver et al., 2008; Ashfield et al., 2010; Elliott et al., 2010).

Cortoni, 2010) and children and young people[19] (Erooga and Masson, 2006; Hackett et al., 2013). Contemporary public and official discourses, however, have tended to be narrowly framed within the context of a number of dominant interrelated risk paradigms within which children are characterised as the victims rather than the perpetrators of HSB.

One is the overarching notion of the 'predatory stranger' (Cowburn and Dominelli, 2001) which lies at the top of the offending hierarchy and is deemed to epitomise the ultimate risk to children. The others are related to 'institutional child abuse' committed by adults in a position of trust (Gallagher, 1998; McAlinden, 2006), 'online grooming' and abuse committed by strangers (Gillespie, 2001; McAlinden, 2012a) and child sexual exploitation and 'localised grooming' (Beckett, 2011; Ost and Mooney, 2013). One of the central arguments of this book, however, is that the cyclical nature of the social and political focus on adult perpetrators, and in particular 'predatory paedophiles', as the predominant source of potential risks to children has been largely reactive in nature. As a result, contemporary discourses on risk have tended to obscure broader offending patterns related to HSB concerning children, including potential offending behaviour committed by children and young people themselves.

In relation to the first of these paradigms, sexualised risks to children have been framed in terms of the 'predatory sex offender' whereby children and young people are deemed to be at the greatest risk of victimisation from 'the anonymous stranger' (Williams and Hudson, 2013: 221; see also Soothill and Walby, 1991; Greer, 2007; McCartan, 2010), rather than representing a risk themselves. As noted earlier, the notion of children posing a risk to others also conflicts with deep-seated cultural notions concerning the innocence and passivity of children[20] and the need to protect them at all costs (McAlinden, 2014b). Within the United Kingdom, such perceptions have been constructed and reconstructed within the popular imagination via media coverage of high-profile cases of the abduction and murder of young children, primarily young girls, by known sex offenders, including those of Sarah Payne,[21] Milly

[19] See notes 2–4 and accompanying text.

[20] See the similar arguments made in relation to the 'culture of denial' and minimisation concerning sexual offending by females: Hetherton (1999); Denov (2004).

[21] Eight-year-old Sarah Payne was abducted and murdered in Sussex in July 2000 by known paedophile Roy Whiting. The case led to the former '*News of the World*' newspaper's campaign

Dowler[22] and Holly Wells and Jessica Chapman (Kitzinger, 2004; Jewkes, 2010; Thakker, 2012).[23] Such socially constructed versions of sexualised forms of risks to children, which privilege sexual offending by adult males against young children who were previously unknown to them over other forms of sexual offending, have also become institutionalised within policy and legal frameworks. For example, a range of legislative and organisational measures have been put in place in the United Kingdom and elsewhere to manage the risk posed by released sex offenders in the community, including most notably, sex offender notification (Shute, 2004; McAlinden, 2006) and Multi-Agency Public Protection Arrangements (MAPPA) (Kemshall and Maguire, 2001; Lieb, 2003). Moreover, a spate of recent high-profile cases stemming from Operation Yewtree,[24] concerning Jimmy Savile and a host of other celebrities, has also tended to reinforce the predatory nature of sex offending concerning children and related social constructions of 'blame' and 'blamelessness' surrounding those deemed worthy of legitimate victim and offender status.

In relation to the second offending paradigm, over the past two decades, high-profile cases of institutional child abuse have emerged in a number of jurisdictions, including the United States (John Jay College, 2004, 2011), Canada (Law Commission of Canada, 2000), Australia (Family and Community Development Committee Victoria, 2013), the Netherlands (Commission of Inquiry, 2011), England and

for a 'Sarah's Law', calling for the authorities to identify the names and whereabouts of known sex offenders (see Ashenden, 2002; Silverman and Wilson, 2002). A Child Protection Disclosure Scheme was introduced throughout the UK, following a successful pilot scheme (Kemshall et al., 2012), allowing parents or carers to check the criminal histories of those with unsupervised access to their children.

22 Thirteen-year-old Milly Dowler was abducted and murdered by Levi Belfield on her way home from school in Surrey in March 2002.

23 Ten-year-old schoolgirls Holly Wells and Jessica Chapman were murdered in Soham in August 2002 by school care taker Ian Huntley who was previously known to the police for a string of allegations of sexual offences against women and young girls. The case led to the Bichard (2004) Inquiry and reform of the law on pre-employment vetting and barring via the Safeguarding Vulnerable Groups Act 2006, as amended by the Protection of Freedoms Act 2012, Part V (see McAlinden, 2010). See also the Safeguarding Vulnerable Groups (NI) Order 2007.

24 The Metropolitan Police Service established Operation Yewtree in October 2012 to investigate widespread allegations of sexual abuse by the late British media personality Jimmy Savile. The initial report of the investigation into Savile was published as *Giving Victims a Voice* (Gray and Watt, 2013). Yewtree was extended against a number of other high-profile British celebrities resulting in the prosecution and convictions of Stuart Hall, Max Clifford, Rolf Harris and Gary Glitter.

Wales (Warner, 1992; Utting, 1997, Waterhouse, 2000)[25] and the Republic of Ireland (Murphy et al., 2005; Commission to Inquire into Child Abuse, 2009; Commission of Investigation, 2009, 2011).[26] These cases of institutional abuse (encompassing physical, emotional and sexual abuse and neglect) have stemmed from a wide variety of child-care contexts in both secular and religious settings including care homes, nurseries and schools (Reder et al., 1993; Corby et al., 2001; Parton, 2004). The key recommendations emerging from these inquiries have led to changes in the legal and policy frameworks on pre-employment vetting and barring designed to stop would-be predatory 'professional perpetrators' (Sullivan and Beech, 2002) from obtaining access to children and the vulnerable through organisations (McAlinden, 2010). However, in underscoring the potential abuse of trust and power by an adult perpetrator within institutionalised contexts, these discourses also tend to obscure the risks of grooming and abuse between peers and the complexity of the victim-offender relationship within organisational settings. For example, some official inquiries into institutional child abuse establish that peers as well as adults abused victims, where abuse became part of the organisational culture (Shaw, 2007: 31–32; Commission to Inquire into Child Abuse, 2009: Vol. 3, para 9.57; McAlinden, 2012a: 182). As discussed further in Chapter 6, the range of sexual offending concerning children and young people in institutional contexts may involve children as offenders, as well as victims, as 'insiders' or parties to the abuse.

In relation to the third paradigm, 'digital risks' related to Internet grooming and abuse by predatory sex offenders (Gallagher et al., 2003, 2006; McAlinden, 2012a) are one of the most publicly prominent risks to children (Davidson and Gottschalk, 2011; Martellozzo,

[25] More than 75 inquiries or reviews have been conducted or are ongoing into allegations of institutional child sexual abuse concerning the late Jimmy Savile and others stemming from Operation Yewtree. The principal Savile inquiries or investigations relate to those concerning the BBC (Smith, 2016), Broadmoor Special Hospital (Kirkup and Marshall, 2014), Stoke Mandeville Hospital (Johnstone and Dent, 2015; Vize and Klinck, 2015), the Leeds Teaching Hospitals (Leeds General Infirmary, St James's Hospital, Chapel Allerton Hospital, Seacroft Hospital) (Proctor et al., 2014) and Duncroft School (Savell, 2013, 2015), nearly all of which were convened posthumously. For a critical overview, see Erooga (2017). The Independent Inquiry into Child Sexual Abuse, with an overarching remit to examine the failure of state and non-state organisations to protect children from abuse and exploitation, published its interim report in April 2018 (Jay et al., 2018).

[26] During the period of fieldwork, two such inquiries were ongoing in Northern Ireland and Australia: the *Inquiry into Historical Institutional Abuse* in Northern Ireland reported in January 2017 (Hart et al., 2017). The *Royal Commission into Institutional Responses to Child Sexual Abuse* in Australia reported in December 2017. For a critical comparative overview, see McAlinden and Naylor (2016).

2012; Staksrud, 2013; Shariff, 2015). Such harms have been framed predominantly in relation to child pornography or child abuse images (e.g. Taylor and Quayle, 2003; Akdeniz, 2008; Quayle and Ribsil, 2012) as well as sexual grooming (e.g. Ost, 2009; McAlinden, 2012a). Legislation to cover online grooming, for example, has been enacted in several jurisdictions, including the United States, Canada, Australia, New Zealand, Singapore, Norway, Sweden, the Netherlands and throughout the United Kingdom.[27] These offences are also related to the stereotypical offending paradigm whereby an adult offender grooms an unsuspecting much younger victim with a view to sexual offending either online or in a prearranged offline, face-to-face meeting. Moreover, a number of international policing bodies have been established, such as the Child Exploitation and On-line Protection Centre (CEOP) and the related Virtual Global Task Force (VGT) to combat sexual offending via the Internet (Gillespie, 2008). Such policy initiatives, however, also tend to reinforce the stranger danger paradigm, impeding consideration of a broader range of virtual risks to children and young people, including those posed by peers in virtual settings. As Ringrose et al. (2012: 7) have demonstrated, for example, within the context of sexting, 'the primary technology related threat' for young people is not the dangerous stranger, as propagated by the mass media, but 'technology-mediated sexual pressure from their peers'.

The fourth offending paradigm stems from cases that have variously been termed 'street', 'on street grooming' (McAlinden, 2012a), 'localised' (CEOP, 2011: 5) or, more recently, 'group localised grooming' (Ost and Mooney, 2013) within the context of inquiries into CSE (Berelowitz, 2012, 2013, 2015). Recent high-profile cases including those in Derby (Galley, 2010),[28] Rochdale

[27] For a jurisdictional overview, see McAlinden (2012a: 5–7). In England and Wales, for example, s 15 of the Sexual Offences Act 2003 (as amended by s 36(1) of the Criminal Justice and Courts Act 2015) captures the offence of 'meeting a child following sexual grooming'. See also the equivalent offence in Northern Ireland: Sexual Offences (NI) Order 2008, art 22 (as amended). This model has also been broadly replicated in the legislative frameworks throughout the United Kingdom and in New Zealand and Singapore.

[28] See 'Derby Sex Gang Convicted of Grooming and Abusing Girls', *BBC News*, 24 November 2010, www.bbc.co.uk/news/uk-england-derbyshire-11799797. Of 13 men charged in relation to Operation Retriever, 9 were convicted of offences ranging from rape and sexual activity with a child to false imprisonment. See sentencing case note for the two 'ring leaders', Abid Mohammed Saddique and Mohammed Romaan Liaqat, sentenced at Nottingham Crown Court on 7 January 2011, www.thelawpages.com/court-cases/court-case-search.php?action=search&mode=1.

(RBSCB, 2012, 2013a, 2013b),[29] Oxford (OSCB, 2015)[30] and Rotherham (Jay, 2014; Casey, 2015)[31] have involved multiple perpetrators working in groups grooming primarily female adolescents into a range of sexually exploitative situations from organised/networked exploitation to prostitution or 'internal' or 'domestic trafficking' (Chase and Satham, 2005; Barnardo's, 2009: 16, 2011: 6). Such cases also tend to promulgate over simplified versions of victimhood and offending identities and mask the highly complex relationships between victims and offenders. Beckett (2011) and others (Montgomery-Devlin, 2008; Barnardo's, 2011) have described 'the boyfriend model' of sexual exploitation resulting from the girl's initial perception of the relationship as one freely entered into. As a result, girls may not perceive themselves as victims and consequently may not be considered as such by others (CEOP, 2011: 88; Jago et al., 2011: 50; Ost and Mooney, 2013: 438). Moreover, young people are also used to recruit or groom other children and young people into exploitative situations (Montgomery-Devlin, 2008: 393; CEOP, 2011: 87). In becoming complicit in their own grooming and victimisation and that of others, the young person is both a victim and a potential perpetrator of CSE. However, these 'nonideal' (Ost and Mooney, 2013) or 'compliant victims' (Lanning, 2005) who are not 'completely innocent' (Von Hentig 1948; Mendelsohn, 1956) or without blame have tended to pose unique challenges for law enforcement chiefly in terms of victim credibility (Pearce, 2009; McAlinden, 2012a: 213–21). As such,

[29] See 'Rochdale Grooming: "Shocking" Failure over Sex Abuse', *BBC News*, 20 December 2013, www.bbc.co.uk/news/uk-england-manchester-25450512. Nine men were sentenced in May 2012 as part of Operation Doublet for a range of sexual offences against young girls, including trafficking and conspiracy to engage in sexual activity with a child. See sentencing remarks of His Honour Judge Gerald Clifton, *R* v. *Hassan and Others* (unreported), Liverpool Crown Court, 9 May 2012, www.judiciary.gov.uk/judgments/hassan-others-sentencing-remarks-11052012/.

[30] See 'Oxfordshire Grooming Victims May Have Totalled 373 Children', *BBC News*, 3 March 2015, www.bbc.co.uk/news/uk-england-oxfordshire-31643791. Following investigations as part of Operation Bullfinch, two pairs of brothers were among seven men convicted at the Old Bailey in June 2013 of a range of offences including rape, trafficking and arranging the prostitution of young girls. See sentencing remarks of Judge Peter Rook QC, *R* v. *Akhtar Dogar, Anjum Dogar, Kamar Jamil, Mohammed Karrar, Bassam Karrar*, 27 June 2013, www.judiciary.gov.uk/judgments/dogar-and-others-sentencing-remarks/.

[31] Following Operation Central, five men from the Asian community in Rotherham were jailed in November 2010 for a range of sexual offences against underage girls. The case prompted a high-profile independent inquiry into the handling of allegations by the local authorities (Jay, 2014). See 'Rotherham Child Abuse: The Background to the Scandal', *BBC News*, 5 February 2015, www.bbc.co.uk/news/uk-england-south-yorkshire-28934963.

they have tended to be overlooked and located low down on interventionist hierarchies of risk and victimhood.

Indeed, a highly moralised public and official discourse concerning victim blaming often emerges in relation to the guiltiest (Von Hentig, 1948; Mendelsohn, 1956) of child victims who do not fit the model of the ideal victim of child sexual abuse or exploitation.[32] Such cases distort well-established hierarchies of victimhood and offending identities, blur the traditional victim-offender divide and the related tension between victim agency/responsibility and coercion (see generally Hoyle et al., 2011). The book aims to confront tensions evident in societal, policy and legal conceptualisations of and responses to risk concerning children and child sexual abuse or exploitation. In challenging contemporary social, policy and legal constructions of such risks, the book also underlines the need to reframe the regulatory agenda on risk, taking account of the capacity and decision-making ability of children as well as their inherent vulnerability (see Chapter 8).

FRAMING THE DEBATES

In recent years, sexual offending against children has dominated 'punishment rhetoric' and penal practice (Simon, 1998; Lynch, 2002; Hebenton and Seddon, 2009; McAlinden, 2012b) and generated considerable academic literature (see e.g. Matravers, 2003; McAlinden, 2007a; Boer et al., 2011; Harrison and Rainey, 2013). In common with contemporary public and official discourses, the majority of recent scholarship on child sexual abuse and exploitation has focused on the broad spectrum of issues involving online forms of sexual offending against children by adult perpetrators (e.g. Sheldon and Howitt, 2007; Livingstone, 2009; Davidson and Gottschalk, 2010, 2011; Martellozzo, 2012; Staksrud, 2013) including child pornography (O'Donnell and Milner, 2007; Akdeniz, 2008) and sexual grooming (Quayle et al., 2008; Ost, 2009; McAlinden, 2012a; Quayle and Ribsil, 2012). Other texts on offline forms of child sexual abuse and exploitation have also focused on children and young people as victims rather than perpetrators (Pearce, 2009; McAlinden, 2012a; Finkelhor, 2014).

[32] See e.g. *R* v. *Neil Wilson* [2013] EWCA Crim 2544 at 12 and 15, where both the prosecutor and the Crown Court judge described a 13-year-old victim of sexual offending as 'predatory' as she had previous sexual experience.

There is a relatively small literature on HSB by children and young people concentrated among a core group of scholars. This has tended to focus on key themes including the behavioural aspects of adolescent sex offenders (e.g. Kaufman et al., 1996; Leclerc et al., 2008; Hackett et al., 2013; Masson et al., 2015); offending trajectories (Craisatti et al., 2002; Lussier and Davis, 2011; Van den Berg et al., 2017); and family, community and organisational responses to this particular offender group (Erooga and Mason, 2006; Hackett and Taylor, 2008; Hackett et al., 2014; Hackett et al., 2015). Against this broader research context, other studies have focused specifically on cyberbullying in an international context (Li et al., 2012; Smith and Steffgen, 2013), while others are written from a broad psychological perspective as practical guides to educate parents and organisations about identifying and responding to the risks of cyberbullying (e.g. Kowalski et al., 2012; Patchin and Hinduja, 2012). As noted earlier, some broadly quantitative studies on cyberbullying and sexting have demonstrated the growing incidence and prevalence of these phenomena, based on survey work or focus groups with children or young people (Kofoed and Ringrose, 2012; Ringrose et al., 2012; Shariff, 2015). To date, however, there is little qualitative research on the broader range of risks of child sexual exploitation and abuse stemming from children and young people. The primary research underpinning this text seeks to address this deficit within the literature by exploring the construction and complexities of such risks from an institutional perspective.

Indeed, no empirical data currently examines all aspects of sexual exploitation and abuse involving children and young people (including in both offline and face-to-face contexts). A central argument of this book is that dominant contemporary discourses on sexual offending – particularly the restricted focus on the sexual abuse or exploitation of children by strangers – have obfuscated or displaced other important dimensions of child sexual abuse and exploitation, including risks stemming from children and young people themselves. What follows presents a more nuanced, multidimensional understanding of harmful sexual or exploitative behaviours by children including both contact and non-contact forms that occur in a range of intra-familial and extrafamilial contexts, such as within families and between peers. While there is limited existing research on peer-to-peer grooming (e.g. McAlinden, 2012a: 133–36, 182–84), the book will also explore this process in some detail as the means by which such behaviours may occur. In examining a wider and more nuanced spectrum of sexualised forms of risk and harm concerning children and young people, alongside the range of social, policy, legislative and organisational responses, the research findings are intended to broaden contemporary discourses related to sexual offending against children, better capturing the complexity of this important societal problem.

A BRIEF NOTE ON THE PRIMARY RESEARCH

Within this study, theoretical and policy arguments on risk concerning sexual exploitation and abuse by children and young people are informed and illustrated by original primary data derived from interviews with professionals across Northern Ireland who work with children and young people displaying harmful sexual or exploitative behaviours. This material informs the discussion in Part II of the book in particular. Other jurisdictions, such as England and Wales, Scotland, the United States, Canada and Australia are considered for comparison and illustration. In particular, comparisons are made with regard to cultural and legal responses to criminalising children as well as policy responses to HSB.

In total, 32 in-depth confidential and anonymous semi-structured interviews were conducted throughout Northern Ireland, predominantly in but not limited to Belfast (February–November 2016.) The sample size was determined by the principle of 'saturation' (Glaser and Straus, 1967) – when the collection of further data will not lead to any 'new' information related to the core themes of the study. The range of participants included professionals from a diverse selection of agencies and professions across the criminal justice and voluntary sectors, such as the police, social services, youth justice, the judiciary, the Public Prosecution Service, the Education Authority, Child and Adolescent Mental Health Services (CAMHS), paediatricians and general practitioners, sexual health and public health nurses, forensic and clinical psychologists, children's charities and victim support organisations. Such a diverse range of professional voices was necessary to ascertain the views of the multiple stakeholders who are integral to the assessment, management and treatment and support of children and young people displaying or affected by HSB. It was also considered appropriate to understand the complexities surrounding these behaviours and to examine, at the level of praxis, where the threshold of risk is deemed to lie. Further details of the methodology, including the sampling and interview procedures, are provided in the Appendix.

RECURRENT THEMES

The book considers the principal themes and debates concerning popular and state-led responses to child sexual exploitation and abuse in general as well as harmful sexual or exploitative behaviours committed by children and young people. The conceptual framework draws upon a range of distinct literatures including the sociology of childhood, media discourses and moral panic theory, sociological and technocratic discourses on risk, victim-offender hierarchies and victim blaming, and the gender-centric debates concerning the impact of 'new media' involving interactive digital technology on popular and youth culture. These respective literatures are critically examined across a diverse range of behavioural contexts, including harmful sexual or exploitative behaviour among peers within familial, institutional (schools and residential care homes), online (sexting/cyberbullying) and public/street-based settings (gangs/party culture). A number of specific cross-cutting themes extend throughout the book.

Against the backdrop of wider social discourses on risk (Giddens, 1990; Beck, 1992) and public panics about the perilous state of contemporary childhood (Scott et al., 1998; Palmer, 2007), the book locates debates about sexual offending related to children within the context of evolving technocratic and managerialist concerns in the area of crime and justice such as risk (Ericson and Haggerty, 1997; Parton et al., 1997; O'Malley, 2010) and pre-emptive regulation (Braithwaite, 2000; Zedner, 2009). As part of the 'new penology' (Feeley and Simon, 1992, 1994), the assessment and management of dangerous violent and sexual offenders have become a core concern, particularly within the context of post-release control (Kemshall and Maguire, 2001; McAlinden, 2007a). From at least the late 1990s, a plethora of risk-averse policies has attempted to apply the logic of precaution (O'Malley, 2004a; Ericson, 2007) and respond pre-emptively (Zedner, 2009) to all potential risks posed by sex offenders (Hebenton and Seddon, 2009; McAlinden, 2010). Within such situational approaches to sex offender risk management, centred on the adult male offending paradigm, children and young people are deemed to be 'at risk' of victimisation rather than constituting a risk themselves. This also helps to explain the fewer specialised treatment programmes and facilities for young sexual abusers, despite the fact that children and young people account for a growing proportion of those who sexually offend against children. Throughout the analysis, the centrality of risk to current regulatory approaches to child sexual abuse and exploitation is also juxtaposed with rights-based discourses which recognise the potential agency of children and their competence as decision-makers (see e.g. Mason and Urquhart, 2001; Lundy and McEvoy, 2012). Therein, it is argued that a delicate balance needs to be struck between the freedom and protection of children and young people, particularly within the context of sexting and their use and ownership of mobile devices and the online environment.

The book also examines the role of the media in creating myths and misconceptions about sexual crime and the consequences of this for discourses on risk and child protection. Through sustained coverage of high-profile cases, the media have helped shape the history of public and political concerns relating to sex offending against children and young people (Sampson, 1994; Silverman and Wilson, 2002; Greer, 2003). This has ranged from the dominance of the stranger danger paradigm and the risk posed by predatory paedophiles in the community through to the emergence of online forms of such risks. In particular, the concept of sex offenders as 'predatory paedophiles' and 'monsters' and the related notions of the child as 'angel' or 'innocent' (Wardle, 2007; McAlinden, 2014b) have become the primary definers of accepted societal understanding of victimhood and vulnerability related to sexual offending. This public and political desire to safeguard children from the risks posed by predatory strangers is juxtaposed with the emergence of a highly sexualised popular culture, often related to new media, promoting subliminal messages and gendered accounts of 'normal' sexual behaviour among peers. This book highlights how these tensions underlying social and cultural constructions of 'at risk' children and 'risk anxiety' (Scott et al., 1998: 689) related to childhood and adolescence have become deeply embedded within social discourses and regulatory frameworks concerning sex offending against children. In highlighting new and emerging forms of harmful sexual or exploitative behaviour by children and young people, it argues that there is a fundamental disconnect between the culturally *constructed* identities of children as victims and the *actual* identities of offenders and lived experiences of victims within the context of harmful sexual or exploitative behaviour.

Indeed, a further related theme encompasses the nuanced tension between assumed victim and offender status concerning child sexual abuse and exploitation and cultural and professional understandings of childhood more broadly. Oppositional discourses on 'innocence' and 'blame' have informed respective cultural hierarchies of victimhood and offending concerning legitimate or ideal victim and offender status (see generally Christie, 1986; Rock, 1998; Walklate, 2007; McEvoy and McConnnachie, 2012). Children, by virtue of their age and inherent innocence and vulnerability, are often portrayed as the ultimate victim, lacking in sexual agency. Harmful sexual behaviour by children and young people, however, blurs the traditional victim-offender dichotomy and inverts long-standing hierarchies of victimhood and offending behaviour (McAlinden, 2014a). Furthermore, there is a related cultural confusion and ambiguity concerning childhood (Jewkes, 2010: 5) stemming from the cultural premature and 'hyper sexualisation' (Egan and Hawkes, 2012: 298; see also McRobbie, 2004; Coy, 2009; Coy and Garner, 2012) of contemporary childhood. In many new or emerging forms of HSB by children and young people presented in this book, such as within the context of peer-to-peer grooming, sexting and child sexual exploitation, children and young people who have broken 'the taboos of childhood' (Brownlie, 2001: 526) lie in the middle ground between the polarities of accepted victim and offender status. The research examines the institutionalisation of such binary identities concerning those deemed worthy of the label victim or offender and the unique challenges for police and legal professionals in terms of the credibility of children and young people as both offenders as well as victims.

Such dyadic constructions of victim and offending identities are also reflected in and sustained by broader dyadic gender-based cultural stereotypes which link femininity with victimhood and masculinity with aggressive or offending behaviour (Mottier, 2008: 9; Oakley, 2015: 77). Against this broader backdrop, the book also explores the impact of binary heteronormative gendered assumptions (see Chase and Statham, 2005; Pearce, 2009; Hoyle et al., 2011; Melrose, 2013; Cree et al., 2014) on the willingness of children and young people to self-identify as a victim concerning peer-to-peer forms of abuse. That is, those who do not fit neatly within accepted victim categorisations, based principally on age or traditional gender and heterosexual identities, may be reluctant to seek protection. In highlighting how victims and perpetrators of child sexual abuse and exploitation are often represented as a false dichotomy, the analysis makes the case for overcoming these artificial and monochromatic distinctions about perceived risk, deeply embedded in the notions of childhood, agency, gender and vulnerability to develop more effective responses to harmful sexual or exploitative behaviour concerning children and young people.

STRUCTURE OF THE BOOK

The book is divided into three parts, the first of which provides the theoretical and policy context. Chapter 2 elaborates more fully on themes raised within this introductory chapter. It charts the evolution of the issue of sexual abuse or exploitation concerning children and young people as a societal problem. In examining the cyclical nature of moral panics (Cohen, 1972) related to sexual offending against children, it argues that the repetitious emphasis on a number of core themes helps to explain why the notion of children as posing a risk to others had failed to capture the attention of legislators and policymakers until relatively recently. These relate principally to the 'othering' of sex offending and the ostensibly public nature of the sexual victimisation of children by adult stranger perpetrators. This narrow cultural construction of harm has also informed legislative and policy frameworks concerning sexualised forms of risk to children (see e.g. McAlinden, 2007a, 2010), masking a broader range of interpersonal and more intimate risks to children which occur in private settings such as within families and between peers.

Chapter 3 critically examines the core cultural and ideological notions underpinning the social and political construction of sexual offending concerning children. This includes discourses on childhood and the sexuality and sexualisation of children and young people; the construction of blame whereby children and childhood are deemed synonymous with innocence, passivity and vulnerability; and the dichotomous construction of victim and offending hierarchies concerning sexual offending epitomised as young, usually female children, and adult male strangers respectively. It explores these tensions in relation to young people who display HSB wherein bifurcated and oppositional versions of victimhood and offending behaviour may combine to form a 'hierarchy of blame', which cannot easily accommodate children and young people as 'deviant' victims or 'vulnerable' offenders (McAlinden, 2014a: 182). Moreover, the human rights dimension and the relevance of children's rights are also central to regulatory debates. In this respect, the chapter highlights the tension between justice responses and thresholds of risk that may criminalise children and wider public health approaches that seek to engage and educate children around expressions of sexual identity and navigating their emerging sexuality.

Having considered the theoretical and policy framework, Part II of the book examines the range of specific issues raised by harmful sexual or exploitative behaviour by children and young people. This part of the book draws on original primary research to inform the theoretical and critical discussion on the nature and extent of such behaviours and how they are perceived and responded to within social, legal and organisational contexts. Chapter 4 examines the emergence of HSB among peers as a distinct societal problem. While the earlier chapters largely concentrate on the principal reasons why peer-to-peer forms of abuse have largely remained hidden, this chapter considers some of the nuances and complexities relating to why HSB has recently emerged. This includes consideration of the impact of technology on modes of interpersonal and social communication and the influence of the media and constantly changing cultural norms and social practices related to sex and sexuality among adolescents in particular which challenge prevailing historical and biological assumptions about children and childhood. The chapter also highlights how the normalisation of 'risky' sexual behaviours among children and adolescents means that the dividing line between coercion and consent becomes very difficult, to define both for children and adults. As a counter to the preponderance of literature which focuses on the sexualisation of children along heteronormative, gendered lines, the analysis also suggests differential experiences among children and young people along the multiple dimensions of gender and sexual identity (LGBTQ) as well as personal resilience.

Chapter 5 unpacks the concept of 'peer-to-peer grooming' and how it features as part of the normalisation of 'harm' within HSB. Given the dearth of previous theoretical and empirical research on peer-to-peer forms of grooming, this chapter takes as its starting point my previous definition of 'grooming' (see earlier), originally conceived within the context of adult-child forms of grooming, and considers whether and how it may apply with children and young people. It will be argued that many of the core dynamics of grooming remain consistent when extended to this specific context, including its use in a range of interpersonal and social contexts, to establish trust or normalise harmful sexual behaviour to entrap the child in an abusive situation. There are, however, important differences relating principally to the varying sources of power differentials as well as vulnerability, including differential emotional and cognitive development and personal and family circumstances, which may stem from not only the victim but also the child perpetrator.

Chapter 6, examines the nature and extent of peer-based exploitation and abuse in relation to age and gender, as well as factors underlying the 'dark figure' of peer-based abuse. In considering some of the complexities surrounding the threshold of where risk might crystallise, as highlighted in the earlier chapters, the chapter also provides a taxonomy of harm along a continuum of normal/healthy-problematic/experimental-harmful sexual behaviour which is categorised as *peer-based relationships*, *peer-based recruitment* and *peer-based risk*. This is illustrated further through an analysis of harmful sexual or exploitative behaviour within a range of contexts including sibling abuse, institutional abuse and forms of CSE such as within gangs or party culture. It examines sexting and sexualised cyberbullying as new and emerging forms of online harmful sexual or exploitative behaviour by children and young people, highlighting the complexities of these behaviours and the enhanced difficulties they pose for identifying, capturing and responding to potential risk.

Chapter 7 analyses legal and societal responses to children and young people who display HSB. It demonstrates that many of the core cultural assumptions surrounding childhood and victimhood identified in the first part of the book, relating in particular to blame and blameworthiness, have become institutionalised, impacting victim and offender credibility and status within the legal process. The chapter draws out the legal, policy and cultural challenges these behaviours present. In so doing, it explicates the myriad difficulties of evidencing harmful intent and consequences, of separating out victims from perpetrators in complex forms of HSB or CSE and of policing new media, as well as the difficulties for communities, families and wider society in coming to terms with young sexual offenders in their midst (see e.g. Hackett et al., 2014, 2015).

Given the difficulties of clearly demarcating normative, risky and harmful sexual behaviours between peers, it is argued that criminal law and policy are limited in their response to what has become a highly significant component of child sexual abuse and exploitation.

Ultimately, therefore, broader policy and societal efforts are required to address risk on a more proactive basis. In challenging contemporary public and official paradigms of sexual offending concerning children and young people and in broadening and deepening understanding of sexualised forms of harm, a need arises to move beyond risk in formulating social and policy responses to harmful sexual or exploitative behaviours by children and young people. The final chapter considers how the current regulatory agenda surrounding child sexual abuse and exploitation could be reframed to better capture the complexity of such risks. This would include in particular developing a range of educative approaches to engage children as well as parents in preventative discourses about potential risks and which take account of children's developing emotional and cognitive maturity and their emerging sexuality and diverse sexual identities. In so doing, it draws out the theoretical and policy implications of balancing risk with children's rights and responsibilities and of broadening our cultural and policy understandings of risk, vulnerability and protection.

2

CHILD SEXUAL EXPLOITATION AND ABUSE: A CONTEMPORARY HISTORY OF CONCERNS

> Societies appear to be subject, every now and then, to periods of moral panic. A condition, episode, person or group of persons emerges to become defined as a threat to societal values and interests; its nature presented in a stylized and stereotypical fashion by the mass media ... the condition then disappears, submerges or deteriorates and becomes more visible. Sometimes the panic is quite novel, and at other times it is something which has been in existence long enough but suddenly appears in the limelight. Sometimes the panic is passed over and is forgotten ... at other times it has more serious and long lasting repercussions and might produce such changes as those in legal and social policy or even in the way society conceives itself.
>
> (Cohen, 1972: 28)

This chapter aims to address why the notion of children 'as risk', as opposed to 'at risk', has failed to capture the attention of legislators and policymakers for so long. It seeks to contextualise the recent history of public and political concerns surrounding child sexual exploitation and abuse and the episodic cultural and political construction of a series of 'panics' relating to the 'risk' of child abuse. A number of core elements have underpinned the study of moral panics as encapsulated in the opening quotation: the stereotypical presentation of a threat or concern, which emerges in cyclical fashion and which often produces long-lasting effects in terms of changes in social or legal policy or to fundamental cultural values and perceptions (see generally Goode and Ben-Yehuda, 1994; Young, 2009; Cree et al., 2014).

The central argument of this chapter is twofold: (i) that the cyclical nature of public and political concerns about the threat posed by sexual offending behaviour relating to children has fixated on a number of stereotypical assumptions concerning the 'othering' of sex offending, the ostensibly public nature of sexual victimisation and the adult–child nature of the sexual contact; and (ii) that the recurrence and confluence of these themes, and the influence of the archetypal predatory stranger paradigm in particular, have resulted in a narrow, homogeneous version of risk in which the child is constructed as 'victim', masking a broader range of interpersonal and more intimate risks to children, including those stemming from other children and young people. These arguments help to explain why, until relatively recently, the notion of children and young people displaying harmful sexual or exploitative behaviours has been a neglected dimension of public and political discourses concerning the risks of child sexual exploitation and abuse. Moreover, they also help to illuminate how and why, in the context of peer-to-peer abuse and exploitation, children and young people may not regard behaviours such as sexting as 'risky' or themselves as 'at risk' or potential victims.

Indeed, public and professional awareness about sexual offending related to children tends to be characterised by a series of 'extreme positions' (Conte, 1994). An historical cycle of 'discovery and suppression' of child sexual abuse is underpinned by 'cultural disassociation' (Olafson et al., 1993) and a history of social denial about sexual offending concerning children (Summit, 1988; see generally Cohen, 2001). As Clapton et al. (2013: 201) argue, 'a tendency to both react to and participate in moral panics is a persistent feature of social work but especially child protection.' The waves of public 'panic'[1] (Cohen, 1972; see also Hall et al., 1978) surrounding high-profile cases of child physical and sexual abuse often result in increased levels of legal and professional intervention. These concerns often diminish once the case fades away to become less prominent in both public and professional consciousness until the next high-profile case emerges when there is a renewed call for legal and policy intervention.

Within Western societies, concerns about sex offending related to children, and indeed children and childhood more broadly (Hendrick, 1997; Cunningham, 2014; James and Prout, 2015), are not fixed since

[1] Note, however, that the concept of 'moral panic' has also been subject to sustained critique chiefly in terms of the vagueness of the concept and its overuse as a shorthand pejorative label which overemphasises the subjective element of societal reactions and impedes meaningful discussion of moral issues (see e.g. the criticisms of Waddington, 1986, in relation to the work of Hall et al., 1978; see also Goode and Ben-Yehuda, 1994; Hunt, 1997; Ungar, 2001; Garland, 2008; Hier, 2008; Young, 2009).

they are socially and politically constructed and so tend to evolve and fluctuate over time (Conte, 1994; Smart, 1999). As Conte (1994: 226–27) argues, although child sexual abuse has been 'a problem both over time and across cultures ... complex psychological, cultural, and political processes are involved in recognizing and responding to childhood sexual abuse' (see also Jenkins, 2004). This chapter charts the contemporary history of sexual offending against children – its emergence, formulation and reformulation as a 'recognisable, problematic and harmful behaviour' (Smart, 1999: 393). It serves as a necessary precursor to more detailed theoretical analysis of the complexities involved in the social, cultural and political construction of 'risk' relating to children and young people and child sexual abuse and exploitation which will be undertaken in the next chapter and indeed much of the rest of the book.

Academic accounts of the public panic concerning sexual crime in the United States (e.g. Freedman, 1987; Best, 1993; Jenkins, 2004) have demonstrated that '[o]ne reality prevailed until it was succeeded by another' (Jenkins, 2004: 2). In the context of the United Kingdom, however, and consistent with Hall et al.'s (1978: 211–22) broader thesis on moral panics, a series of 'discrete moral panics' and images of the child sex offender have tended to progress through various interdependent periods of concern which have 'mapped together' to produce 'an increasingly amplified threat to society'. The chapter begins with a brief examination of the early emergence of 'child abuse' within the United States, Europe and Great Britain, before moving to chart the intermittent waves of public panic relating to the risk of sex offending concerning children. These surges of panic have centred upon the predominant 'stranger danger' paradigm and the risk posed by predatory 'paedophiles' in the community, institutional child abuse within a range of quasi-intra-familial child care settings, grooming and abuse via the Internet by online predators and organised forms of child sexual exploitation.

THE EARLY EMERGENCE OF CHILD ABUSE: INTRA-FAMILIAL ABUSE

Child sexual exploitation and abuse are not new phenomena. While the past four decades have witnessed a dramatic increase in public and professional concerns about child sexual abuse and exploitation, there is a much longer history of concerns about child abuse and in particular cruelty to children and physical injury inflicted by parents (Radbill,

1968; Parke and Collmer, 1975; Kalisch, 1978). Writing in 1867, for example, French physician Ambroise Tardieu describes post-mortem findings of sexual abuse. Within Great Britain, the existence of child sexual abuse has been traced to the Victorian period (Jackson, 2000).

In the historical construction of the 'child victim' of sexual abuse, however, the medical profession tended to 'desexualise' the problem and view harm in physical rather than moral terms, while the justice system was similarly reluctant to conceptualise child sexual abuse as real trauma to the victim meriting a formal legal response (Smart, 1999; Jackson, 2000). As Jenkins argues, '[c]hildren were often regarded as seducers who provoked such offenses for their own psychological reasons' (2004: 2). Indeed, as discussed at length in Chapter 7, such approaches which tend to minimise the impact of abuse on children and instead place responsibility and blame for the abuse on errant non-typical victims are still in evidence today. Several social historians have attributed the historical reticence to formally recognise child abuse to the absolute power that fathers had over their children in most pre-industrial Western societies such as France (Donzelot, 1979) and Great Britain (Behlmer, 1982; Rose, 1991). These writers note how 'institutionalized patriarchy' (Herman, 1981) was gradually eroded with increasing industrialisation bringing about a change in family relationships and a focus on the role of the mother.

The formal recognition of child physical abuse is generally attributed to the American Henry Kempe and his colleagues who first publicised the issue in the paper 'The Battered Child Syndrome' (Kempe et al., 1962). This was later extended to include neglect, non-organic failure to thrive[2] and emotional abuse (Garbarino and Gilliam, 1980). However, it was not until the late 1970s in the United States that awareness of the possible extent of the problem of child sexual abuse heightened among professionals and the public (Kempe, 1978; Finkelhor, 1979). Finkelhor (1979) suggests that this recognition came about as a result of the growth of feminism and campaigns for the protection of children which highlighted children's vulnerability in the private sphere. This perspective was also given impetus by the development of the wider concept of 'family violence' and several subcategories of this more general rubric, such as 'domestic violence' (Straus, 1974; Pfohl, 1977; Gordon, 1988).

[2] This is defined as decelerated or arrested physical growth associated with poor developmental and emotional functioning and usually occurs where a child younger than age 2 has no known underlying illness or medical condition (Skuse, 1985).

In Europe in general, an awareness of child sexual abuse did not come about until some years later (Jones et al., 1987: 42–50; Bagley and King, 1990: 25–37). Catholic cultures such as France and Southern Germany were slower to recognise sexual abuse as a moral, legal and social problem, compared to Protestant or secularised cultures such as the United States, England, Canada, Sweden, Norway, the Netherlands and Northern Germany (Chesnais, 1981). These differences in regulatory responses to child abuse have been attributed to the respective religious traditions underlying Protestantism and Catholicism which reveal a tension between 'a rhetoric of strong penal repression' and 'soft authoritarian paternalism' (Melossi, 2001: 412; see also McAlinden, 2012b). Even the latter group of countries, however, failed to record occurrences of the sexual abuse of children with other criminal statistics until the late 1970s (Chesnais, 1981).[3]

Social and professional change in the area of child sexual abuse has been slow, and it was not until the twentieth century that issues concerning child abuse, child protection and the rights of children came to public notice (Bagley and King, 1990; Ferguson, 1990, 2004), and even then only intermittently (La Fontaine, 1990: 39–40). This reconceptualisation of childhood, recognising the child as 'innately and structurally vulnerable' (Goldson, 1997a: 12), was initiated by the formation of the humane movement and the development of the juvenile court system (Olafson et al., 1993). As Kennedy et al. (1990) note, for centuries the Common Law only recognised three serious breaches of sexual morality: rape, sodomy and bestiality. In the United Kingdom, legislation relating to other types of sexual offence, including those involving children, was added only during the Victorian period in the latter part of the nineteenth and early twentieth centuries.

The National Society for the Prevention of Cruelty to Children (NSPCC) was founded in the United Kingdom in 1884, bringing the maltreatment of children to public attention and campaigning for changes in legal and public attitudes to the care and treatment of children (Corby, 2012: 12). During this period, for example, the age of consent for girls was raised from 10 to 13 years in 1875 and finally to 16 years in 1885[4] because of mounting concern from the Purity

[3] The first survey on the incidence of child sexual abuse was carried out in Britain between 1977 and 1978 (Mrazek et al., 1981). The rest of Western Europe lagged behind, although an earlier German study of incest offenders implied that many of the victims had been children (Maisch, 1973).

[4] Via the Criminal Law Amendment Act 1885.

Movement about child prostitution (Walkowitz, 1980; Simpson, 1988; Smart, 1999). Criminal prohibitions against incest are now almost universal, but prior to the Punishment of Incest Act 1908 such cases were dealt with by the ecclesiastical courts, as offences against morals and religion (Turner, 1952; Wolfram, 1983). Between 1910 and the late 1960s, the issue of child abuse as a major societal problem became a 'dormant issue' in Great Britain (Corby, 1987; Gordon, 1988; Costin, 1992). Indeed, it was only in the early 1970s and late 1980s that child abuse was 'rediscovered' in Great Britain (Parton, 1985; Murphy, 1995: 9–16).

Although the term 'child abuse' may cover a range of harms encompassing physical, sexual and emotional abuse and neglect (Bernstein et al., 1994; Finkelhor et al., 2005), the predominant focus during this period was on physical forms of intra-familial abuse and neglect. Parton (1981, 1985) pinpoints a wave of cases concerning baby battering as being among the first examples of moral panic in relation to the abuse of children and young people in Great Britain. From the late 1970s onwards, a number of public inquiries followed the deaths of children who had been subjected to severe and sustained child physical abuse (Hill, 1990). The cases of Maria Colwell (DHSS, 1974), Jasmine Beckford (BBC and BHA, 1985) and Tyra Henry (LBL, 1987) placed child abuse firmly back on the policymaking agenda.[5] The Colwell inquiry in particular 'proved crucial in establishing the issue as a major social problem and introducing fundamental changes in policy and practice' (Parton, 1985: 12; see also Hutchinson, 1986).[6] However, as La Fontaine (1990: 38, 42) asserts, 'sexual abuse was not even mentioned in the Department of Health circulars until 1980', and it was not until the wave of cases of suspected child abuse in Cleveland in 1987 that 'the problem of the sexual abuse of children exploded into the public domain' (see also Nava, 1988; Kitzinger, 1996).

The Butler-Sloss Report into the Cleveland inquiry concluded that paediatricians and social services that took the children into care had misdiagnosed sexual abuse in most of the cases (DHSS, 1988). Media coverage of the inquiry was 'extensive and without precedent' (Franklin and Parton, 1991: 191) and formed a key part of the

[5] Around the same period, similar concerns about intra-familial child physical abuse stemming from a handful of high-profile cases also arose in other Anglophone countries such as Australia and the United States (Critcher, 2003: 95–98).

[6] Seven-year-old Maria Colwell was beaten to death by her stepfather, after suffering a period of physical abuse and neglect.

'formidable backlash' concerning the 'overreaction to child abuse' (Olafson et al., 1993: 18, citing Gardner, 1991: 115–16). Similarly, in the early 1990s the Orkneys case in Scotland involved allegations of satanic ritual child sexual abuse by parents which were later proven to be unfounded (La Fontaine, 1998).[7]

In the aftermath of these cases, child protection frameworks were replete with 'tensions and contradictions' (Parton, 1997); as a result, legal and professional intervention, and social work in particular, tended to retreat from the private sphere (Scott, 2001). Such cases also provide a useful illustration of the pendulous nature of public and professional concerns surrounding child abuse which tend to oscillate between denial and minimisation of allegations or suspicions on the one hand and overzealous 'witch-hunts against innocent victims' (Conte, 1994: 227) on the other (see also Finkelhor, 1994a; Myers, 1994). As will be argued further in the next chapter, it is precisely because the sexual abuse or exploitation of children tends to evoke such deep-seated, powerful, moral and emotive reactions, particularly those stemming from the innocence of children and the need to protect them at all costs, that public and official responses to the issue have tended to be characterised by such extreme positions.

More recently, high-profile cases of intra-familial abuse which featured heavily in the media have also involved extreme physical cruelty and neglect of children, rather than sexual abuse, at the hands of adults who were tasked with caring for them.[8] Eight-year-old Victoria Climbié was tortured and murdered by her aunt and her aunt's partner, leading to the most comprehensive review of child protection services for decades (Laming, 2003). This case was followed within a few short years by that of Peter Connelly (initially known as 'Baby P') which, like the Climbié case, also occurred within the remit of Haringey Council in North London, as well as those of Khyra Ishaq and Daniel Pelka. Seventeen-month-old Peter Connelly died as a result of a series of horrific injuries inflicted by his mother, her partner and her partner's brother (LSCB Haringey, 2009). Seven-year-old Khyra Ishaq was starved to death and beaten by her mother and her mother's partner in 2008 (BSCB, 2010). Daniel Pelka died at age 4 after being physically

7 There were parallel concerns across the same period about ritual child sexual abuse in the United States (Nathan and Snedeker, 1995), Canada (Marron, 1988), New Zealand (Hood, 2001), Australia (Guilliatt, 1996) and the Netherlands (Jonker and Jonker-Bakker, 1997), including within day nurseries (see generally La Fontaine, 1998; de Young, 2004).

8 For a thematic overview of recent cases of high-profile child deaths following abuse and media responses, see Fitzgibbon (2011).

abused, neglected and starved by his mother and stepfather (CSCB, 2013).

In all cases, the children were known to a host of professionals, including police and social services, their general practitioner (GP) or paediatric services at the local hospital. As Lord Laming's follow-up report highlights, concerns about risk of harm should have been apparent but were not officially followed-up or acted upon due to 'widespread organisational malaise' (Laming, 2009: para 1.20). While acknowledging the changing social mores and professional contexts over the intervening years, both academic (Parton, 2004) and official voices (Laming, 2009) have noted the similarities between the earlier and more recent cases and the fact that the inquiries were making the same recommendations to strengthen child protection arrangements several decades on. These observations denote the hidden nature of more intimate forms of child abuse and lead one to question whether any real societal or institutional lessons have actually been learned.

Indeed, such cases have had a number of undesirable effects on the popular imagination concerning the societal understanding of risks related to child sexual exploitation and abuse. First, the victims in these cases did not come from a traditional nuclear family – most often, they were separated from one or both parents and were being cared for by a single parent or another relative along with the partner of their primary carer. These features help society to dismiss these cases as an aberration and as a by-product of dysfunctional families as part of a 'feral underclass' (Fitzgibbon, 2011: 43) rather than accepting that they may be symptomatic of a wider, more systemic problem concerning more intimate forms of abuse. This is also reflective of the notion of contemporary moral panics as 'ordering practices' (Hier, 2003: 19), where in trying to account for and respond to broader symptoms of social decay (see also Fitzgibbon, 2011: Ch. 3), the community 'remain[s] emotionally and physically intact' (Jewkes, 2010: 16).

Second, they are a resounding reminder of 'adultism' – of the power of adults, their abuse of positions of trust and the relative vulnerability and powerlessness of children and the status of the child as 'victim' (see Davis and Bourhill, 1997: 35–44; Goldson, 1997a: 12). This, however, is not to deny the intrinsic vulnerability of children due principally to their age and the power differentials between child victims and adult perpetrators which are integral to the onset and maintenance of many forms of child abuse (Finkelhor, 1994b; Kitzinger, 1997; Paolucci et al., 2001). Rather, it is to highlight the impact and significance of such stereotypes which may obfuscate any concerns about risk of harm stemming from children themselves.

Third, in highlighting physical and emotional abuse and neglect, they tend to obscure the 'incest taboo' (Tidefors et al., 2010) and render 'incest abusers . . . invisible' (Itzin, 2001: 35). Intra-familial *sexual* abuse is thought to account for between 80 per cent (Grubin, 1998; McGee et al., 2002) and 90 per cent (Radford et al., 2011) of all sexual offending against children and may include sibling incest (Adler and Schutz, 1995; Carlson et al., 2006) or sibling abuse (Wiehe, 1997; Hoffman and Edwards, 2004; Caffaro, 2013) as well as father–daughter/other parent–child incest (Phelan, 1995; Itzin, 2001). As discussed further in Chapter 6, the former can include sexual abuse between older and younger children (Kaufman et al., 1996) or between adolescent siblings (Tidefors et al., 2010) and is thought to account for about half of child-to-child sexual abuse (Tidefors et al., 2010).

Several scholars have argued that the largely hidden nature of intra-familial sexual abuse, despite the fact that intimate abuse accounts for the vast majority of sexual offending against children, can be attributed to the societal need to preserve the 'normal' family unit and the home in particular as a sphere of safety and protection (Parker and Aggleton, 1999; Saraga, 2001). In Young's (2009: 13) terms, '[a] moral panic is a moral disturbance centring on claims that direct interests have been violated.' As a result of the traditional cultural unwillingness to visualise risk to children in a domestic context, public discourses have appeared to 'reverse the order of danger' (Jackson and Scott, 1999). As feminist scholars have argued, sexual offending committed by strangers is privileged over most other forms of child sexual abuse or exploitation (Cowburn and Dominelli, 2001; see also Newburn and Stanko, 1994), resulting in a minimalist version of sexualised risks to children.[9] As discussed further, within children's own landscapes and internal theorising of risk and safety, the distinction is readily made in practice between the public and the private spheres. The private sphere of the home is viewed in terms of safety and security, whereas vulnerability is in turn associated with the public sphere (Harden, 2000; Jewkes, 2010). This, however, does not easily accommodate risks

[9] McCartan (2004), however, has argued that the public does have the capacity to disassociate from the media's portrayal that sexual crimes are committed exclusively by strangers. See also Greer (2003), who argues that the public does accept that the risk of sexual victimisation by a stranger is slight so that the issue again becomes one of reluctance.

which lie in between in terms of those stemming from peers or people or places with which children and young people are familiar.

EXTRAFAMILIAL ABUSE: THE PREDATORY STRANGER

Whereas the early recognition of child abuse stemmed from the private sphere and concerns with intra-familial abuse, within neo-liberal societies such as the United States and the United Kingdom,[10] there has been a discernible postmodern paradigm shift in which the paedophile has been 'reconstruct[ed] . . . as the dangerous stranger' (Cowburn and Dominelli, 2001: 399). From the early 1990s onwards, a series of cases have highlighted the prevalence of 'stranger danger' and the risk posed by the omnipresent, 'anonymous' (Williams and Hudson, 2013: 221) and eponymous stranger in the community (see also Kitzinger, 1999a; Greer, 2003). Despite the diversity of types of sexual offending concerning children, including those perpetrated by women and children, the cultural construction and proliferation of '"the paedophile" as an external threat' (Cowburn and Dominelli, 2001: 400) has led to the conflation of categories of risk within media and public discourses in particular.

While there are 'multi-disciplinary definitions and understandings of "paedophilia"' (Harrison et al., 2010: 481; see also Ames and Houston, 1990; Feelgood and Hoyer, 2008), a range of writers have discerned the influence of medico-legal discourses on paedophilia within the contemporary media portrayal of sex offending concerning children (e.g. Soothill and Walby, 1991; Kitzinger, 1999b; Greer, 2003). Medical frameworks broadly define the term 'paedophilia' as a 'sexual attraction towards pre-pubescent children' (Rosen, 2003; APA, 2013), which has become a blanket term for all sexual offending against children (see Rind et al., 1998; McCartan, 2008). That is, sexual offenders are seen as being synonymous with the 'predatory paedophile' – male, adult offenders who have a proclivity for preying on young victims who were previously unknown to them. The media depiction of this primary offending paradigm concerning sexual offending against children, which has resonated internationally, can be distilled further into three broad categories of risk concerning sexual offending against children.

[10] Cavadino and Dignan (2006), for example, identify the hallmarks of this type of 'political economy' as a dominant penal philosophy of incapacitation, high rates of imprisonment and the social exclusion of deviants.

The first type of case relates to what can be termed 'known official risks', that is, sex offenders officially known to the local police and who are likely to be subject to notification requirements (or the so-called sex offenders' register)[11] but about whom the public may not know. Cases on both sides of the Atlantic provide illustrations of this type of case involving the sexual murder of children – Sarah Payne and Megan Kanka (Lieb et al., 2011). Eight-year-old Sarah Payne was abducted while she was playing in a field near her grandparents' home and murdered in Sussex in July 2000 by known paedophile Roy Whiting. In New Jersey, some years earlier, 7-year-old Megan Kanka was raped and murdered by her neighbour in July 1994, convicted sex offender Jesse Timmendequas. Within the popular imagination, such cases have become 'signal crimes' (Innes, 2004) and have come to epitomise the risks to children from predatory strangers.[12] As discussed further, concerns about particular victims have in turn been used to spearhead legislative campaigns for increased regulation of the whereabouts and behaviour of sex offenders against children in the community. The resulting laws – 'Megan's Law' and 'Sarah's Law' – have become emblematic of the rhetorical political and moral crusade against child sex offenders in the name of victims.

The second category fits with what Zedner (2009: 47), adopting the now infamous terminology of former US Secretary of Defence Donald Rumsfeld, referred to as 'known unknowns' – the risks we know that we don't know about – that is, suspect sex offenders about whom police have concerns but for whom allegations have never been formally prosecuted or adjudicated.[13] By way of example, in England and Wales, seven-year-old Sophie Hook was murdered by suspected paedophile Howard Hughes after being abducted from a tent while she camped out in her uncle's garden in July 1995. Following Hughes's trial, it was revealed that he had previously been known to police for multiple incidents of similar attacks on children, but police had been

[11] Within the United Kingdom, sex offender notification which requires certain classes of sex offender to provide their personal details to the police and any changes to these details was first provided for by Part I of the Sex Offenders Act 1997 and since strengthened by Part II of the Sexual Offences Act 2003, replacing the earlier provisions.

[12] See also the German case of 7-year-old Natalie Astner, who was murdered by a convicted sex offender who had been released from prison on parole fourteen months earlier (Albrecht, 1997; Dessecker, 2008). The ensuing campaign for 'Natalie's Law' ultimately resulted in a range of harsher measures for sex offenders.

[13] In a study by the late Keith Soothill and colleagues, this category of those 'strongly suspected of serious sex crime and future danger' (Soothill, 2005; Soothill et al., 2005) accounted for one-third of repeat sex offenders against children coming to the attention of police.

unable to prosecute either because of a lack of evidence or because the victims' parents had been unwilling to pursue the case to spare their children the further ordeal of giving evidence in court.[14] Similarly, the 'Soham murders' of a pair of ten-year-old schoolgirls, Holly Wells and Jessica Chapman, in Cambridgeshire in August 2002 by school care taker Ian Huntley received sustained media attention. The Bichard Inquiry (Bichard, 2004) into police handling of intelligence and information-sharing systems highlighted that Huntley was also previously known to the police for a string of allegations of sexual offences against women and young girls, but no action was eventually taken.

The third type of case relates to what Zedner (2009: 47) terms 'unknown unknowns' or those risks we don't know that we don't know about. This covers the serial 'geographically transient' (Wilson, 2009: 226) sex offender whose modus operandi involves travelling around different locations to escape notice or avoid detection. Serial sex offender Michael Fourniret was tried and convicted in 2008 for the rape and murder of at least seven young girls in both France and Belgium and possibly more European countries over a fourteen-year period. Within the United Kingdom, Levi Belfield was convicted in 2011 of the murder of thirteen-year-old Milly Dowler who was abducted and murdered on her way home from school in Surrey in 2002. At the time of his conviction in 2011, Belfield was serving time in prison for the murders or attempted murder of a number of other girls or young women who had been abducted in various parts of the country. One of the most infamous cases of serial predatory sexual offending and murder of young children involves Robert Black. While serving time for the abduction and sexual assault of six-year-old Mandy Wilson in 1990, Black was charged and convicted in 1994 for the murders and attempted abduction of a number of other children (Wyre and Tate, 1995; Wilson, 2009: Ch. 9). Black was a delivery man whose job took him all over England and Scotland and whose daily mobility allowed him both to scout for and apprehend potential victims and to dispose of their remains.

It is well documented that the tabloid media as 'primary definers and claims makers' (Crichter, 2003: 134–36) tend to have 'a distortive effect' in framing public perceptions about risks related to sexual crime (Williams and Hudson, 2013: 221; see also Soothill

[14] Note that the trial occurred prior to the introduction of the Youth Justice and Criminal Evidence Act 1999, Part II of which introduced a range of 'special measures' to facilitate the giving of evidence for vulnerable witnesses, including children. See further Chapter 6.

and Walby, 1991; Kitzinger, 2004; Jewkes, 2010; Willis et al., 2010; Berry et al., 2012; Thakker, 2012). The cumulative effect of these various types of cases has been a convergence of public concerns and heightened awareness of the dangers posed by predatory strangers to 'threatened children' (Best, 1993). Collectively, such cases help to augment public anxieties about the omnipresent risk related to sex offending concerning children, 'crystalliz[ing] fears over ... the predatory child sex offender' (Greer, 2007: 28) and placing the media and the public 'on "paedophile alert"' (Jewkes, 2010: 9).

These socially constructed versions of sexualised forms of risks to children, which equate the sexual victimisation of children with abuse by a predatory stranger in the public sphere, have also become institutionalised within legal and policy frameworks. Indeed, as I have discussed at length elsewhere, concerns with the presence of predatory sex offenders in the community have shaped contemporary legislative and policy debates on the risk related to sex offending against children, spawning a plethora of regulatory measures in the United States and the United Kingdom (McAlinden, 2007a, 2010, 2012b). The proliferation of this disproportionate and narrow version of risk and the resulting ambiguities concerning levels and types of risk operate to the detriment of effective risk management and the development of broader more viable policies concerning child protection.

Moreover, constructing and framing the overall risk posed by sex offenders as external to the community or the family help to maintain the public/private divide. As Jewkes (2010: 16) contends, 'the moral panic over "paedophilia" has perpetuated the notion that sexual dangerousness resides in strangers and that those strangers are not like "us."' This inevitably results in the 'othering' (Becker, 1963; Garland, 2001) of sex offending against children and helps to obscure broader patterns of risk and victimisation that lie outside adult–child sexual relationships and occur within interpersonal relationships including those between peers. As Gordon (1988: 223) has argued, 'the dominant stereotype of the "stranger" perpetrator ... completed the reconstitution of the pedophile, thereby concealing the continued predominance of sexual assault within the family.' The location of risk in the public sphere has also tended to mask risks to children from within intra-familial or quasi-intra-familial contexts such as organisational child-care settings.

INSTITUTIONAL CHILD ABUSE

In parallel with ongoing concerns about predatory strangers, from the early 1990s onwards, a new wave of cases highlighted the vulnerability of children within environments traditionally considered secure such as children's homes, clubs and schools (Reder et al., 1993; Corby et al., 2001; Parton, 2004). Institutional child abuse has emerged as a hybrid category of child sexual exploitation and abuse which lies somewhere between extrafamilial and intra-familial forms of abuse. That is, despite the fact that institutional abuse is generally classed as a subcategory of extrafamilial abuse, in that the abuser comes from outside the family, there are also shared features with intra-familial abuse which make the issues much more complex (McAlinden, 2015). One is the proximate and ongoing relationship between adults and children within an organisational environment, where adults may have sole responsibility for the welfare of children, which 'often place[s] them *in loco parentis*' (Sullivan et al., 2011: 58; see also Colton, 2002; Leclerc et al., 2008). The other is the imbalance of power between adult perpetrators and child victims which is thought to be exaggerated by the offender's 'caring role' and the 'traumatic or abusive histories' of a particularly vulnerable group of children and young people (Erooga et al., 2012: 62).

Institutional and institutionalised forms of child sexual abuse have tended to provoke an opprobrious reaction on the part of the media and the public due principally to the abhorrent breach of trust and abuse of power and authority (McAlinden, 2012a: Ch. 5) and the 'corruption of care' (Erooga, 2009: 39–40) by adults charged with the welfare and protection of children. Such forms of quasi-intra-familial abuse also present as deeply problematic and unpalatable for society chiefly because they underscore the risks of more intimate forms of abuse within private interpersonal contexts. At the same time, and somewhat paradoxically perhaps, although institutional child abuse bridges the public/private divide, its broad categorisation as a form of extrafamilial abuse also provides a measure of reassurance for society about the relative safety and sanctity of the traditional family unit and home.

The phenomenon of institutional child abuse is also one which has resonated worldwide (Colton et al., 2002; Skold and Swain, 2015). Although the term encompasses a range of abusive and harmful behaviours towards children (physical, emotional and sexual abuse and neglect), the predominant public focus has been institutionalised forms of child sexual abuse. However, whereas societal awareness and perceptions of the risk posed by predatory strangers tend to derive from media and public discourses, much of our knowledge and understanding about institutional child abuse stem from official discourses and public inquiry reports. Over the past few decades, there have been a number of high-profile inquiries into institutional child abuse in a range of jurisdictions including the United States (John Jay College, 2004, 2011), Canada (Law Commission of Canada, 2000), Australia (Family and Community Development Committee Victoria, 2013), the Netherlands (Commission of Inquiry, 2011) and Scotland (Shaw, 2007). During the course of the fieldwork, there were recently completed or ongoing inquiries into historical institutional abuse in Northern Ireland[15] and Australia[16] which have since been reported (see McAlinden and Naylor, 2016). England and Wales and the Republic of Ireland have had a lengthy and more concentrated history of inquiries into institutional child abuse.

In the former jurisdiction, cases have stemmed from a variety of secular and religious organisations in both residential and non-residential settings including care homes, nurseries and schools (see e.g. Warner, 1992; Kirkwood, 1993; Utting, 1997, Waterhouse, 2000; Nolan, 2001).[17] In the latter jurisdiction, public and political concerns have been dominated by a string of high-profile inquiries involving the Catholic Church (Murphy et al., 2005; Commission to Inquire into Child Abuse, 2009; Commission of Investigation, 2009, 2011), although abuse is by no means confined to this particular religious context.[18] The Ryan Report, for example, generated widespread media coverage and provoked public outcry throughout Ireland and internationally (Brennan, 2008; Arnold, 2009; Flannery, 2009). It highlighted the fact that the abuse of children and the failure of

[15] In Northern Ireland, the *Inquiry into Historical Institutional Abuse* reported in January 2017 (Hart et al., 2017).

[16] The *Royal Commission into Institutional Responses to Child Sexual Abuse* in Australia reported in December 2017. The final report is available here: www.childabuseroyalcommission.gov.au/. Australia has had a broader history of concerns relating to institutional child abuse which has included the forced removal of indigenous children from their families producing what has been termed the 'Stolen Generation' (see e.g. Australian Human Rights Commission, 1997; see also Nagy and Kaur-Sehdev, 2012).

[17] For a critical overview of these inquiries, their main findings and principal recommendations, see e.g. Parton, 2004; McAlinden, 2006, 2012a: Ch. 5.

[18] For a critical overview of the background and aftermath of these Irish inquiries, see Keenan, 2011; McAlinden, 2013. There is an ongoing *Commission of Investigation into Mother and Baby Homes* in the Republic of Ireland run by the Catholic Church on behalf of the Irish state due to report finally in February 2019.

Church and State authorities to adequately respond to the problem were *systemic* in Irish childcare institutions (Commission to Inquire into Child Abuse, 2009: Vol. 4, paras 6.09–6.18).

In the course of this series of public inquiries into institutional abuse which served to cement the link between institutions, such as care homes, and the sexual abuse of children, a number of key themes have emerged which help to embed the notion of omnipresent risk and the deep-rooted nature of sexual offending related to children. These include that the abuse normally took place over a number of years and its extent went unrecognised for some time; usually more than one victim was involved, and often more than one offender; there was often a culture of acceptance or disbelief of the existence of the problem; and many complaints were not formally reported by victims or acted upon by the relevant authorities (Gallagher, 2000; McAlinden, 2006, 2012a: Ch. 5). The latter criticisms have been made in particular within the context of sexual abuse within churches or faith communities (Berry, 1992; Francis and Turner, 1995; McAlinden, 2013).

Indeed, the emphasis on the religious or spiritual context of sexual offending against children in many of these cases also tends to insulate the problem and remove it from everyday, real-world, secular contexts. Moreover, victims of institutional child abuse have also tended to be in the older age range of adolescents rather than young children (see e.g. Loftus and Camargo, 1993; Haywood et al., 1996; Sullivan and Beech, 2004, Sullivan et al., 2011). A number of these themes including the failure to recognise abuse, initial disbelief of victims or official denial or minimisation of allegations of abuse and disregard of the older child or adolescent victim are also pertinent for the contemporary social and political construction of child sexual exploitation and abuse by children and young people and will be discussed further in Part II of the book.

The social construction of risk within institutionalised contexts and the othering of sex offending concerning children have also become embedded further within official discourses. Within the United Kingdom in particular, for example, high-profile cases have led to a series of wide-ranging changes to the legislative framework on pre-employment vetting and barring (McAlinden, 2010) including most recently the Safeguarding Vulnerable Groups Act 2006.[19] Such

[19] The legislation was enacted in response to the Bichard Inquiry (2004) and scaled back under the Protection of Freedoms Act 2012, Part V. See similarly the Safeguarding Vulnerable Groups (NI) Order 2007.

regulatory activity tends to further ensconce social and cultural stereotypes about the predatory and insidious nature of sex offending – that many 'professional perpetrators' (Sullivan and Beech, 2002) will deliberately seek out employment and opportunities that involve access to children and the vulnerable through organisations where they can 'groom' children, staff and the wider environment to safely abuse in relative anonymity and secrecy (see McAlinden, 2012a: Ch. 5).[20]

The consensus within popular and political discourse surrounding this particular category of child sexual abuse has further promulgated dominant cultural stereotypes about risk which have in turn helped to mask other forms of child victimisation by peers within the organisational environment. In particular, these relate to the adult perpetrator-child victim dichotomy and the cultural categorisation and compartmentalisation of victim and offender identities relating to sexual abuse involving children. However, both of these constructs have been challenged by a handful of inquiry reports. Several inquiries have highlighted the existence of peer-to-peer abuse where children were also abused by other children as well as adults within childcare institutions where abuse had become part of the organisational culture (see e.g. Shaw, 2007: 31–32; Commission to Inquire into Child Abuse, 2009: Vol. 3, para 9.57). Moreover, as discussed further in Chapter 6, 'the vulnerability of organisations' (Erooga, 2009: 38), or what Hall terms 'the institutional syndrome' (Hall, 2000: 159), as opposed to individual victims may also facilitate a continuum of sexual offending within the institutional environment which may involve children as offenders, as well as victims, as 'insiders' or parties to the abusive process.

ONLINE GROOMING AND ABUSE

Within the past few years, public and political perceptions of risk have converged around the Internet where online grooming and abuse have emerged as the 'new sit[e] of social anxiety' (Hier, 2003: 3; see also Ungar, 2001). Anxiety over children's and young people's use of the Internet has emerged as the 'contemporary 21st century' moral panic (Clapton et al., 2013: 197) and the new vanguard of risk management

[20] In fact, not all institutional sex offenders, or indeed sex offenders in general (Smallbone and Wortley, 2000), are predatory or 'preferential' in deliberating targeting victims but may be motivated instead by situational factors or opportunity once ensconced in an institution (Sullivan and Beech, 2002, 2004; Erooga et al., 2012).

and child protection. As Jewkes (2010: 5, 10) contends, 'the online sexual abuse of children' has become 'one of the most feared phenomena of the age' where children and young people are considered vulnerable to victimisation by those wishing to abuse or exploit them. In short, risks to children in the online world have become the contemporary public as well as academic orthodoxy in sexual offending concerning children and have been reimagined as the 'new' or modern edifice of 'stranger danger'. In consequence, 'the family' and intimate interpersonal relationships are once again seen 'as a defensive bastion, under threat from abusive strangers rather than harbouring abuse' (Pratt, 2005: 280).

Durkin (1997: 14) has suggested that there are four main purposes for which the Internet may be misused by those with a sexual interest in children: (i) trafficking of child pornography, (ii) locating children to abuse, (iii) engaging in inappropriate sexualised communications with children and (iv) communicating with other offenders. Whereas the last of these behaviours has been the subject of public concerns about virtual forms of sexual abuse and 'the pedophile subculture online' (Holt et al., 2010),[21] it is the first three which have dominated public and official discourses on online forms of sexual offending concerning children. In this respect, 'the problem' of sexual offending via the Internet has been largely confined to child pornography (O'Donnell and Milner, 2007; Akdeniz, 2008; Ost, 2009; Quayle and Ribsil, 2012) and online grooming of children (Davidson and Gottschalk, 2010; Martellozzo, 2012; McAlinden, 2012a).

As Williams and Hudson (2013: 220) have argued, grooming and abuse via the Internet are 'highly synonymous with stranger abuse, a conflation often reinforced by the tabloid media'. Academic, public and policy discourses have highlighted a number of pertinent features of online forms of child sexual abuse and exploitation. These precipitate concerns with stranger danger, simultaneously amplifying public concerns over the risks to children and young people within the virtual environment and distorting perceptions of risk on the part of children and young people. First, the stereotypical case which appears in the media involves an older adult male sex offender who tries to make

[21] See e.g. the high-profile 'Wonderland' international police investigation which resulted in simultaneous arrests in twelve countries (including the UK, Belgium, Austria, France, Italy, Finland, Norway, Australia and the United States) involving an estimated 145 male offenders: see e.g. D. Casciani, 'World's Largest Paedophile Ring Uncovered', BBC News, 6 March 2011, www.bbc.co.uk/news/uk-12762333; D. Shaw, 'How "Vile" Paedophile Ring Targeted Victims', BBC News, 22 April 2015, www.bbc.co.uk/news/uk-32413508.

contact with much younger victims, typically girls, to subsequently abuse them either online or offline (Gallagher et al., 2006; Hörnle, 2011; Webster et al., 2012). In tandem with this, there have also been a number of public campaigns on the safe use of the Internet aimed at increasing the awareness of children and parents about the dangers of 'online strangers' (O'Connell, 2001; Davidson and Martellozzo, 2008a).[22] Moreover, as noted in the opening chapter, legislation to criminalise online forms of grooming has been enacted in several jurisdictions (see also McAlinden, 2012a: 5–7), and international policing bodies have also been established to combat sexual offending online (Gillespie, 2008). The existence of these regulatory frameworks also speaks to the structural and institutional entrenchment and policy prioritisation of fears about the online predatory stranger in the unsafe space of the public sphere.

Second, the anonymity of offenders within cyberspace is seen as the defining feature of online forms of child sexual exploitation and abuse. The Internet may enable 'offender metamorphosis' (Taylor and Quayle, 2003: 97–119) and allow sex offenders to assume an 'electronic double' (Davidson and Gottschalk, 2010: 4) perhaps misrepresenting their identity as a like-minded child or young person (Quayle and Taylor, 2001; Davidson and Martellozzo, 2008a: 282) to prey on unwitting victims. This may simultaneously enhance the opportunity of offenders and the vulnerability of children in online contexts (Quayle and Taylor, 2001; Davidson and Martellozzo, 2005; Kierkegaard, 2008; Hörnle, 2011).[23] In this sense, anonymity may serve not only to mask the potential risks to children online, but it may also cause children to 'lower their guard', especially if their online interaction with the offender or indeed their peers does not fit their impression of stranger danger.

Third, in an age of domestic Internet access, the accessibility of potential victims is also augmented by the fact that the Internet has become central to many aspects of our social and domestic lives, particularly those of children and young people.[24] With 'twenty-four

[22] See e.g. 'Young People Take the Lead in Nationwide Safer Internet Day Campaign', UK Safer Internet Centre, 9 February 2015, www.saferInternet.org.uk/news/young-people-take-the-lead-in-nationwide-safer-Internet-day-campaign.

[23] Note, however, that while the Internet may provide user anonymity, the 'digital trace' (Davidson et al., 2010: 2) or 'footprint' (McLaughlin, 2009: 12) also facilitates the likelihood of prosecution (see generally McAlinden, 2012: Ch. 6).

[24] A range of studies with children and young people has demonstrated the extent of their computer literacy as well as their use of the Internet (Livingstone and Bober, 2004; Davidson and Martellozzo, 2008a; Livingstone, 2009). See e.g. Webster et al. (2012: 16–20, 101–18) who found in focus group research with young people age 11 to 16 in the UK, Italy and

seven' access (Middleton et al., 2006) in both 'fixed' and 'mobile' environments, 'as such services grow, so do the risks associated with them' (Warren, 2008: 165; see also Nair, 2006: 180). The risk of sexual victimisation, therefore, is seen as being much more acute and prolific in the virtual environment in that it may emanate from anywhere in the world and where the use of technology enables the victim-offender interaction to become 'increasingly private, intimate and controlled' (Gallagher et al., 2006: 42). The fact that this form of child sexual exploitation and abuse has become one of the most challenging for society to countenance is in large part due to the fact that the Internet allows strangers to become 'virtual friends' (Davidson and Martellozzo, 2005: 1). As such, it also assuages the boundary between the risks associated with the public sphere and the perceived safety of private domestic spaces by bringing potential risk into most family homes and the everyday lives of children.

A range of labels has been used by academics to describe the various forms of online contact between potential offenders and victims which are often used interchangeably within the literature. These include 'cybersexploitation' (O'Connell, 2003), 'cyber sex' (Döring, 2000; Quayle and Taylor, 2001), 'online child sexual abuse' (Jewkes, 2010; Martellozzo, 2012; Quayle and Ribsil, 2012), 'Internet child abuse' (Davidson and Gottschalk, 2011) or 'Internet exploitation' (Gallagher et al., 2003, 2006). However, even though online forms of sexual offending against children may entrench public concerns about the predatory nature of sex offending against children, at the same time they also 'challenge traditional views of what constitutes child sexual abuse in the real world' (Davidson and Martellozzo, 2008b: 351). As Jewkes (2010: 10) notes more generally, 'the Internet has become something of a scapegoat for a myriad of deviant human behaviours and conditions.' Indeed, online forms of grooming and abuse are considerably more complex than contemporary media portrayals might suggest (Gallagher et al., 2003: 9; see also McAlinden, 2012a: Ch. 4). Not least is the fact that they belie the complexities of offending and victim identities and the often highly complex relationships between victims and offenders in virtual contexts in a number of significant ways.

First, it is important to note that not all adults who are interested sexually in children use the 'subterfuge' of posing as teenagers or

Belgium, that time spent online ranged from five minutes to six hours, and that virtually all young people used Facebook, with 'friends' ranging from 50 to 1000.

children online (Powell, 2007: 118). Although there will inevitably be cases where adult offenders will try to 'target teens and seduce victims into sexual relationships' (Davidson and Gottschalk, 2010: 39; see also Choo, 2009: 32), many offenders are truthful and open about their identity, including their age and sexual intentions towards children (see also Wolak et al., 2004: 428; Webster et al., 2012: 8, 46–48). By way of example, nearly half of the victims in Wolak et al.'s study were described as 'being in love with or feeling close bonds with the offenders' (2004: 428). Such findings serve to highlight inaccurate stereotypes relating to the use of a range of deception or grooming techniques by male adult predatory paedophiles previously unknown to the child victim (McAlinden, 2012a). As discussed further, '"compliant" or "statutory" victims' (Wolak, et al., 2004: 432) who may have developed strong emotional attachments to offenders, particularly where the age gap between victims and perpetrators is one of only a few years, pose unique challenges for law enforcement and for prevention efforts in particular.

Second, online forms of sexual offending do not always fit within the traditional social constructions of victimhood in which children and young people are the 'innocent' victims of online sexual abuse. In common with institutional forms of child sexual abuse as highlighted earlier, victims are typically older children or adolescents rather than younger children and are predominantly female.[25] In a study by Wolak and colleagues, for example, 99 per cent of victims were between ages 13 and 17, and 75 per cent were female (Wolak et al., 2004: 428). In relation to offenders, while the overwhelming majority of Internet sex offenders are adult males (Wolak et al., 2004: 428; Gallagher et al., 2006: 42; Choo, 2009: xii; Davidson and Gottschalk, 2010: 39), a growing number of online sexual offences are committed by children and young people (Finkelhor et al., 2000; Choo, 2009: xiii; Elliott et al., 2009). Some of the most recent manifestations of these online behaviours are sexting and sexualised forms of cyberbullying. In the contemporary focus on online forms of grooming and sexual offending by predatory strangers, however, the fact that other forms of sexual

[25] In relation to the gendered nature of online forms of sexual offending, while females are at a much higher risk of receiving sexual solicitations online (Mitchell et al., 2001, 2007; Gallagher et al., 2006: 41–42), a minority of studies have found significantly higher proportions of male victims and female perpetrators of online grooming. In one American study, for example, a quarter of victims were male (Wells and Mitchell, 2007).

exploitation and harm to children may also be occurring online, such as exploitation and abuse between peers, can be overlooked.

Third, some elements of online sexual offending further distort the traditional victim-offender dichotomy. As with offline or face-to-face forms of sexual offending (McAlinden, 2006: 347; Montgomery-Devlin, 2008: 393), children who have themselves been victimised online may also be used to procure and groom other child victims for offenders (O'Connell, 2003: 11; Palmer and Stacey, 2004: 23). As O'Connell (2003: 4, 11) notes, where the child has been involved in not only looking at but also in the making of indecent images of children, technically they may be said to have become both the producer and distributer of child pornography. Online sexual solicitation, however, may be perceived as less serious or threatening by children because it often involves non-contact forms of offending. As discussed further in Part II of this book, these particular dimensions of online forms of harmful sexual behaviour also have important implications for how children view certain forms of sexualised contact, including in the virtual world, and how they may perceive risky behaviour and themselves as victims. More broadly, it also has resonance for how law and society perceive non-contact forms of sexual exploitation and abuse in the absence of tangible harm.

CHILD SEXUAL EXPLOITATION

The most recent incarnation of social and political concerns about harmful sexual behaviour concerning children and young people, and one of the highest-profile constructions of 'risk' to emerge within the United Kingdom, is child sexual exploitation. Despite the fact that academics have noted the complexity of the term 'child sexual exploitation' (see e.g. Melrose, 2013), as noted in the first chapter, it is generally taken to mean a form of child sexual abuse 'in which children are sexually exploited for money, power or status'.[26] Scott and Skidmore (2006: 1), for example, explain as follows:

> Sexual exploitation incorporates a spectrum of experience ranging from what is generally referred to as 'child sexual abuse' at one end, to 'formal prostitution' at the other. Many young people are first drawn into 'informal exploitation' where sex is exchanged for drugs or somewhere

[26] See www.nspcc.org.uk/preventing-abuse/child-abuse-and-neglect/child-sexual-exploitation/what-is-child-sexual-exploitation.

> to stay. Many young women become engaged in a coercive relationship with an adult man who sometimes grooms them for more formal prostitution.

While concern around sexual exploitation of children is not new and predates recent cases (Lerpiniere et al., 2013; Cree et al., 2014), the terminology has evolved over time and has included 'juvenile or teenage prostitution' (Melrose et al., 1999) or 'child prostitution' (Lee and O'Brien, 1995; Shaw and Butler, 1998) and, most recently, 'sexual exploitation' (Kosaraju, 2008; Pearce, 2009) and 'child trafficking' (Rafferty, 2007; Cree et al., 2014).[27] All of these terms, however, tend to denote exploitation of children at the hands of adults and largely omit consideration of sexually exploitative behaviours and relationships among children and young people where they may manipulate or coerce another into engaging in some form of sexual activity (see further Chapters 5 and 6).

Most of what is known about this form of child sexual abuse derives from media coverage of a number of recent high-profile cases and a handful of research studies (e.g. Clutton and Coles, 2007; Pearce, 2009; Twill et al., 2010; Beckett, 2011; Beckett et al., 2013, 2014; Pearce et al., 2013) and related inquiries or policy reviews (e.g. Scott and Skidmore, 2006; Barnardo's, 2009, 2011, 2012; CEOP, 2011, 2012; Berelowitz et al., 2012, 2013, 2015; Brodie and Pearce, 2012; Home Affairs Committee, 2013, 2014) which brought the issue to public and political attention. Although there are very few reported cases, academic and policy studies generally indicate that 'what we are aware of is only "the tip of the iceberg"' (Beckett, 2011: 48; see also CEOP, 2011). While the emerging picture is 'complex and ambiguous' (Melrose, 2013: 161), the dominant paradigm involves the sexual grooming, exploitation or abuse of children or young people by adults who are initially unknown to them.

Beckett's (2011) study of the problem in Northern Ireland adopts a comprehensive definition of child sexual exploitation which outlines some of its broader purposes: 'a form of sexual abuse in which children or young people are exploited, coerced and/or manipulated into engaging in some form of sexual activity in return for something they need or desire and/or for the gain of a third person' (Beckett, 2011: 3). This 'something' which the child or young person receives is further defined as including both tangible items (e.g. food, somewhere to stay, drugs,

[27] For a critical overview of the changing use of language in this field, see Melrose (2013: 158–61).

alcohol, cigarettes or money) and more intangible 'rewards' (e.g. affection, protection or a sense of value or belonging). The tangible and intangible nature of the rewards surrounding sexual exploitation are illustrative of not only the broader processes of sexual grooming (McAlinden, 2012a: Ch. 4) but also much of the innocuous and surreptitious nature of such forms of offending against children prior to the manifestation of harm and the realisation of victim status on the part of victims.

A number of recent cases of child sexual exploitation have occurred in the North and Midlands of England including those in Derby, Rochdale, Oxford and Rotherham[28] where gangs of men have worked in groups grooming primarily female adolescents into a range of sexually exploitative situations from organised/networked abuse to prostitution or internal or domestic trafficking (Chase and Satham, 2005; Barnardo's, 2009: 16, 2011: 6; Ost and Mooney, 2013: 429–30). Such cases have generated a moral panic over South Asian gangs preying on white girls, propagating the notion of South Asian men as 'folk devils' (Gill and Harrison, 2015). As a result, these cases have given rise to the labels 'street', 'on street grooming' (McAlinden, 2012a), 'localised' (CEOP, 2011: 5; Williams and Hudson, 2013) or more recently 'group localised grooming' (Ost and Mooney, 2013) which denote a number of characteristics about this particular form of child sexual abuse: namely, that the abuse happens in a localised public space – where victims are typically accosted on the street by perpetrators who were previously unknown to them – and normally involves multiple perpetrators working in networks or 'abuse rings'. The perceived situational nature of sexual offending also helps wider society to disengage from the problem and the more complex range of risks concerning child sexual exploitation. Moreover, the media association of child sexual exploitation with particularly vulnerable children, including the emphasis on the link between exploitation and 'looked-after children' in institutional care (Beckett, 2011), also serves to distance the problem from the lives of most 'normal' people and families.

While such cases challenge and confront the stereotypical notion of the offender as 'a rootless drifter or a "sexually degenerated old man"' (Olafson et al., 1993: 14, citing Gordon, 1988: 223), they also tend to reinforce and further entrench the stranger perpetrator paradigm

[28] See Chapter 1, notes 28–31 and accompanying references.

portrayed in this instance in the guise of 'foreigner'.[29] Both public and academic discourses have emphasised the racial element of these crimes and the stark cultural differences within mainstream white popular culture and Asian communities respectively (Moghal et al., 1995; Gilligan and Akhtar, 2006; Cowburn et al., 2015), in terms of how child sexual abuse and victims more generally are viewed and responded to.[30] There are divergent views on the centrality of race and culture to the recent cases of child sexual exploitation and localised grooming.[31] This tension, however, has also contributed to the 'othering' (Garland, 2001) of sexual offending concerning children, creating 'culturally-specific notions of hegemonic masculinity' (Gill and Harrison, 2015: 34) and diverting attention and resources from other forms of child sexual exploitation and abuse.

In this vein, Beckett (2011) has further highlighted a number of models of child sexual exploitation denoting the often highly complex relationships between victims and offenders. These include abuse of a child through prostitution, the 'party house scenario' and the 'sexually exploitative relationship'. The last two are of particular relevance for social and legal responses to peer-based child sexual exploitation, both in terms of how such victims are perceived by wider society and how victims may perceive themselves. The party house scenario involves perpetrators inviting young girls to parties where there are free alcohol or drugs where the 'exchange of favours' (Kosaraju, 2008: 15) via sexual acts is usually 'demanded or forcefully taken retrospectively' after a period of fun and grooming (Beckett, 2011: 5). Within the sexually exploitative relationship, or what others have termed 'the boyfriend model' (Montgomery-Devlin, 2008: 392; Barnardo's, 2011: 6; CEOP, 2011: 10), the young person perceives 'the relationship' as a 'consensual romantic' one that they have freely entered into (Beckett, 2011: 5).

[29] See e.g. the similar argument made by Pearce (2011) in relation to child trafficking.

[30] Gilligan and Akhtar (2006), for example, contend that in some ethnic minority communities, in common with some white communities, there are cultural inhibitors to disclosure, including reluctance to discuss the issue as a 'taboo' or 'hidden' subject, lack of appropriate vocabulary and relatively high levels of denial in relation to child sexual abuse. More broadly, this can also be attributed to the roles of shame and honour within patriarchal Asian cultures which have generally high levels of intolerance for deviant behaviour (Zhang, 1995; Vagg, 1998) often resulting in victim blaming (Cowburn et al., 2015).

[31] One author, for example, has argued that the Rochdale gang should have been prosecuted as perpetrators of a hate crime (Walters, 2013), while others have argued that the racial dimension has been constructed by the media and essentially overplayed (see e.g. Cockbain, 2013; Salter and Dagistanli, 2015). As Ost and Mooney (2013: 437) note, this broad tension has also been evident in views expressed to the Commons Select Committee on Localised Child Grooming: see Home Affairs Committee, 2013.

As Ost and Mooney (2013: 426) have argued, 'those who groom children in this context are far from strangers to victims; they are individuals whom victims have come to trust and often love' (see also Berelowitz, 2012: 48). The fact that victims may have become involved in some sort of relationship with their abusers, however this may have begun, can undermine the societal recognition of the harm suffered. As discussed further in Chapters 6 and 7, this can lead to victims being perceived as having been in some way complicit and even instrumental in their own abuse.

More broadly, however, these dominant models of child sexual exploitation may obscure the complexity of the forms of sexual exploitation which children and young people experience in the twenty-first century. In this respect, what Melrose (2013: 161) terms the 'pimping and grooming' model, as highlighted earlier, may coexist with other forms of child sexual exploitation including those in the context of peer relations. As with institutionalised forms of child abuse, the offending culture surrounding these forms of sexual offending may facilitate a continuum of sexual exploitation in which sexually exploitative and abusive behaviours become normalised so that young people may be simultaneously both perpetrators as well as victims of abuse. As discussed further in Chapters 5 and 6, peer-based sexual exploitation is also emerging as an area of growing professional and policy concern (Barter and Berridge, 2011; Beckett et al., 2012, 2013; Firmin, 2013). Peer-to-peer forms of grooming and abuse may take the form of young people recruiting or grooming others into exploitative and abusive networks (Montgomery-Devlin, 2008: 393; CEOP, 2011: 87) as young people are apt to feel safer and be more trusting of a like-minded child of the same age rather than an adult (Montgomery-Devlin, 2008: 393; Barnardo's, 2011: 7; CEOP, 2011: 87). In such instances of peer recruitment, the young person becomes both a victim as well as a potential perpetrator of child sexual exploitation. Indeed, a further inhibiting factor for young people preventing them from reporting the abuse and extricating themselves from the abusive situation is that 'they are told implicitly and explicitly that they are as guilty as the adults' (Montgomery-Devlin, 2008: 393).

Peer-based sexual exploitation and violence within gang culture have also emerged as a lesser-known subset of child sexual exploitation. Research by Beckett and colleagues (2012, 2013, 2014) has examined gang-associated sexual exploitation and violence which have become 'part and parcel of sexual activity within the gang environment'

(Beckett et al., 2013: 6). In a similar vein, the partying lifestyle of young people has also emerged as a further subset of sexual exploitation among peers, where vulnerable young women in particular will exchange sex in return for popularity (Melrose, 2013). The normalisation of these patterns of sexual victimisation and violence among young people also 'blur[s] the boundaries' between their experiences of being either a victim or a perpetrator of sexual violence, with many young people (including young women as well as young men) experiencing both (Beckett et al., 2013: 7). In consequence, it can also become increasingly difficult for the victim to distinguish between risky or harmful sexual behaviours and normal interactions between peers. As discussed further in Part II, for a range of cultural and institutional reasons, including those related to victim stereotyping and blaming, incidences of this form of peer-on-peer sexual exploitation are not being reported by young people or proactively responded to by professionals.

CONCLUSION

Although changing permutations of panic related to the sexual abuse and exploitation of children have led to mutations of risk in evolving social contexts, by and large the perceived nucleus of the problem and its central cultural constructs have remained unchanged. These have included, most notably, the adult-child nature of the sexual contact, the public nature of sexual victimisation of children and risk as being 'other' than, rather than 'of', intimate relationships related to the family, peers and home. Framing the problem of child sexual abuse around particular panics and in such narrow terms tends to divert attention and resources from a broader heterogeneous range of risks to children and young people. In particular, the predatory stranger has become the meta-narrative for discourses on sexual abuse and exploitation concerning children.

At a time of perceived social anxieties concerning risks to children or threats to established family values, paedophiles as folk devils have provided 'a necessary external threat' and a means of boundary affirmation (Jenkins, 1992: 7, citing Cohen, 1972). Indeed, perhaps the defining feature of a 'moral panic' is that it tends to 'mark the moral boundaries of society' (Critcher, 2003: 5; see also Garland, 2008) and, in the case of sexual offending concerning children and young people specifically, the contours of what is deemed risky behaviour. The cultural denial or disassociation of behaviours which appear to threaten these moral boundaries can be discerned in each of the main forms of child sexual abuse and exploitation examined in this chapter. It is against this backdrop of the cyclical nature of concerns about sexual offending and the social disavowal of more interpersonal and intimate forms of sexualised risks against children that the notion of peer-based harmful sexual or exploitative behaviour has emerged.

Indeed, concerns about sexting and sexualised forms of cyberbullying and other forms of risky sexual behaviours among peers have become the new forms of moral panic concerning sexual offending and children. As one senior social work practitioner in the study commented:

> What we want to do is beware of moral judgements. From a sociological perspective . . . it used to be teddy boys, then it was rockers and all that. We have to be careful we don't demonise a whole generation of young males and victimise a whole generation of young females. So I think it is problematic.[32]

As explored further in Chapter 6, the notion of children as perpetrators rather than victims of sexual offending is problematic for society, and also for some professionals, as it tends to generate a 'moral disturbance because of conflicts in values' (Young, 2009: 4) about childhood.

As reflected in the quotation at the beginning of the chapter, the media creation of stranger danger has also had 'serious and long lasting repercussions' producing changes in both 'legal and social policy [and] . . . in the way society conceives itself' (1972: 28). While the social and political obfuscation of sexual forms of risk emanating from children and young people can be attributed in large part to the public prominence and recurring nature of other types of sexualised risks concerning children as highlighted in this chapter, it can also be attributed to a range of cultural and ideological concerns relating to victims and offenders more broadly as well as the nature of children and childhood. Such concerns have had a number of knock-on effects for how society and law perceive children and how children experience childhood, irrespective of actual risks of victimisation, as discussed further in the next and subsequent chapters.

[32] Interview 23, 24 June 2016.

3

THE SOCIAL AND POLITICAL CONSTRUCTION OF SEXUAL OFFENDING CONCERNING CHILDREN

> They [the public] probably are not as difficult around males between fifteen and eighteen who commit sexually abusive behaviour. I think actually the public would probably accept that ... boys at that age are always thinking of sex, so it is not so much of a challenge. And as for children, it so doesn't happen ... I think then if you would also ask them do they sexually harm each other. So I think the difficulty is ... firstly the sexual bit. And the second bit is, but could that be harmful? ... So there's a few things in there in terms of gender, sexual development, sexuality, and the aggressiveness of boys.[1]

While concerns about sexual offending related to children are not fixed but have rather fluctuated and evolved over time, as outlined in the previous chapter, so too have concerns about children and childhood more broadly (Hendrick, 1997; James and Prout, 2015). In his seminal text *Centuries of Childhood*, French academic Phillipe Ariès (1962) highlighted the shifting nature of childhood, arguing that childhood is not a historical constant but a social and economic construct embodying the prevailing cultural concerns of a given time (see generally James and James, 2004; Cunningham, 2006, 2014; Heywood, 2013). Despite the fact that later scholars have questioned many of Ariès's core assumptions, subsequent work advancing a 'new sociology of childhood' (Prout and James, 1997; Lavalette and Cunningham, 2002; James and Prout, 2015) has retained the notion of childhood and adolescence as social constructions.

[1] Interview 16, 9 June 2016, Independent Social Work Consultant.

Since childhood is a social construction, it is also 'subject to a continuous process of (re)invention and (re)definition [wherein] current ideas about children are underpinned subtly by the attitudes of our forebears' (Jewkes, 2010: 8). Within the context of this broader literature, this chapter critically examines the central components of the contemporary social and political construction of sexual offending concerning children and young people. It argues that contemporary cultural concerns about the risk of sexual offending related to children stem from several core historical ideologies about the nature of children and childhood. In brief, although academic discourses have generally shifted away from viewing children as passive objects towards a view of children as important and competent social actors (see e.g. Alderson, 1995, 2000; Mason and Urquhart, 2001; Farrell, 2005; Lundy and McEvoy, 2012), policy and social discourses have lagged someway behind.

A number of underlying themes emerge which link this chapter to the previous one. First, central to an understanding of the cultural construction of children and childhood is, as Brooks (2006: 16, citing Professor Al-Aynsley Green[2]) observes, a 'deep ambivalence' towards children. This cultural confusion and the 'highly ambiguous' ideology contextualising children and childhood (Jewkes, 2010: 5) is evidenced, for example, in the stark tension between the contemporary premature cultural sexualisation of children and the proliferation of public and political concerns about predatory sex offenders. It is also illustrated more broadly by the fundamental disconnect between societal concerns about risks to children and a deeper discussion of the nature of contemporary childhood and adolescence.

Second, analogous to 'moral panics' (Cohen, 1972) about sexualised forms of risk related to children and young people, there is also evidence of what Brooks (2006: 16) has termed 'child-panic'. Within what has been broadly characterised as 'an age of anxiety' (Holloway and Jefferson, 1997: 255), children have become the locus of contemporary adult anxieties about a series of dangers related to sex, consumerism, technology, strangers and safety. In essence, public concerns about sex offending related to children 'serve as the ideological embodiment of deeper anxieties' about risks to children (Hier, 2003: 6). Whereas the previous chapter examined the intermittent waves of public panic

[2] Prof. Al Aynsley-Green coined this phrase marking his appointment as the first Children's Commissioner for England in 2005. See L. Ward. '"Child-Unfriendly" England Served Notice', *The Guardian*, 2 March 2005.

premised around stranger danger and related risks to children, this chapter examines the core cultural viewpoints about children and childhood which underlie such panics.

Third, it will be demonstrated that concerns about the parlous state of childhood are also characterised by extreme positions: '[c]hildhood is seen to be corruptible or corrupted, and between these poles there lies a shrinking habitat for young people of average virtue' (Brooks, 2006: 17). Indeed, the oppositional nature of the childhood conundrum also has particular implications for children and young people who perpetrate harmful sexual or exploitative behaviour. Such children bridge the dichotomous conception of childhood and adulthood, as well as victimhood and offender identities related to sexual offending behaviour, as blameless versus blameworthy, respectively.

In this respect, the chapter argues that a number of core cultural and ideological tensions underly the contemporary social understanding of the nature of children and childhood which impede or at best problematise public and policy discourses on sexualised forms of risk stemming from children and young people. These relate to the sexuality and sexualisation of children and young people; the polarised construction of 'innocence' and 'blame' whereby children and childhood are deemed synonymous with 'innocence', passivity and vulnerability; and the dichotomous and highly moralised discourse concerning the construction of victim and offending hierarchies of sexual offending. The chapter also explores these themes and tensions in relation to young people who display harmful sexual behaviour. These notions have manifested themselves in turn in criminal justice policies in which children are deemed primarily to be 'at risk' of harm from sexual offending rather than constituting a risk of harm to others. The chapter also examines the relevance of the children's rights discourse which has become subsumed within the broader rhetoric of 'risk' yet which is also fundamental to how society and law view expressions of children's sexual identities via sexting and other potentially harmful sexual behaviours. The chapter begins with a brief overview of the dominant theoretical conceptions of childhood as a preface to more detailed consideration of these core arguments.

CONCEPTUALISING CHILDHOOD

Childhood is a relatively recent concept. Ariès (1962: 128), for example, as one of the early theorists on childhood, notes how in medieval society the notion of childhood as a distinct stage in the life cycle did not exist, and that an awareness of childhood and the needs of children as being separate from those of adults did not emerge until the seventeenth century (see also James et al., 1998).[3] There are a range of conceptual frameworks on childhood including historical perspectives (see e.g. Steedman, 1995; Cunningham, 1998, 2014; Gittins, 1998; James and James, 2004; Heywood, 2013), biological essentialist perspectives (see e.g. Piaget, 1929; Gelman, 2003), and social constructionist perspectives (see e.g. Parson and Bales, 1955; Ariès, 1962). A detailed exposé of the historical construction of childhood and the shifting cultural position of children within the social, political and economic landscape is beyond the scope of this book. It is of broader relevance, however, in understanding the evolving concept of the child reflecting the social conditions of the time as well as the prevailing 'roots of contemporary anxieties' (Cunningham, 1998: 1195). In this respect, some of the key themes from this perspective will be considered further in this chapter, illustrating how social understanding of children and childhood is highly contingent on time and place. They will be revisited in Part II of the book in terms of tensions within the historical construction of childhood by the law, the courts and the legal profession. Of most relevance for present purposes, however, are the latter two perspectives – the psychological and sociological paradigms – and the inherent tension between them.

Regarding the first perspective, several evolving historical constructs of childhood related to the 'natural child', the 'romantic child', the 'evangelical child', 'the factory child' and the 'delinquent child' (see generally Hendrick, 1997, 2005). With links to biological essentialism described more fully later, writing in the late seventeenth century, early modern philosophers emphasised the innate goodness of the child with Locke in 1693 (Locke, 1812) specifically rejecting the idea of infant depravity.[4] Jean-Jacques Rousseau, writing in the latter half of the eighteenth century (1762) in *Émile: or On Education*, during a period of increasing literacy and Romanticism, espoused the notion of the 'romantic child' stemming from the natural purity and innocence of

[3] Note, however, while the terms 'children' and 'childhood' are used interchangeably within the literature, some scholars also differentiate them. Broadly speaking, while children are human beings shaped by their cultural, political, social and economic backgrounds, childhood is a period of 'becoming' which precedes adulthood (see generally Jenks, 1996: 9; Denzin, 2010: 2).

[4] A marked difference, however, between this view and that of biological essentialists is that children were not regarded as being all the same but were subject to individual differences (see Hendrick, 1997).

children and their inherent vulnerability. This can be juxtaposed with the 'evangelical child', emerging in the nineteenth century with the growth of the Evangelical movement, which depicted the innate wickedness of children and childhood as being inherently corrupt and in need of overt control and correction (see also Walvin, 1982). In the late eighteenth and early nineteenth centuries, during a period of growing industrialisation in Great Britain when cheap labour was required, the concept of the 'factory child' emerged (see also Silver, 1977). Critics, however, objected to the use of child labour, projecting the 'notion of a "natural" and "innocent" childhood' (Hendrick, 1997: 40), which eroded through long hours of work. In the mid-nineteenth century, the birth of reformatory and industrial schools to deal with 'depraved', 'delinquent' children cemented the relation between youth and crime and highlighted the reformative effects of education in restoring children to their 'true position' as 'natural' and 'innocent' (Hendrick, 1997: 45). The notion of 'childhood' as a distinct and 'special' period of development only consolidated in the late nineteenth century with the introduction of compulsory state schooling, which ended the worst excesses of child labour (Hendrick, 1997: 45–47). As discussed further later, subsequent noteworthy definitions of childhood in the late twentieth century include the child as 'victim' and the child as 'threat'.

A unifying theme which transverses these varying historical constructs is the overwhelmingly moral tone of public and official discourses on children and childhood. The principled nature of the debates is couched in absolute terms and reflects in particular the good versus evil dialectic (McAlinden, 2014a). Moreover, adults have always been the primary definers of the moral status of children (Dwyer, 2011) and how childhood has been written about and understood. Traditionally, 'the socialisation of the child' and what is considered 'appropriate development [are] not open to negotiation, except between "knowledgeable" adults' (Scraton, 1997b: 164; see also Jenks, 1996; James et al., 1998). As Cunningham (1998: 1195) notes, the construction and reconstruction of childhood have 'variably stood for innocence, hope, niaveté, incapacity, or evil, or has embodied ... nostalgia for times past'. As discussed later, these themes underlying historical conceptions of the 'imagined' child are of particular relevance to contemporary social constructions of hierarchies of blame surrounding victim and offender identities related to sexual offending behaviour. As such, they present significant social and policy challenges when children and young people engage in harmful sexual or exploitative behaviours.

In relation to the second perspective, proponents of biological essentialism, influenced by the philosophies of Aristotle and Plato on human nature (Ambler, 1987), suggest that human behaviour is anchored in 'immutable biological roots' (Miller and Costello, 2001: 592) and that 'our destiny is in our genes' (de Melo-Martin, 2003: 1184). According to this view, children were to be regarded as 'natural rather than social phenomena' and childhood as a 'pregiven essential nature' and a 'universal experience' (James et al., 1998: 17, 139). The work of psychologist Jean Piaget (1929), for example, writing in the early twentieth century highlighted a 'genetic epistemology' (Piaget and Duckworth, 1970) in which the naturalness and universality of childhood were characterised by 'discrete, age-related . . . stages of development' (Haydon and Scraton, 2000: 417). Reflecting the notion of the 'becoming child' (Brownlie, 2001: 523–24) – in which children are not viewed as subjects in their own right but as 'future adults' – puberty in particular was seen as signifying the end of childhood and as representing 'a bridge between childhood and adulthood' (Oakley, 2015: 83). Although this theory is focused primarily on the biological aspects of child development, it is also implicitly underpinned by the influence of social factors on the development of knowledge (DeVries, 2000: 190; Matusov and Hayes, 2000: 215).

This perspective is also characterised by a 'shift' in sociopolitical thinking from viewing nonconformity in children's behaviour as 'deviant' to 'risky' and as an accepted part of developing personal and social identities. That is, within this broader framework, 'risky behaviours' are thought to be the 'hallmarks' of adolescence (Kelley et al., 2004: 27), which is itself viewed as 'a time of heightened vulnerability' for risk-taking behaviour which generally declines into adulthood with the augmented capacity for self-regulation (Steinberg, 2007: 55). While the expectations and parameters attached to youth may also be 'culturally produced and sustained' (Brown, 2005: 5), demarking childhood and adulthood by fixed age-related boundaries is an important consideration for the legal construction of childhood and legislative and policy responses surrounding, for example, the age of consent. However, this reductionist account of adolescence and its association with 'risk taking and novelty seeking', including sexualised behaviours, within the literature (see e.g. Kelley et al., 2004: 27; see also Steinberg, 2007; Lee et al., 2013) serves to contribute to the 'panic' concerning sex and young people. Moreover, it also tends to pathologise potentially harmless sexual behaviours and obscure the lived experiences of children and young people and the 'messy' realities of their lives.

In particular, it does not take a full account of childhood, and especially adolescence, as key stages of personal and social development which entail the negotiation of personal identity and finding one's place in the social world. Indeed, there is a sizeable literature which documents the staged biological and psychological development of children and their evolving physical and emotional maturity and capacity for reasoned decision-making (see e.g. Erikson, 1950; Mann et al., 1989; DeHart et al., 2000; Jacobs and Klaczynski, 2006). This also inevitably means that children and adolescents are often not equipped to navigate the complexities or ethics of interrelationships, appreciate nuanced social complexities or fully understand sexual themes. Further, as they are prone to making mistakes, they cannot be judged by the same standards or held to the same expectations as those concerning adults. In such a context, therefore, risk-taking behaviour is not to be viewed as problematic or burdensome but rather as an inevitable and vital part of children's development in providing important experiential opportunities for learning, exploration and personal growth. As discussed further in Chapter 7, this is also an argument which militates against the blanket criminalisation of behaviours such as sexting.

In relation to the third perspective, advocates of the social constructionist perspective contend that contemporaneous social and cultural factors shape childhood experience, challenging the previous orthodoxy expounded by Piaget (1929) on the universality and immutable nature of childhood (see e.g. James et al., 1998).[5] The temporal 'cultural construction of ideas to do with childhood' (Cunningham, 1998: 1195) and the related notions of the complexity and 'plurality of childhoods' (Qvortrup et al., 1994: 5) wherein children are thought to be products of social processes are generally attributed to Ariés (1962). According to Ariès, two early influences on the conceptualisation of childhood emerged between the fifteenth and seventeenth centuries. The first was 'a new emotional ethic ... concerning the care of children' (Brooks, 2006: 6), known as 'coddling', by which the child 'on account of his sweetness, simplicity and drollery' became

[5] A number of theorists have also challenged the simplicity of Piaget's paradigm. See e.g. the work of behavioural scientist Lev Vygotsky (1962, 2004) who focused on the interaction between social development and cognitive development in children.

a source of amusement for adults (Ariés, 1962: 131). The second came from those outside the family and the churchmen and moralists 'eager to ensure disciplined, rational manners' (Ariés, 1962: 132–33). In the eighteenth century, these two elements were extended by an emerging concern for the physical health and safety of children. This marked the beginning of what has subsequently been termed the 'child study movement', which led to social reforms including child labour laws, the establishment of juvenile courts and the treatment of 'at risk' children (Hendrick, 1997: 47–49).[6] Similarly, the work of American sociologist Talcott Parsons (Parson and Bales, 1955) on the socialisation of the child emphasised the primacy of the family in preparing the child for integration into adult society.

While Parsons's theory has been subject to criticism in terms of furthering 'a naturalistic reduction' of the child (Jenks, 1996: 18), it has been influential on the development of education and social care provision (Qvortrup et al., 1994: x). On one level, the demographic changes to household structures and the modern cultural configuration of the family at the beginning of the twenty-first century displaces the role of the 'traditional' or nuclear family unit as the primary vehicle for the social regulation of children. On another level, however, the cognitive, psychological, moral, emotional, social and sexual development and behaviour of young people are also deeply embedded within their interactions with families as well as peers and broader social structures and context – an argument which recurs throughout the book. Put another way, it can be the very powerful and formative influence of cultural and environmental factors which create the conditions for children to display 'risky' behaviours or become vulnerable to victimisation by others (see further Chapter 5). Moreover, the impact of these factors can affect children differentially at various stages of their development. This also underscores the power of ongoing supportive, nurturing contexts for children and young people.

While both of these latter paradigms have been influential on the development of contemporary academic and policy discourses on children and childhood and are of relevance for the broad arguments presented in the course of this chapter, they are overtly positivistic and deterministic in nature in that neither perspective

[6] Ariès work, however, has been subsequently challenged on a number of grounds including the fact that it tends to trace the development of an upper- or middle-class version of childhood while ignoring the experiences of poor and working class children. See e.g. Stone (1974); Wilson (1980); Vann (1982); Ben-Amos (1995); Cunningham (2014: Ch. 3).

harnesses the agency of children. As Shaw and Butler (1998: 180) have contended, 'adult myth-making about children and childhood reflects and maintains the relative powerlessness of children and ensures that they have little recognition as potential authors of their own biography.' A core critique underpinning previous paradigms on childhood, which presuppose that the behaviour of children and the nature of childhood may be variously biologically determined or socially constructed, is that they negate the potential for the individual agency and autonomy of children. This capacity for 'choice' and self-determination is central to the transition to adulthood as well as interactions with peers including those concerning potentially harmful or risky sexual behaviour. As discussed further in Chapter 8, the provision of age-appropriate education is key to equipping children to make such competent choices and determinations.

SEX, SEXUALITY AND THE SEXUALISATION OF CHILDREN AND YOUNG PEOPLE

The dichotomy of biological essentialist versus social constructionist approaches to childhood is also reflected in discourses on the sexuality of children and young people and indeed discourses on human sexuality more broadly. The former approach determines that human behaviour and sexual identity are 'natural, inevitable and, biologically determined' (DeLamater and Hyde, 1998: 10), whereas the latter espouses that humans are influenced by cultural values and socialisation processes which play a central role in shaping and informing individual meaning and identity. Some theorists have synthesized biological and social influences within a single theory as part of an 'interactionist' or 'conjoint' approach (see e.g. Berscheid and Walster, 1974; Tuzin, 1995). DeLamater and Hyde (1998: 10) are dismissive of the 'true conjoining of essentialism and social constructionism'. Other scholars, however, agree that a coordinated account of adolescent sexual maturation is likely to contain elements of both (see e.g. Plummer, 1982, 2003; Tolman and Diamond, 2001). Accepting this broader perspective, I would argue that discourses on children's sexuality and behaviour need to be cognisant of both biological and psychological factors stemming from puberty, gender differences and maturation, as well as social and cultural influences such as those stemming from peers and within the family.

In relation to the first approach, adolescence in particular is a life stage associated with social and sexual exploration and the development of wider personal and social relationships. According to theorists such as Freud, the biological explanation of sexuality holds that within Western societies, 'sexual instincts' and sexuality are 'absent in childhood' with sexual maturation emerging 'at the time of puberty' and manifesting as an interest in romance and sex in adolescence (Freud, 1975: 135, cited in Davidson, 1987: 262; see also Martinson, 1994; Giordano et al., 2006; Booth et al., 2015).[7] This position gives rises to two core assumptions: that children are 'asexual' until the time of puberty and that the 'natural order' of things is that children will develop an attraction for the opposite sex (Davidson, 1987). This approach, therefore, potentially countenances sexualised behaviours by adolescents but specifically not prepubescent children.[8] Taking this view further, any perceived diversion from these norms which is outside 'the limits that are regarded as normal' is defined as a 'perversion' (Freud, 1975: 158, 162, as cited in Davidson, 1987: 269). With links to the 'romantic child' referenced earlier, children and young people who are 'sexually mature' before their age are seen as a threat to the 'pure state' (James and Jenks, 1996: 320) and 'cherished ideals of childhood' (Jackson and Scott, 1999: 99). As a result, instances of harmful sexual or exploitative behaviour by children and young people can be dismissed easily by society as an aberration rather than being regarded as symptomatic of a wider societal problem as part of 'an attempt to cling onto traditional accounts of what children are' (James and Jenks, 1996: 324). Moreover, according to this perspective, while the predominant concern within popular discourses is the threat of the predatory stranger, the premature cultural sexualisation of children makes children more likely to be 'at risk' of sexual victimisation, rather than constitute a risk themselves.

Feminist scholars, however, have critiqued biological essentialist theory as promoting a highly gendered and heterosexual view of sexuality and as being responsible for 'male-female difference and male dominance' (Bem, 1993: 6; see also Thorne and Luria, 1986;

[7] Within other cultures, however, the sexual interests and activities of children may continue throughout childhood (Mirkin, 1999). See e.g. Malinowski (1932), who describes sexualised practices among children of the Trobriand islanders. Similarly, Oakley notes that within Arapesh culture, girls as young as 9 or 10 are already betrothed and it is generally accepted that unsupervised adolescents will have sexual intercourse (Oakley, 2015: 83).

[8] Some studies, however, show that children can express their sexuality before the physical benchmark of puberty (see e.g. Goldman and Goldman, 1982; Vanderburgh, 2009).

Coppock et al., 1995; Corteen and Scraton, 1997; Mort, 2000). Although the limits of 'normal sexuality' in adolescence, and what is deemed 'appropriate' and 'healthy' (Bancroft, 2009: Ch. 5; McNeely and Blanchard, 2010), are to some extent biologically determined by factors such as puberty and age, they are also socially defined by cultural influences and the 'sexual rules' and norms of a given society (Shoveller et al., 2004; Moore and Rosenthal, 2006). As other scholars have argued, adolescence in itself is 'a cultural invention' (Ben-Amos, 1995) and the tension between normal and acceptable sexual interactions between young people is also subject to variation between societies and cultures. As discussed later, regulating and responding to sexualised forms of risk posed by children and young people must also be considered within the context of the often rapidly changing cultural norms and broader social milieu of the time.

Indeed, in contrast, according to the social constructionist approach, 'sexual desire' and what comprises the 'sexual' varies between cultures and across historical periods (Giles, 2006; Oakley, 2015). Various composite theories underlie this approach to sexuality. Foucault (1978), for example, contends that sexual expression is fashioned around prevailing cultural norms. Similarly, underlining the importance of language and metaphor, Simon and Gagnon (2003: 492) have argued that 'sexual scripts' provide a 'conceptual space within which some of the fundamental aspects of human activity could be examined'. That is, knowledge, desire and meaning related to sex derive, not from 'the relatively constant physical body' but from 'the historical situation of the body' grounded in 'economic, political, familial and social conditions' (Simon and Gagnon, 2003: 492, xii). Even though research has found no strong correlation between family structure and context and individual adolescent sexuality (see e.g. Davis and Friel, 2001), it is the broader sociocultural conditions which help shape children's understanding of their own sexuality and sexual behaviour as well as their societal understanding more broadly. In line with the biological essentialist viewpoint of sex and sexuality being 'categories loaded with heterosexual meanings' (Thorne and Luria, 1986: 176), the social constructionist stance, however, has also tended to produce stereotypical and mythical accounts of gender and sexuality (Corteen and Scraton, 1997; Mort, 2000) (see further Chapter 4).

In this respect, conventional social understandings of sexuality have produced what has been termed an 'institutionalised hierarchy of sexuality' (Coppock et al., 1995: 19) based on a number or heteronormative values surrounding gender roles. In particular, males are deemed to display 'aggressive, dominant behaviour' and be 'naturally promiscuous' (Mottier, 2008: 9, 49) stemming from an innate, 'biological ... uncontrollable, sexual drive' (Stanko, 1985: 9), while females are presumed 'dependent, passive, unaggressive and submissive' (Oakley, 2015: 77). The social entrenchment of such stereotypes surrounding 'violent boys and precocious girls' (Walkerdine, 2000) may also influence young men's attitudes towards young women and their acceptance of 'myths about sexual aggression' (Coy and Horvath, 2011). Such a view, however, can produce over-simplistic accounts of sexualised behaviours between children and young people, delimiting girls' agency and capacity to make sense of and negotiate their own identity (Renold and Ringrose, 2011; Duschinsky, 2013; Egan, 2013) and excluding the notion of harmful sexual or exploitative behaviour by young females. As discussed in Part II, while both young males and young females can commit harmful sexual or exploitative behaviours, there are clear gendered dimensions to sexualised behaviours such as sexting (Ringrose and Barajas, 2011). These 'polarised gendered stereotypes' (Papadopoulos, 2010: 5) have also shaped how children and young people view sexual identity and intimate relationships as well as sexual violence, pornography and harmful sexual or exploitative behaviours more broadly (see further Chapter 4).

Such culturally entrenched stereotypes about masculinity and femininity have also become institutionalised impacting political agendas and legal structures. These consequences have been felt most keenly in relation to the social and legal acceptance of cultural 'rape myths' and 'victim blaming' (Gurnham, 2016), contributing in part to the attrition rate regarding sexual assault (Temkin and Krahé, 2008). Women who do not correspond to the 'real rape stereotype' (Stewart et al., 1996: 135) are regarded as 'encouraging the men's behaviour' (Stanko, 1985: 1998) and, consequently, denied full status and protection as 'innocent victims' (Coppock et al., 1995: 31). This is well illustrated, for example, by the backlash following the recent #MeToo campaign, wherein victims who had come forward alleging sexual harassment or sexual assault by men have been derided for using sex for personal gain. Furthermore, within this broader context, sexual coercion of males is often taken less seriously than sexual coercion of females (see also Huitema and Vanwesenbeeck, 2016). As discussed further in the next chapter, gendered myths have permeated popular discourses on victim and offender identities and hierarchies concerning sexual offending behaviours involving children and young people.

However, as Jewkes (2010: 7) contends, 'there is a significant degree of cultural hypocrisy in our attitudes to sex, risk and young people.' Despite the fact that stories of trafficking or other sexual offences concerning children seek to 'reclaim and safeguard a state of childhood innocence . . . they do so by titillating; they excite at the same time as encouraging moral outrage' (Cree et al., 2014: 431, citing Gittins, 1998). A range of fundamental cultural anomalies surround the premature sexualisation of children and young people which are fundamentally at odds with policy and professional attempts at child protection or the management of risk to children from sexual offenders. In the main, as I have argued previously, there is a 'current barrage of mixed messages regarding children's sexuality and appropriate behaviour' (McAlinden, 2012a: 293). Strong cultural and political views concerning the need to protect children from sex offenders are at variance with many forms of contemporary popular culture, most notably the music and fashion industries, which tend to overtly sexualise children from a young age (Durham, 2009; Levin and Kilbourne, 2009; Papadopoulos, 2010) (see Chapter 4). Kincaid (1998: 21) succinctly captures the problem as follows: society simultaneously 'regards children as erotic' and 'an erotic response to children . . . as criminally unimaginable'. The upshot of this tension is twofold: first, stemming from the social and political panic concerning the omnipresent predatory sex offender, is the normalisation of the eroticism of children wherein 'almost any picture of a naked child is likely to be considered sexual and pornographic' (Mirkin, 1999: 5). Second are the cultural confusion and the blurring of boundaries across society, as well as for children and young people, about what is considered within the realms of appropriate and 'normal' sexual behaviour by children.

In this vein, public policy concerns about the sexualisation of (female) childhood have been recognised in England and Wales and Scotland (see e.g. Buckingham et al., 2010; HM Government, 2010; Papadopoulos, 2010; Bailey, 2011). Such concerns generate additional challenges for professionals in responding to new and emerging forms of sexualised behaviours between children and young people particularly in differentiating those which are deemed normal and benign from those which are potentially inappropriate, coercive or harmful (Ashurst and McAlinden, 2015). They also generate pragmatic difficulties for professionals in engaging with children and young people in discourses on potentially harmful sexual behaviour. As discussed in the final chapter, this also underlines the need to re-evaluate children's and adults' knowledge and understanding of sex, sexuality and sexualisation in the contemporary context, primarily via education and outreach programmes in schools.

HIERARCHIES OF BLAME: SEXUAL OFFENDING AND VICTIMISATION CONCERNING CHILDREN

A further tension underlying the social and political construction of sex offending concerning children is the hierarchy of blame and blamelessness which attaches to victims and offenders. Within the past few decades, victims of crime have become the bastion of discourses on 'law and order' (Elias, 1993; Dubber, 2006) and have been used rhetorically to 'lever up punitiveness' (Zedner, 2002: 447). Criminal justice policy-making, particularly regarding violent and sexual offences, has been characterised by 'zero sum thinking' (O'Malley, 2004b: 323; see also Garland, 2001; Dubber, 2006) in which it is assumed that the enactment of retributive penal policies will punish the offender and vindicate the victim. This results in what Tilly (2008: 33) has termed a 'double game' of credit and blame. Further, victims are often perceived as 'the mirror' or 'binary opposite' (Rock, 1998: 195; McEvoy and McConnachie, 2012: 527–28) of perpetrators of sexual crime. What Rock (1998: 195, citing Merleau-Ponty, 1973: 31) terms the 'indissoluble dialectic' is founded on the young, 'innocent' and unsuspecting victim who represents the 'antithesis' of the older, adult, predatory male 'monster'.

Critical victimologists have emphasised, however, that the attribution of the label and status of victim is a social process (Miers, 1990; Mawby and Walklate, 1994). Within this broader context, there is a 'hierarchy of victimhood' (Carrabine et al., 2004) which polarises the distinction between the 'good' and 'bad' victim (Madlingozi, 2007). The 'ideal' (Christie, 1986: 18) or 'imagined' victim (Walkate, 2007) of child sexual abuse or exploitation appears as 'young, pure, passive and blameless' (McAlinden, 2014a: 185). Reflecting earlier historical concerns outlined earlier, a contemporary conservative moral politics is premised on the 'sacralisation' of children (Zelizer, 1994) and the 'veneration of the innocence of childhood' (Furedi, 2013: 45). Perceived risks to particularly 'innocent children' thus become the catalyst for legal and policy reform, providing the impetus for 'moral panics and moral regulation' (Hunt, 2011; see also Hier, 2003). A burgeoning amount of regulatory measures related to adult sex offenders who prey on young children are designed to address the loss of children's innocence or the 'theft or violation of childhood' (Kitzinger, 1988: 78).

A number of features underpin contemporary social constructions of children as 'innocents' and what Kitzinger (1988: 79) has termed 'real childhood'. First, children are regarded as intrinsically vulnerable (Furedi, 2013: 42) and therefore entirely pure or 'blameless', simply by virtue of their age or status as children. Age typically signifies the power imbalance between victim and offender, thereby highlighting the culpability and depravity of the sex offender. As Tilly (2008: 95) contends in relation to offenders, 'the younger the victim, the greater the blame'. Second, analogous to the literature on rape cited earlier (e.g. Stewart et al., 1996; Temkin and Krahé, 2008), the child deemed 'deserving' of the status of victim will have been abused by someone previously unknown to him or her. What I have previously termed 'the "real child abuse" stereotype' (McAlinden, 2014a: 184) usually takes place in a public setting, involving an aberrational abduction of a child victim by a stranger perpetrator. Third, there is also a gendered dimension to contemporary constructions of childhood sexual victimisation, suggesting high levels of victimisation among girls, which runs counter to research demonstrating patterns of victimisation among both boys and girls.[9]

As discussed in the previous chapter, stereotypical cases involving children abused or murdered by predatory sex offenders, such as those of Sarah Payne or the 'Soham murders', have become 'signal crimes' (Innes, 2004) in shaping public attitudes about child sexual abuse, precipitating legislative and policy change (Silverman and Wilson, 2002). Notably, in both cases, the victims were young girls who were in a public space and engaged in the routine activities of childhood at the time of the offence and the perpetrators were adult males with a history of sex offending. However, these cultural narratives concerning sexual offending against children and 'legitimate' victim status suffer from three core deficits – they tend to discount the sexual victimisation of older children or adolescents; they privilege the

9 For example, earlier large-scale research by Elliott et al. (1995) demonstrated that 58 per cent of adult sex offenders targeted girls; 14 per cent targeted boys; while the remaining 28 per cent targeted both boys and girls. See also Chapter 5 in relation to the gendered nature of sexualised behaviours between young people.

victimisation of children in extrafamilial settings or by strangers over more intimate forms of abuse, including that within families and between peers; and they preclude consideration of the sexual victimisation of young males.

In contrast, the 'ideal' or archetypal sex offender as 'paedophile' 'symbolises the antithesis of the sacred child' (Furedi, 2013: 40) and is premised on the parallel notions of evil, guilt and their deserving of contempt. As Furedi and others have contended, while the legitimate or deserving victim of child sexual abuse is predicated on the veneration of the sanctity of childhood, this is matched with 'a universal loathing for the child abuser' (Furedi, 2013: 45) and the conception of child sexual abuse as 'the supreme evil of our age' (Webster, 1998: 39). Reflecting the same oppositional cultural discourse, key structural attributes of the contemporary construction of 'the child sex offender' are conversely related to their age, gender and predatory nature. As discussed in the previous chapter, this is manifested in the cultural mantle of the older adult male dangerous stranger.

Indeed, it is the notion of sex offenders as 'outsiders' (Becker, 1963) or 'other' (Garland, 2001) which has become the defining characteristic of public and political discourses on sexual offending concerning children. The media propagate the 'othering' process by perpetuating the notion that sexual crime is committed by 'fiends' or 'beasts' as opposed to 'ordinary' men (Soothill and Walby, 1991; Kitzinger, 1999a; Stanko and Lee, 2003). Wardle (2007), for example, differentiating the media juxtaposition of victims and offenders of sexual offending against children as 'angels' and 'monsters', notes how pictorial depictions of sex offenders are used 'to make the "other" appear particularly immoral, bizarre [and] subhuman' (Wardle, 2007: 273). This 'otherness' of offenders is commonly juxtaposed with the 'ordinariness' of victims which simultaneously serves to reinforce the social boundaries between childhood and adulthood and good and evil more broadly.

Although the representation of sex offenders as 'pure evil' remains a powerful notion in advanced Western societies (Baumeiser, 1996, cited in Wardle, 2007), this moralising public discourse leaves little room or tolerance for attempts to contextualise sexual offending or to differentiate between levels and types of risk. As feminist scholars have contended, the casting of the sex offender as a subhuman and malevolent stranger helps to maintain the dichotomy of 'normal' and 'deviant' men (Cowburn and

Dominelli, 2001; see also Newburn and Stanko, 1994) and a view of risk and the threat to children's innocence 'as coming from somewhere beyond the boundaries' (Lynch, 2002: 560). However, the fact that child sex offenders may be 'of us' rather than 'other than us' and may also include children and young people is a deeply unpalatable truth for society to countenance. As Girard (1982: 87) observes, part of the function of 'scapegoating' is to shift the blame to others, thereby absolving us of any guilt or responsibility.

The cultural power of the 'othering' has also shaped legal and policy discourses concerning sexual offending against children. In what I have previously termed 'a politics of purification' (McAlinden, 2014a: 189), state-sanctioned punishment sustains populist notions of the victim/offender divide by reinforcing the sanctity of childhood and the depravity of the offender (Spencer, 2009: 219–20; see also Simon, 1998). Lynch (2002: 545), for example, in her analysis of federal legislative debates on sexual predator laws in the United States, pinpoints a moralising discourse underpinned by fears of contamination from a noxious supernaturally dangerous outsider (see also Hacking, 2003; Pratt, 2005). Such concerns have been translated into a range of broadly exclusionary measures, such as sex offender notification, which have been put in place within neo-liberal societies such as the United States and the United Kingdom aimed at the targeted surveillance and control of dangerous violent and sexual offenders (McAlinden, 2012b). Once more, the legislative enactment of such policies is also heavily based on the notion that the 'known' risks posed to children reside largely in the public sphere where they can be more readily directed and controlled, thereby protecting the sanctity of childhood and the inner sanctum of the family and home.

The neat classification of victims and offenders as 'reified and distinct' categories (McEvoy and McConnachie, 2012: 527), however, is not always possible. That is, victim or offender status is not fixed but is often fluid and subject to oscillation over time. As highlighted in the previous chapter and discussed at length in Part II of the book, there is a range of instances in which children and young people may move from being a victim to becoming a perpetrator of child sexual abuse or exploitation within the context of relationships with peers. This includes, for example, within the domain of online interactions, street or localised grooming or the context of institutional child abuse. Moreover, relationships between victims and offenders in the context of sexual offending, particularly between adolescent peers, are often highly complex so that these core categories cannot always be demarked so unambiguously.

Indeed, social and legal discourses cannot easily countenance unorthodox or 'deviant' (Karmen, 1983) victims, since they fall between the two stools of accepted victim and offender status. As discussed further in Part II, the typical oppositional stance held by the public surrounding 'disputed victims' (Reid, 2015: 211) is as expressed by one independent safeguarding professional:

> You primarily get the discourse that's about, you know, these are kind of really evil people, or . . . it's the kind of more negative side of it. You also get a bit around these poor children too. But most of it, particularly round those who sexually harm, is about how appalling it is that they are so evil and whatever, so young.[10]

Moreover, such deep-seated and culturally entrenched oppositional hierarchies of innocence and blame may also be internalised by children and young people. By way of example, a study which used vignettes of juvenile female prostitution with undergraduate students found that students with stronger sexist attitudes were more likely to blame the young girl and less likely to recommend restorative interventions. However, if the students were told about a background history of victimisation, they were less likely to attribute blame (Menaker and Miller, 2013). In such instances, therefore, there is more of a cultural tendency to attribute culpability where children's own behaviour would seemingly threaten the moral positioning of children by bridging the innocence/blame divide which attaches to victims and offenders and indeed childhood and adulthood more broadly.

As James and Jenks (1996: 322–24) argue, children and young people who participate in harmful or other exploitative behaviours have been 'removed from the category of "child" altogether'. This also helps to contextualise public vitriol and official condemnation following high-profile cases of violent or sexual offending by children. Such cases are frequently denounced as 'pure evil' or as representing 'the loss of innocence' since they cannot otherwise be accommodated within the cultural hierarchies of innocence or blame (McAlinden, 2014a: 190).[11]

[10] Interview 6, 25 April 2016.

[11] See e.g. some of the newspaper headlines following high-profile murders or attempted murders of children by other children: 'An Act of Unparalleled Evil', *The Independent*, 25 November 1993 (citing Mr Justice Moorhead at the trial of 10-year-old Robert Venables and Jon Thompson for the murder of 2-year-old James Bulger in Merseyside, Liverpool); and, more recently, 'The Truth About the Edlington Devil Brothers', *Anorak*, 23 January 2010, www

Indeed, children, and women, are typically placed at the bottom of the offending hierarchy due principally to their cultural status as victims (see also Newburn and Stanko, 1994; Cowburn and Dominelli, 2001; Denov, 2003; McAlinden, 2014a). Thus, it takes extreme forms of offending for both of these groups to transgress the normative boundaries attached to their age or gender and reach the top of the offending pyramid. This view was also expressed by a number of professionals in the study. An independent forensic psychologist stated: 'Unless it is extreme and unless there's a death with it, such as in Jamie Bulger or some of the better known cases, then I think that the public are kept away from harmful sexual behaviour within adolescence.'[12] A senior social work practitioner also expressed a similar view:

> There's a denial about it . . . it's not a comfortable topic. They don't like to go there, to think that children can do any of these things . . . And then there's also a horror with it, where I think they kind of view it as very extreme, that they must be absolutely evil predators that could do horrendous things. Or they have been so badly abused themselves that they do this. But I kind of experience it at one end of the scale or the other, you know. Total disbelief that this could be happening . . . And at the other end, it must be horrific.[13]

These reflections underline not only the decidedly moral tone of public discourses on peer forms of abuse but also the marked tendency to at best pathologise and at worst negate the notion of children and young people as 'perpetrators' of child sexual abuse.

Cultural hierarchies of innocence and blame concerning sexual offending against children can similarly be discerned within the legal system which acts as an 'echo chamber for conversations about credit and blame' (Tilly, 2008: 35). As I have argued previously, it is the institutionalisation of blame via legal processes of blame allocation which reproduces and reinforces the popular bifurcation of those deemed 'innocent' and 'blameworthy' (McAlinden, 2014a: 181). It will be demonstrated that the blame-blameless dichotomy which attaches to sex offending concerning children would also appear to be couched in absolute terms leaving no room for 'degrees of blame' (McAlinden, 2014a: 186). Consequently, children who do not present

.anorak.co.uk/237229/news/the-truth-about-the-edlington-devil-brothers-vile-pictures.html/ (following the 'Edlington case' in South Yorkshire where two brothers ages 10 and 11 brutally attacked and sexually assaulted two other boys, leaving them for dead).

[12] Interview 2, 18 April 2016. [13] Interview 1, 16 February 2016.

as 'completely innocent' (Von Hentig, 1948; Mendelsohn, 1956) or pure may be deemed undeserving of the 'victim' label. As discussed further in Chapter 7, this is also reflected in the legal and policy frameworks governing children and young people who display harmful sexual behaviour and in the responses of legal and other professionals and jurors.

In particular, it will be argued that a number of factors appear to dilute the moral positioning and vulnerability of some victims as sexual innocents and place them at the bottom of the victim hierarchy. These include the fact that many victims of Internet offending or street grooming are typically older children or adolescents (Finkelhor et al., 2000; CEOP, 2011), who may have become involved in some sort of relationship with their abusers, or who may have engaged in some form of harmful or risky sexual behaviour, and who are therefore perceived by legal and other professionals as 'participating victims' (Olafson et al., 1993: 14) – as having been complicit or instrumental to some degree in their own abuse or that of others. In this respect, '*non-ideal* adolescent victims' who fail to conform to 'the idealised social construction of the "normal" child' (Ost and Mooney, 2013: 441–42), may be perceived as having consented to their own victimisation.

CHILDREN AT 'RISK' AND THE RELEVANCE OF CHILDREN'S RIGHTS

A final tension to emerge is that between protectionist and participatory discourses on children and childhood. From the late twentieth century, 'risk' has become systemic to conceptualising the social problems and dynamics of advanced industrial societies (see in particular Giddens, 1984, 1990; Beck, 1992) across the diverse arenas of 'politics, law, science, technology, economy and everyday life' (Beck, 2002: 41). Within the 'risk society' (Beck, 1992: 260; Ericson and Haggerty, 1997; Giddens and Pierson, 1998), risk and security are increasingly thought of as not only as things to be proactively identified but also classified and controlled. A defining feature of this 'reflexive modernity' (Beck, 2009: 19–21) is the social and political construction of 'new risks' in which perceived risks are often manufactured or produced (see also Giddens, 1984, 1990; Beck, 1992; Ungar, 2001). There are in turn attendant complexities surrounding 'the globalisation of doubt' (Beck, 1992: 2; see also Giddens, 1999) in the form of 'non-knowing' which can lead in turn to increased security and scrutiny by the state (Rostoks,

2010) to 'control . . . the uncontrollable' (Beck, 2002: 41). This is evidenced, for example, in the global response to terrorism post-9/11 (Ignatieff, 2004; Zedner, 2005) and in the spread of regulatory, exclusionary measures within neo-liberal societies to protect the public from both dangerous violent and sexual offenders (Seddon, 2008; Hebenton and Seddon, 2009).

The institutionalisation of risk and security is exemplified clearly within the sphere of crime and justice (O'Malley, 1998; Garland, 2001), where risk has become the fulcrum of the contemporary working practices of key criminal justice agencies such as the police (Ericson, 1994; Johnston, 2000), probation (Hudson, 2001' Robinson, 2002) and social services (Kemshall et al., 1997).[14] Against this broader backdrop, two potentially competing versions of risk related to children have emerged – the first, relating to children 'at risk' of victimisation by predatory sex offenders and the second, concerning 'risky children' in 'conflict with the law'.

In relation to the first of these manifestations, public panic about sexual offending more broadly and child panic about the perilous state of contemporary childhood, as discussed in this and the previous chapter, mean that children are seen as being at risk of sexual offending rather than constituting a risk themselves. Notions of the child as 'innocent', 'asexual' and as 'at risk' have in turn been reflected in criminal justice policy and practice related to child protection and sex offender risk management. As part of the 'new penology' (Feeley and Simon, 1992), broader societal concerns about the presence of sex offenders in the community have fed into and sustained a technocratic version of risk premised on the social control of 'dangerous offenders' (Rose, 2000) and 'actuarial justice' (Feely and Simon, 1994).[15] Similarly, a 'new order' of child protection has emerged based on the likelihood of the child suffering significant harm (Ferguson, 1997, 2004; Wattam et al., 1997; Brandon and Thoburn, 2008). The policy framework on risk governance has thus moved from 'dangerousness' to 'risk' (Castel, 1991) and subsequently to 'precaution' (Ewald, 2002; Ericson, 2007), characterised by the imperative of governing 'worst case scenarios' and all permutations of future risk before they occur (Zedner, 2009).

[14] See also its application to a diverse range of social fields by subsequent scholars as envisaged by Ulrich Beck, such as environmental issues (e.g. Lash et al., 1996; Strydom, 2002) and the corporate sector (e.g. Kytle and Ruggie, 2005; Peterson, 2011).

[15] Actuarial justice is characterised by a quantitative approach to risk assessment, typified by assessment scales designed to evaluate future dangerousness and the probability of reoffending.

In policy and legislative terms, this manifested as the introduction of multi-agency public protection arrangements (MAPPA)[16] to risk assess, manage and treat known sex offenders and a host of regulatory measures to control the whereabouts and behaviours of sex offenders in the community (Kemshall and Maguire, 2001; McAlinden, 2010). 'Memorial laws' (Valier, 2005) on sex offender notification, for example, 'Megan's Law'[17] in the United States or 'Sarah's Law'[18] in the United Kingdom, were named after specific child victims yet designed to protect all amorphous future child victims as 'vulnerable citizens' (Ramsay, 2010). Criminologists have argued, however, that expansive forms of state regulation are leading to increasingly volatile, contradictory and incoherent penal policies on risk (O'Malley, 1999; Crawford, 2006; McAlinden, 2010). In tandem with this view, the spread of risks stemming from a highly sexualised contemporary popular culture and the social and leisure activities among children and young people make them less amenable to criminal justice, as opposed to educative or welfare, interventions.

In relation to the second formulation of risk relating to children, the polarised 'moral landscapes of childhood' (Valentine, 1996), highlighted earlier, and the governance of so-called 'risky' children have been a mainstay of debates about youth justice over the past few decades (Kelly, 2000; Armstrong, 2004; Fionda, 2005). Broader concerns related to child welfare (Stainton-Rogers and Stainton-Rogers, 1992; Parton, 1998) have been displaced by concerns with 'risky children' and 'out of control' or 'troublesome' youth (Muncie, 1984; Pearson, 1984; Scraton, 1997a; Baron, 2003; Goldson, 2011). In the United Kingdom, the 1993 murder of 2-year-old James Bulger by 10-year-olds Jon Thompson and Robert Venables became the locus of a demonising and authoritarian public and political discourse. This centred on the notion of 'children as criminals', being symptomatic of a broader loss of innocence (Davis and Bourhill, 1997), moral decline and '"families" in "crisis"' (Coppock, 1997) and provided the impetus

16 See the Criminal Justice Act 2003, ss 325–27 in England and Wales and the equivalent in Northern Ireland for the Public Protection Arrangements Northern Ireland (PPANI): Criminal Justice (NI) Order 1008, arts 49–51.

17 At the Federal level, sex offender registration and community notification are governed by the Adam Walsh Child Protection and Safety Act 2006.

18 See s 327A of the Criminal Justice Act 2003 which places a duty on MAPPA to consider disclosure to particular members of the public of an offender's convictions for child sexual offences where there is a risk of serious harm to a particular child or children. See also art 50 (2A) of the Criminal Justice (NI) Order 2008.

for radical policy and law reform (see generally, Goldson, 1997b; Haydon and Scraton, 2000).

Policy concerns about childhood (Scraton, 1997a) or youth in crisis (Goldson, 2011) were translated into root-and-branch reform of the youth justice system beginning in the late 1990s with the introduction of 'restorative justice'.[19] Indeed, the risky or threatening child is consistently perceived in very narrow terms as being in conflict with the law in public spaces and frequently characterised as part of wider social anxieties about antisocial behaviour and, more specifically, 'hoodie' or 'yob' culture (Robinson, 2009; Hier et al., 2011). This is illustrated further by the more recent example of the riots in London and Birmingham and other towns and cities in England during the summer of 2011 (Ashe, 2014; Newburn, 2015), which 'brought forth an outpouring of angst about the state of modern youth' (Newburn, 2012: 331). Moreover, such policy concerns within youth crime and justice also resonated internationally with the 'globalization of crime control' (Muncie, 2005). Within Northern Ireland, as discussed further in Chapter 7, additional cultural tensions and challenges stem from 'the conflict'[20] and the legacy of the conflict relating to criminalising children and young people and protecting children's rights (Carr and McAlister, 2014; Haydon and Scraton, 2016).

These two versions of risk related to children, however, are potentially conflicting – in the first, the child assumes the role of victim and in the second, the status of wrongdoer. In this respect, dominant cultural and policy discourses on children and childhood, highlighted throughout this chapter, are often presented in dichotomous terms, reflecting the broader tension between 'fear for' and 'fear of' children (Holland et al., 2008: 4). Children and the state of childhood are polarised as either being 'at risk' or 'as potentially threatening' (Scott

[19] The legislative basis for the youth justice systems in Northern Ireland and England and Wales were overhauled via the Youth Justice (NI) Act 2002, Part 4 and the Youth and Criminal Evidence Act 1999, Part I respectively, with a paradigm change from custody to diversion and the embedded use of the restorative justice ethos. In brief, a number of restorative disposals were introduced including diversionary or court-ordered youth conferencing (see arts 57–60) which, in keeping with the inclusivity, problem-solving and reintegrative principles of restorative justice (see e.g. Braithwaite, 2003; Van Ness and Strong, 2014; Zehr, 2015), aims to balance the needs of the victim and the young offender by agreeing to a plan of action which allows the young person to make amends and stop committing crimes. For a critical overview, highlighting an underlying tension between retributive and restorative aims within the legislative reforms, see e.g. Ball, 2000; Gelsthorpe and Morris, 2002; Goldson and Muncie, 2006.

[20] 'The conflict', or what is also known euphemistically as the 'Troubles', is a contested term for the civil/political unrest that occurred in Northern Ireland from the late 1960s to the mid-1990s.

et al., 1998: 689; see also Stainton Rogers and Stainton Rogers, 1992). It is perhaps the former premise, however – social anxieties about at risk children – which is more clearly reflected in contemporary discourses on sexual offending behaviour by children and young people.

As Staksrud (2013: 168, citing Slovic, 2000: 191) observes, '[r]isk can also be a surrogate for social or ideological concerns.' In this respect, many of the broader themes and tensions surrounding risk discourse, as highlighted at the outset of this section, are evident in contemporary social and policy responses to harmful sexual or exploitative behaviours by children and young people: there is a broad range of evolving (adult) concerns about the safety of and risks to children across a diverse range of social contexts including those relating to strangers, technology and consumerism – these perceived anxieties about childhood are also highly contingent on broader social changes in the late twentieth century (Giddens, 1991). Sexualised risks relating to children and young people and their status as at risk victims are to a large extent socially and culturally determined based on innate assumptions about the nature of children and childhood. Given the difficulties of separating out risky/harmful sexual behaviour among peers from that which is more normal/experimental or benign, there are significant 'unknowns' in terms of where risk is thought to crystallise (see further, Chapter 6).

Indeed, 'risk anxiety' (Scott et al., 1998: 689) about children and their perceived vulnerability has become a defining feature of contemporary childhood in which a series of moral panics about sexual offending concerning children, as set out in the previous chapter, appear to be inextricably entwined with a broader range of perceived risks and social anxieties related to children and young people. Childhood has always been 'embroidered with myth, steeped in nostalgia . . . it has always reflected the prevailing anxieties of the age' (Brooks, 2006: 18). In consequence, and reminiscent of a previous 'golden age' (Pearson, 1984; see also Davis and Bourhill, 1997) in which children and childhood were seen as less corruptible and corrupt, 'we hang on to the ideal of children as precious innocents who must be protected from the sordid and the spoiled' (Jewkes, 2010: 16).

'Growing up in the risk society' (Furlong and Cartmel, 2007: 8), and in the face of a series of radical social changes which have impacted the everyday lives of children, has inevitably meant that children and young people in the modern world face new and ever changing risks as well as opportunities. Peer-based sexual behaviours, particularly within the context of risks stemming from the use of social media and web-based technologies, present as challenging because they epitomise 'the uncontrollable and incalculable dangers that are direct effects of human action and technology' (Peterson, 2012: 20, citing Beck, 1999). In essence, it becomes difficult for professionals and for children and young people to identify and manage such 'technological risk' (Staksrud, 2013: 59–61) on a proactive basis.

Reactionary, risk-based discourses governing contemporary behaviours by and towards children, however, have been a retrograde step in terms of our holistic understanding of modern childhood, children's behaviour and children's rights. Indeed, the downside of such protectionist discourses on risk and what has become known as a 'paternalistic' approach' (Kitzinger, 1988: 81) to children and childhood is effectively the subjugation of rights-related discourses. As outlined earlier, adults have traditionally been the primary definers of childhood and what constitutes a risk to children (Dwyer, 2011) where concerns are propagated and scaffolded by the media and policy frameworks (see e.g. Crichter, 2003: 134–36). In turn, public discourses rarely include children's own voices or opinions.

This broad argument is underpinned by two key notions: first, and central to the theorising of risk, is the public/private divide where the association of risk and vulnerability with the public sphere (see generally Goffman, 1971) and safety with the private sphere of the family and home is shared by both adults (Saraga, 2001) and children (Harden, 2000) (see Chapter 2). Second is that children are classed in 'collective group terms' (Staksrud, 2013: 172) as 'immature, naïve, vulnerable and a danger to themselves' (Harden, 2000: 44, citing Pilcher, 1996) and incapable of self-regulating risk. As Giddens (1991: 123–24) contends, while anxieties about risk are shaped by public discourses and global insecurities, they are also subject to 'the reflexive self' – that is, the individualisation of experience among young people and the personal capacity and resilience of individual children to assess risk and make competent decisions about engaging in risky behaviour for themselves (see further Chapter 4). For the most part, however, within social and policy discourses on risks to children, including sexualised risks, 'the element of choice, responsibility and reflexivity', prized by adults, is denied to children (Harden, 2000: 47).

As Egan and Hawkes (2009) note, 'the problem with protection', which objectifies children as victims, is that it leaves little room for consideration of the sexual agency of children. A 'culture of overprotectiveness of children' (Faulkner, 2010: 108) and a related emphasis on risk to children and their vulnerability mean that the focus is often upon 'curtailing the freedom of potential victims' to keep them safe (Kitzinger, 1988: 81). As Scott et al. (1998: 689) have stated, 'risk anxiety' about children may have 'material consequences for children's daily lives and for everyday adult-child negotiations around . . . protection and autonomy'. Extending this argument further, I contend that a blanket protectionist ethos, which underlies regulatory debates on sexual offending, may be flawed from both a practical and an ideological standpoint. It will not protect children from 'unknown' risks which manifest within the context of interpersonal relationships with peers, and from within the family and home; it may also undermine the rights of children and adolescents, including the right to freedom of expression concerning their sexual identity.

The broader issue of balancing *participation* with *protection* hinges on the 'welfare principle'[21] and the question of who arbitrates 'the best interests of the child', particularly with regard to evolving capacity for decision-making, including that related to sexual behaviour (see further Chapter 6). Even though the United Nations Convention on the Rights of the Child (1989) governs both protection rights (such as from neglect, abuse and exploitation) as well as participatory rights (to be respected as full and active members of their family and society) (Alderson, 2008: 17),[22] there is a delicate balance to be struck. Staksrud (2013: 169) poses the question thus in the context of 'children in the online world': 'Are they considered to be innocent and in need of protection? Or competent and willing learners in need of advice?' To date, a broadly protectionist regulatory approach has held sway. As Gillespie (2013: 642) explains in the context of sexualised practices among children and young people such as sexting, it is assumed that children under age 18 'may not yet have the capacity to understand the dangers involved in posing for sexualised images'.

As discussed further in Part II of the book, scholars have argued that sexting in the form of an adolescent freely taking a sexualised photograph of him- or herself and sending it to another may be viewed as

[21] See the United Convention on the Rights of the Child 1989, art 1; and the Children Act 1989, s 1 and its equivalent, the Children (NI) Order 1995, art 3, which enshrine the welfare/paramountcy principle.

[22] Note that the Convention also covers a third type of right: *provision* rights such as access to goods and services (Alderson, 2008: 17).

a form of sexual expression, particularly when the child has reached the age of consent (see e.g. Lööf, 2012; McLaughlin, 2012; Gillespie, 2013). According to this view, while sexting may be said to technically breach the criminal law governing child pornography in terms of taking, possessing or distributing an indecent image of a child,[23] as a form of sexual identity it should be governed by a rights rather than a risk-based framework as a 'proportionate response' to harm (Gillespie, 2013: 641–42). Moreover, studies have also shown that adolescents consider sexting to be 'another way of expressing yourself' (Karaian, 2012: 67) and as a form of 'flirting' (Phippen, 2012). Non-consensual sexting, however, and behaviour which is clearly abusive, coercive or harmful in its intent or effects present as more challenging. The crux of the issue, therefore, for regulatory discourses and for legal and other professionals, becomes one of being able to reliably differentiate different types of risky behaviour within peer-based relationships as potentially harmful, exploitative or benign.

More broadly, it will be argued further that increasing the capacity of children and young people to understand the potential dangers and harmful effects of peer-based behaviours is key to affecting this balance between protection and participation. A proportionate response to sexualised forms of risk concerning children depends on the legal and social status children are afforded in contemporary society. The arguments presented in the course of this chapter demonstrate how adults 'as moral agents' have traditionally ascribed inferior moral and political status to children (Dwyer, 2011). The envisaged approach to balancing risk and rights, or protectionist and participatory discourses, however, invites consideration of children as moral beings with capacity for autonomy and agency in the determination of their own lives. This calls for the development of 'bottom-up' as opposed to 'top-down' formulations of rights (see e.g. Matthews, 2003; Thomas, 2007; Ballet et al., 2011), which takes cognisance of the individual voice, agency and competency of children. Moreover, it also necessitates putting in place social and structural supports, such as education programmes, to enable children to make appropriate and informed decisions regarding their personal interactions with each other and with adults.

[23] See the Protection of Children Act 1978 (as amended), extended to Northern Ireland as the Protection of Children (NI) Order 1978 which now applies to indecent photographs of children under age 18 (previously age 16). See Chapter 6.

CONCLUSION

This chapter has critically examined the core constructs underlying the social, cultural and political understanding of risks concerning sexual offending related to children. It is the confluence of these core cultural and ideological notions – related to the sexual innocence and vulnerability of children and their hierarchal status as the ultimate 'victim' – which obscure or distort meaningful public and policy discourses on sexualised forms of risk stemming from children and young people. In essence, it is precisely because child sexual abuse is 'so central' to our thinking 'as a society' (Olafson et al., 1993: 19) that 'denial, minimization, and rationalization' have played a sustained and central role in the societal response (Conte, 1994: 227).

In this sense, 'moral' or 'child panics' tend to polarise views about risk, 'victimising some and demonising others' (Cree et al., 2014: 432). The notion of 'innocence' is particularly problematic because it can be used 'to deny children access to knowledge and power' (Jackson, 1982) and, at the same time, may 'stigmatize the knowing child' (Kitzinger, 1988: 80). Indeed, childhood and sexuality remain 'contested terrains' where constructions of the former tend to constrain and even deny the latter (Corteen and Scraton, 1997: 82; see also Robinson, 2013). This is exemplified by 'regulatory discourses' on sexuality and the persistent unwillingness of adults or institutions such as churches and schools to engage in meaningful discussions with children on sexuality and sexual behaviour (Haydon and Scraton, 2002). This ultimately creates a circuitous problem in that for children, the chief source of information on sex and sexuality is more likely to stem from their peers or the media (Measor, 2004; Brown and Strasburger, 2007; Lagus et al., 2011) as a tool for 'sexual learning' (Buckingham and Bragg, 2003: 9). As discussed further in the next chapter, the difficulty stemming from this position is that the media and popular culture tend to promote 'sexual' (Gagnon and Simon, 1987) or 'social' (Ashurst and McAlinden, 2015) 'scripts' which skew messages about healthy sexual norms and behaviour.

As also examined further, childhood is also interpreted and defined through social and legal institutions such as the school, the family and the legal system (Qvortrup et al., 1994: 3). It will be argued that the 'deep ambivalence' (Brooks, 2006: 16) and 'conflicting notions of childhood' (Jewkes, 2010: 5) which have always underpinned societal norms are also evident within contemporary legal and policy responses to children and young people who display harmful sexual or exploitative behaviours. At the same time, however, we also need 'to take account of the social and cultural factors [and] historically changing norms of sexual behaviour' (Melrose, 2013: 165) that continually shape the sexual practices of children and young people in any given era.

The crux of current risk-based configurations of children's sexual behaviour is the emphasis on 'fear', 'deviancy' and 'shame' whereby children are often left to self-navigate risk in peer-based settings without appropriate knowledge to support their decision-making (Haydon and Scraton, 2002). The debates concerning children's rights demonstrate the importance of empowering children and allowing them space to negotiate risk and construct their own social and personal identities, including sexual identities. As Sidebotham (2013: 153) has contended, 'rather than simplistically labelling individuals as victims or perpetrators, or as culpable or not culpable', we should seek a more rounded version of children and childhood that recognises their 'culpability, vulnerability, agency and potential'. This demands consideration of the child, not as 'risky' or 'at risk', or as 'victim' or 'perpetrator', but as 'individual'.

Indeed, as discussed in Part II of the book, children construct their own hierarchies and identities within peer-to-peer relationships, including those within gangs or other group settings and potentially exploitative and harmful interpersonal relationships. In recognising and affording space to the rights and agency of children and young people within regulatory debates on harmful sexual or exploitative behaviours, it becomes imperative for policymakers and professionals, therefore, to try to separate out behaviour among peers which is potentially risky or harmful from that which is not. Moreover, it also necessitates equipping children, who have evolving autonomy and capacity for decision-making, with protective knowledge to better make this distinction for themselves.

PART II

CHILDREN AS 'RISK': CHILDREN AND YOUNG PEOPLE WHO DISPLAY HARMFUL SEXUAL OR EXPLOITATIVE BEHAVIOUR

4

THE EMERGENCE OF HARMFUL SEXUAL BEHAVIOUR

> The normalisation of sexual language and images. I think that is happening slowly, but I think there is a pop culture that is very, very sexualised. The song language is sexualised. Videos are sexualised, tele programmes are sexualised.[1]

Having considered the theoretical and policy framework, Part II seeks to examine the range of specific issues raised by harmful sexual or exploitative behaviour by children and young people. It will draw on original primary research to inform the theoretical and critical discussion on the contemporary emergence of peer-based sexual behaviours, the nature and scope of such behaviours and how such 'risks' are perceived and responded to within social, legal and policy frameworks and, indeed, by children and young people themselves. This chapter examines some of the nuances and complexities surrounding the emergence of the principal forms of peer-to-peer child sexual exploitation and abuse in advance of a more detailed examination of the nature and extent of such behaviours – including sexting and cyberbullying as two of the most recent 'panics' concerning potentially harmful sexual behaviour (HSB) by children and young people – in the following chapters.

Part I sought to examine the social and political construction of sexualised forms of risk to children more generally and the range of cultural and ideological notions which have traditionally coalesced to obfuscate or diminish such risks as stemming from children and young people. This chapter extends this discussion by examining the converse – why

[1] Interview 2, 18 April 2016, Independent Forensic Psychologist.

potentially harmful sexual behaviours by and among children and young people have more recently emerged. This includes an analysis of the impact of technology on modes of interpersonal and social communication and the influence of the media and constantly changing cultural norms and social practices related to sex and sexuality among adolescents in particular. Perhaps unsurprisingly, the evidence emerging from the primary data supports the thesis that a premature cultural sexualisation of children is occurring. However, the data also suggests differential experiences among children and young people along the dimensions of gender and sexual identity and personal resilience. It will be argued further that the resulting normalisation of sexualised culture and behaviours and the associated distortion of the boundaries between problematic-harmful and healthy sexual behaviours among peers has dual implications – for effective social, legal and organisational responses to risk, as well as for children and young people in undertaking risky behaviours and in making informed choices and protecting themselves from potential risks.

THE EMERGENCE OF THE PROBLEM

As outlined in Chapter 2, although child sexual abuse as a whole was only recognised as a distinct societal problem beginning in the second half of the twentieth century, a number of scholars have traced its history to at least the Victorian period, beginning in the early nineteenth century (see e.g. Rush, 1980; Smart, 1999; Jackson, 2000). Similarly, while there are various traceable permutations of concerns about sexually abusive behaviour by children and young people stemming from the late 1980s and early 1990s (Brownlie, 2001),[2] child perpetrators of sexual abuse have only emerged as a distinct 'problematic deviant category' (Okami, 1992) at the tail end of the twentieth century. Brownlie (2001) locates the advent of the 'risky child' as being symptomatic of broader social anxieties about childhood which juxtapose children as either victims or threats and which view the unregulated child as 'dangerous'. Indeed, as outlined in the previous two chapters, risk has remained central to the

[2] Brownlie (2001: 520) gives a range of examples which focus on the masturbating child (Walling, 1909); the sibling incest offender; the sexually deviant young person (Krafft-Ebing,1914); and the sexually aggressive/traumatised child within Freud's seduction theory (1896). See also examples of American studies which trace adolescent sex offending from the early 1940s, particularly in relation to males: Doshay (1943); Shoor et al. (1965).

contemporary societal understanding of childhood (see e.g. Jenks, 1996; Ferguson, 1997; Scott et al., 1998), underpinning a sustained societal discourse and biological essentialist view of childhood aimed at protecting the innate sexual immaturity and innocence of children (Zelizer, 1994; Hendrick, 1997; Furedi, 2013). Such social constructs have also worked to keep the notion of the child or adolescent sex offender in cultural abeyance.

The slow burn in terms of the incremental societal recognition of sexualised 'risky' children can be related to the fact that to acknowledge such risk is to 'break the taboos of childhood' (Brownlie, 2001: 526). In this vein, the early societal recognition and professional awareness of risks stemming from children and young people who display HSB have been confined to two narrow domains: sibling abuse/incest (Justice and Justice, 1979; Russell, 1986; Adler and Schutz, 1995) and child victims of sexual abuse becoming victimisers themselves as part of the 'intergenerational transmission' (Kaufman and Zigler, 1989) or cycle of abuse (Finkelhor, 1990; Watkins and Bentovim, 1992; Dhawan and Marshall, 1996). More recently, concerns about a pattern of sexual offending in adult males stemming from adolescence (Hanson and Slater, 1988; James and Neil, 1996; Skuse et al., 1998) were extended to cognisance of younger children as perpetrators (Johnson, 1988; Gil and Johnson, 1993; Calder et al., 1997).

One of the first reports to highlight the issue within the United Kingdom was the 1992 *National Children's Home Report* (NCH, 1992) which documented the high levels of denial and minimisation of the problem of children and young people who sexually harm other children as a matter of public concern (NCH, 1992: 7), and the lack of coordinated responses to the problem (NCH, 1992: 8). While children and young people who display HSB had emerged as a central component of child protection frameworks by the mid- to late 1990s (Calder et al., 1997), in tandem with academic and policy discourses more broadly, the focus was confined to young male perpetrators with young female perpetrators being given scant attention (see exceptionally, Johnson, 1989; Carrington, 1993; Matthews et al., 1997). Indeed, as examined further, the range of harmful sexual behaviours by children and young people includes male and female perpetrators within a range of interpersonal and social settings, including within the context of families, peer-based relationships, institutions and online settings.

A pivotal factor underlying the contemporary emergence of peer-to-peer abuse is the premature cultural sexualisation of children and young people in which discourses on sex and sexuality have become 'the wallpaper of children's lives' (Bailey, 2011: 12). As Rich (2011: 6) has argued, harmful sexual behaviour 'does not develop in a vacuum' but rather 'occurs in a social and developmental context, not absent of interactions with the environment'. What Palmer (2007) has referred to as 'toxic childhood' relates to a broad range of social changes which are harming children and the traditional notion of childhood. These include changes to the social and leisure activities of children as well as changes to eating and clothing habits. While there may be evidence of an independent childhood culture among younger primary schoolchildren 'in the playground', as Opie (1993) has argued, among older children and adolescents there is evidence of the cultural erosion of the sanctity of childhood (Zelizer, 1994; Furedi, 2013). Within this specific context, it would seem that the blurring of the boundaries between childhood and adulthood has been made possible by the cultural sexualisation of children. This has in turn fostered the potential onset of harmful sexual or exploitative behaviours between children and young people via the normalisation of popular social discourses on sex and sexuality among peers.

As Ashurst (2013) has argued, sex is in the very fabric of society. References to and images about sex permeate print and broadcast media (newspapers, magazines and television) and the entertainment industries (music, films and computer games). Sexually suggestive and erotic images or messages are frequently used as an advertising tool, 'selling . . . product[s] with a sexual innuendo',[3] including those related to the perfume, alcohol, food, soft drink, fashion and car industries. Within this broader framework, there are also those products aimed specifically at younger consumers, including advertisements for clothes by American brands such as Abercrombie and Fitch, American Apparel and Calvin Klein, and British Brands such as Jack Willis, which have relied on the depiction of young, semi-naked models in sexualised or provocative poses (Brown and Strasburger, 2007).[4] Such advertisements are also highly 'gendered' (Goffman, 1979) – the underlying messages about sex provide a blue print for social and sexual norms related to body image and in particular dyadic gendered stereotypes and the expected sexual roles to be played by males and females. In turn, they may also impact how children and young people think and talk

[3] Interview 13, 31 May 2016, Public Health Nurse.

[4] See e.g. '"Sexualised" Jack Willis Catalogue Is Banned by Advertising Watchdog', *BBC Newsbeat*, 1 June 2016.

about sex and how they may perceive the 'unwritten rules' (Powell, 2010a) about sex, including healthy and consensual sexual relationships. In short, the determination of whether sexual behaviour is normal or risky or harmful then becomes a very difficult one for children to make.

A range of specific factors appear to underpin the contemporary 'emergence of a hypersexualised culture' concerning childhood and adolescence (Egan and Hawkes, 2012: 278; see also McRobbie, 2004; Coy, 2009; Coy and Garner, 2012), many stemming from postmodern changes in communications technology (Postman, 1994). The broad existence of such a culture is generally supported by the existing literature. The following discussion seeks to analyse the specific thematic nuances underlying this emergence stemming from an analysis of the primary data. While there is a degree of overlap between these themes, they are differentiated and unpacked here for the purposes of critical analysis.

The Media and a 'Culture of Sex'

Many interviewees pinpointed the presence of an 'overtly sexual media'[5] in contemporary society and the fact that children and young people are 'constantly bombarded with sexualised images'.[6] The media, including television, newspapers or magazines, radio and billboard platforms, are central to our social understandings of sex, gender and sexuality (Attwood, 2017). What Attwood (2017) terms 'sex media' or 'technosexualities' have a powerful influence on the sexualisation of childhood (Buckingham and Bragg, 2003; Faulkner, 2010; Gunter, 2014), eroding the basic distinction between childhood and adulthood by destroying the information hierarchy among adults and children and exposing children to a broad range of adult themes (Postman, 1994), including sex and promiscuity. At the same time, however, the depiction of sexualised content in the media is rarely accompanied by 'any mention of the risks or responsibilities' which are associated with sexual activity (Brown and Strasburger, 2007: 485). A number of interviewees pointed to reality television programmes such as *Celebrity Big Brother*[7] and newspaper and magazine coverage of high-profile celebrities which

[5] Interview 32, 2 November 2016, Police Officer.

[6] Interview 29, 10 October 2016, Police Officer

[7] *Celebrity Big Brother* is a reality television programme which follows a number of celebrity contestants, known as 'housemates', who reside in a custom-built house for a number of weeks during which housemates are evicted by a public vote until there is one eventual winner. The series takes its name from the character in the novel *1984* (Orwell, 1949).

tend to promote the message that sex is 'glamorous, fun and risk free' (Brown and Strasburger, 2007: 484). As a senior practitioner who works with children and young people affected by child sexual exploitation explained:

> I mean that's very much influenced by celebrities as well. All these celebrities that have sex tapes, you have pop stars who have very, very explicit language. There's the likes of Geordie Shore, which completely normalises sex and lots of sex with lots of different people . . . Even this morning, Miss Great Britain was on Lorraine Kelly because she was on Love Island and had sex on TV . . . It is like a TV event now . . . So sex gets you places. And that is reality when you look at it.[8]

For other interviewees, the significance of the media, and television programmes in particular, was related to its being a key source of information about sexual norms and practices for children and young people (Brown and Strasburger, 2007). As a police officer explained:

> If you are a teenager growing up, and go . . . I'm going to ask Johnny out. And you switch on the TV or you switch on the Internet. What do I do? And they see this portrayed . . . and I think for a teenager who is growing up . . . If they look at all of this, they think, right, OK, this is what I've to do.[9]

As explored further later, while the media have always been among the primary definers about risks related to sex offending concerning children, as set out in Part I of the book, new forms of media stemming from Internet-based or digital technologies bring with them a new set of risks and challenges.

Several interviewees pinpointed what they termed 'a culture of sex'[10] or 'a very sexualised culture in that sex is talked about constantly'[11] and where there is 'much more of a freedom around experimenting . . . and [where] there is very little of emotional attachment to it'.[12] The essence of this culture and the norms which it tends to promote was explained succinctly by two interviewees: 'the normalisation of casual sex'[13] and 'the culture of sex now is that you can have sex and it's OK. You can have sex with many different people, many different partners, and it is

[8] Interview 21, 23 June 2016, Social Work Practitioner. [9] Interview 31, 17 October 2016.
[10] Interview 2, 18 April 2016, Independent Forensic Psychologist.
[11] Interview 14, 2 June 2016, Sexual Health Nurse.
[12] Interview 16, 6 June 2016, Social Work Consultant.
[13] Interview 6, 25 April 2016, Independent Safeguarding Consultant.

OK.'[14] Other interviewees explained further in terms of this being central to the self-presentation and aspirational identities of children and young people and their standing with their peers:

> So if you are not having sex it is either you are missing out on this amazing, unknown thing, or there is something wrong with you and you are not attractive. And I think being attractive and being sexually mature and experienced is a real golden nugget. It is something that you have that other people don't have, and that's what people aspire to.[15]
>
> I think what happens with any generation of young people is, they have to define themselves as different . . . We are more able to talk about sexual stuff, which means that there's not as much of a taboo . . . I think social constructs are different and I think the media has influenced that . . . it almost changed the discourse from being, you shouldn't do it at all, you know, until you are in the right sort of situation . . . to, you must do it at all times, at all cost, sort of thing. I think youngsters struggle more nowadays with not wanting to do it, but not knowing how to say 'no'.[16]

This shift in social discourse tends to endorse the idea that 'under age sex' and 'sex with randoms is the norm' (BASW, 2016: 7) rather than being confined to a 'warm and loving relationship'.[17] As discussed further in Part III, it also accentuates the need to empower children with the capacity for decision-making around healthy sexual relationships and, at the same time, the attendant difficulty in engaging children in discussions about behaviours that they do not regard as particularly unwelcome, risky or harmful.

'New Media': Social Media, Mobile Phones and Changing Modes of Communication

As Grabosky (2001: 243) argued more than a decade ago, 'the convergence of computing and communications has begun to change the way we live, and the way we commit crime.' The Internet has created an alternative social space and has fundamentally and irrevocably changed the nature of interpersonal communication, among adults as well as children, which is predominantly played out online. Moreover, these changes in communication have also had knock-on effects for communication within families and between children and parents during what

[14] Interview 2, 18 April 2016, Independent Forensic Psychologist.
[15] Interview 14, 2 June 2016, Sexual Health Nurse.
[16] Interview 6, 25 April 2016, Independent Safeguarding Consultant.
[17] Interview 27, 3 August 2016, Senior Social Work Practitioner.

would formerly have been considered as 'family time'. As one police officer in the study reflected: 'some of the rules of engagement in our house was, family time is family time. TV off, phones off, we will talk about our day . . . But I think something is lost in today's society around that.'[18] This in effect may remove the social space between adults and children in terms of daily or regular discourses about well-being and awareness of potentially harmful or risky behaviours.

For children and young people, the binary distinction between online and offline settings, or virtual or face-to-face contacts, is by no means clear cut (see e.g. Livingstone, 2009). Rather, they tend to 'mi[x] communication from different sources and media' (Ringrose et al., 2012: 15) which has in turn reshaped the processes of social and sexual identity within their peer group (Ringrose and Barajas, 2011: 134). This fusion of experiences also helps to explain the potential crossover between online and offline forms of HSB among peers (see further Chapter 6). Increased levels of socialisation into 'virtual peer groups' has resulted in decreased socialisation into 'physically proximate groups' (Surette, 2015: 12; see also Yar, 2012; Sun et al., 2013). Research also demonstrates that 'virtual peer associations' may be as important as face-to-face peer associations in predicting deviant behaviour (see e.g. Miller and Morris, 2016) and that the use of smartphone dating apps is a risk factor for sexual victimisation (Choi et al., 2016).

Moreover, the Internet may provide an alternative social space for negotiating peer-based identity which is fluid, negotiable and often different from the real world (Jewkes, 2010: 10; see also Jewkes and Sharp, 2003; Valkenburg et al., 2005; Brown, 2011). The same police officer explained the significance of the 'real self' and the 'virtual self' (Spears et al., 2013: 194–95) in the context of posting on social media: 'they can be anything they want to be in their rooms. And they can, you know, channel Beyoncé or Kim Kardashian or whatever, and the sexual agenda is up there. Which is why I think so many of them get into hot water.'[19] In brief, the faceless nature of cyberspace is potentially more facilitative of harmful sexual behaviour because it completely alters the nature of social and personal interaction and distorts social norms and parameters about what is appropriate in terms of the content of communications and generalised behaviour. As one interviewee explained: 'there is an addictive quality to using technology now, and it dulls boundaries, blurs boundaries, dulls sensitivities among young people.

[18] Interview 29, 10 October 2016. [19] Ibid.

And when you link it in with risk taking, which is a normal part of adolescence, you can see why people are now saying, well what is the social norm here?'[20]

Indeed, social norms, self-regulation and social responsibility have different meanings in the online world which may leave children exposed to higher levels of risk. In the absence of visual (Short et al., 1976; Wells and Mitchell, 2007) or social cues (Kiesler et al., 1984; Sproull and Kiesler, 1986), 'trust' within virtual settings must be built solely through communication (Whitty and Joinson, 2009: 97–108). In particular, without 'social context cues ... to regulate social interaction ... people's behaviour will also become uninhibited [and] anti-normative' (Whitty and Joinson, 2009: 22; see also Webster et al., 2012). As Davidson and Martellozzo (2005: 10) state, 'the Internet is more than just a medium of communication it constitutes a new virtual reality, or a cyberworld with its own rules and its own language.' This is conveyed particularly through the style and speed of writing and responses, including the use of punctuation, abbreviations and emoticons (Mantovani, 2001). In brief, digital forms of communication, and social media in particular, are 'both facilitating behaviours and changing those behaviours' among peers.[21] As discussed further later, this dynamic is also played out through two further factors – changes in dating or 'courting' practices and the ready accessibility of pornography online. For teenage boys in particular, power relationships and peer hierarchies are negotiated within digital peer networks and subsequently verified in their offline lives at school and within their neighbourhoods (Harvey et al., 2013). Indeed, the construction and performance of youth masculinities and femininities, particularly regarding sexual identity, within contemporary youth culture is far more complex than some academic and public discourses might suggest.[22]

Previous research has documented widespread computer literacy and the ubiquitous use of social media and mobile phones among children and young people (Livingstone and Bober, 2005; Wolak and Finklehor, 2011; Webster et al., 2012).[23] This includes the use of multimedia

[20] Interview 24, 6 July 2016, Independent Treatment Professional.

[21] Interview 15, 3 June 2016, NSPCC Worker.

[22] For a critical discussion of classic neo-liberal accounts of masculinity and femininity, see e.g. Butler, 1993; Messerschmidt, 1993; Connell and Messerschmidt, 2005; Nayak and Kehily, 2013.

[23] A study commissioned by the National Literacy Trust in which 85.5 per cent of 17,000 schoolchildren surveyed in the UK, between ages 7 and 16 had their own mobile phone:

messaging apps such as Snapchat, Instagram, WhatsApp, Facebook and tumblr.[24] A number of interviewees in the present study also highlighted this issue as a significant problem: 'In the last five years since we have had 4G phones, smart phones . . . that nearly all children in post primary school have, that have the availability to access everything, anywhere, anytime. That has definitely brought huge issues.'[25] In reality, however, this growing facet of social behaviour is by no means confined to children, as adults also engage in social media and Internet use to a prolific extent. There are thought to be at least 140 million users of social media sites worldwide, which includes 10 million users within the United Kingdom and where 80 per cent of access is via smartphone (Turgoose, 2016). Children and young people tend to define themselves by the amount of 'likes' or 'friends' they receive via social media as a key constituent of their social identity and indicative popularity: 'the number of friends they have or competition to be liked by people, this kind of thing, that's how they lead their lives.'[26] Having a large number of 'friends', however, and particularly where settings are not private, also augments the risks to which children and adolescents are potentially exposed.

Recent Irish-based research comparing the use of social media by children and adults within the specific context of cyberbullying found that while both adults and children may engage regularly with social media as a means of communication, children tend to use different platforms than their parents (O'Higgins Norman and McGuire, 2016). Parents most often favoured Facebook and WhatsApp, whereas children favoured Twitter and Instagram. Moreover, there were generally low levels of awareness of potential risks and monitoring of children's use of social media by parents: only 18 per cent regularly monitored such use regularly, and only 53 per cent knew of the risk and were happy that their children were safe. The lack of knowledge and monitoring by parents and the contrasting patterns of social media use between adults and children more generally also illustrate that parents are highly dependent on what their children tell them in their assessment of

reported in G. Paton, 'Children "More Likely to Own a Phone than a Book"', *The Telegraph*, 26 May 2010.

24 In a study of children's use of the Internet and mobile environments across seven countries (Denmark, Italy, Romania, United Kingdom, Ireland, Portugal and Belgium), nine in ten Irish children ages 15 to 16 and just under 40 per cent of 11- to 12-year-olds have a social network profile, despite the age restriction for such sites being 13 (O'Neill and Dinh, 2015: 4–5).

25 Interview 3, 20 April 2016, Education Authority Professional.

26 Interview 15, 3 June 2016, NSPCC Worker.

risks. In addition, such findings may also indicate a skewed view of the problem in that parents more often view risk in terms of their child being 'at risk' of online victimisation rather than constituting a risk themselves as a potential perpetrator of harmful sexual or exploitative behaviour.

A preponderance of interviewees in the present study pointed to the rise of social media, its centrality to the everyday lives of children and the gulf between adults and children in this regard as among the primary contributory factors underlying the contemporary normalisation of peer-based sexual behaviours: 'We have young people who have been born into the digital age'[27]; 'young people are also much more au fait and much better at social media than we are. They are streets ahead. They are always one step ahead'[28]; 'I would say it is more to do with the social media. The young people these days live in a different world to my generation. They convey their lives through the Internet, social media, texting, all that sort of thing. That's how they communicate'[29]; and 'Social media is such a part of children's lives now, even the wee ones that are coming in. It is quite amazing. And ... as we all know it has just rocketed without any controls or whatever. It is about catching up all the time, I suppose.'[30] As the latter interviewee attests, the significance of the use of social media by children and young people is that it allows them to openly and explicitly communicate with one another often without adult supervision or censorship.

In addition to the prolific use of social media, the other interrelated factor is the centrality of mobile phones to the lives of children and young people where 'they conduct their whole lives on their phones.'[31] Indeed, many of the interviewees commented on children's ownership of their mobile phone to the extent that it becomes 'an extension' of themselves and a core part of their personal and social identity. As one police officer asserted:

> Teenagers will not leave their phones down. So even if you advise, look, do you want to switch your phone off, or do you want to get rid of your phone ... It is like taking an arm off them. They are so dependent on it and it is so part of their everyday-ness that ... even when they know they

[27] Interview 27, 3 August 2016, Senior Social Work Practitioner.
[28] Interview 9, 25 May 2016, Youth Support Worker.
[29] Interview 6, 25 April 2016, Independent Safeguarding Consultant.
[30] Interview 4, 21 April 2016, Senior Social Work Practitioner.
[31] Interview 16, 6 June 2016, Social Work Consultant.

> don't want to look at it, they do look at it. It is like us wearing a watch, I suppose.[32]

Similarly, a senior social work practitioner commented on the potential difficulties this poses for parents in trying to monitor risk and keep their children safe:

> This is the new normal for our young people. They are on their phones 24–7. And everyone's question is, what should we do about this? … Should we take the phone off them? And the first response from a parent, from any parent is, this is risky, I will take the phone off them. And for our young people, you might as well ask them to cut their arm off.[33]

Another police officer framed this issue in terms of the potential criminogenic effects and the facilitation of indecent images: 'It is just an extension of your hand, your phone, take a picture and send it on. In the bathroom with your bits out, send it on. It literally doesn't take five seconds, which is where the difficulty is.'[34] As discussed further in Chapter 6, this feature of mobile phone use also has important consequences for policing and the investigation of cases. Children, and victims in particular, who are reluctant to relinquish their phone for forensic scrutiny may also be less willing to report potentially harmful sexual behaviour or more likely to withdraw an initial complaint.

Changes in Dating and Courting Rituals: The 'Third Hand Removal of Emotion'

Twenty-first-century changes in modes of social communication more generally have also had effects on interpersonal modes of communication between children and young people, including within romantic relationships. As outlined in Chapter 2, the development of romantic relationships in adolescence, post-puberty, are central to the maturing social and sexual identities of teenagers as 'emerging adults' (Martinson, 1994; Giordano et al., 2006; Booth et al., 2015). An older, generally American literature has delineated courtship practices and a range of classifications for romantic relationships between adolescents such as 'dating' and 'going steady' with the underlying ideals of love and commitment and the eventual transition towards marriage (see e.g. Waller, 1937; Herman, 1955; Gordon and Miller, 1984). In the contemporary context, however, 'romance' and 'sex' in adolescence

[32] Interview 31, 17 October 2016. [33] Interview 27, 3 August 2016.
[34] Interview 32, 2 November 2016.

bring both 'opportunities' and 'risks' (Booth et al., 2015) which are augmented in 'digitized' peer-to-peer networks (Ringrose and Barajas, 2011). That is, in one sense young people, and young women in particular, may no longer be constrained by expected dyadic gender-based roles within opposite-sex peer relationships (e.g. as passive recipients of romantic male attention, and having sex only within the confines of marriage with a male partner). On the other hand, however, related dangers stem from the removal of emotion inherent within modern sexual and romantic relationships among children and adolescents in digitally mediated settings. Indeed, the majority of sexually active American teenagers have also had sexual relationships outside of a 'normal' romantic relationship where there is a significant crossover between engaging in both 'romantic' and 'non-romantic' sexual experiences over time (Manning et al., 2005; Giordano et al., 2006).

Within this broader context, a new impassive parlance has emerged which includes phrases and abbreviations such as 'friends with benefits'[35] (Kan and Cares, 2006), 'hook ups'[36] and 'MILF'.[37] These terms denote the blurring of boundaries within sexual relationships among young people – between both friends and potential romantic partners and between adults and children. Moreover, the keeping of 'inside' secrets (Goffman, 1959: 141–43) relating to sex or other taboo adolescent behaviours is facilitated by the 'digital networked world' (Schneier, 2011). The notion of peer relationships as 'a secret club that the adults don't tend to get into'[38] serves to reinforce group belonging and social identity among peers (see also Cottle, 1980; Bok, 1983). Within virtual settings, a number of terms have developed to denote various types or stages of peer-based relationships such as 'ghosting'[39] and 'insta-flirting'.[40] A specific jargon and set of shorthand terms are used among children and young people to make reference to sex or sexual practices and to exclude parents from this discourse. This includes terms such as '143' (I Love You), 'GYPO' (Get Your Pants Off), 'GNOC' (Get Naked on Camera), 'WTTP' (Want To Trade Pictures), 'ASL' (Age/Sex/

[35] Friends who have an occasional, casual sexual relationship with no emotional involvement.

[36] A 'hook up' is a one-off sexual encounter with a peer with whom you are not in a relationship.

[37] This colloquial term means 'Mother I'd Like to F***'.

[38] Interview 29, 10 October 2016, Police Officer.

[39] 'Ghosting' is a form of 'breaking up' when a person cuts off all contact with another teen without warning.

[40] 'Insta-flirting' is flirting via social media by liking their photo and posting favourable comments. See 'The Secret Dating Life of Teens', *Bella* Magazine, 27 September 2016.

Location), 'CD_9' (Code 9 or parents nearby) and 'KPC' (Keep Parents Clueless) (see Ashurst, 2014).[41]

This fundamental change in how children and adolescents experience dating practices and romantic relationships was stressed by a number of professionals in the study. One NSPCC professional explained: 'Whereas now every child has a mobile phone in their hand or whatever . . . When you and I were growing up, if you wanted to date a girl you had to phone the house and speak to the parent. Parents now have no idea who is talking to their children, really.'[42] A medical professional explained further in terms of the use of dating apps:

> For youngsters between texting and apps . . . and in terms of our world of sexual health, have changed things dramatically. You only have to think of all these apps, Tinder and Grinder and whatever. Essentially . . . you can find out who is across the street, who is available to have sex. So you don't even need to have the chat up any more.[43]

Such views also hark back to the paternalistic, romantic view and 'golden age' (Pearson, 1984) of childhood, as outlined in the previous chapter, where children were invariably regarded as being safer and subject to less menacing influences in times past. In reality, however, as one interviewee attested: 'teenagers . . . have from time immemorial, a different language, a different way of thinking that the old people don't understand.'[44] In relation to sexting, for example, while adults commonly use the term, young people often prefer alternative terms such as 'nudes', 'nude selfie' or 'naked selfie' (Ringrose et al., 2012: 6; Crofts et al., 2015: 28). As the same interviewee conceded, echoing the views of a number of professionals, within the context of the technological revolution stemming from the Internet, the key issue then becomes one of adults as 'the changeover generation', 'playing catch up all the time, whilst the whole technology thing is so speedy that it is really hard to keep up'.[45]

Moreover, the routine use of social media and texting between peers has tended to remove any degree of emotion within interpersonal relations. The use of social media as the mainstay of social communication means that children are losing the ability to communicate face-to-

[41] See also 'Is Someone NIFOC telling your Child IWSN? Police Force Reveals Secret Texting Codes Every Parent MUST Know to Keep Their Kid Safe', *Mail Online*, 9 January 2017.
[42] Interview 15, 3 June 2016.
[43] Interview 12, 26 May 2016, Nurse Consultant in Sexual Health.
[44] Interview 6, 25 April 2016, Independent Safeguarding Consultant. [45] Ibid.

face, creating in the process automatic, reflexive and impassive forms of communication. As noted earlier, digital communication is by its nature characterised by faceless forms of interactions devoid of visual (Short et al., 1976; Wells and Mitchell, 2007) or social cues (Kiesler et al., 1984; Sproull and Kiesler, 1986). A police interviewee explained the often unemotional and dispassionate nature of peer-based interactions in which the online medium serves as a form of emotional filter in terms of how children and young people think about and view sex:

> And it is that sort of third hand removal of emotion. You know, kids are seeing this stuff. They think they are learning all this sexual knowledge. And then they are trying to re-enact it in the real world, not realising that people don't do that, people don't want to do that, that's not normal, people aren't normally that size, they don't look like that, they don't sound like that. But they are exposed to it in this sort of three-dimensional thing. And I think that is so impactful in how they view their own world. Their whole world views are so skew whiff.[46]

While there are older debates on the precise effects of media stories about sex (see e.g. Soothill and Walby, 1991; Duggan, 2000; Greer, 2003: 43–60), or viewing pornography (Allen et al., 2006; Twohig et al., 2009), on negatives attitudes and aggressive behaviours related to sex, these are largely superseded by the cultural pervasiveness of subliminal messages about sex in the contemporary digital era. As discussed further in Chapter 7, this emotional displacement in relation to virtual peer interactions is also evidence of 'moral disengagement' (Almeida et al., 2012; Perren and Gutzwiller-Helfenfinger, 2012) and may impact how legal and other professionals view potential victims and how they conceptualise or negate risk of harm even in the aftermath of an alleged or suspected sexual offence.

Access to Pornography: 'Two or Three Clicks Away'

Several interviewees in the study emphasised the experiential element of harmful sexual behaviour in terms of children and young people either being exposed to sexual images or a highly sexualised environment or experiencing abuse directly themselves (see also Carson, 2015). That is, they highlighted how for those children who had not experienced abuse directly, exposure to pornography is 'massive'[47] or 'at the bottom of most cases'.[48] The use of Internet-enabled digital media

[46] Interview 29, 10 October 2016. [47] Interview 31, 17 October 2016, Police Officer.
[48] Interview 32, 2 November 2016, Police Officer.

was also seen as a facilitator and enabler of accessing pornography (see also Horvath et al., 2013) where children and young people 'are only about two or three clicks away from something inappropriate'[49]: 'Now this stuff is all over the web and there is this, for some, an addictive element'[50]; 'I think pornography . . . it is at the end of your hand . . . type in sex you are probably going to have hard core porn within two clicks . . . And if you go, what's that? . . . You just put it into a phone and you are going to find out what it is'[51]; and 'anything is possible on the Internet . . . The children nowadays, everything is at their fingertips . . . they have access to anything.'[52]

The latter viewpoint also highlights the issue of accidental as well as intentional exposure to online forms of pornography, where the former is often more prevalent (Horvath et al., 2013). Indeed, there has been an increase in both the rate of consumption (Carrol et al., 2008) and exposure to pornography by children under age 13 (Sun et al., 2016). Research in the mid-1980s documented that the average age of first exposure to pornography was 11 for boys (Bryant, 1985). More recent research suggests that this figure may be lower with the advent of Internet literacy (Livingstone and Bober, 2005; Johnson et al., 2010) and, moreover, that exposure and access to pornography increase with age (Horvath et al., 2013). As discussed further later, there are also known gender differences in that boys are more likely than girls to be exposed to and deliberately access or use pornography (Horvath et al., 2013).

As Sun et al. (2016: 983) argue in the context of adults, 'pornography has become a primary source of sexual education.' Similarly, interviewees in the present study articulated the scope of this problem in relation to children and adolescents: 'their sexual development . . . their whole sexual knowledge, their whole experience of what a relationship is, what your body image is, how everything works, is all based on pornography'[53]; 'children, even from the ages now of prepuberty . . . are looking at sexual imagery and seeing it as part of their normal experience'[54]; and where for boys in particular, 'young males watching porn and thinking that that is a realistic expectation of a relationship. Their notions of sex and relationships are completely derived from

49 Interview 4, 21 April 2016, Senior Social Work Practitioner.
50 Interview 15, 3 June 2016, NSPCC Worker.
51 Interview 32, 2 November 2016, Police Officer.
52 Interview 22, 10 June 2016, Children and Adolescent Forensic Mental Health Professional.
53 Interview 1, 16 February 2016, Service Manager, HSS Trust.
54 Interview 24, 6 July 2016, Independent Treatment Professional.

porn.'[55] The problem, however, lies not in the viewing of pornography per se, but the fact that the age at which children do so is usually vastly out of kilter with their stage of emotional and cognitive development:

> Children of 10 and 11 now know about pornography, they know about sex, they know about anal sex ... They use expressions now that we would never have heard ... I would never have heard of until I was much older, an adult. And they hear those expressions, they see that information, they observe things, but they are not mature or adult enough to be able to process what that means at that stage. They aren't. They haven't got the life experience and they haven't got the intellect at that stage.[56]

As noted earlier, while the links between exposure to pornography and acceptance of 'rape myths', in relation to adults for example, are far from being clear cut (see e.g. Kutchinsky, 1991; Russell, 1998; Allen et al., 2006; Ferguson and Hartley, 2009), there is substantial research evidence to support the harmful effects of pornographic material on both young adults (Sun et al., 2016) and adolescents (Horvath et al., 2013). The mainstreaming of and ready access to sexual or pornographic material online (McRobbie, 2004; Carroll et al., 2008; Papadopoulos, 2010; Lööf, 2012) promote a 'homogeneous script' (Sun et al., 2016: 293) which depicts the themes of power over and aggression towards women. Indeed, pornography use among adolescents is linked to the development of 'risky sexual scripts' and distorted attitudes towards sexual coercion (Tomaszewska and Krahé, 2016) which distort beliefs about gender and sex and objectify women (see also Horvath et al., 2013).

Furthermore, the use of pornography has also been acknowledged by the judiciary as a significant risk factor in cases coming before the courts of serious harmful sexual behaviour by children as young as 11, where there is an attempt at re-enactment of sexual scenes with both same sex and opposite sex victims.[57] A more nuanced view was also expressed by a judge in the present study who reflected upon the use of 'extreme pornography' in the most serious cases:

> It wasn't an experimental thing, or at least not in the innocent sense. I felt this could only have happened as a result of a young man watching

[55] Interview 21, 23 June 2016, Social Work Practitioner.

[56] Interview 3, 20 April 2016, Education Authority Professional.

[57] See e.g. J. Tozer, '"Gay Porn" Computer Searches of Boy Rapist, 11', *Daily Mail*, 22 October 2016; R. Perrie, 'Web Porn Lad, 15 Rapes School Girl', *The Sun*, 28 February 2013, where the judge noted that the 'trigger' for the offence was 'experimentation' following previous access to Internet pornography.

> pornography, watching extreme pornography. Because nobody gets it in their head to try . . . there are certain things that just . . . are so far off the scale . . . Young men have always been interested in young women and that's the way of it, and as you grow up hopefully your interests remain within what might be termed normal, normal tramlines. But I remember this one, and it had violence and sexual assault.[58]

Indeed, together with the previous factor – concerning social media and mobile phones – the ready access to pornography was the most common cultural factor identified by professionals in the study as ultimately promoting increased engagement in risky sexual behaviours among children and adolescents. For many of the interviewees, this was tied to the promotion of gendered norms concerning masculinity: 'they see this as . . . this is what men do.'[59]

However, the viewing of pornography, and by young males in particular, would appear to shape not just those behaviours at the most serious end of the spectrum which are criminalised as sexual offences and which would eventually come before the courts but also more routine interactions between children and young people. A police officer recounted an experience after giving a talk in a secondary school:

> A wee fifteen-year-old girl came up after the lesson and . . . shared with us the fact that she had had her first early sexual experience with what she considered was a boyfriend, a consensual and to her an age-appropriate experience, albeit that it was under the age of consent. And what started as a consensual sexual act, midway the young lad started beating on her, pulling her hair, punching her. She withdrew her consent at that stage and told him to stop. He didn't. So that went from a consensual act to a rape, effectively. The child had been raped. So it was progressed as an investigation. And it transpired that the young fella had been exposed to a lot of extreme pornography and he thought that was what you did.[60]

This scenario illustrates the ideation of a 'sexual' (Gagnon and Simon, 1987), 'social' (Ashurst and McAlinden, 2015) or 'mental script' (Horvath et al., 2013; Sun et al., 2016), wherein the use of pornography becomes the benchmark for sexual behaviour and experiences.[61] The same police officer explained further:

[58] Interview 26, 1 August 2016, District Court Judge.
[59] Interview 5, 22 April 2016, NSPCC Worker. [60] Interview 29, 10 October 2016.
[61] See e.g. Sun et al. (2016) whose research with American college men ages 18–29 concluded that the more a man views pornography, the more likely he is to use those 'scripts' during real-life sexual encounters.

> I think young boys have always looked at pornography magazines and sort of . . . the bra and pants section of catalogues . . . I think it is a natural progression in terms of puberty and understanding your sexuality. But I think that . . . the extreme nature of what is being sexted and viewed is so concerning in terms of a young person's sexual script. Because I think we are raising a generation of potential offenders . . . And that is laying down a sexual script for your lifetime . . . I do worry for that generation of males because they are so exposed to so very, very much that I do believe the sexual script is slightly off kilter in terms of what we would understand as normal sexual functioning. So their ability to embrace what is normal is so far away from what you or I would know as normal. They are more accepting of anything.[62]

Indeed, many of the interviewees in the study voiced concern about the long-term impact of exposure to pornography in terms of 'warping sexual boundaries'[63] or 'skewing their view of normality'[64]: 'because how do you know what is normal after you have seen all that?'[65] While this may not ultimately result in society 'raising a generation of potential offenders' as the police officer cited earlier feared, it certainly has enormous potential for 'distorting people's norms about what is acceptable'[66] and to impact developing adolescent sexuality and attitudes to and expectations about sex within peer-based relationships. In particular, it may diminish the ability of children and adolescents to differentiate confidently and conclusively normal-healthy behaviours from those which are more risky-problematic or indeed potentially harmful. Moreover, as discussed further in Chapter 6, while professionals share concerns about *access* to pornography by children and adolescents, such concerns have also mutated into the *creation* of digital sexual content by teenagers.

'Corporate Paedophilia': Video Games and Music Videos as 'Pornography'

In addition to pressures to conform to culturally specific 'idealised forms of femininities and masculinities' (see Chapter 3), young people are also 'managing globalised consumer . . . cultures of consumption' (Ringrose et al., 2012: 8). Several interviewees underlined 'the

62 Interview 29, 10 October 2016.
63 Interview 4, 21 April 2016, Senior Social Work Practitioner.
64 Interview 3, 20 April 2016, Education Authority. 65 Ibid.
66 Interview 32, 3 November 2016, Police Officer.

pressures they [early adolescents] are under, not only from their peers but from media, the music they listen to, the videos they watch, the films they have access to'.[67] Within the broader rubric of what has been termed 'visual criminology' (Hayward, 2009; Carrabine, 2012), some scholars have questioned the extension of 'the grammar of the pornographic' and the '"porn" suffix . . . to a greater and greater selection of visual representations', displacing the erotic within our cultural understandings of the pornographic (Dymock, 2016: 1–2; see also Tait, 2008; Hester, 2014). However, it is undeniable that the emergence of what has been termed 'corporate paedophilia' (Bray, 2008; Egan and Hawkes, 2008b) by feminist scholars utilises children as a major economic force in consumerism, including the music,[68] fashion[69] and gaming[70] industries. This phenomenon has tended to promote highly gendered sexually explicit messages or images or age-inappropriate products which readily sexualise childhood and adolescence (Buckingham et al., 2010) and where childhood innocence is often presented as the ultimate 'fetish' and commodity (Faulkner, 2010).[71] A particular concern, however, relates to deeper cultural influences stemming from not only the promotion of explicit messages and values about sex and identity but also the tacit affirmation of abusive, violent and sexualised norms which result in increased aggression and decreased empathy and prosocial behaviour (see e.g. Anderson et al., 2010) leading to the denial or minimisation of potential harm. In relation to video games, for

[67] Interview 7, 13 May 2015, Former Police Officer.

[68] In addition to the range of explicit lyrics which promote sex and violence by artists such as Eminem, Lady Gaga and Beyoncé, see e.g. Rihanna's 2010 stage appearance in New York which simulated sex and masturbation before an audience of pre-teen and adolescent girls: G Littlejohn, 'Is This What Mike Stock Was Talking About? Rihanna Continues to Shock with Raunchy Moves in Front of Young Fans', *Mail Online*, 14 August 2010, www.dailymail.co.uk/tvshowbiz/article-1302822/Rihanna-continues-shock-raunchy-moves-young-fans.html; see also Miley Cyrus's infamous 2013 'Wrecking Ball' music video.

[69] See e.g. the public furor which erupted when Primark, a UK high-street fashion chain, started selling padded bras for children: S. Poulter, 'Primark Shamed into Axing Padded Bikinis for Girls of 7 after Being Accused of "Disgraceful" Sexualisation of Children', *Daily Mail*, 14 April 2010. See also the controversy over the £50 pole-dancing kit that leading supermarket Tesco included within its toy section in 2006 with an advertising slogan that read 'Unleash the sex kitten inside . . . simply extend the Peekaboo pole inside the tube, slip on the sexy tunes and away you go': 'Tesco's "Toy" Pole Dance Kit', *The Mirror*, 23 October 2006.

[70] Within the gaming industry, top-selling computer games such as the 'Grand Theft Auto' series (now in its fifth iteration) are heavily premised on a highly masculinised culture which glorifies violence and objectifies and overtly sexualises females. For a critical overview, see Bryce and Rutter (2003); Taylor (2009).

[71] See e.g. the 1998 debut single and music video for Britney Spears's 'Hit Me Baby One More Time' in which she appears in a school uniform. See also Gwen Stefani's (2004) 'Hollaback Girl' and Beyonce's (2011) 'Move Your Body' music videos which are both set within American high schools.

example, these have been termed 'cultural zones of exception [which] provide alluring and experimental landscapes' and in which 'social rules can be more or less abandoned' (Atkinson and Rodgers, 2016: 1291).

A minority of interviewees drew on contemporary examples within the music video industry:

> So the likes of Rihanna who had that video with all the S&M. She was tied up and saying hurt me, hurt me. You just think, is this what we are selling to young people? Is this what is to be accepted that they are just subjected and objectified? So all of those things are really concerning ... We have become so desensitised that it is nearly ... it is normal to have these sorts of videos with people writhing around the place, with the really aggressive rape lyrics and violence towards women.[72]
>
> You talk about pornography, but music videos are the big thing ... because we say 'what pornography?' And they say 'we never watch pornography.' 'Well what music videos do you watch?' ... I can't remember half the names of them. But I remember we had to go and look them up and what's that ... twerking ... And that's what they are watching and that's what they see as normalised. And because it is not seen as pornography, it is not hidden.[73]

In a similar vein, many of the interviewees in the study drew attention to the potentially harmful effects of hidden messages about sex and sexual norms which are contained within video games and the fact that they are often not viewed as harmful in comparison to 'clear' or more traditional forms of pornography: 'It is that game thing. There really should be much more public awareness of them, because they are horrific, absolutely horrific. And people think, oh pornographic ... clear porn, oh that's terrible ... But I think the other is far more insidious, really.'[74] Examples were frequently cited of the depiction of violence in games such as 'Call of Duty' and sexualised violence in 'Grand Theft Auto' where 'women are hos and pimps and they are being raped and beaten, and that this is normal.'[75] As with more traditional forms of pornography, as set out earlier, the dangers for children and young people around these forms of entertainment are that 'their norms are distorted by what they see online ... I just wonder what we are doing to boys actually in terms of what they see. You think

[72] Interview 8, 23 May 2016, Senior Practitioner, Rowan SARC.
[73] Interview 5, 22 April 2016, NSPCC Worker.
[74] Interview 4, 21 April 2016, Senior Social Work Practitioner.
[75] Interview 8, 23 May 2016, Senior Practitioner, Rowan SARC.

of all those violent games . . . and the normality of what they see online and how that impacts on their normative values.'[76]

A safeguarding professional articulated the problem in terms of the challenges it presents for professionals and parents: 'Gaming is a massive one for us in terms of people are buying their kids 18 games and really not understanding what happens in Grand Theft Auto.'[77] The fact that these activities are being used among their peers and are branded as 'a game' may lead parents to negate 'risk' and assume that regulators are being overly cautious in issuing an '18 certificate', based on the age-rated content of the video game. As articulated further, this also reinforces the need to engage parents and carers around greater knowledge and understanding of what their children are viewing or have access to both online and offline.

'Gang' or 'Partying Culture'

A minority of interviewees referred to the issue of drug or alcohol misuse among adolescents which may act as a 'disinhibitor'[78] by increasing their vulnerability and decreasing their capacity to make appropriate or safe choices. The literature establishes that the emergence of the 'gang' (Beckett et al., 2012, 2013, 2014), or 'partying' culture (Melrose, 2013) may encourage children and young people to exchange 'sex for popularity' (Melrose, 2013: 162; see generally Pitts, 2008; Firmin, 2011; Beckett et al., 2013). Peer pressure among older children or adolescents has always been around and has been principally related to the under-age consumption of cigarettes, alcohol or marijuana and engagement in antisocial behaviour (Steinberg, 1987; Hansen and Graham, 1991). A number of professionals who work with children and young people across a range of spheres articulated the contemporary concern around sexual behaviours and the pressure for social conformity:

> It is all these things to conform. The peer group is the most powerful group in the world, and what young people do to fit in. And they do some very hateful and harmful things to other people, just to be part of the group. Just to belong to something.[79]
>
> And it is that peer pressure. It has got so normal. So if you get to sixteen and you haven't had sex, you are a freak. So no acceptance of choosing not [to have sex]. It is just a given, that it has to be. And so I

[76] Interview 15, 3 June 2016, NSPCC Worker. [77] Interview 11, 26 May 2016.
[78] Interview 23, 24 June 2016, Social Work Service Manager.
[79] Interview 21, 23 June 2016, Social Work Practitioner.

> think that's an enormous pressure for that particular group of young people. And that might start younger than sixteen; that could be from whatever age.[80]

A defining feature of modern adolescence within the literature, as discussed in the previous chapter, is risk-taking behaviour (Kelley et al., 2004: 27; Steinberg, 2007: 55) or experimentation (Furlong and Cartmel, 2007: 101) and the bringing to bear of peer pressure around engagement in sexual activity, alcohol and drugs. In essence, as the prevalent social culture and norms change, so does the nature of the pressures associated with them.

The significance of this party culture, however, is that it may feed into and reinforce the contemporary 'culture of transient sex' and sexual experimentation as discussed earlier. Several interviewees articulated this problem: 'I think that young people, where the party is concerned . . . hold parties for the purpose of sexual activity'[81]; 'it is definitely more relationship based. It is about introducing that person who thought they were in a relationship, say to a house party and then, you know, do you want drugs, do you want alcohol? It's that kind of passing around that happens. And we see that house party model more.'[82] Other interviewees explained this further: 'We do have peer on peer where adolescents would maybe out at parties, house parties, they have had drink and drugs and older adolescents would take advantage of that and sexually assault them.'[83] This also underlines the scope for sexual exploitation among peers and the very real pragmatic difficulties in separating out experimental from more risky and potentially problematic and harmful sexual behaviours:

> I think it's more in a situation where there is a group of young people . . . where there is alcohol, drugs . . . there is an element maybe of experimentation going on. And I know that's one of the issues as well, in general, trying to distinguish between experimentation . . . what is experimental and when does it become abusive? And now what's regarded as experimentation has widened so much. I mean . . . peers have always experimented and that is normal behaviour. I suppose whenever it gets to the point of alcohol and drugs being involved, there is a greater risk of people behaving, then, in an aggressive way or even having an element of gang sex involved. And if there is a

[80] Interview 12, 26 May 2016, Nurse Consultant in Sexual Health.
[81] Interview 2, 18 April 2016, Independent Forensic Psychologist.
[82] Interview 11, 26 May 2016, Safeguarding Professional.
[83] Interview 8, 23 May 2016, Senior Practitioner, Rowan SARC.

> vulnerable young person in the middle of all that, they are going to be the victim. Whether they are a boy or a girl. But quite often it is a girl.[84]
>
> I suppose the biggest thing is the complete normalisation of what is sexually harmful behaviour and lack of understanding around that. The complete lack of understanding on giving and getting consent as well. How it manifests itself with young people is, there is this kind of assumption that young people go to a party, boys would maybe provide drugs and then girls would have sex with them. Now it is not necessarily that they are being passed around, but what we do see a lot of is, one girl will have a boyfriend for two weeks, then that will change and they will maybe have another boyfriend for the next two weeks . . . There's young people who have actually been raped on their first night of being with someone, and then going on to have a relationship with them, because they don't actually recognise that it is wrong.[85]

As Melrose (2013: 162) points out, within the context of such peer-based sexual exploitation and abuse, victims may not see themselves as victims but rather as exercising agency and their engagement in sexual activity as 'just having a good time'. Further case examples of peer-to-peer abuse within the context of gang or party culture will be considered in Chapter 6.

A small body of academic and policy research has identified the prevalence of 'rape myths' among young people in England and Wales and their failure to identify rape and sexual assault from a range of fictional scenarios (see e.g. Coy et al., 2013; Gurnham, 2016). These studies acknowledge, somewhat unsurprisingly perhaps, that such views are particularly prevalent among younger teenagers (13- to 14-year-olds) who will have generally less knowledge and experience of sex and relationships. However, the widespread confusion and ambiguity surrounding the giving and receiving of consent within the context of a partying culture is also prevalent among older adolescents.

This was well illustrated in a BBC television programme aimed at examining the views of young people on what constitutes rape.[86] A mixed group of twenty-five male and female 16- to 18-year-olds was shown a film depicting a fictional sexual encounter during a house party scenario and asked to decide if they thought this was rape or if consensual sexual activity had taken place. The protagonists in the

[84] Interview 24, 6 July 2016, Independent Treatment Professional.
[85] Interview 21, 23 June 2016, Social Work Practitioner.
[86] 'Is This Rape? Sex on Trial', *BBC Three*, broadcast on 2 November 2015.

scenario – a teenage boy and girl – knew each other, having previously been in a relationship; they were both drunk; and the sexual act in question involved the boy climbing into bed with the sleeping girl and an act of oral sex. The participants were then asked to vote anonymously on three questions reflecting the legal criteria on consent.[87] On the first question – 'did the girl consent?': 13 per cent voted 'yes', 54 per cent voted 'no' and 33 per cent voted 'don't know'. On the second question – 'did the boy believe he had consent?': 54 per cent voted 'yes', 39 per cent voted 'no' and sixteen per cent voted 'don't know'. On the final question – 'is this rape?': 87 per cent voted 'yes', 4 per cent voted 'no' and 9 per cent voted 'don't know'.

In brief, many of the participants were initially reluctant to conceptualise the scenario as rape. Throughout the group discussions, the young people used phrases such as 'semi-rape' or 'not a full rape' and there was 'no intentional rape' because 'it wasn't violent' and that the 'girl was not completely innocent' and 'gave him signs'. Moreover, their views were also suffused with cultural stereotypes of rape and sexual offending linked to the predatory stranger paradigm, as depicted in Chapter 2. As one boy put it: 'You think of a vile monster, not a boy who did one bad thing.' Such views and comments were evenly split among the boys and girls. At the end, a criminal barrister, who had helped devise the scenario for the documentary, explained to the group that under the law this would be considered rape and that the boy would likely be found guilty.

A police officer in the context of the present study summarised the problem succinctly in relation to the mindset of children and young people and skewed perceptions of potential risk:

> Again a lot of kids think, you know, your average sex offender is some oul geezer in a brown mac jumping out of a hedge with a bag of sweets in one hand and a puppy in another. Whereas they have no concept of abuse even being within their own peer group. I mean we have 15-year-old girls talking to us about having anal sex because that doesn't get you pregnant. That just blows my mind. At 15 years of age![88]

These findings are broadly illustrative of a number of core arguments and themes presented in the course of this book: they demonstrate the prevalence of victim-offender typologies and hierarchies surrounding sexual offending including the acceptance of rape myths among

[87] See the Sexual Offences (NI) Order 2008, arts 3 and 5. See further Chapter 7.
[88] Interview 29, 10 October 2016.

children and young people – young people also appear to draw heavily on the stereotypes of sexual crimes committed by strangers (see also Coy et al., 2013: 22), which in turn leads them to negate risk as coming from within their peer group; there is a lack of clarity surrounding normal and potentially harmful sexual behaviour among peers in routine social settings, including those within the context of an already established relationship; and crucially, there is a lack of awareness of the law related to what constitutes the act of rape and in particular what counts as consent.

THE EXPERIENTIAL SEXUALISATION OF CHILDREN

Collectively, this amalgam of contemporary cultural factors underpinning the postmodern social construction of childhood undermines and effectively displaces historical and biological essentialist perspectives on the nature of children and childhood. As set out in the previous chapter, these latter perspectives tend to negate risk as stemming from children and young people and instead prize childhood as an inherently moral and highly inviolable life stage. In effect, there is a stark tension between traditional cultural suppositions concerning the innate sexual innocence of children (see e.g. Rousseau, 1762; Hendrick, 1997) and the premature social sexualisation of childhood (Olfman, 2008) which has come to increasingly define contemporary experiences of childhood. One professional succinctly stated: 'They grow up too quick' [sic].[89] Similarly, a judge expressed this sentiment as follows: 'All the children that come into my court, they all want to be treated as older than what they are.'[90]

The upshot of this experiential sexualisation of childhood is essentially twofold: one, 'a blurring of the lines between sexual maturity and immaturity' and reversal of traditional adult-child roles whereby children are presented in 'adultified' ways while adult women are 'infantilised' (Papadopoulos, 2010: 6; see also Dines, 2008) and two, a further distortion of the boundaries between consent and pleasure on the one hand and violence and control on the other. As detailed earlier 'there has been a "sexing up" of contemporary culture', in which 'abusive and/or exploitative sexual practices may have become "normalised"' (Melrose, 2013: 163, 166).

[89] Interview 9, 25 May 2016, Youth Support Worker.
[90] Interview 26, 1 August 2016, District Court Judge.

In consequence, the cultural salience and proliferation of images of and messages about sex may influence cultural norms and impact the ability of children and young people to make informed and healthy choices relating to normal and appropriate interpersonal relationships and behaviours. There is a broad and well-documented link between exposure to sexual media (whether in print, on screen or via music) and sexual attitudes and behaviours among teens, including future intentions to be sexually active (Brown, 2002; Brown et al., 2006; L'Engle et al., 2006; Martino et al., 2006; Strasburger et al., 2010; Cougar et al. 2012).[91] In this vein, the media have been said to function as a kind of 'sexual super peer' that promotes early and premature sexual activity among teens (Brown et al., 2005; Strasburger, 2012). Some important nuances, however, related principally to gender and sexual identity and resilience, emerge from an analysis of the primary research conducted for this study.

Gender and Sexual Identity

In tandem with the deep cultural ambivalence towards children and childhood (Brooks, 2006: 16), as discussed in the previous chapter, there is a 'deeply ambivalent construction of the middle-class white girl' (Egan, 2013: 265) which juxtaposes a protectionist and condemnatory social discourse. On one level, evidence suggests that sexuality is 'a contaminant of young femininity' (Duschinsky, 2013: 255) and that the 'premature or hyper sexualisation of the child' (Renold and Ringrose, 2013: 247) and what has variously been termed 'porn chic' media (Vares et al., 2011: 139) or the 'raunch culture' (Levy, 2006) may impact young girls disproportionately (see e.g. Driscoll, 2002; McRobbie, 2009; Vares et al., 2011; Egan, 2013; Renold and Ringrose, 2013). Several scholars have underlined the premature and excessive sexualisation of girlhood within predominantly Western 'commodity' or 'popular culture' (Driscoll, 2013: 286).[92] Cougar et al. (2012), for example, demonstrate that sexually explicit lyrics have a deleterious effect on young girls and young women, leading to the enforcement of gendered stereotypes which objectify females and encourage them to judge their personal worth on a sexual level only.

[91] Strasburger (2005: 270), for example, notes that in the context of the United States, the 'average child' sees nearly 15,000 references to sex on television alone and that 80 per cent of popular teen shows contain references to sex.

[92] See also, however, the highly sexualised depiction of young girls in post-feminism Japan in male-authored Manga comics and cartoons (Gwynne, 2013).

On another level, girls are also said to be subject to the 'double-pull of countervailing gender norms' which demand that 'young women display both desirability and innocence' (Duschinsky, 2013: 262, 255). As a result of this 'gendered double standard' (Ringrose et al., 2013; Lee and Crofts, 2015: 458–59), girls who 'sext' or send images of themselves may be judged more harshly than males as they have infringed on 'moral expectations of what "good girls" should and should not do' (Crofts et al., 2015: 18). In such circumstances, girls are also said to experience 'layers of shame' (Davidson, 2014: 34) around sexual reputation where the personal, social and emotional consequences of behaviours such as sexting tend to outweigh any possible legal ramifications.

At the same time, however, as discussed in the previous chapter, boys are traditionally seen as 'dominant' sexual 'aggressors' (Mottier, 2008: 9) and girls as 'passive' and 'submissive' (Oakley, 2015: 77). Replicating the broader hegemonic construction of victim and offender identities concerning gendered and sexualised violence (see Chapter 3), boys are represented as 'problematic and risky' (Harvey et al., 2013: 2) and girls consequently are seen as being at risk. Such binary and oppositional constructions of young girls as '"passive victims" of a "sexualized" media' (Vares et al., 2011: 140), however, leave little room for agentic considerations of the decision-making potential of young girls and women. In this respect, there is also what Butler (1990) has more broadly deemed a 'performative' aspect to gender identity among young girls. Indeed, as discussed further later, within the contemporary noxious sexual culture, girls, including 'tweens' or pre-teen girls (Vares et al., 2011), navigate their sexual identities and femininities within digital and real world peer-to-peer networks in increasingly complex, fluid and culturally diverse ways. That is, girls may display 'schizoid subjectivities' which transverse discourses on 'sexual knowingness and innocence, often simultaneously' (Renold and Ringrose, 2011: 389) and where they may variously demonstrate 'porno-chic performance' as well as be the 'innocent' victims of sexualised cyberbullying (Ringrose and Barajas, 2011: 122).

Echoing the protectionist stance, several of the interviewees voiced concern related to the cultural prevalence of gender stereotypes and their impact on young women in terms of both the pressure to behave in highly sexualised ways and how they are perceived by society:

> I think it is disproportionate for girls. I think there's more weight put on girls to act and behave in certain ways and I think you see that through

> what people describe as 'the porn star experience' now. So you've got the pouting, you've got selfies, they must be able to perform these certain acts.[93]
>
> I think that things have gotten worse because I think we have taken backward steps for gender equality in the way that women are treated in the media and in society in general . . . When I hear young fellas the way they talk about girls, I definitely think it has got worse. And I think that's where a lot of problems are coming from, is that women are not valued at all, and particularly young women.[94]

One interviewee also drew out the differential effects of this for young women and young men in the context of 'romantic' relationships more generally:

> Young women seem to be more ready to enter into his whole life and his friends and everything and maybe leave some of their own behind. Whereas young men, and that is gender stereotypical but I think it is true, that young women are more investing in a relationship. You know I laugh at young men in the clinic. The question is, are you in a relationship? No, no, not really. So how long are you seeing her? Oh about a year. And you're like, she's bought the ring! And you are not even calling her your girlfriend! So there is a different language that they use as well.[95]

However, as also acknowledged in the previous chapter in relation to the polarity of such social stereotypes, there is also a 'concomitant impact on boys' stemming from the gendered and sexualised subculture in terms of 'the hyper-masculinised images and messages that surround them' (Papadopoulos, 2010: 3). Previous research has shown that the construction of a 'mad' or 'sad' masculine self-identity is fashioned around the consumption of drugs and crime and the values of toughness and respect on the street (Collinson, 1996). Research has also shown in relation to substance misuse that while the effects of peer approval and social bonds were more evident for girls, peer pressure mattered more for boys (Whaley et al., 2013, 2016). Indeed, many of the interviewees in the study attested to the impact of the blurring of boundaries surrounding the age of girls and young women and the disproportionate impact of this on boys and young men. As the same health professional quoted earlier and another explained:

[93] Interview 2, 18 April 2016, Independent Forensic Psychologist.
[94] Interview 10, 25 May 2016, Youth Support Worker.
[95] Interview 12, 26 May 2016, Nurse Consultant in Sexual Health.

> Well I would say the big thing for me is . . . young women. You see them one day in their school uniform . . . and the next day all dressed up in makeup and brows and more maintenance than I ever knew in a lifetime. And it is obvious that they look eighteen or nineteen. So that scenario of the young fellas . . . the actual blurring of what does a 15-year-old look like any more . . . I think, is difficult.[96]
>
> And that's what we would see a lot now, is where the young men are quite afraid, because it is all or nothing they would say. Professionals . . . would say the young men are afraid of the young women. Because you can have a 12-year-old now that can dress so well and do their make up so well, with their bloggers and their YouTubers or whatever, that they actually look about 17 or 18. And it is frightening and it is scary.[97]

This issue, however, is not solely a social and cultural one but also has legal ramifications surrounding the age of consent and the criminalisation of peer-based sexual behaviours (see Chapter 7). As discussed further in Chapter 6, there are also case examples of females as sexual aggressors across a range of contexts, including sexting and 'where a young woman may coerce a young man to have sex with her, as opposed to the other way about'.[98] In essence, however, given the arguably greater cultural and often competing social pressures which girls are subjected to, there is an underlying tension between coercion and agency within practices such as sexting (Phippen, 2012; Ringrose et al., 2012; Lee and Croft, 2015).

In relation to the use of pornography, the literature generally establishes that young males are more likely than young women and girls to use peers and pornographic materials as a source of information and learning about sex (Flood, 2007; Phippen, 2012) in preference to formal sex education (Epstein and Ward, 2008). Whereas young women claimed they accessed pornographic materials only once, whether out of curiosity or under encouragement from a boyfriend, boys and young men are encouraged to view pornography by their male peers and are more likely to view a variety of types of images on a repeated basis (Flood and Hamilton, 2003). Moreover, within this broader context, the 'contemporary sexual norms of many young people, particularly young males, are initiated, distorted and scaffolded by social media' (Ashurst and McAlinden, 2015: 377). The literature, therefore, generally tends to promote a highly gendered and reductionist perspective on the use, effects and acceptance of a 'pornified' culture

[96] Ibid. [97] Interview 13, 31 May 2016, Public Health Nurse. [98] Ibid.

(Paul, 2005) by young males which simultaneously disempowers young girls. Indeed, taken as a whole, social and policy narratives on the cultural sexualisation of children and young people have tended to reinforce an overly deterministic and simplified version of risk stemming from 'a gendered account of childhood, sexuality and danger' (Duschinsky, 2012: 715).

A consideration of gendered dimensions, or 'doing gender' (West and Zimmerman, 1987), is considerably more complex, however, than existing narratives might suggest. By way of example, in contrast to existing research, a minority of interviewees made reference to how the accessing of pornography 'creates unrealistic expectations on both sides of the coin'.[99] As a forensic mental health professional explained:

> For a lot of the boys that we do assessments on, even those that haven't engaged in harmful sexual behaviour, when we do a psychosexual history on them, they have access to pornography. That's kind of what they expect from their girlfriends. They expect them to be porn stars. And even some of the girls, when we do their psychosexual history, they would be saying that they are engaging in anal sex but yet they would be still claiming to be a virgin. And oral sex ... and it is just par for the course with these young kids now. And I do think it is what they are accessing and what their boyfriends are accessing on the Internet; that they expect that that's the norm.[100]

The gendered aspects of harmful sexual and exploitative behaviours among peers will be considered further in Chapters 5 and 6 in relation to diverse patterns of harmful sexual or exploitative behaviours across a range of social contexts, as well as victimisation profiles and differences in reporting practices.

A further sub-theme, which is little considered in the existing literature, is the LGBTQ (lesbian, gay, bisexual, transgender and queer[101]) aspects of sexual identity among children and young people. A minority of studies have highlighted the issue of enhanced vulnerability of adolescent boys in particular who are 'same-sex attracted' and questioning their sexuality in engaging in risk-taking behaviour, particularly in online contexts (see e.g. Hillier and Harrison, 2007; Lööf,

[99] Interview 28, 16 August 2016, Senior Voluntary Sector Interviewee (victim support).

[100] Interview 22, 10 June 2016.

[101] The 'Q' is frequently added to the LGBT acronym where the term 'queer' is used to refer to those who are questioning their sexual identity or who are not specific as to their gender or sexual orientation.

2012).[102] In this vein, a number of interviewees highlighted 'confusion about sexuality'[103] against the backdrop of a sexualised culture which promotes experimentation as a key additional factor underlying both the emergence of potentially harmful sexual behaviour among peers as well as instances of victimisation. This was believed to be particularly enhanced in relation to young men:

> I think, the HSB young people, are struggling with their sexual orientation. Because it has transpired that some of them have then come out as being gay ... That they have ... issues going on ... because I know, still the message is that being gay is not right. I know it is changing and whatever, but I am wondering if there is stuff going on there that they are struggling with, on top of it all.[104]
>
> I would probably say it might have been more young men who were coming to terms with their sexuality and maybe more young gay men who are not out and that have found themselves in vulnerable places. But again I think it is about a lack of self-esteem and confidence in that emerging sexuality that you have that maybe puts them at a lot more vulnerability.[105]

One interviewee referred to the related transgendered aspects of emerging sexuality among children and how this may effectively mean that issues around developing sexual identity come into play much earlier: 'Transgender is a big, big area, especially for our schools ... And transgender would be completely different to your LGB in that the young person actually experiences their sexuality earlier. I am talking, three or four years of age.'[106] This more nuanced view of gender stemming from the transgender aspects of peer-based sexual behaviours as well as those which relate to children and young people who self-identify as lesbian, gay or bisexual also reinforces the over-simplified and rather one-dimensional accounts of gender and sexuality which dominate social and even some policy and academic discourses concerning gender and peer-based sexual behaviours. Moreover, although not explicitly highlighted by the primary research for this study, an

[102] By way of example, in a study conducted by the Swedish Youth Council, members of the LGBT group were three times as likely to post sexualised images or videos of themselves online (18.8 per cent versus 6.8 per cent) and were twice as likely to have sex with someone that they had first met online (31.9 per cent versus 16.3 per cent); see Swedish Agency for Youth and Civil Society (2009).

[103] Interview 18, 14 June 2016, Senior Voluntary Sector Interviewee.

[104] Interview 10, 25 May 2016, Youth Worker.

[105] Interview 12, 26 May 2016, Nurse Consultant in Sexual Health.

[106] Interview 13, 31 May 2016, Public Health Nurse.

intersectional approach to youth sexuality (see generally, Daley et al., 2007; Taylor et al., 2010; Button et al., 2012) also necessitates additional consideration of social categorisations such as race, ethnicity or class, and the complex interplay among them, which may also impact power relations within 'hierarchies of sexuality' (Coppock et al., 1995: 19).[107] This also reinforces the need to promote key messages for children and young people around confidence and self-esteem as well as sexual identity and healthy sexual and interpersonal relationships which transverse homogeneous Western cultural norms on gender and sexuality.

Resilience

The potential impact of the reified gendered stereotypes and effects identified earlier may be mitigated by a further factor. That is, while teens may overestimate the sexual activity of their peers based on information obtained from the entertainment media (Cougar et al., 2012), the relationship between sexualised media content and children's sexual behaviour is not always linear and one dimensional. Several studies have identified a number of factors underpinning the longer-term resilience of survivors of child sexual abuse, including positive self-image, strong emotional supports and external attributions of blame (see e.g. Valentine and Feinauer, 1993; Bouvier, 2003; Wilcox et al., 2004). In this vein, the family and the personal competency and autonomy of children, who will have varying degrees of emotional, social and cognitive development, may be important factors in mediating the influence of cultural and societal sexualised media content (Buckingham and Bragg, 2003; Papadopoulos, 2010). The latter theme is pertinent to countering the 'social scripts' (Ashurst and McAlinden, 2015: 377) which are influencing children and to developing proactive efforts at prevention as discussed in the final chapter. This argument may also help to explain, to some extent at least, why some children and young people are negatively influenced by their peers and cultural messages about sex while others are more resilient.

In relation to children and young people more generally, for a minority of interviewees, the impact of the presence of cultural messages about sex on the behaviour of children and young people has perhaps been overstated:

[107] See further Chapter 6, note 2 and accompanying text.

> I think while it is out there, teenage pregnancy is on the decrease, which is a good thing. So I think there are a lot of fears out there that are unjustified about young people. I think if young people get good, fact based information, then they will make appropriate choices for where they are at.[108]

Several interviewees in the study drew attention to the structure-agency nexus and the differential impact of cultural factors on individual children. One professional explained this in relation to the viewing of pornography: 'For a lot of kids . . . viewing online pornography is very prevalent and for a lot of children they get desensitised to it and . . . a lot of them are not viewing that.'[109]

Others explained the issue of 'resilience' in relation to those who had previously been victimised with echoes of the broader debates which demonstrate that not all children who are abused will go on to become abusers themselves (see e.g. Craissati et al., 2002; Hackett et al., 2013; Lambie and Johnson, 2016)[110]: 'So the resilience factors that help young people get through other childhood problems equally apply to young people with harmful sexual behaviour . . . what other compensatory factors are around?'[111]; 'then you have the kids that don't do it. They go through that abuse but they have the resilience to go in a different direction.'[112] Interviewees involved in assessment and therapeutic services, while acknowledging that abuse 'could be very intrusive, it could be very impactful',[113] explained this further with reference to cases they had experienced:

> I think the problem is that it depends on each child. You know some kids will bounce back from an experience because of all the other resilience factors in their lives. And I have seen it in child protection where a child has been horrifically raped, but has recovered in a way that a child who . . . has had experience of indecent exposure, has not recovered from that because they don't have anything else in their system that would help them with resilience. So . . . it depends very much on the victim.[114]
>
> It entirely depends on the victim, on the abuser, on the length of time that the abuse happened, and the emotional and psychological impact that abuse had on the victim . . . And oftentimes the relationship

[108] Interview 19, 16 June 2016, Youth Worker, FPA.

[109] Interview 15, 3 June 2016, NSPCC Worker.

[110] Craissati et al. (2002) reported that almost half of those convicted of sexual offending against children had been abused as children. See also Hackett et al.'s (2013) study of 700 young sexual abusers which reports similar percentages.

[111] Interview 24, 6 July 2016, Independent Treatment Professional.

[112] Interview 1, 16 February 2016, Service Manager, HSS Trust. [113] Ibid. [114] Ibid.

> between the victim and the abuser will also impact on the outcome for the victim.[115]

The differing levels and types of impact on victims also underline the importance of not being prescriptive in terms of what may constitute 'harmful' or 'risky' sexual behaviour among peers as 'harm' cannot be viewed by purely objective criteria, without being mindful of the consequences for individual victims and the particular contexts in which the abuse occurs (see further Chapter 6). Moreover, as discussed further in Part III of the book, it also highlights the need to develop resiliency factors among children and young people related, for example, to peer empathy and appropriate levels of social and familial support (Lambie and Johnston, 2016).

One interesting sub-theme, raised by a small number of interviewees, relates to the relationships between changing modes of social communication, considered earlier, and resilience:

> At the end of the day, we are now in a virtual world. So reality and virtual are so intertwined, whereas a lot of young people get them both confused. And their communication and ... their social life now is evolved round a screen. And that in itself has reduced resilience. It can knock confidence so much that you wouldn't darken the door, or you wouldn't leave the house or whatever. They just don't know how to communicate any more.[116]

These arguments related to resilience also accentuate the need to not only enhance parental awareness and controls on what children are accessing online but, moreover, to augment children's personal resilience to cultural pressures around sex and their ability to negotiate their own sexual identity, as considered further in Chapter 8.

NORMALISATION AND THE 'NEW NORMAL'

The foregoing discussion has established that evolving cultural norms and consequential social behaviours are changing the nature of interactions among children and young people at a broad level. An analogy may be drawn with the debate around the normalisation of recreational drug use as part of youth culture at the turn of the millennium. On the one hand, the normalisation thesis held that drug use was so prevalent

[115] Interview 28, 16 August 2016, Senior Voluntary Sector Interviewee.
[116] Interview 13, 31 May 2016, Public Health Nurse.

among youth that it had become normalised activity (Parker et al., 1995, 2002). On the other hand, this view was thought to both over-exaggerate and over-simplify the extent of the problem devoid of the actual normative context in which the problem occurs (Shiner and Newburn, 1997, 1999). That is, while not *every* child or young person is engaging in underage sexual activity or practices such as sexting, the normative context around peer-based sexual behaviour is clearly changing.

The sexuality and sexualisation of children and adolescents in the digital culture and social media age (Moore and Rosenthal, 2006; Boyd, 2014; Saleh et al., 2014) have produced a new set of cultural norms surrounding what is deemed appropriate or normal sexual behaviour, particularly among adolescents. One police officer explained the problem in relation to children and young people more generally and how this may be more acute with children who have been abused or are in care:

> So I think there is a lot to do with the societal norms now, for teenagers, about sexual health and what is a healthy relationship. And it is different from when we were growing up. There is almost like . . . this is the way you do it. And you know, you have sex. You don't hold hands and kiss. You go straight into sex. And there is this expectation. And that's for children who haven't maybe experienced trauma. So for children who have maybe, for long periods, been sexually abused by people who are supposed to love them, it is normalised behaviour. It is looking for love. It is looking for care. It is looking for TLC. It is looking for company, attention, all sorts of reasons, so it is very common.[117]

As discussed further in Chapter 6, the difficulties surrounding the normalisation of sexualised language and behaviour are also particularly pertinent in relation to online forms of HSB such as sexting or sexualised cyberbullying.

Indeed, the rapid pace of technological, normative and behavioural change has inevitably created a culture of confusion about what is 'acceptable' among male and female adolescents growing up in 'today's highly sexualised landscape' (see Jewkes, 2010: 5).[118] It is this culture of confusion which also augments the vulnerability of children and young people to sexualised forms of harm and simultaneously diminishes their

[117] Interview 31, 17 October 2016.
[118] Chris Cloke, then Head of NSPCC's Child Protection Awareness, cited in Papadopoulos (2010: 12).

capacity to make judicious choices about risk of harm to self and others with conviction. At the same time, however, as highlighted earlier, individual children and adolescents may be impacted differently. As one professional succinctly put it: 'young people are all so different, so what's normal for someone is completely un-normal for somebody else.'[119]

The crux of the problem for children and young people, as well as for society more generally, is that 'the culture of confusion' generates potential challenges along two primary fronts. The first relates to the dilution of the individual agency and competence of children to say 'no' to unwanted behaviours or experiences and, moreover, societal reluctance to accept this fact:

> So I think in terms of agency, I think agency is a massive area that we are not prepared . . . we are not having the discourse about. And it is almost like it is dirty. It is a dirty word, because that means they . . . they rang them, they put a thing on Facebook saying they were available for a blow job. They said they would be in such and such a carpark. But like come on, let's look at what these children have experienced. Let's look at what their norm is.[120]

This is also broadly reflective of the victim-offender dichotomy, discussed at length in the previous chapter, in that victim acquiescence in such activities may ultimately detract from their social status as victims, particularly where young girls are concerned.

The second issue relates to the far-reaching and lasting consequences stemming from the inadvertent infringement of legal norms. A youth worker explained in relating to sexting and the sending of indecent images between peers: 'I think more young people will be criminalised because of things that they think are normal, but they are not. Like putting photographs on. I think that more young people will get criminal records because of that.'[121] Similarly, a police officer explained:

> Sexting is very, very normalised. And there is a difficulty then in managing that for us as a Public Protection Unit, in that they [children] don't realise that it is unhealthy, or possibly unlawful, depending on what the context is. But trying to manage then, that this is what they see

119 Interview 14, 2 June 2016, Sexual Health Nurse.
120 Interview 11, 26 May 2016, Safeguarding Professional.
121 Interview 10, 25 May 2016, Youth Worker.

> as normal behaviour . . . a lot of it is to do with ignorance, not realising what they are doing is wrong.[122]

As discussed further in Chapters 5 and 6, normalisation can also lead to lax sexual boundaries among peers with no cognisance of potential harm or the legal ramifications following the commission of a potential crime.

A related difficulty is that although adults may have traditionally framed what is considered normal or abnormal sexual behaviour and development in children and young people, as outlined in the previous chapter, what is considered normal by adults may not be considered so by children: 'I don't think anybody knows what is normal now. I mean I could move forward and say to you what you thought was normal about having access to sex or knowing about sex in your day, well you know that is not the experience now.'[123] This may also be the case even in professional contexts where there is often a lack of understanding of peer-based sexual behaviours: 'a lot of professionals . . . really cannot get their head round it, because they just feel it is so against what they think is the norm . . . I think people find it really hard to understand.'[124]

As I have argued previously, before professionals or society or parents can respond appropriately, they need to take account of how both norms for sexual behaviour and norms within cultural appetites, including within content in communications about personal and sexual matters, are 'continually changing and at a very rapid pace' (Ashurst and McAlinden, 2015: 375).[125] As Horvath et al. (2013) have noted, contemporary normative behaviours among young people reflect radical departures from norms and experiences of youth in earlier times, raising pertinent questions for adults about the plausible distinction between normative and potentially harmful behaviours. Several of the interviewees in the study articulated this problem: 'Perhaps professionals who are looking in at this view it very differently [from] the young people who are involved in the culture of it. And I think we need to work out what that is. And I think we need to have a look at how that

[122] Interview 31, 17 October 2016. [123] Interview 3, 20 April 2016, Education Authority.

[124] Interview 17, 7 July 2016, Independent, former Youth Justice Professional.

[125] See e.g. the public uproar and court case surrounding the UK publication of D. H. Lawrence's (1960) *Lady Chatterley's Lover* in which Penguin Books was acquitted after being prosecuted under the Obscene Publications Act 1959: *R* v. *Penguin Books Ltd* [1961] Crim LR. 176. This can be contrasted, for example, with the publication of *Fifty Shades of Grey* by E. L. James (2012) which depicts sadomasochism and became the fastest-selling paperback in history, selling more than 100 million copies worldwide.

fits within a young person in 2016, and not react.'[126] Similarly, a police officer reflected on such difficulties rhetorically: 'It is very difficult for us . . . and we have gone through the . . . what is normal, what would you expect? But maybe the boundaries of what's normal are changing as well. Is it normal for a 14-year-old girl to send a picture of herself topless? I think unfortunately it is.'[127] In proactively addressing the problem, it becomes imperative, therefore, to raise pertinent questions for both adults, especially those involved in the front line of child protection and intervention services, and children and young people about the distinction between potentially harmful and healthy contemporary sexual behaviours.

In short, in an age in which Western societies are increasingly characterised by multiculturalism and constantly evolving social mores, there is a need for professionals and parents to take continual account of what may be the 'new normal' for children and young people at any given time. Furthermore, the dual problems stemming from the normalcy and evolution of sexualised behaviours in the everyday lives of children and young people also pose challenges for legal and policy responses which seek to identify and respond to risk and impose sanctions for the infringement of social and moral norms (see Chapter 7). As discussed at length in Chapter 6, however, the distinction between normal-problematic-harmful sexual behaviours, even within professional discourses, is not always immediately clear-cut or an easy determination to make.

Given the prevalence and normalisation of the contemporary sexualised culture, the divergent impacts on individual children and adolescents and the constant evolution of cultural norms underpinning teen culture, there is a need to develop a range of tailored, age-appropriate messages for children and young people around sex and healthy relationships, on a more wide-ranging basis (see Chapter 8). Moreover, there is also a related danger of adult complacency concerning the normalisation of peer-based sexual behaviours and a need, therefore, to engage professionals as well as parents in similar discourses around potential risks and what constitutes healthy or harmful sexual behaviour. In relation to sexting, for example, and the exchange of indecent images between adolescents, several practitioners cautioned: 'there is a danger there, that as professionals we don't dig a bit deeper and look at

[126] Interview 2, 18 April 2016, Independent Forensic Psychologist.
[127] Interview 32, 2 November 2016.

what that's about'[128]; and 'so do you change the category a bit? I would argue no, because we can't let it become normalised.'[129]

CONCLUSION

This chapter has demonstrated how, from the early emergence of harmful sexual or exploitative behaviour among children and young people as a distinct societal problem, a confluence of factors has combined to normalise the onset of peer-based sexual behaviours. These are related, inter alia, to changes in dating and courting practices, the proliferation of popular culture with both explicit and more innocuous sexual messages, the growth of a partying culture, changing modes of communication stemming from the rise in the exponential use of social media and mobile phones (among children as well as adults) and ready access to pornography or exposure to subliminal messages related to pornography. Taken together, these social norms have influenced the identity and behaviours of children and young people along three plains: how they view and define themselves and negotiate their social identity more generally, how they then behave within the context of interpersonal relationships with peers and how they think about and view sex specifically.

Indeed, these factors have collectively impacted sexual and social norms, including the behavioural 'rules' for sex in the twenty-first century, arguably undermining the need to think about relationships and sex in a consensual way. In consequence, there has been a gradual blurring of boundaries between consensual or coercive relationships, between the expected role and behaviours of adults and children, and even traditional roles between males and females. As considered further in the next chapter, these shifting social, cultural and gendered norms may impact a child's vulnerability and make them more susceptible to grooming and abuse by weakening their personal autonomy and capacity for decision-making. Moreover, the resulting ambiguities about what constitutes risky sexual behaviour among peers also has onward consequences for professional, policy and legal responses to such risks (see further Chapter 7).

A fundamental tension has also emerged from an analysis of the primary data which illustrates the dichotomy between these cultural

[128] Interview 18, 14 June 2016, Senior Voluntary Sector Interviewee.
[129] Interview 32, 2 November 2016, Police Officer.

messages about sex and the attendant premature sexualisation of children and young people and what I have termed 'experiential sexualisation'. That is, emerging and important insights challenge traditional reductionist, binary constructions of gender identities, particularly in relation to 'doing girlhood' (Driscoll, 2013: 286) (e.g. that girls can behave as sexual aggressors as well as boys) or the lived experiences of contemporary teenage masculinity (e.g. the blurring of the boundaries of consent stemming from the older physical appearance of young girls) and in terms of how individuals experience such pressures within their immediate social environment stemming from their own personal resilience. In essence, the extent to which children and young people may be at risk of peer-based harmful sexual or exploitative behaviour in contemporary society across a diverse range of contexts may be as much to do with their family environment (see Chapter 5) and agentic factors which may mediate broader structural and cultural influences.

In this respect, given the cultural prevalence of images of and messages about sex and the ready availability of and access to pornography, a key challenge is 'how you build that resilience ... and protective factors'[130] and increase the capacity of children and young people to make healthy and informed choices about safe and appropriate sexual behaviours. More broadly, this is also reflective of the notion of the 'being child' (as opposed to the 'becoming child' underpinning socialisation models as considered in Part I of the book) (Brownlie, 2001: 523–24). The former notion recognises the complexity of factors surrounding children's decision-making and children as agentic beings in their own right rather than as adults in waiting. The next chapter considers further some of the risk or vulnerability factors underlying the aetiology of harmful sexual or exploitative behaviours among children and young people. How society can move from a focus on social risk of harm to increasing the personal resilience of children and young people – in short how we balance *risk* with *resilience* or vulnerability factors with protective factors – will be considered further in Part III of the book.

[130] Interview 13, 31 May 2016, Public Health Nurse.

5

PEER-TO-PEER GROOMING: A REAPPRAISAL

> I think a lot of it for young people is their confidence. A lot of it is peer pressure. A lot of it is feeling isolated . . . wanting to feel loved. A lot of them think they are in a relationship. They want to please. They want to be valued. It is something they feel they are maybe good at and they don't feel they are good at anything else. They might feel they are a bit cool, they are popular, everybody likes them. I reckon some of them, only afterwards, even recognise what has happened.[1]

The aim of this chapter is to provide an in-depth examination of the complexities of peer-to-peer grooming, within the broader context of the normalisation of harmful sexual or exploitative behaviour, as it might apply with both children and adolescents. The term 'grooming' is generally taken to refer to the process whereby would-be abusers will 'set up' opportunities to abuse and subsequently prevent victim disclosure (see generally Salter, 1995, 2003; Craven et al., 2006; McAlinden 2006, 2012a). In this vein, the process has been likened to 'emotional seduction' (Salter, 1995: 274) or 'entrapment' (Howitt, 1995: 176; Gallagher, 1998, 2000) and has been deemed 'a ubiquitous feature of the sexual abuse of children' (Thornton, 2003: 144). While subsequent empirical work has challenged the universality of this claim across all abusive contexts (e.g. within families, institutions and online), grooming has nevertheless been retained as a core variable underpinning sexual offending against children and appraised as one that 'deserves its place in the lexicon of sexual offending' (McAlinden, 2012a: 284).

[1] Interview 9, 25 May 2016, Youth Support Worker.

To date, however, the dominant and extant thread of public and official discourses on grooming has been within the context of adult-child abuse which occurs online ('internet/online/cyber grooming') (see e.g. Gillespie, 2001, 2008; Gallagher et al., 2003, 2006), within childcare institutions ('institutional grooming') (McAlinden, 2006; see also Gallagher, 1998), or within the context of child sexual exploitation (CSE) ('localised' or 'street grooming') (Beckett, 2011; Ost and Mooney, 2013). This belies the important fact that grooming also occurs, and usually more often, in more intimate, private, face-to-face settings (McAlinden, 2012a: Ch. 4). Indeed, as a reflection of broader public discourses on 'stranger danger' and children as being 'at risk' rather than presenting 'as risk' themselves (see Chapters 2 and 3), academic and legal and policy discourses have, by and large, been narrowly focused on the grooming *of* children by adults, rather than grooming behaviours *by* and *among* children and young people.

A small number of studies have included some focus on the grooming behaviours of adolescents, rather than younger children (see e.g. Kaufman et al., 1996, 1998; Leclerc et al., 2008). Other studies have considered grooming by peers as a minor theme within the context of a broader research agenda. These can be broadly grouped into two strands: (i) studies on adults grooming children within the confines of child sexual abuse (McAlinden, 2012a), child pornography (Ost, 2009), online sexual exploitation (O'Connell, 2003; Palmer and Stacey, 2004), or CSE in offline contexts (Montgomery-Devlin, 2008; Ost and Mooney, 2013) where children who have themselves been victimised are groomed to 'recruit' other victims; and (ii) studies on the aetiology of harmful sexual behaviour (HSB) by children and adolescents (Taylor, 2003; Vizard et al., 2007). Key findings from some of these studies as they relate to the modes and methods of grooming among peers are drawn on further later. Notwithstanding these isolated examples, to date, however, the empirical foundation for examining peer-to-peer grooming is rather limited.

Previous empirical research conducted by the author in 2012 espoused a new definition of grooming, based on extensive reading of the subject and primary research. This definition sought to better capture the complexity of the process and the multiple manifestations of grooming, including grooming between peers:

> (1) the use of a variety of manipulative and controlling techniques (2) with a vulnerable subject (3) in a range of inter-personal and social

> settings (4) in order to establish trust or normalise sexually harmful behaviour (5) with the overall aim of facilitating exploitation and/or prohibiting exposure. (McAlinden, 2012a: 11)

This research, which also concentrated predominantly on the grooming and abuse of children by adults, found that peer-peer-grooming and abuse between the 13- to 17-year-old age group was among the growth areas of concern for criminal justice professionals, including police, across the United Kingdom (McAlinden, 2012a: 134).

In general, however, the complexities of the grooming process among peers have not previously been examined within the contemporary context of changing modes of social communication which privilege the negotiation of personal identity and social relationships within 'digital peer networks' (Harvey et al., 2013) in the social media age (see previous chapter). This chapter sets out to remedy some of these gaps in the existing literature by undertaking an in-depth examination of the dynamics of peer-to-peer grooming and its potential role in harmful sexual and exploitative behaviours among children and young people and in peer-based social behaviours more broadly.

A number of themes presented earlier in the book recur within the course of this chapter. These relate to the cultural orthodoxies surrounding 'the ideal victim' (Christie, 1986: 18; Walklate, 2007) and the challenges of classifying children and young people who groom others, and who may themselves be subject to a range of personal and social vulnerabilities, as 'deviant victims' or 'vulnerable offenders' (McAlinden, 2014a: 182) (see Chapter 3), and the impact of a highly sexualised popular culture (Papadopoulos, 2010; Bailey, 2011) which promotes ever evolving sets of contemporary sexual norms and resulting 'risky' practices among peers (see Chapter 4). Indeed, following on from the previous chapter, the discussion also considers whether 'virtual peer associations' (Miller and Morris, 2016: 1543) and the prevalence of sexting within the broader contemporary 'culture of transient sex' might negate or displace the need for specific grooming strategies among peers in some cases.

Mindful also of the problems of applying an adult-centric language of 'offending' and the rubric of 'risk' to children and young people (Calder, 2002; Hackett et al., 2006, 2015), as outlined in the first chapter, this chapter takes as its starting point my earlier definition of grooming as presented here. With these challenges and complexities in mind, the chapter provides an in-depth reappraisal of this original definition and its five individual components within the specific context of peer-to-peer abuse. Notwithstanding the degree of overlap between them, they are examined separately for the purposes of critical analysis. To begin, however, it is useful to provide a contextual framework for this analysis by undertaking a brief comparison of the key similarities and differences with adult-child forms of grooming stemming from the primary research.

CONTEXTUALISING PEER-TO-PEER GROOMING

'Grooming' has become a catch-all term within public discourses on sexual offending concerning children and synonymous with 'risk' relating to adult-child contact, inflating levels of suspicion and fear within the popular imagination.[2] Indeed, in conjunction with wider debates on peer-to-peer forms of abuse (see Part I), grooming among peers features much less in public consciousness, as it is a term commonly associated with predatory adult behaviour. A professional in the present study explained this popular linkage: 'It does definitely come back to that thing where people don't think anything of harmful behaviour by children . . . You would maybe think of bullying or antisocial behaviour, but you are still not looking at the potential for HSB with kids. Whereas with adults, we are much more suspicious of an adult who is interested in kids.'[3] There are, however, a number of shared characteristics between adult-child and peer-based forms of grooming which merit specific consideration.

Similarities: Problems in Defining Scope and Pinpointing Intention

First, and in the main, there are difficulties surrounding the precise meaning and scope of the term 'grooming' (see generally Gillespie, 2004: 586; McAlinden, 2006: 341–42). In this vein, several interviewees articulated their understanding of the term 'peer-to-peer grooming' which conveyed an implied element of at least latent coercion or manipulation with an end goal of some form of sexual exploitation. Some typical definitions included: 'it is really just one young person bringing another to meet their own needs and desires'[4]; 'it is a way of

[2] See e.g. the range of typical newspaper headlines which denote the public 'panic' around grooming: 'Child Grooming Occurs in "Every Town"', *BBC News*, 31 December 2014; 'Dinner Lady's Child Grooming Warning Over Biscuit', *The Belfast Telegraph*, 8 October 2010.

[3] Interview 1, 16 February 2016, Service Manager, HSS Trust.

[4] Interview 28, 16 August 2016, Victim Support Professional.

engaging with others sexually . . . and where there is an intent to exploit or coerce somebody into doing something they don't want to do'[5]; 'when someone tricks you and when they say they like you in order to sexually use you[6]; and 'it is about establishing, you are going to do what I want, whatever way round I choose to do that.'[7]

However, while on one level these conceptualisations of peer-to-peer grooming might appear to map onto adult-child forms of sexual grooming, the term is not always apt with peer-to-peer abuse where potentially harmful sexual behaviours are perhaps more difficult to pinpoint and define. Rather, it needs to be used in a considered and measured way with peers, mindful of the context of the behaviours since 'the motivations and methods and materials are quite often very different'[8] and, moreover, may also change over time as 'it isn't always necessarily them starting out to exploit.'[9] This view was expressed by several professionals underlining the dangers associated with transposing the adult vernacular onto children and the need to look at the underlying motivations:

> Grooming is something that we talk about . . . which adults will do. With children we have to look at what is it they were doing and why were they doing it? If it is to get to a position where they could be alone with somebody and they could do things . . . which they know to be wrong, then you could describe it as grooming. But if it is part of trying to develop a relationship, and then they made bad decisions about what they did in the relationship, then that's different . . . So, I think there are difficulties with grooming, when you apply it to children. I don't think that we should just take the language from adults and apply it to children. I think that we need to look at the actions and the behaviours and analyse them to see what the purpose of it is. Is it malign or is it positive?[10]
>
> I think there's a difference between normalised behaviour and this sort of peer-to-peer consent, where . . . well everybody's doing it . . . Or, my best mate did it, so I have to do it. I think there is a slight naiveté in that in comparison to the sinister peer to peer exploitation of targeting, pressurising . . . 'you will do. This is what I want you to do.' There is a big difference, I think, between the two of them. And again every circumstance has to just be looked at to see what the story is behind it.[11]

[5] Interview 2, 18 April 2016, Independent Forensic Psychologist.
[6] Interview 21, 23 June 2016, Social Work Practitioner.
[7] Interview 6, 25 April 2016, Independent Safeguarding Consultant.
[8] Interview 2, 18 April 2016, Independent Forensic Psychologist.
[9] Interview 16, 6 June 2016, Social Work Consultant.
[10] Interview 23, 24 June 2016, Social Work Service Manager.
[11] Interview 31, 17 October 2016, Police Officer.

Second, and following on from the previous point, there are difficulties in identifying potential risk or a harmful motivation prior to the occurrence of actual harm. Since much of the early stages of grooming looks like 'befriending' or 'getting to know someone', it is essentially a behaviour that is only usually identifiable with the benefit of contextual hindsight (McAlinden, 2012a: 97). In relation to children and young people, this in itself stems from the problems of identifying a harmful or exploitative intention which is over and above their 'normal' everyday peer-to-peer interactions. Notwithstanding that the identification of a harmful motivation on a proactive basis is also systemic to adult-child forms of abuse (see generally McAlinden, 2012a: 9), such problems are seemingly enhanced with peer-based forms of abuse:

> I think grooming can happen in normal relationships as well and I think that where it becomes exploitative, that is the difficult part . . . It has to be something that is happening along with the other stuff. Because if we look at the other behaviours they are quite normal in quite a lot of relationships. At the start it tends to be one person that's more controlling than the other. If we are very honest about sexual relationships when they start, we do have an interest in others sexually and therefore we might do things like taking them out for meals or we might buy them things, presents and things like that. So we are very careful about what we are saying that is and how we explain that to young people.[12]

As this same professional continued, 'so it's about the behaviour, it's about the impact and it's about the effects.'[13] In this sense, peer-to-peer grooming among children and young people may be akin to 'what are ostensibly courting behaviours' (Fernandez, 2006: 191). From the point of view of identifying and managing potential risk, the pivotal issue becomes, therefore, one of establishing context and the age-appropriateness of the behaviour with the target person (see further Chapter 6).

Differences: Proximity and Speed

At the same time, there are also important differences between adult-child and peer-to-peer forms of grooming where a number of differential variables are at play. One such difference is that there are a smaller number of cases involving peers where grooming features in the traditional sense of the word in terms of a pre-planned conscious mode of

[12] Interview 2, 18 April 2016, Independent Forensic Psychologist. [13] Ibid.

manipulative and preparatory behaviour. A professional engaged in assessment and therapeutic work with younger children reflected on previous cases: 'I couldn't think of any in that deliberate sense of grooming, you know.'[14] Similarly, another professional from the Sexual Assault Referral Centre reflected on cases which are generally at the more serious end of the spectrum and which potentially enter the justice system:

> We hear things out there, but very few cases would be coming through here . . . So it might be somebody has been groomed in school or through a friend's network or whatever. But small numbers . . . Barnardo's obviously, they would see quite a lot of it, and they would say that's probably their growing area, which isn't surprising if you think about the house party scene and all the rest of it. But in terms of what we see, it is one of our smallest categories probably.[15]

On one level, the small number of cases coming through to referral may be indicative of the effectiveness of peer-to-peer grooming in that victims may not realise they have been victimised and so are more reticent to report. On another level, however, and in common with intra-familial forms of adult-child sexual abuse (see generally, Craven et al., 2006: 293–94; McAlinden, 2012a: 284), there is perhaps less practical need for children and young people to deliberately and actively groom for access purposes as they may already be proximate to other children within their immediate peer group and where they have 'the advantage of already having some kind of established relationship'.[16] Several professionals shared this view both in relation to peers more broadly as well as siblings specifically, highlighting the attendant difficulties of identifying grooming within the context of preexisting relationships:

> If you take the grooming in terms of what it is, obviously it does happen. I think my issue is that because these young people are interacting anyway, unlike if you have an adult to get access to this child, they do have to take a much more active role to get closer to that child. But if these peers are already out and about interacting in their day-to-day play, going to school and all of that, you have less need to be close to that person . . . So I find there is a grooming through the sense of the word, but I think we need to see it within the context of they are physically

[14] Interview 4, 21 April 2016, Child Care Centre Professional.
[15] Interview 8, 23 May 2016, Rowan SARC Professional.
[16] Interview 1, 16 February 2016, Service Manager, HSS Trust.

> having contact anyway. They are sexting anyway . . . They use a lot more of those tactics.[17]
>
> Within families . . . you don't really need to groom. The opportunity is there in so many ways. And he was looking after the personal care of this child. So I suppose the only grooming would be in getting her to go along with what he was doing. And he was actually sharing a bed with her . . . So, I am not sure that he needed to do a lot of grooming.[18]
>
> It possibly is less obvious on the outside than it would be with an adult . . . You are not going to query a 16-year-old in school talking to a 14-year-old or whatever. And I think they can do a lot of the grooming as part of normal social interactions, which is much harder, I think for adults to identify because it is, I think, less obvious.[19]

For a small number of interviewees, this was also relevant to a broader 'gang' (Beckett et al., 2012, 2013, 2014), or 'partying' culture (Melrose, 2013) (see further Chapter 4): 'So someone, because of their name, because of their kudos, can just kind of sit there and they don't have to do any grooming. It is just a given. If somebody goes in and says "right, you are with me tonight", you go.'[20] In this instance, the power base or latent coercion may be derived from the differential social status among peers rather than any overt methods of grooming. As discussed further, it is this normative feature of peer-based relationships which may mitigate or negate perceptions about risk in the minds of children and young people. Grooming in such contexts, therefore, becomes less about access, and more about the maintenance of control. As sexual behaviours become normalised, children become less wary of the risks stemming from peers or those closest to them and, as a result, often 'there is a lack of a sense of me being exploited'[21] or it is seen as 'less threatening . . . less risky . . . [as] there is a safety, associated with peers.'[22]

In common with online forms of adult-child sexual grooming and abuse which generally occur within a much shorter time frame (see Gillespie, 2007: 3; Kierkegaard, 2008: 43; CEOP, 2010: 14; McAlinden, 2012a: 114), peer-to-peer grooming which takes place before the occurrence of HSB is a much more expeditious process. This feature was generally explained by professionals as being related to two

[17] Interview 16, 6 June 2016, Social Work Consultant.
[18] Interview 24, 6 July 2016, Independent Treatment Professional.
[19] Interview 1, 16 February 2016, Service Manager, HSS Trust.
[20] Interview 21, 23 June 2016, Social Work Practitioner.
[21] Interview 16, 6 June 2016, Social Work Consultant.
[22] Interview 1, 16 February 2016, Service Manager, HSS Trust.

core factors – the peer group dynamic and routine interactions between children and young people, as well as changing modes of communication such as 'texting' and 'sexting' which have 'created new opportunities for deviance and victimization' (Wolfe et al., 2016: 614) (see generally, Chapter 4). In relation to the first of these factors, a social work consultant explained:

> So you are finding it is a shorter period of time in terms of having to do it . . . it can be more direct and it doesn't have to be as subtle. Because they are already in the company, but also because they do a lot of their communication through text, there is a flirtatiousness that comes in there anyway . . . Whereas an adult to a child wouldn't have that same freedom with texting and social media, they are straight to the point because they have already got some sort of a contact with each other . . . there is less going round the houses with it . . . And then if she doesn't do it, they just move on to somebody else. There is a speed with it that's different, that we need to acknowledge.[23]

This facet of HSB among children and young people accords with Smallbone and Wortley's (Wortley and Smallbone, 2006; Smallbone et al., 2008) theory of the situational nature of sexual offending. That is, rather than being 'predatory', much of sexual offending behaviour is often 'opportunistic' or 'situational' and occurs in certain circumstances. This is also broadly reflective of the 'routine activities theory' which in brief holds that 'crime' or harmful behaviour occurs as a result of a confluence of three factors: a motivated offender (whether this is a conscious or subconscious motivation), a suitable and available victim and the absence of a capable guardian (see generally, Cohen and Felson, 1979).[24]

In relation to the second factor, another legal professional linked the speed with which peer-to-peer grooming can occur to changing modes of social and interpersonal communication derived principally from mobile phone use: 'Grooming is so much quicker now. Grooming used to take time. Now it doesn't even take seconds. Young people are used to instant communication . . . Like it is OK to talk about very personal things very quickly with somebody, because we are used to that.'[25]

[23] Interview 16, 6 June 2016, Social Work Consultant.

[24] See e.g. the multi-nation study by Näsi et al. (2017) which found that routine activities theory is a useful predictor of online victimisation of people ages 15 to 30 in the USA, Finland, Germany and the United Kingdom.

[25] Interview 30, 12 October 2016, Senior Prosecutor PPS.

The previous discussion has established that grooming among peers is different in several respects from adult-child forms of grooming, including most notably in relation to the questionable necessity of deliberate grooming strategies over and above routine interactions among peers and the speed of the onset of harmful sexual or exploitative behaviours in some cases. The discussion will now move to consider the dynamics of each of the elements of the broad definition of grooming presented earlier in relation to peers. These are distilled to a shorthand list encompassing what are deemed to be the core ingredients of grooming: power and control, vulnerability, the exploitation of personal and social contexts, trust and normalisation and entrapment. In brief, it will be argued that the purpose and process of grooming may operate among peers in much the same way as it does between adults and children in relation to the last three variables. However, it is the first two in particular – power and control and vulnerability – which present greater complexities for discourses on peer-to-peer forms of grooming, and indeed on risk more broadly, within the context of harmful sexual or exploitative behaviours.

POWER AND CONTROL

The first element of the definition seeks to encapsulate the essence of grooming – *the use of a variety of manipulative and controlling techniques*. Previous research on the pre-abuse grooming of children by adults has established that this is often a staged process, beginning with befriending a child and getting to know his or her interests, progressing to establishing an 'exclusive relationship' which isolates the child from protective others and culminating in the introduction of sexualised themes and eventually sexual contact (see e.g. Conte et al., 1989; Elliott et al., 1995; Salter, 1995, 2003; McAlinden, 2006, 2012a). As noted at the outset of the chapter, there is a small body of research on the grooming strategies used by children and young people. Of this research, two such studies which have considered the grooming variable as part of a wider research study on HSB by children and young people are those conducted by Taylor (2003) and Vizard et al. (2007).

Taylor's (2003) study involving a sample of 227 cases of HSB, reports high percentages of coercion as part of the grooming process: 39 per cent used physical force to gain victim compliance or ensure their secrecy and a further 11 per cent used threats of either 'harm' or 'blame' to avoid disclosure. Only 19 per cent had persuaded their victim into compliance without force or threats, which is indicative of more covert grooming strategies.[26] Moreover, in just under 15 per cent of cases, the children and young people acted with an accomplice.[27] In most of these cases, there were reports of the use of force or the threat of violence prior to and throughout the grooming and abuse (Taylor, 2003: 65). The latter finding also lends tentative support to the argument that when children and young people interact collaboratively, such as within institutions or gangs, the hegemonic group or social dynamic among peers may contribute to the onset and escalation of more entrenched patterns of grooming and aggressive forms of HSB.

Vizard et al. (2007: 66) found instances among their slightly larger sample of 280 cases of isolating the victim from adults. This included inviting the victim to go up to their bedroom to 'play', including playing on their computer. Approximately one-third exhibited prior grooming of the victim (34 per cent). Just over one-third (36 per cent) used verbal threats to obtain victim compliance in the abuse or ensure their silence following abuse. A minority, however, used physical force or threats of harm. For example, 8 per cent used excessive force to gain victim compliance; 4 per cent abducted their victim; 3 per cent used a weapon; and a further 1 per cent physically restrained their victim by tying them up.

These previous studies have established that HSB between children and young people inevitably entails a degree of coercion or the exercise of power and control (see also Ashurst, 2016). Contrary to the existing literature, however, there was generally a split in the views of interviewees in the present study in terms of the use and type of coercive or controlling techniques used by children and young people in the course of HSB. In line with the two studies described here, for the majority of interviewees who made reference to peer-to-peer grooming, the use of physical force or threatening behaviour, as opposed to more insidious grooming, emerged as a key attribute of HSB both within extrafamilial and intra-familial contexts where the motivation 'is about power and control over the other person'[28] and where 'very little of it is actually about sex.'[29] The pre-abuse behaviours were variously described 'absolutely as abusive'[30] and, in some cases, 'very much about violence and

[26] See also earlier American studies by Fehrenbach et al. (1986) and Kahn and Chambers (1991) who report higher percentages of youth using or threatening physical force or violence of 45 per cent and 42 per cent, respectively.

[27] See also Vizard et al. (2007: 68) who report a similar percentage (14 per cent) of children and young people 'acting with co-abuser(s)'.

[28] Interview 28, 16 August 2016, victim support Professional. [29] Ibid.

[30] Interview 11, 26 May 2016, Safeguarding Professional.

control',[31] or 'quite forceful ... bullying and threatening'[32] and 'not necessarily any less coercive'.[33] Several interviewees reflected:

> I think probably one of the concerning things about young people is that ... there is probably more physical force used. And that sort of lack of self-control. Immediate gratification. You know grooming implies a process where you are prepared to wait till you get the opportunity. Where you are prepared to put aside your immediate desires for a longer-term goal. With young people, their actions tend to be, I think, generally more impulsive. Maybe less restrained ... Some type of coercion would be, I think, more common.[34]
>
> I haven't got the sense there has been a lot of grooming leading up to what they have done. It has been opportunistic sometimes ... Some of it has just been quite sudden and aggressive with it. And violence involved with it ... It would have been more threats. You know, 'don't you be telling about this' ... It has been negative consequences of something happening if they tell.[35]
>
> One of the boys who was in the victim situation if you like was a very passive wee boy and the other was quite an aggressive one. So actually what had happened was not the grooming, friendship type thing, but he had groomed him by battering him in the playground to the point that the kid knew, I am stuck in the toilet with him, I have no way out.[36]

For a small number of interviewees, however, violence did not feature as heavily in the prelude to abuse by children and young people unless this was at the end of a longer period of time and where violence took place in conjunction with more covert grooming techniques. A NSPCC worker represented this view recounting his experience of a number of cases:

> We see very little violence, apart from that one where I was saying to you that the wee boy was threatened. But he was also cajoled ... not unlike how an adult would groom. Normalising it, or educative ... 'I'm going to show you. This is what adults do' ... We had another one where there was a boy, he was 19, where he was describing when he was 17, texting an 11- to 12-year-old. And waiting for two years. He said 11 was too young. But when she was 14 he said that was fine in his head, and that he was grooming her from [when] she was 11 and was sending her texts and

31 Interview 1, 16 February 2016, Service Manager, HSS Trust.
32 Interview 4, Child Care Centre Professional.
33 Interview 1, 16 February 2016, Service Manager, HSS Trust.
34 Interview 24, 6 July 2016, Independent Treatment Professional.
35 Interview 25, 25 July 2016, Consultant Paediatrician.
36 Interview 6, 25 April 2016, Independent Safeguarding Consultant.

> stuff ... He set up the situation, went to the party, gave her drink and so on ... And when she showed some resistance, then he used force.[37]

Indeed, although many of the dynamics may be similar to adult-child abuse in terms of the 'relationship' between the parties and the 'secrecy' underlying the abuse, peer-based preparatory strategies as a prelude to harm have emerged within previous studies as being subtler or more experimental and less well developed than with adult perpetrators (see also McAlinden, 2012a: 135), at least at the early stages of the relationship.

A further theme which emerged from the interviews in terms of controlling strategies, which has not previously featured in the existing literature, was the difference between grooming or pre-abuse behaviours among younger and older children, particularly in relation to virtual contexts: 'In the primary school age there doesn't seem to be overt grooming on [the] Internet, but certainly in the older ones you would see that'[38] and 'with younger children it is definitely more along the line of experimentation ... and not an opportunistic situation ... [where] there's a big difference in terms of the developmental stage, the emotional ... and cognitive capacities ... the cause and the intent all seem to be very different between the younger ones and even the older teens.'[39] Another safeguarding professional also supported this view by emphasising the small age difference in the cases of peer-based grooming and abuse among adolescents they had come across:

> I think that goes back to our social expectations of what a young person should be capable of at a certain age. So if you have a 16-year-old male who is grooming a 14/15-year-old girl. I am not having to say it is 10, 12, 13 ... They are only a year difference.[40]

Recent research conducted by Leclerc and Felson (2016) has shown that adolescent offenders adopt similar strategies to adults but are better able to use games and 'routine' activities as a prelude to sexual abuse. Indeed, while the underlying motivations or broad approach of children or adolescents may well be different from those within adult-child abusive or exploitative relationships, child 'perpetrators' still have to circumvent the 'external inhibitors' and the 'victim's resistance'

[37] Interview 5, 22 April 2016, NSPCC Professional.
[38] Interview 20, 20 June 2016, Rowan SARC Professional.
[39] Interview 1, 16 February 2016, Service Manager, HSS Trust.
[40] Interview 11, 26 May 2016, Safeguarding Professional.

(Finkelhor, 1984) to abuse. This argument was supported by a forensic psychologist:

> I mean definitely adults are selecting children to groom for sexual activity. You know, clearly that is coercive ... but that is not to say that adolescents don't do the same thing ... you can't just say it is an adult behaviour and this is an adolescent behaviour. There is a crossover and ... it is more to do with the intent that's behind it, the motivation, and the harm that can be caused by it.[41]

The grooming techniques used by children and young people may, therefore, lack the sophistication of those used by adults, who may have had the chance to hone their grooming skills over a longer period of time but may nonetheless be no less (even if inherently) coercive or harmful.

On one level, the age differential between the groomer or abuser and those being groomed or abused, which would usually amplify the power imbalance between the parties, may be much less in comparison to adult-child sexual exploitation or abuse. By way of example, according to the Northern Ireland 2010 Young Life and Times Survey, 12 per cent of 16-year-olds who took part in the survey reported that the person who tried to groom them was 'about their age', that is, not more than two years older than them and almost a further 20 per cent were only three to four years older than the intended victim.[42] On another level, however, as Palmer's (1997) well-cited definition of HSB outlined at the outset of the book makes clear, power imbalances can manifest in a variety of ways, other than age. This includes disparities in 'emotional maturity, gender, physical strength, intellect' which are often pivotal to the dynamics of HSB. To this list can be added social status and the fear of social marginalisation (Firmin and Curtis, 2015: 5) which often lie at the heart of peer-based relationships.

Two further sub-themes which emerged from the study and which relate to this first component of the definition are worthy of note: One, in tandem with what I have previously termed 'a continuum of offending' (McAlinden, 2014a: 186), is that there may also be a related 'continuum of power imbalances' in which 'young people who abuse their peers have power and control over the young person they are harming' but 'may be simultaneously powerless in relation to some peers who are encouraging their behaviour or in the home where they are

[41] Interview 2, 18 April 2016, Independent Forensic Psychologist.

[42] See www.ark.ac.uk/ylt/. See also See also Beckett (2011: Ch. 5).

being abused' (Firmin and Curtis, 2015: 5). Many professionals in the study, working in both therapeutic and justice contexts, drew attention to this continuum and the potential crossover from being a victim to becoming an abuser within the specific contexts of CSE, the broader party culture and institutional forms of peer abuse:

> We know some of the CSE young women now that we are working with, may well be both ... They started off being the victims but ended up involved in the whole grooming process and involved in recruiting peers and younger ones coming through.[43]
>
> Children who are at risk of exploitation, who are going to parties, having drugs, having drink and then engaging in sex with whoever is there, they will then bring their friends across to it, and their friends ... will be taking drink and drugs and before you know it engaging in sex with older boys or usually younger men ... [they] would probably be grooming ... but those girls are also being exploited, they are being victimised, because they don't realise they are victims.[44]
>
> I think it is very common in our children's homes. And we have had it kind of going between two particular children's homes for a while where the kids were taking in the new residents and bringing them out on the street ... Or then we had an incident in one of the units where this girl was arrested for abusing other children. And it was very definitely she was abusing them and getting them to be available for the guys, just to save herself for a while. So there's definitely that. But I think it is more for our children in care or ... where it is on the street, and that's where kids have been recruiting other children.[45]

This complex interplay of power differentials among peers may mean that the dividing line between agency and consent on the one hand and abuse of power and coercion on the other may be difficult to identify. As Firmin and Curtis (2015: 5) argue, 'we have to recognise the risk they [children] pose to others as well as the risk they may face.' This underscores the need to move away from rigid monochromatic distinctions between victims and perpetrators of abuse (McAlinden, 2014a) which are ultimately unhelpful as a frame of reference in responding to the risks presented by HSB. As one practitioner explained: 'in terms of the perpetrator and the victim, it is very difficult. I think it is so grey. And I think how we then classify people; I don't think that helps in terms of moving forward or

[43] Interview 9, 25 May 2016, Youth Support Worker.
[44] Interview 32, 2 November 2016, Police Officer.
[45] Interview 1, 16 February 2016, Service Manager, HSS Trust.

helping those people.'[46] As discussed in the final chapter, this approach involves embracing a more complex and nuanced understanding of victimhood and of peer forms of sexual abuse and exploitation that more accurately capture the lived experiences of children and young people and better frame our resulting legal, social and policy responses to risk.

The other related point is that while the original generic definition of 'grooming', as set out earlier, implies an element of overt or direct compulsion for the victim to acquiesce to the harmful sexual behaviour, there may also be a more covert element of indirect compulsion underlying peer-to-peer abuse. That is, the highly sexualised messages and gendered norms stemming from the hyper-sexualised contemporary popular culture (Egan and Hawkes, 2012: 278), as outlined in the previous chapter, and the hegemonic group dynamic among peers stemming from this, may also entail a distinct element of latent coercion or indirect compulsion underlying HSB. In this respect, a minority of interviewees pinpointed the effects of the media and popular culture on grooming practices as part of the prelude to abusive or exploitative behaviours which also potentially exposes children and young people to more risk: 'the media does the grooming here . . . and then young people just kind of live out the roles that they think are expected of them through media'[47]:

> They are being groomed by society which makes it easier for the perpetrators that we talk about to kind of pick them up. The sort of very natural stuff that goes on developmentally where teenagers don't want to talk to their parents and they want secrecy and privacy to do all their teenage stuff . . . the way they socialise. There are a lot less real people in their world and a lot more unreal people. And it is like they don't seem to have necessarily the ability to discriminate that the virtual person I am talking to there is not the same as somebody I talk to here.[48]

This argument is in part further supported by research which demonstrates that young people experience a higher volume of violence, sexual harassment and sexually abusive acts in schools or residential care, where there is constant and concentrated exposure to 'harmful social norms related to gender, relationships and consent' (Firmin and Curtis, 2015: 4, citing Frosh et al., 2002; EVAW, 2010; see also HC

[46] Interview 14, 2 June 2016, Sexual Health Nurse.
[47] Interview 21, 23 June 2016, Social Work Practitioner.
[48] Interview 6, 25 April 2016, Independent Safeguarding Consultant.

Women and Equalities Committee, 2016: 10–11).[49] As Hackett and Taylor (2008) have noted, this highlights the vitally important role of schools in preventing the onset of sexually abusive behaviour and in particular in building the personal capacity of children and young people to make healthy choices around sexual behaviour and in equipping them to make a disclosure in the event that they are victimised. However, as discussed further later, the exercise of manipulative and controlling techniques and resulting power imbalances may also augment the vulnerability of children and young people to abuse and exploitation in a wider range of interpersonal and social contexts other than schools and residential care.

VULNERABILITY

The second element of the definition refers to who may be targeted – *[with] a vulnerable subject*. As discussed in Part I of the book, age in particular is a key inherent attribute informing social and cultural conceptualisations of children's victimhood and vulnerability. Children are regarded as intrinsically vulnerable (Furedi, 2013: 42) by virtue of their age or status as children. Within this broader context, research demonstrates that any child or young person may be a victim of peer-on-peer abuse, but that some children are inherently more vulnerable to abuse than others. The research base on grooming and abuse between adults and children establishes a 'differential vulnerability to abuse' (Sas and Cunningham, 1995: 67) where background factors within the histories of individual victims may increase their vulnerability to being targeted, groomed and abused (see generally, Salter, 1995; see also Elliott et al., 1995: 584; Gallagher, 1998: 808–11; Powell, 2007: 34–35). Similarly, a range of inherent or experiential vulnerabilities are known to increase the susceptibility of children and young people to peer-on-peer abuse. These include a history of intra-familial abuse (Berelowitz et al., 2012); young people being in care, including residential care; and experiencing bereavement through the loss of a parent, sibling or friend (Beckett, 2011; Berelowitz et al., 2012). More broadly, however, children with 'unmet emotional, social

[49] For example, evidence from the House of Commons inquiry into 'Sexual Harassment and Sexual Violence in Schools' found that 59 per cent of girls and young women ages 13 to 21 had faced some form of sexual harassment at school or college in the past year; almost a third (29 per cent) of 16- to 18-year-old girls had experienced unwanted sexual touching at school; and 41 per cent of girls ages 14 to 17 experienced some form of sexual violence within an intimate relationship (HC Women and Equalities Committee, 2016: 7).

or physical needs' (Montgomery-Devlin, 2008: 383) are also vulnerable and open to manipulation and exploitation by others.

On the other hand, children and young people who are abused or exploited do not always exhibit 'underlying vulnerable factors or the current risk indicators' (Montgomery-Devlin, 2008: 388) which also makes it more difficult to predict which children and young people might be vulnerable to victimisation. As Firmin and Curtis (2015: 4) point out, while many of these vulnerability factors may make children or young people more visible to professionals as well as to those who might abuse or exploit them, those without such outward characteristics that bring them into contact with professionals (e.g. being in care) may be more vulnerable to abuse or exploitation as a result of their invisibility. Therefore, it is not these underlying vulnerabilities on the part of victims per se which make peer abuse or exploitation possible but rather the exploitation of these particular vulnerabilities by those minded to take advantage of an opportunity or environment.

Indeed, consistent with adult-child sexual abuse, children and young people who display HSB also appear to exploit personal weaknesses in their peers. A small number of interviewees pinpointed this more traditional view of grooming behaviours in terms of a considered process of victim identification and selection. This was related to 'preexisting vulnerabilities' stemming from 'a physical disability, a learning disability or . . . extensive mental health presentations'.[50] A child and adolescent mental health professional explained further in terms of children identifying 'who won't tell':

> In that one case I said to you about the boy who came forward himself, there was definitely evidence of him buying games for some of his little brother's friends, because he knew he liked them. And also he seemed to be very, very good at picking out a vulnerable child that he would have access to . . . We said to him 'well why that boy and not that boy?' 'Oh well he'd shout and squeal and tell everybody.' Whereas he was able to identify that . . . and that is a form of grooming, isn't it, to be picking out who won't tell.[51]

As discussed in the previous chapter in relation to gender and sexual identity, 'confusion about sexuality'[52] against the backdrop of a wider sexualised culture which promotes 'experimentation' emerged as

50 Interview 8, 23 May 2016, Rowan SARC Professional.
51 Interview 22, 10 June 2016, Children and Adolescent Forensic Mental Health Professional.
52 Interview 18, 14 June 2016, Senior Voluntary Sector Interviewee.

a prominent factor underlying instances of peer-based victimisation. A sexual health nurse explained, reflecting the views of many of the front-line health professionals:

> Where young people who are gay or maybe wanting to explore relationships and those feelings, they are very vulnerable and isolated. So to me you are looking at exploitation and grooming. They are people that are probably easy to identify. But then because they don't maybe want people to know their sexuality, then they are easy to control as well.[53]

As Sas and Cunningham (1995: 67) have noted in relation to adult-child forms of grooming and abuse, but which would also appear to apply equally to peer-to-peer forms, the issue of 'differential vulnerability to abuse' is a highly complex one that is not easily studied.

In this vein, and moving from a discussion of victimisation to those who might be *vulnerable to offending*, a diverse range of factors underlying children's vulnerability may also have a role to play in the *commission* of HSB. Many children and young people displaying HSB 'have histories of multiple abuse and disadvantage' (Ashurst, 2016: 3) coming to the attention of child welfare agencies prior to the emergence of HSB. Earlier research has established the existence of 'abusive histories' and a range of familial, educational, emotional and behavioural difficulties among children and young people presenting with HSB (Bischof et al., 1995; Graves et al., 1996; Taylor, 2003; Vizard et al., 2007). By way of example, Vizard et al.'s (2007) study referred to earlier established a range of 'salient vulnerability factors' and a comprehensive list of 'psychosocial and behavioural characteristics' among children and adolescents which underlie the onset of HSB. These included a dysfunctional family environment which was present in some form across the entire sample,[54] inappropriate sexualisation, being removed from the family home/taken into care at an early age, educational or neuropsychological difficulties, physical and mental health problems and a history of antisocial behaviour. These findings also accord with earlier American research which found that physical and sexual abuse, neglect and loss of a parental figure were commonplace in the histories of a national sample of 'sexually abusive youths' (Ryan et al., 1996).

[53] Interview 14, 2 June 2016, Sexual Health Nurse.

[54] The impact and significance of a history of family dysfunction on HSB is often explained by reference to attachment theory and the disruption to normal attachment processes. See e.g. in the context of studies of adult sexual offending Ward et al. (1996); Marshall (2010).

Similarly, a study of HSB involving 700 children and young people carried out by Simon Hackett and colleagues, as one of the largest samples internationally, also found that children and young people who 'sexually abuse others are a diverse group with a complex set of motivations, background experiences and varying types of abusive behaviour' (Hackett et al., 2013: 232).[55] Of particular note are the findings that a significant proportion of the sample (38 per cent) were identified as learning disabled; and there were high rates of both sexual and non-sexual victimisation in the backgrounds of those children and young people referred for displaying HSB – two-thirds had experienced some kind of abuse or trauma such as physical abuse, emotional abuse, severe neglect, parental rejection, family breakdown, domestic violence and parental drug or alcohol abuse. Approximately half had experienced sexual abuse. As such, understanding and responding appropriately to children who display HSB need to be placed in a wider context which recognises the broader 'structural and cultural inequities that they face in their lives, including their own victimisation' (Barter, 2013: 118).

Ashurst (2016: 3) explains the significance of this cycle of vulnerability, or what she terms the 'dual sexual abuse experience' (see also Hackett et al., 2013: 241, citing Bentovim, 2002; Hackett, 2002), in that younger children in particular presenting with HSB 'have a high probability of having been sexually abused themselves' whereby they may re-enact their direct experiences of abuse (see also Veneziano et al., 2000). Notwithstanding the fact that not all young people who are sexually exploited or abused go on to become perpetrators (Craisatti et al., 2002; Taylor, 2003; Lussier and Davies, 2011; Hackett et al., 2013; Lambie and Johnson, 2016; Levenson et al., 2016; Jennings and Meade, 2017), there is the possibility of oscillation between perceived 'victim' and 'perpetrator' categories within particular contexts such as familial or institutional settings or gang culture (see further Chapter 6).

For the small number of females (3 per cent) in Hackett et al.'s study, however, a history of childhood sexual abuse was 'more a marker of vulnerability than a risk of sexually abusive behaviour in adulthood' (Masson et al., 2015: 19).[56] These complexities underlying the

[55] A wide range of abusive behaviours was perpetrated – ranging in order of prevalence from touching other's private parts (84 per cent), penetration/attempted penetration (52 per cent) to non-contact sexual behaviours (50 per cent), and sexual abuse involving physical violence (18 per cent).

[56] Among adult female sexual offenders, however, the prevalence of adverse childhood experiences is disproportionately high in comparison to female non-sexual offenders: see Levenson et al. (2016).

individual, family and abuse characteristics of child and adolescent sexual offenders, as Hackett et al. (2013) argue, underscore the need for a comprehensive, nuanced approach to risk and intervention that encompasses both care and control aspects (see also Morrison and Henniker, 2006; Chaffin, 2008). Such an approach must also take account of the gendered aspects underlying peer-based grooming, abuse and exploitation and the broader differential socialisation processes for males and females which may impinge upon individual vulnerability, agency and autonomy (see Chapters 3 and 4) (see also Lane and Lobanov-Rostovsky, 1997; Robinson, 2005).

Turning to the findings from the present study, there was broad acknowledgement, in the words of a forensic mental health professional, that 'all of the children that we are assessing, they are victims in some way themselves . . . They certainly experienced some kind of trauma in their lives. They have had complex upbringings.'[57] Interviewees articulated a seemingly more expansive range of vulnerabilities in the backgrounds of children and young people who display HSB. These were generally related to two main strands of experiential or social vulnerability: (i) vulnerabilities stemming from their family background and (ii) a broader range of social and emotional vulnerabilities impacting children and young people more generally. In relation to family factors, these were framed by professionals in terms of general 'life experience'[58] relating to 'victimisation and their own abuse'[59] and where 'physical violence is a very common feature, but sexual assault you will see time and time again.'[60] An NSPCC professional explained as follows: 'there is invariably, but not always, a victimisation or a sense of victimisation in the past . . . and we will look for the static factors . . . You know the "toxic trio", domestic abuse, mental health, substance abuse. And generally we get them all.'[61] For other professionals the lack of clear social and familial norms relating to appropriate sexual behaviour were also a key underlying variable:

> Very sexualised environments in their backgrounds is another key thing. So that's about the sort of social rules in their house. So if there's lots of very confusing sexual information around, or no real boundaries about what is appropriate to watch or talk about in front of children and

[57] Interview 22, 10 June 2016, Children and Adolescent Forensic Mental Health Professional.
[58] Interview 6, 25 April 2016, Independent Safeguarding Consultant.
[59] Interview 4, 21 April 2016, Child Care Centre Professional.
[60] Interview 26, 1 August 2016, District Court Judge.
[61] Interview 5, 22 April 2016, NSPCC Professional.

> teenagers, then they kind of just learn that. So it is about the rules, the norms that they learn from their parents.[62]

This latter factor was believed to be particularly pertinent with younger children in the sense that 'there is experimentation where you have young, vulnerable children who ... because of their own experiences, don't have the same boundaries or insight, and it can be that kind of experimentation just getting out of their own control if you like.'[63] This was thought to be particularly acute within cases of sibling or other forms of intra-familial abuse (such as between cousins) where 'some of it is a degree of experimentation, out of sexual curiosity'.[64] In terms of the impact of these background vulnerabilities on individual children and young people, this was generally identified in terms of 'learned behaviour, damaged relationships, addiction, attachment issues, that the perpetrator is emotionally damaged, they have issues of anger or control, isolation, depression or anxiety, or they are involved in other illegal acts'.[65]

In addition to the highly sexualised popular culture (see previous chapter), other interviewees pinpointed a broader range of vulnerabilities among children with no underlying trauma or abuse in their histories and which might potentially affect children and young people more generally. These included 'social and emotional issues, you know, like loneliness, wanting to be loved, wanting to be accepted'[66] and where they 'haven't the strength or whatever, to recognise that maybe this isn't OK ... I think with the older kids that peer pressure is enormous and wanting to be liked and ... going along with what's asked of them'.[67]

In essence, the broader range of contextual issues underlying the vulnerability of those who display HSB can be distilled to a single factor which was pinpointed by a small number of interviewees – that of 'neglect' in terms of having a 'lack of support networks'.[68] A public health nurse explained in the following terms: 'It's neglect, to be honest with you, neglect in the first instance is the main trigger ... physical neglect and emotional neglect ... if there is neglect, you need then to

[62] Interview 6, 25 April 2016, Independent Safeguarding Consultant.
[63] Interview 4, 21 April 2016, Child Care Centre Professional.
[64] Interview 26, 1 August 2016, District Court Judge.
[65] Interview 28, 16 August 2016, Victim Support Professional.
[66] Interview 14, 2 June 2016, Sexual Health Nurse.
[67] Interview 4, 21 April 2016, Child Care Centre Professional.
[68] Interview 9, 25 May 2016, Youth Support Worker.

be on alert.'[69] The significance of 'emotional neglect' is that 'if you have never experienced empathy, it is actually quite hard to demonstrate it. And that makes it easier, then, for you to commit offences of all sorts, because . . . you haven't got the ability to put yourself in somebody else's shoes.'[70]

From the perspective of grooming, this range of ostensible vulnerability factors tends to reinforce the relevance of grooming to peer-based forms of abuse in the sense that the abusive histories and victimisation experiences of children and young people may have become internalised and normalised and are then re-enacted with someone else. On the other hand, however, this range of vulnerabilities relating to children and young people who display harmful sexual or exploitative behaviour does not account for why some of those children with abusive or traumatic histories go on to become abusers while others do not.

Indeed, a minority of interviewees emphasised the need to move away from the notion of 'dysfunctionality as being a reason',[71] as a growing number children presenting with HSB come from '"normal" families where mum and dad are still together . . . where there are good incomes and well-meaning families and children who are going to good schools, but who are engaging in all sorts of unusual activity'.[72] This was particularly thought to be the case with online forms of HSB:

> And I think we need to now not see it as more from dysfunctional families. That young people in their own right are being bombarded about their sexuality. They don't know how to manage it and they are doing things online . . . and they are doing that without a dysfunctionality within their family. So I think more and more I think we have to review the causes when we see their online activity.[73]

Other interviewees referred to this factor as 'affluent neglect'.[74] This latter argument also reinforces the need to avoid overreliance on highly pathologised, deterministic accounts of victim or perpetrator vulnerability and to instead concede the significance of broader social and cultural influences on the onset of HSB among peers, beyond the immediate family environment.

More recent research has also highlighted the fact that a complex range of social and contextual risk factors, as well as personal

[69] Interview 13, 31 May 2016, Public Health Nurse.
[70] Interview 6, 25 April 2016, Independent Safeguarding Consultant.
[71] Interview 16, 6 June 2016, Social Work Consultant. [72] Ibid. [73] Ibid.
[74] Interview 11, 26 May 2016, Safeguarding Professional.

characteristics, combine to form a 'causal model' of HSB (Ashurst, 2015). Without wishing to oversimplify the complexity of this model, it is essentially composed of social and contextual risk factors (including the 'culture of sex' and 'transient sex' identified in Chapter 4 of this book), together with personal characteristics (including mental and psychological factors, personal traits and skills and intellect) which ultimately combine to influence and promote the onset of HSB. As discussed further in the next chapter in relation to a typology of harm, this model also has implications for how we identify and respond to potential risk.

Moving from social and background factors to a consideration of the personal characteristics of those children and young people deemed to be perpetrators, in addition to lack of confidence and self-esteem, low levels of intellect or cognitive ability were a prominent theme emerging from the present study. Several interviewees articulated this point in relation to children presenting with HSB who had some form of learning difficulty coming to the attention of the justice system:

> All his friends were starting to have girlfriends. He felt he couldn't have a girlfriend and he couldn't interact with girls. He felt his friends were never including him anymore. They had all turned 14 and they were going off and doing things with girls. And he was being left out. And he just said, I wanted to know what it was like.[75]

A youth court judge also explained this feature of HSB in relation to its impact on the ability of the young person to interact with their peers socially and at the same level:

> Well certainly in the greater number of cases I can think of, I would say that the perpetrator has been a person with . . . I am reluctant to use the word learning difficulties, but certainly hasn't attained terribly well educationally. Also I think socially they don't have a good range of friends, or friends of their own age. That sort of thing comes across quite often. Sometimes you wonder are they grooming younger people, but I think it's actually . . . I can think of a case of a 12-year-old who was running around with an 8-year old. That was a male, assault by a male on a male. And whenever we looked at it . . . they were comparable in terms of mental ages and ability. It wasn't that he had picked on an 8-year old because he would be easier to manipulate. He had no friends at his own level. So those sorts of things seem to go together: lack of educational

[75] Interview 17, 7 June 2016, Independent, former Youth Justice Professional.

> attainment, social functioning ... Just difficulties in meeting friends, that sort of thing.[76]

This facet of HSB also serves to problematise the first aspect of the definition of grooming identified earlier, in that it is more difficult to assert in such circumstances that the perpetrator was exercising power or manipulation in a deliberately manipulative and controlling sense. Moreover, the fact that many children displaying HSB face significant social and emotional issues, such as wanting 'to be accepted or loved', reinforces the potentially different relational motivation underlying peer-to-peer abuse, as distinct from sexual gratification or the exertion of power and control.

Taken as a whole, therefore, the body of research examined here, including new findings from the present study, highlights the issue of 'dual vulnerability' (derived from social/situational as well as personal characteristics) which may be a pertinent factor for both potential perpetrators and victims of peer-to-peer abuse and exploitation. This ultimately underlines the greater complexity of grooming within the onset of HSB or CSE among children and adolescents. More broadly, it also once again points to the futility of dichotomous victim-offender distinctions and the often extremely challenging nature of some cases which necessitate tailored and holistic specialist interventions (see e.g. Righthand and Welch, 2001; Veneziano and Veneziano, 2002) with individual children and families, and with children and young people more generally (see further Chapter 8).

THE EXPLOITATION OF PERSONAL AND SOCIAL CONTEXTS

The third element of the definition denotes the context within which grooming can occur – *in a range of interpersonal and social settings*. Grooming in general can occur in a wide variety of contexts, including within intra-familial/quasi-intra-familial or extrafamilial settings and may be online (Gillespie, 2001, 2008; Gallagher et al., 2003, 2006) or face-to-face (Gallagher, 1998; McAlinden, 2006, 2012a). In a similar vein, 'environments, contexts and relationships' (Firmin and Curtis, 2015: 6) can all limit the decision-making powers and the capacity of children and young people to make safe choices which protect their own well-being. In addition to experiencing abuse within the context

[76] Interview 26, 1 August 2016, District Court Judge.

of their family and home (via, for example, intra-familial or sibling abuse), or within the school setting (Frosh et al., 2002; Hackett and Taylor, 2008), violence and exploitation among peers have also been linked to abuse of their partners or peers (see e.g. Chung, 2005; Barter et al., 2009; Barter, 2015). Potentially abusive contexts and environmental factors, however, can also extend to public as well as more private spaces.

For example, the involvement of young people in gangs has led to an increased exposure to street-based violence (Young and Hallsworth, 2011; Beckett et al., 2012, 2013), and young people have also been sexually exploited by peers in a range of public places including in parks, bus or train stations, shopping centres or arcades (Berelowitz et al., 2012). Some manifestations of grooming have occurred within the context of 'street' or 'localised grooming' in which young girls may groom others into exploitative or abusive networks (Montgomery-Devlin, 2008; Beckett, 2011; Ost and Mooney, 2013). Moreover, the emergence of a range of online-based sexual behaviours between children and young people, such as sexting and sexualised cyberbullying and the sharing of images via social media and other platforms, also demonstrates that the context can include virtual as well as real-world settings (see further Chapter 6).

The significance of the context for the exploitation and abuse is that, in common with adult sexual offending against children (see generally Wortley and Smallbone, 2006; Leclerc et al., 2011), the strategies used by adolescents in particular for peer-to-peer forms of HSB are strongly influenced by situational factors and the location of the abuse. Previous research has demonstrated that the most likely setting for adolescents to use manipulative or grooming strategies was within their own home while they were alone with another child or young person (Ashurst and McAlinden, 2015: 379; see also; Taylor, 2003: 65; Vizard et al., 2007: 66; Leclerc et al., 2008). Nonetheless, there are documented differences in the grooming methods used both within and outside the family by adolescents. Within intra-familial settings, in which an older child may groom a younger sibling as a precursor to abuse, perpetrators were more likely to give gifts to establish trust (Kaufman et al., 1996). Within extrafamilial settings, however, in common with adult sexual offenders, drugs and alcohol were more commonly used to gain the victim's compliance (Kaufman et al., 1998). In addition, as might be expected, young people who engage in HSB with both boys and girls adopt a wider array of grooming strategies than those who abused only boys or only girls (Kaufman et al., 1996).

In the context of the present study, further insights have emerged in relation to grooming or preparatory strategies among peers within the context of 'intimate' relationships surrounding CSE. As noted in Part I of the book, previous research in the Northern Ireland context has established the existence of the 'boyfriend model' (Montgomery-Devlin, 2008: 392; Barnardo's, 2011: 6) of CSE, or the 'sexually exploitative relationship' (Beckett, 2011: 28), due to the girl's initial perception of the relationship as that of 'boyfriend' and 'girlfriend'. Following the bestowing of gifts (typically money and mobile phones), and often the use of alcohol and drugs, the girl is taken to hotels or 'party houses', where over a period of time involvement in sexual acts is eventually sought as 'an exchange of favours' (Kosaraju, 2008: 15)[77] which also encourages dependency and 'entraps' the young person further.

Extending these previous findings further, many of the interviewees highlighted the existence of a 'softer' or more insidious approach to grooming within the context of CSE which focuses on exploiting the perceptions of children and young people within peer 'relationships':

> I think it is young women who think it's a boyfriend. And then all of a sudden they are at parties with other people. So I would say that grooming is very important and I would say, because the young women are very vulnerable, they are looking for love, I think it works really well for the young fellas who are doing all this. I think they are very clever and that they know that the young women are so vulnerable and what they want is someone to love them unconditionally. And I think it is very easy to do it that way.[78]
>
> I think to start to understand why they kept going to that house or why they got into that car, that's not just about grooming. We also need to accept what made them feel good. Because this might have been the only person who for the first time made them feel as if they were important ... So I think in terms of young people, if it was a peer they don't see it as harmful ... if there was very little age difference. So if you are talking getting in a car with a 17-year-old and that's a 15-year-old, that's a boyfriend-girlfriend. In the same way as they would have still said to you, 26-year-old that's boyfriend-girlfriend ... But certainly young

[77] For further discussion of this model, see McAlinden (2012a: 116–17).
[78] Interview 10, 25 May 2016, Youth Support Worker.

> people in the CSE, if it was within a four- or five-year gap, that was a peer. And they saw that as . . . what's the big deal?[79]

As the latter quote attests, as a result of negligible age differences and the perception of 'being in a relationship', victims in such peer-to-peer contexts may not perceive themselves as such or, moreover, may not be considered vulnerable or at risk by professionals (CEOP, 2011: 88; Jago et al., 2011: 50; Ost and Mooney, 2013: 438).

Peer-to-peer forms of grooming which exist within the context of other face-to-face and virtual contexts were also highlighted by a number of professionals in the study. In relation to face-to-face contexts, interviewees drew on examples from a range of interpersonal and social contexts, including school and residential care where it may often be more difficult to proactively identify behaviours as 'harmful':

> For me it is in terms of similar ages and possibly similar networks, is how I see peer-to-peer grooming. You know, where we are encountering it is kids in the neighbourhood or in the same school, where they bring each other into it . . . And certainly, you definitely see it . . . they have groomed the victim in it, whether it's through friends or family.[80]
>
> So in that sense, with grooming, what might happen is I will spend a bit of time . . . say for example you and I are the odd kids in school and we don't really have large social circles. And you are particularly isolated. If I come along and befriend you and spend time with you, protecting you and standing up for you, you now feel very connected to me. And I might then suggest some games that we can play. I want to be low level but lead us in and then escalate, escalate, escalate. By this point you are stuck because you haven't got any other friends, you have no other way out of this.[81]
>
> And another one is institutions, our care homes. There's a 15-year-old involved there too. So it's a fine line in it, but you can definitely see the grooming there that's going on and so on, but then they are living together, they are interacting together. The age difference isn't such a big thing because their whole environment is with each other. All their activities are with each other, just because of the unit. That's certainly an issue that comes up. But it is hard to prove it is not consensual.[82]

Previous research conducted by the author has pinpointed a process of 'institutional grooming' (McAlinden, 2006, 2012a: Ch. 5). This term is

[79] Interview 16, 6 June 2016, Social Work Consultant.
[80] Interview 1, 16 February 2016, Service Manager, HSS Trust.
[81] Interview 6, 25 April 2016, Independent Safeguarding Consultant.
[82] Interview 1, 16 February 2016, Service Manager, HSS Trust.

used to describe the process whereby would-be perpetrators make unique use of the organisational environment as a cover to target and sexually abuse children and to groom organisational systems and professionals, which may act as the gatekeepers of access, into viewing them as posing no danger to children (McAlinden, 2006). In particular, the pervasive features of organisational contexts such as power, anonymity, opportunity, secrecy and trust work to both facilitate abuse via a process of normalisation and prevent discovery or disclosure. In this respect, the findings of the current study serve to reinforce and extend this broader concept by providing further examples of the dynamics of this process as they might relate to peers and which also appear strongly tied to environmental and situational risk factors such as proximity, opportunity and trust.

In relation to digital contexts, a small number of interviewees drew attention to grooming practices and emerging risks associated with online gaming which involves boys and young men in particular:

> In terms of boys and young men, you can see them in the criminal justice system; you can see them in terms of that grooming online. And online gaming is another one, certainly in my research to date that is coming up. Online gaming is another route in for boys and young men, which maybe girls aren't into as much.[83]

This also reinforces the broader argument made earlier that risk and opportunity for harm can stem from ordinary everyday routine interactions among peers and from activities which are at the centre of the social and leisure activities of children and young people. One such high-profile case which exemplifies the risk inherent in online multiplayer games among peers (such as Minecraft, World of Warcraft, Call of Duty and Battlefield) is that of 14-year-old Breck Bednar who was groomed and then murdered by an 18-year-old male he met through online gaming.[84]

Much of the research on peer-to-peer grooming conducted to date, however, was conducted well before the advent of online platforms for communication such as social media and smart phones. As one professional explained in relation to the onset of HSB among peers: 'it is the accessibility to the Internet . . which has everything on it and it is children's accessibility and exposure to that that has changed our lives

[83] Interview 18, 14 June 2016, Senior Voluntary Sector Interviewee.

[84] See 'Gamer Admits "Sexual" Murder of 14-year old School Boy He Groomed On-line', *Metro*, 25 November 2016.

completely in the last five years, since the invention of the smart phone and 4G and Wi-Fi and all of that. And alongside that is the capability of peers to share.'[85] As such, this generally older literature on pre-abuse grooming predates some digital forms of peer-to-peer abuse or exploitation such as sexting and sexualised forms of cyberbullying, both of which are technology dependent. To date, therefore, existing discourses on grooming have not considered or taken account of how sexting and the rapidly evolving nature of contemporary modes of interpersonal communication, and the resulting 'removal of emotion' from romantic and non-romantic relationships (see further Chapter 4), may change the norms, precursors and patterns of abusive or exploitative behaviours among peers.

Two further findings from the literature support the hypothesis that virtual contexts may significantly alter the grooming and abusive strategies among peers, as well as potentially increase the prevalence of online forms of peer-based harmful sexual or exploitative behaviour. One is the finding that peer abusers 'adopt specific sets of strategies' for grooming and abuse 'once they assess the costs and benefits involved' (Leclerc et al., 2008: 58). Online methods may therefore well become the means of choice for grooming since sexualised or risky virtual communications are often perceived by young people to be safer than face-to-face interactions (see e.g. Wolak and Finkelhor, 2011 more generally; and Phippen, 2012, in the context of sexting) (see further Chapter 6). The other is the fact that the prevalence and normalisation of sexting in particular can facilitate risk-taking behaviours by children and young people which are traditionally associated with adolescence (Kelley et al., 2004: 27; see also Steinberg, 2007; Lee et al., 2013). This can simultaneously obscure the identification and management of risk concerning HSB on the part of both professionals and children and young people themselves.

TRUST AND NORMALISATION

The fourth and fifth elements of the definition denote the dual purposes of the grooming process. The fourth aspect seeks to capture the initial purpose of pre-abuse grooming in ensuring victim access and compliance – *to establish trust or normalise sexually harmful behaviour*. As noted at the outset of the chapter, at its most basic level, grooming includes

[85] Interview 3, 20 April 2016, Education Authority Professional.

manipulation and control to make the abuse or exploitation possible. In common with the grooming process more generally, which has been distilled to the three central variables of access, compliance and secrecy (Craven et al., 2006: 297), peer-to-peer grooming is not only an 'entry point' into the domain of HSB but is also a means by which young people may both cause harm and maintain their harmful sexual behaviour and its controlling effect on the victim (Ashurst and McAlinden, 2015: 379). This was also articulated clearly in the present study:

> I think it is that entry part to harmful sexual behaviour . . . It enables the young person to cause harm, but more realistically in the real world it enables them to maintain harm. And I think that's really, really important because peer to peer grooming keeps people in relationships where they can be abusive and keeps victims in relationships that they can't get out of.[86]

For the most part, however, the neglected dimension of discourses on grooming is to explicitly consider *how* access, compliance and secrecy are secured and maintained prior to, throughout and following abusive sexual behaviour among peers.[87]

In this respect, the entire grooming process can perhaps be distilled to a single word – normalisation. At its most powerful, grooming behaviour may operate to the extent that victims often do not even realise that they are being or have been exploited or abused. Indeed, normalisation was a theme relating to peer-to-peer forms of abuse that came through strongly in the primary research. This was again related principally to the perception of victims that they are in some form of relationship or friendship with their abuser:

> Nine out of ten victims of peer-to-peer grooming are completely unaware that they are being groomed. So they will see it as, that person loves me, they care about me, this is a healthy relationship. They are doing and saying these things because they worry about me and they want to keep me safe. Or they are showing me love, or whatever. But when they find out that they have been the victim of exploitation by a peer, unfortunately they become further isolated.[88]
>
> He has always been in my gang of friends. Or I was there and he is my brother so what do you mean? He has already got contact with me. And

[86] Interview 2, 18 April 2016, Independent Forensic Psychologist.

[87] See Salter, 2003; McAlinden, 2012a: Ch. 4 for isolated examples in relation to adult-child grooming.

[88] Interview 28, 16 August 2016, Victim Support Professional.

> I did go with him into his room. And I did play the games . . . Or we were drinking that night. And I think that's where there's less of a sense of it being a danger, of being another person . . . if it is people within their peer setting . . . there is an agreement of what we have already done together. Therefore, why would I suddenly say, well I didn't want that bit. And that's the confusing bit . . . So that's why to then say, but I was groomed just for that bit . . . it just doesn't make sense for them.[89]

As the latter quote also attests, it is the insipid and conventional nature of the grooming process among peers which masks awareness of harm and makes self-identification of risk extremely difficult. As discussed in the previous chapter, the process of normalisation also presents as particularly challenging for parents and professionals because of the chasm between what is regarded as normal or problematic by children and by adults which may evolve on a regular basis with changing social mores and cultural practices. In essence, as argued earlier in relation to inherent 'power and control', due to the proliferation of social and cultural norms related to sex, children and young people on one level may have less to do in seeking to normalise HSB. The pivotal construct, however, which ultimately underlies the normalisation process and which unites the range of contexts in which HSB may occur is 'trust'.

The creation and subsequent abuse of trust helps the abuser to overcome protective factors, stemming from the child or protective others, which may act as barriers to abuse (see generally Wyre, 2000; van Damn, 2001; McAlinden, 2006). Notwithstanding the fact that definitions of the term can vary (McAlinden, 2006), a preponderance of scholars, such as Johnson-George and Swap (1982), Luhmann (1988) and Coleman (1990), all define trust as a behaviour or attitude which permits risk-taking behaviour. Adult sex offenders may make use of the creation and subsequent betrayal of trust as they seek to groom both children and significant others and even the environment (McAlinden, 2006, 2012a: Ch. 2). Arguably, however, the use and abuse of trust are even more pertinent within the context of peer-based abuse as children and young people are likely to be less cautious and more trusting of like-minded peers than of perceived adult predatory strangers. Several interviewees in the study supported this argument:

[89] Interview 16, 6 June 2016, Social Work Consultant.

> In grooming, like identifying someone to groom and then gaining trust . . . Those sorts of things aren't necessarily sexual. They are usually not. It is wanting to be loved. It is all of those things. It is like survival.[90]
>
> The young person who is doing the grooming will build a relationship and build trust. Now sometimes it is even easier for a peer because their relationship might already be there . . . So it is just about building trust and slowly introducing their ideas and what is acceptable, what is not acceptable. How you show love, how you show friendship, what it means to be a good friend, what we should do for each other.[91]

In essence, therefore, within the context of close interpersonal relationships among peers, children and young people either may not be as cognisant of the risks posed by peers or may not perceive their own actions as risky behaviour.

It is useful to examine further some of the key themes from the work of Ben-Yehuda, as one of the most notable scholars in the area of betrayal and trust, as they might relate to the dynamics of peer-to-peer grooming: First, trust can appear in varied intimate and social settings, including interpersonal, group and organisational contexts (Ben-Yehuda, 2001: 6–7; see also Luhmann, 1988; Friedrichs, 1996; Kramer et al., 1996; Oliver, 1997). This factor illustrates that trust has resonance not only at the micro level within interpersonal relationships – such as those between individual children or young people – but also at the macro level (Coleman, 1990) in terms of how relationships might operate between would-be perpetrators and wider society, including within organisational units or settings such as families and schools.

Second, trust invokes the concepts of 'reliability' and 'faithfulness' and assumes such relationships as loyalty, friendship and belief (Ben-Yehuda, 2001: 11–31). These are the necessary preconditions that the perpetrator must cultivate to establish intimate and social relationships with those he or she wants to groom. Perpetrators try to create shared interests and identities on a personal level and an imagined sense of community at the collective level. It is this sense of 'belonging' (Ben-Yehuda, 2001: 27–28) or shared membership of the *peer* group that ultimately makes the betrayal of trust possible.

Third, trust is a social construct whose violation amounts to an infringement of a moral code which is often deeply engrained within

[90] Interview 14, 2 June 2016, Sexual Health Nurse.
[91] Interview 28, 16 August 2016, Victim Support Professional.

society (Ben-Yehuda, 2001: 6–7). This argument helps to explain why societal reactions are typically more severe towards harmful sexual behaviour committed by children or young people, where the very act of betrayal of social and cultural norms related to childhood (see Chapter 3) becomes a form of deviance in itself (Ben-Yehuda, 2001: 311). As documented in Part I of the book and as recently articulated by Anne Morrison (2015), public attitudes towards children and young people displaying HSB and the risk they are perceived to present can be deeply ambivalent and are at once minimising, punitive, dismissive and fearful.

ENTRAPMENT

The fifth element conveys the ultimate purpose of grooming – *with the overall aim of facilitating exploitation and/or prohibiting exposure*. The literature reviewed earlier generally establishes that while some of the methods used to facilitate abuse by children and adults may be inherently different, their underlying purpose remains the same – to not only facilitate the abuse but also maintain the victim in a state of compliance while ensuring protection of the groomer from victim disclosure or discovery by others. Previous studies on the disclosure of child abuse by children at the hands of adults have supported the effectiveness of the 'entrapment' dynamic which lies at the heart of the grooming process – children may delay disclosure for months or years after the abuse, even long into adulthood, with many not disclosing at all (Sorensen and Snow, 1991; Berliner and Conte, 1995; Cawson et al., 2000; McGee et al., 2002; Allnock, 2010).

Similarly, the small number of studies on disclosures of peer-based abuse affirms that victims commonly withhold disclosures of their victimisation, particularly to their parents. Factors which impede such disclosures include secrecy, feelings of powerlessness, self-blaming, the child's inherent vulnerabilities, fear of retaliation, fear of losing the relationship if the abuser is a friend and low expectations regarding the effectiveness of telling and of adult interventions (Mishna and Alaggia, 2005). Moreover, in general, girls and boys disclose most often to a peer or friend of their own age, rather than parents (Priebe and Svedin, 2008; Schönbucher et al., 2012). Indeed, those children abused by peers also anticipate more adverse outcomes in the form of less anticipated support from parents and more anger from their mothers (Sperry and Gilbert, 2005). Other motives for nondisclosure to parents include lack of trust and not wishing to burden parents (Schönbucher et al., 2012).

Just as child perpetrators appear to perform a cost-benefits analysis in the lead-up to abuse (Leclerc et al., 2011: 58), victims also appear to perform their own risk assessment around disclosure in 'weighing up the risks' (Mishna and Alaggia, 2005: 217). As the previous analysis establishes, fear of the consequences and in particular the perceived loss of social networks or lack of support may all combine to keep children entrapped in abusive peer relationships. Since reporting the incident is the first step in engaging the justice process, not surprisingly other research has also found that children under age 5, adolescents and those who experience abuse at the hands of peers are all subject to 'lower formal sanction rates' (Bunting, 2008). In this vein, grooming may also account for the delay in prosecution for childhood sexual abuse due to the feelings of betrayal, powerlessness, guilt and self-blame concerning child sexual abuse which inhibit immediate disclosure (Lewis and Mullis, 1999). This body of research generally supports the importance of 'purposeful disclosure' (Sas and Cunningham, 1995: 8) – that is, to not only augment the ability of individual children to come forward and tell someone (whether that be a parent or peer) but also the capacity of that person to respond effectively (see Chapter 8).

Aside from the role and effects of normalisation, one of the additional reasons emerging from the present study as to why children do not disclose peer forms of abuse is that they may not, at least at first, regard the sexual behaviour they are experiencing as particularly unwelcome or harmful. A medical professional articulated this facet of entrapment:

> Well I suppose it depends what keeps them in. Particularly if young people have learned wrong behaviour, and I think it is another big myth … and I am not saying that children aren't traumatised by abuse, you know, but if you discover . . . you have early sexual awakening and it is nice, and children enjoy the abuse. And young people enjoy the abuse … I think a lot of children who are groomed, whether it is by adults or whether it is peer-on-peer, they discover something that is very enjoyable. And it is only then I think, when they go into adulthood and they look back, that they discover, actually this was wrong. So I think once people are initiated, it is not that difficult to keep them in.[92]

[92] Interview 20, 20 June 2016, Rowan SARC Professional.

As such, without wishing to downplay the consequences for children abused in other intra-familial or quasi-intra-familial contexts, the consequences for victims of peer-to-peer abuse in coming to terms with their own victimisation and the associated difficulties in extricating themselves from an abusive situation may well be augmented. For those who do come to realise their victimisation, a strong sense of personal embarrassment and public degradation, including among peers, (Schönbucher et al., 2012) – in addition to the shame and guilt which are integral to child sexual abuse (Finkelhor and Browne, 1985; La Fontaine, 1990; Ginzburg et al., 2009) and sexual victimisation more broadly (West et al., 2000; Sable et al., 2006) – may work to inhibit disclosures of peer abuse in the short term.

Even where disclosures are eventually made by victims, or where a 'discovery' of some form of abuse is made by parents or others, the grooming process may have a lasting impact on victims and impede therapeutic interventions and justice processes. This was explained by a number of participants in the study as represented in the following quote by a safeguarding professional:

> The difficulty then for professionals is about young people understanding that they are a victim. And it is about the time it takes for a young person to understand that the relationship they are in is abusive, and then for them to want to cooperate. So for those agencies who are trying to protect or reduce the risk to that young person, in a period when they do not see themselves as a victim . . . that is hugely difficult. But we know that it can take up to a year and more for a young person, even to be in regular contact with a professional, before they are prepared to even say anything. Because of whatever it is in terms of the grooming that they have experienced or what they are receiving from that relationship that meets a need that they have.[93]

An element of perceived 'agency' on the part of older children or adolescents may combine with more coercive elements to keep them locked in an abusive situation. The consequent lack of self-perception as victim or as being at risk may simultaneously dilute their legitimacy as victims in the eyes of professionals (see generally in the context of CSE, Pearce, 2009; McAlinden, 2012a: 213–21) and, in turn, limit their access to justice or therapeutic services (see further Chapter 7).

[93] Interview 11, 26 May 2016, Safeguarding Professional.

CONCLUSION

This chapter sought, for the first time, to provide a 'thicker' understanding of grooming as it might apply between children and young people within the context of peer-to-peer harmful sexual or exploitative behaviour. In examining my previous generic definition of grooming further in relation to HSB among peers, important differences have emerged relating to the first two components of the definition – *power and control* and *vulnerability*: This analysis has made the broad distinction between *direct* and *indirect compulsion*. That is, in some instances, the presence of a 'hyper-sexualised culture' (Egan and Hawkes, 2012: 278) may work to normalise HSB and negate the need for specific coercive strategies among peers to overcome initial barriers to victim acquiescence. In this sense, much of HSB among peers may be situational or opportunistic, rather than predatory in nature (Wortley and Smallbone, 2006; Smallbone et al., 2008) which stems from routine (peer) activities (Cohen and Felson, 1979). Moreover, there may also be a continuum of power imbalances in which children and young people may be simultaneously 'at risk' as well as presenting 'as risk' to others.

In addition, the notion of vulnerability in relation to peer forms of abuse is rather more enmeshed, intersecting traditional victim-offender dualisms. In particular, 'dual vulnerabilities' may pertain to the social and personal characteristics of both the victim and the perpetrator. This finding also reinforces one of the broader themes of this book relating to the highly contested nature of cultural dichotomous victim-offender discourses on peer-based abuse. At the same time, and as discussed further in Chapter 7, this dual vulnerability may also muddy the moral and legal culpability of children who commit HSB as it invites consideration of the exploitation of the abuser and the contextual nature of their perceived agency.

In sum, while my earlier all-purpose definition of grooming has withstood deeper scrutiny within the context of peer-based behaviours, the role of grooming appears even more complex and nuanced within the context of peer-to-peer forms of harmful sexual or exploitative behaviours. In turn, therefore, while the grooming rubric retains its internal veracity and cogency as a concept and its applied significance with peers, it cannot simply be transposed from broader discourses on child sexual abuse by adults to discourses on peer forms of sexual abuse or exploitation. It thus needs to be used with heightened caution in describing the behaviours of children and young people.

To return to the rubric of 'risk', the significance of the concept of grooming, however this occurs, relates to the normalisation of risky or potentially harmful sexual behaviour among peers to the extent that victims may not be cognisant of being at risk. This also has knock-on effects in terms of legal and organisational responses to sexualised risks stemming from children and young people (see further Chapter 7). Moreover, turning to the next chapter which endeavours to present a 'typology of harm', grooming, in conjunction with other variables such as age or power differentials and the absence of genuine consent among peers, may also be a risk factor in determining where along the spectrum of normal-problematic-harmful behaviour a given sexual behaviour is thought to lie.

6

THE NATURE AND SCOPE OF PEER-TO-PEER EXPLOITATION AND ABUSE: TOWARDS A TYPOLOGY OF 'HARM'

> I know there's advice from the National Police Chief Council that the police should not be out to criminalise young people, but what it then doesn't do is give you some form of assessment or threshold if you like, as to when that is becoming harmful . . . Something might be acceptable but at what point does it become unacceptable? And I don't think you can ever give clear, prescriptive thresholds . . . because you've got to take so much into consideration when making those sorts of decisions.[1]

This chapter seeks to examine the nature and extent of peer-to-peer harmful sexual and exploitative behaviours across a range of interpersonal and social contexts. The chapter has three component parts. It begins with an overview of recent, mainly quantitative, studies on peer-based sexual behaviours, including recent statistical data obtained within the context of the present qualitative study. On one level, this primary data confirms the broad age and gendered dimensions of peer-based harmful sexual behaviour (HSB). On the other hand, however, some important nuances emerge in relation to sexual aggression by young females and increased reporting by young male victims which challenge traditional societal and even professional constructions of 'risk'.

Based on insights from this and the previous chapter, a typology of peer-to-peer harm is subsequently presented along a continuum of *peer-based relationships*, *peer-based recruitment*, and *peer-based risk.* This tripartite discussion seeks to consider where risk and potential harm are thought to crystallise by taking account of a range of contextual factors,

[1] Interview 7, 13 May 2015, Former Police Officer.

including in particular the presence of age or power differentials and coercion. While this framework is potentially useful in differentiating normal-problematic-harmful sexual behaviours more broadly, it will be argued that at the level of praxis, these core categories are not completely discrete but rather mutable and potentially intersecting. Indeed, as part of a continuum of behaviour, individual children and young people may oscillate between these categories, simultaneously crossing the boundaries between assumed victim and offender status.

Finally, utilising theoretical insights as well as excerpts from the primary data, this broad taxonomy of harm is illustrated further through a number of case studies, including sibling abuse, institutional abuse, online forms of grooming and abuse (such as sexting and cyberbullying), child sexual exploitation (CSE) and within the context of gang or partying culture. While some of these forms of peer-based sexual behaviours have emerged from within the confines of the dominant and extant adult perpetrator–child victim paradigms of risk concerning sexual offending, as presented in Part I of the book, others have emerged more recently as new risks and as stand-alone forms of exploitation or abuse among peers. In particular, this section of the chapter highlights new and emerging forms of peer-to-peer harmful sexual or exploitative behaviours within the context of CSE (e.g. 'line-ups') and gang or 'partying culture' (e.g. 'chemsex parties'). Moreover, it also demonstrates the potential for crossover between the different forms of HSB, including from private to public settings and from online to offline contexts.

THE NATURE AND EXTENT OF PEER ABUSE

The abuse or exploitation of children by other children accounts for a growing number of cases of child sexual abuse or exploitation (Berelowitz et al., 2012; Beckett et al., 2014). As noted at the outset of the book, figures of child sexual abuse or exploitation committed by those under age 18 vary between studies, depending on how the phenomenon is defined and measured, with overall estimates ranging from between one-quarter and one-half of all known cases of child sexual abuse (Masson and Morrison, 1999; Taylor, 2003; Erooga and Masson, 2006; Vizard et al., 2007; Finkelhor et al., 2009).

A 2011 report by Barnardo's highlighted that exploitation among peers within age-appropriate relationships has become more prevalent across the United Kingdom, accounting for up to one-quarter of its service provision (Barnardo's, 2011; see also Pearce, 2009: Ch. 4; Beckett et al., 2012). Similarly, following their previous research which found that one in three girls and 16 per cent of boys reported some form of intimate partner violence (Barter et al., 2009), a more recent study found increased levels of sexual coercion among females ages 13 to 17 within the United Kingdom of more than four in ten (Barter, 2015). The scope of HSB is also potentially wide ranging and can extend from contact behaviours (including unwanted touching and penetration) to intimate partner violence or abuse within exploitative situations or contexts and non-contact behaviours (including grooming, exhibitionism, voyeurism, sexting and sexualised cyberbullying) (Ashurst, 2015; Firmin and Curtis, 2015: 2).

Early adolescence appears to be the 'peak time' for engaging in HSB (Finkelhor et al., 2009: 2; Ashurst, 2016: 3) with some notable gender differences between boys and girls (see also Becker and Hicks, 2003; Erooga and Masson, 2006). Vizard et al. (2007), for example, reported that the majority of children and adolescents displaying HSB in their sample of 280 cases were male (91 per cent) and ages 11 to 17 (81 per cent), although a significant proportion (14 per cent) were under age 10. Although both boys and girls may experience HSB, studies suggest that girls and young women are more frequently identified as victims and report it has a negative impact on their lives, whereas adolescent males are more likely to be abusers and less likely to say they are impacted negatively (Barter, 2011; Firmin, 2011).

Hackett et al. (2013) have shown that in just over half of their large sample of cases (664) where gender of the victim was known, child and adolescent abusers had abused females only (51 per cent), 19 per cent had abused males only, and just under one-third (31 per cent) had abused both males and females. Boys, however, report high levels of victimisation within gang-related contexts (Pitts, 2008; Beckett et al., 2013; Barnardo's, 2014). Moreover, in tandem with child sexual abuse more broadly (Hunter et al., 1992; Watkins and Bentovim, 1992; Palmer, 2001; Walrath et al., 2003; Tewkbury, 2007), male victims may be more reluctant to report abuse, particularly in relation to immediate disclosures of abuse. In short, consistent with the broader socialisation of boys and girls (see Chapters 3 and 4), there are clear gendered dimensions to both the experiences and reporting of peer-to-peer abuse.[2]

[2] Some evidence suggests differential rates of victimisation and offending among children and young people according to race, as the overwhelming majority of perpetrators are white (see e.g.

Although adolescent boys account for the majority of perpetrators, a comparison of the limited international data on young females who sexually abuse shows that figures range from 3 per cent (Hackett et al., 2013; Masson et al., 2015) to between 8 and 12 per cent (Ryan et al., 1996; Kubik et al., 2003; Hickey et al., 2008; McCartan et al., 2011) of peer-based abuse. In particular, young female perpetrators tend to be younger than their male counterparts, have higher rates of sexual victimisation, fewer prior convictions and usually fewer victims (Finkelor et al., 2009: 6; Masson et al., 2015).[3] While peer-on-peer abuse is usually experienced by children from ages 10 upwards (Firmin and Curtis, 2015: 3), where there may be only a slight age differential between the abuser and the abused (generally classed as not more than two years' difference in age), other studies have identified child victims of peer abuse as young as ages 4 to 8 at the point of referral,[4] with females generally being referred at a younger age than males (Taylor, 2003; Berelowitz et al., 2012; Hackett et al., 2013) and most victims being known to their abuser (Hackett et al., 2013). The broad age-based divide within professional discourses on referral and intervention between children ages 10 to 12 and children under age 10 (the age of criminal responsibility) is of significance and will be discussed further in the next chapter.

Other studies have tended to concentrate on the onset, incidence and prevalence of non-contact exploitative and abusive behaviours by children and young people in the digital world where figures broadly equate to rates of offline forms of HSB (see e.g. Finkelhor et al., 2000; Elliott et al., 2009). As outlined at the outset of the book, within virtual settings, sexting (Wolak and Finkelhor, 2011; Ringrose et al., 2012) and cyberbullying (NSPCC, 2013) have emerged as among the most publicly prominent and pernicious of online forms of harmful sexual or exploitative behaviour by

Hackett et al., 2013). For example, black and ethnic minorities are often under-identified as victims (Berelowitz et al., 2012, 2013) and overidentified as perpetrators (Palmer and Pitts, 2006). See also the broader literature and evidence base on the cultural under-reporting of abuse among ethnic minority groups (e.g. Gilligan and Akhtar, 2006; Gohir, 2013; Cowburn et al., 2015).

3 Note, however, that Finkehor et al. (2009: 6) found that young females in their study were more likely than young males to be involved in incidents with multiple victims (23 per cent versus 12 per cent).

4 In Vizard et al.'s study, for example, the average age of onset was 9.5 (Vizard et al., 2007: 65). Other studies, however, report lower ages of onset as young as 4 (see e.g. Taylor, 2003: 61) or 5 (Hackett et al., 2013: 235). In the latter study, while the mean age of referral was 14, more than one-third of all referrals related to children age 13 or under (Hackett et al., 2013: 236).

children and young people with the increased availability and widespread use of smart phones and social media. The varied definitions of the phenomenon, however, render accurate comparisons of prevalence rates impossible. Ringrose et al.'s (2012: 11–13) overview of a range of studies on sexting across the United Kingdom, Europe and the United States has highlighted that between 14 and 40 per cent of young people are affected by sexting. More recent National Society for Prevention of Cruelty to Children (NSPCC) figures show that around one in seven young people has taken a semi-naked or naked picture of themselves with more than half subsequently sharing this image with someone else (Martellozzo et al., 2016: 11).[5] Similarly, the prevalence of cyberbullying varies widely across international studies depending on how it is conceptualised within different cultures (see Li et al., 2012).[6] Figures have ranged from as low as 10 per cent to up to 40 per cent (Tokunaga, 2010), though some studies report even higher prevalence rates of 50 to 70 per cent (for an overview, see Shariff, 2008: Ch. 3; Kowalski et al., 2012: Ch. 4; Li et al., 2012; Patchin and Hinduja, 2012: 15–18, 30–33). Within England and Wales, for example, an NSPCC study found that 38 per cent of young people have been affected by cyberbullying (NSPCC, 2013). However, as also noted in Part I of the book, despite the growing breadth of such behaviours and their statistical significance, they are only beginning to emerge as distinct areas of concern within public and even official discourses.

Broadly similar findings emerged from the primary data collected for the present study in Northern Ireland where interviewees generally confirmed the established age and gender dimensions of peer-based HSB across a range of contexts with a number of noteworthy variations. Furthermore, although race or social class did not emerge as distinct themes within the interview narratives, several interviewees emphasised the fact that peer-based sexual behaviour 'crosses all of the divides. Different ages, different social classes and different remits'.[7]

[5] These figures also equate broadly with those in Northern Ireland where, according to one study, 14 per cent of children have sent an image of themselves; 26 per cent have felt pressure to 'sext' and 63 per cent have seen a sext of someone they know: see research commissioned for the *BBC Spotlight Programme*, 11 November 2014.

[6] Note, as outlined in Chapter 1, cyberbullying encompasses a broad range of harmful behaviours which do not always have a sexual element: see Chapter 1, note 15.

[7] Interview 8, 23 May 2016, Rowan SARC Professional.

Age

In relation to the age demographic, around 10 to 12 per cent of the approximately 200 child victims who are referred annually to the Sexual Assault Referral Centre (SARC) are abused by another child or young person under age 18.[8] According to youth justice statistics for 2014–2015, the average age at the date of the offence is 15, with the age of the perpetrator ranging from 12 to almost 18.[9] Similarly, the age parameters of victims and of children who display HSB presenting for professional help can vary according to the precise remit of the specialist service. For example, Child and Adolescent Mental Health Services (CAMHS) take referrals from age 13 to under age 18,[10] whereas the Child Care Centre works with children from ages 3 to 13 or beyond if the child has learning difficulties.[11] Indeed, a forensic psychologist explained further in relation to 'the developmental age of a child' and the fact that age is not always a determining factor: 'you have to think about the age and level of understanding. Is a person old enough to consent?'[12] This interviewee described a typical case presenting for therapeutic services: 'It's probably from about 8 up . . . But sometimes we would have wee ones who are allowed to go out with the bigger brother or sister and maybe 6, 7, and they get caught up in it.'[13] As acknowledged in the previous chapter and in the words of a social work consultant: 'the age of young people presenting with harmful sexual behaviour is getting younger. Because I think there is a sexualisation and I think it is about core messages.'[14]

Many of the cases coming forward for counselling and support services are cases of historical or non-recent child sexual abuse where adults are reporting instances of abuse that occurred when they were children. This coincides with the Inquiry into Historical Institutional Abuse in Northern Ireland which was ongoing at the time of fieldwork during 2016 and which was reported in January 2017 (Hart et al.,

[8] Ibid. See also Buckley (2016). The Rowan SARC was established in May 2013 and offers a province-wide 'one-stop' centre which delivers a coordinated inter-agency response to all victims of sexual assault and rape, including children as well as adults.

[9] Statistics supplied to the author during Interview 17, 7 June 2016, Independent, former Youth Justice Professional. At the time of writing, figures were not available for 2015–2016 or 2016–2017.

[10] Interview 22, 10 June 2016, Forensic CAMHS Professional.

[11] Interview 4, 21 April 2016, Child Care Centre Professional. The Child Care Centre is a multidisciplinary unit which deals with the investigation and treatment of child sexual abuse and is operated by the Belfast Health and Social Care (HSC) Trust.

[12] Interview 2, 18 April 2016, Independent Forensic Psychologist.

[13] Interview 4, 21 April 2016, Child Care Centre Professional.

[14] Interview 16, 6 June 2016, Social Work Consultant.

2017).[15] Of the approximately 500 individuals across Northern Ireland who complete their counselling every year within one victim support organisation, the majority of cases are intra-familial (e.g. abuse by a father (23 per cent of cases) or close relative (24 per cent)) and a large proportion occur in the victims' own home (59 per cent) where 17 per cent involve abuse of a younger sibling by an older brother.[16] These figures also indicate the relationship-based nature of much of sexual offending behaviour concerning children and young people and the fact that 'it is very much centred on relationships that the victim already has.'[17]

As acknowledged earlier, broad age-based classifications need to be treated with caution as they may not take full account of the personal characteristics and developmental stage of the child, which can vary greatly among individual children, particularly among *younger* children or those with a learning disability. Several interviewees highlighted this as a problem within broader policy contexts with the second interviewee clarifying further in respect of a particular case:

> Sometimes the chronological age isn't so good, it is more around their maturity and their experiences, and if they have any cognitive impairments. So we would have, I suppose, generic bandings. So we would be thinking 0–7, 8–13 and then 14–17 and then adults plus. But within those groups you have a lot of variation [such as] a child who had ASD or a learning difficulty . . . or somebody was more shy or outgoing.[18]
>
> I had a 19-year-old assaulting a 14-year-old boy whom she considered herself to be in a relationship with. Now she was operating at a younger age, I think, mentally and emotionally, so she wasn't really . . . mature . . . she was more like still a teenager. That's a general difficulty in the cut-off point at 18 . . . Because we now know from all the brain stuff that has been done, that adolescence probably continues for a longer period of time, into young adulthood. And therefore sometimes when I am working with that 18 plus group, you are working with people who have started their behaviour in adolescence, and then it hasn't been

[15] The terms of reference for the inquiry included, inter alia, an examination of whether there were systemic failings by institutions or the State in their duties towards children in their care between 1922 and 1995. For the governing legal framework, see the written statement to the Northern Ireland Assembly by the then first minister and deputy first minister on 18 October 2012; see also the Inquiry into Historical Institutional Abuse Act (Northern Ireland) 2013. For a critical overview, see McAlinden and Naylor (2016).

[16] Statistics supplied to the author during Interview 28, 16 August 2016, Victim Support Professional.

[17] Interview 28, 16 August 2016, Victim Support Professional.

[18] Interview 8, 23 May 2016, Rowan SARC Professional.

> discovered at that stage. You know, they are 18, 19 maybe, before any victims come forward, or before you know what they have been doing at that age.[19]

Such subjective variances among children and young people may have a deep impact on how the individual child or young person interacts with peers and how the social world is viewed, including the pervasive cultural messages and norms about sex.

Moreover, broader implications stem from societal perceptions about age and what constitutes 'risky' behaviour, particularly relating to *older* children or adolescents. An interviewee who formerly worked in the area of youth justice explained as follows in relation to the response of the young person as well as that of parents and the embedded denial or minimisation of harm:

> There would be a lot of denial . . . I didn't do it or what's exactly wrong with that? I think when it is against a child there's very little denial. I think when it's a 15-year-old maybe against a 13-year-old girl. 'So what?' . . . I think the teenage, peer on peer, there would be a very big . . . 'what's the problem?' Or 'sure she didn't mind.' So that would take a lot of work to get them to see, what you did was totally inappropriate. It was harmful. It hurt someone. And even then some of the parents would be saying 'what's the issue?'[20]

These broad tensions surrounding the age variable are potentially significant on at least two fronts: they serve to problematise age-based legal or policy thresholds for criminalisation or engaging therapeutic intervention with children and young people who display HSB; and they may also work to negate or endorse societal and professional presumptions about risk with younger children in particular 'because of their age they are viewed as less risky',[21] and conversely older children are denied the full protection of the law. This view was expressed by a judge who articulated the tension between legal constructions of age and the inherent vulnerability of some children and young people, particularly female adolescents:

> Age . . . whilst it is a scientific fact . . . you get 16-year-olds that want to present themselves as being an 18- or 19-year-old, but in reality they have the mindset of a 14-year-old. But I know 21-year-olds who are very vulnerable. Young females who are very, very vulnerable, but they don't

[19] Interview 24, 6 July 2016, Independent Treatment Professional.
[20] Interview 17, 7 June 2016, Independent, former Youth Justice Professional.
[21] Interview 4, 21 April 2016, Child Care Centre Professional.

> see themselves as victims. They don't see themselves as being vulnerable and they don't get the level of protection from the law, simply because they are no longer children. They are not under the age of 16.[22]

Such difficulties are particularly acute with regard to the legal demarcations for sexual offences which can vary across different behavioural contexts including those relating to child sexual abuse (age 16) and indecent images of children (age 18) (see further Chapter 7).

Gender

As noted earlier, in tandem with figures on gendered and sexualised violence more broadly (see e.g. Finkelhor, 1990; Grubin, 1998; Lalumière et al., 2005; Kelly, 2013), the majority of children who engage in HSB are male, though the gender imbalance is less pronounced with older children or adolescents. By way of example, most of those who report to the police as victims or come forward for counselling and support in Northern Ireland are female. A professional working in the area of victim counselling and support explained: 'most of the victims that we see, at least 76 per cent of the clients that we see are female, and 24 per cent are male.'[23] Similar figures were reported for specialist therapeutic and investigation services with children between ages 3 and 13 (see also Morrison, 2015). For example, while of the 76 referrals to the Child Care Centre in 2013 for either investigation or therapy, 33 were males and 43 were females, higher percentages of younger male children were engaged in 'explicit sexual play' (Morrison, 2015).[24] Similarly, of those children or young people referred to the Youth Justice Agency for displaying HSB during 2014–2015, almost all were male (93 per cent).[25]

Although the overwhelming majority of children and young people who display HSB are male, and 'females generally tend to be victims',[26] professional interviewees reported a marked increase in cases involving females as perpetrators, including among younger children. As one professional explained within the context of concerning or potentially harmful sexual behaviour within schools:

22 Interview 26, 1 August 2016, District Court Judge.

23 Interview 28, 16 August 2016, Victim Support Professional.

24 Interview 4, 21 April 2016, Child Care Centre Professional.

25 Statistics supplied to the author during Interview 17, 7 June 2016, Independent, former Youth Justice Professional.

26 Interview 24, 6 July 2016, Independent Treatment Professional.

> I was asking the primary schools to mark incidents that were happening, the age and gender ... So as you went through the primary school, the figures in the lower end of the primary school were about a 60/40 split, boys and girls. So the girls were actually carrying out some sexual behaviours. And these wouldn't have been serious sexual assaults, but they had been maybe rubbing their genitals on something or acting out that way. When you get to the top end of the primary school, you know sort of 10, 11, it reverts to what you get in the criminal justice system. It went to sort of about 95 per cent male, 5 per cent female.[27]

Several professionals pinpointed the fact that 'society [and] the world is changing and social media is changing things. So we are having people act very differently than they would have before'[28] and that 'sometimes females can be a lot more emotionally and sexually aggressive, like boys.'[29] One of these interviewees explained further in the context of assessment and therapeutic intervention:

> And I have to say from my experience it is not just males that are practicing this violence. Females can be equally as violent for possession rights, jealousy purposes. I think that we tend to label boys more easily as being the people who hurt others. I do think that they can be physically violent, but if we are talking about emotions and about harmful behaviour, then girls as well can display very similar behaviours.[30]

As discussed later, this has occurred particularly within the context of digital forms of harmful sexual or exploitative behaviour such as sexting where girls may act as the 'initiators' as well as within group or gang settings where they may act as 'recruiters' of other victims and where 'polarised gendered stereotypes' (Papadopoulos, 2010: 5) (see Chapter 4) do not manifest as clearly.

Cultural gendered stereotypes, however, also exist among professionals and are tied to typologies about the 'ideal' victim and 'imagined offender' of child sexual abuse more broadly as discussed in Chapter 3 (see generally McAlinden, 2014a) and 'who society wants to see as victims and who they are prepared to see as perpetrators'.[31] This view was echoed by a number of interviewees in terms of the stereotypical biological assumptions about gender which are reinforced by the differential socialisation of boys and girls and the sexual norms of a given

[27] Interview 6, 25 April 2016, Independent Safeguarding Consultant.
[28] Interview 2, 18 April 2016, Independent Forensic Psychologist.
[29] Interview 16, 6 June 2016, Social Work Consultant.
[30] Interview 2, 18 April 2016, Independent Forensic Psychologist. [31] Ibid.

society (see e.g. Shoveller et al., 2004; Moore and Rosenthal, 2006; Papadopoulos, 2010) whereby 'we expect females to be more nurturing and it is against their nature to see it that other way'[32]:

> Particularly when it is peer on peer, I think the gender stuff comes in. It seems to sit easier for us to see women as victims and females as victims, as opposed to equally as sexually aggressive as some males are . . . Now part of that for me is the social construct in the sense that people don't think girls can do it or women can do it because we don't have penises, so therefore how can we sexually assault anybody? Also we are meant to be nurturers, all that sort of stuff . . . When boys and girls are little they externalise very difficult feelings. But girls learn to internalise very difficult feelings. So as they get older, what you see is higher levels of the girls with self-harm, eating disorders, and you get higher levels of the boys in the offending. And you see that in the sexual offending stats as well.[33]

In a similar way to age, such social and cultural constructions of gender may also work to negate or obscure perceptions of risk relating to both young males and females respectively, where 'people tend to put them in boxes',[34] and 'we have a bias towards young females'[35] and where 'there is still a lack of acknowledgement that it happens to boys too.'[36] As Roesch-Marsh (2014: 222) has argued in the context of Scotland: 'victimisation continues to be culturally "feminized" [while] offending is "masculinised."' Indeed, within the context of the present study, there was also broad acknowledgement of how gender impacts the assessment of risks and needs: 'for young males it is almost automatic they are the perpetrators' and professionals 'very quickly go down that route'[37] and where for young females, they 'are pushed towards CSE'[38] and the status of being vulnerable to or a victim of CSE; 'girls tend to get their behaviour rewritten as their own vulnerability. So they will always get the label of sexually exploited.'[39] This dichotomous discourse among professionals was also clearly shaped by the association of HSB with offending behaviour and the linkage of CSE with victimhood at the opposite end of the spectrum. As argued further, this

32 Interview 5, 22 April 2016, NSPCC Worker.
33 Interview 16, 6 June 2016, Social Work Consultant.
34 Interview 9, 25 May 2016, Youth Support Worker.
35 Interview 14, 2 June 2016, Sexual Health Nurse.
36 Interview 7, 13 May 2015, Former Police Officer.
37 Interview 18, 14 June 2016, Senior Voluntary Sector Interviewee.
38 Interview 5, 22 April 2016, NSPCC Worker.
39 Interview 6, 25 April 2016, Independent Safeguarding Consultant.

represents an over-simplified and one-dimensional view of peer-based sexual behaviours which generally emerges as much more fluid and complex and where both males and females can be victims as well as perpetrators and, moreover, can vacillate between these core categories.

Within the generally small but growing corpus of literature on sexual offending by adult females (see e.g. Vandiver and Walker, 2002; Ashfield et al., 2010; Gannon and Cortoni, 2010; McIvor, 2017), there is a narrower body of work on sexual offending behaviour by young females (see e.g. Fehrenbach and Monastersky, 1988; Matthews et al., 1997; Kubik et al., 2003). This subgroup, however, is typically subsumed within generalist studies on adolescent sexual offending with very small numbers of young females within their overall sample (see earlier, e.g. Masson et al., 2015). As might be expected then, given their comparatively low profile as a distinct 'offending' group, public and policy discourses on the latter (that is, young female sexual abusers) are therefore impacted and shaped by the former (adult female sex offenders). In particular, the broader literature on adult female sexual offending suggests a number of typologies, two of which are of direct relevance for present purposes: predisposed/intergenerational offending (i.e. where there is a history of family violence or abuse) and male coerced/co-offender (where offending takes place in conjunction with a male) (see generally Matthews et al., 1991).[40] While the first of these is evidenced in the critical review of the predominantly quantitative international literature surveyed previously (see e.g. Hackett et al., 2013; Masson et al., 2015), the second of these came through strongly in a thematic analysis of the primary data obtained in the present study.

In this vein, a small minority of professionals voiced the concern that 'there is still an assumption among ... not everybody, but a large number of people ... that she has to have been put up to it. She is a co-worker with a male ... There is also still some reluctance to think that females can do it on their own.'[41] Several professionals reflected on their experience of cases across the age spectrum from younger children to adolescence, where females often acted in cooperation with a male rather than as sexual aggressors in their own right. The second quote

[40] For the sake of completeness, the third branch of this typology, which does not generally apply to children or adolescents as perpetrators, is the 'teacher/lover' where the older woman has abused a position of trust. These broad typologies were based on a small number of female sexual offenders (16), although later studies have supported their validity (Matthews, 1998; Nathan and Ward, 2002; Vandiver and Kercher, 2004).

[41] Interview 23, 24 June 2016, Social Work Service Manager.

that follows also starkly highlights the 'polarised gendered stereotypes' (Papadopoulos, 2010: 5) which tend to characterise discourses on male and female sexuality as highlighted in the previous two chapters:

> The commonality in most of them that we would see is that the gender is always male. We have had a few situations where females have been involved in assisting, playing games and holding other girls down, thinking it was fun and a game to hold other girls down to allow boys to do things to a girl. That sort of behaviour, in reasonably young children, primary school. Maybe not fully understanding the implications of that.[42]
>
> To be fair I have only come across one female that is possibly HSB . . . But I would say the female that I know, if she has done what she is meant to have done . . . well I think she has been coerced into doing it. So the coercion has come from a male. I think that in most cases, for abuse anyway, that there is usually a male somewhere in the background, isn't there? But the males, most of them . . . it has never been an opportunistic thing, it has been more kind of like planned and thought about. And probably a power thing . . . But quite a few are also experimental. But there has to be a certain amount of coercion in that bit as well.[43]

In reality, however, as the same social work professional cited earlier confirms in relation to young females: 'Our experience is that there are some who clearly are doing it on their own. And certainly there have been one or two where we would have thought . . . where there has been a mixed gender pair, that the female would be the driver.'[44] The consequences of this mode of moralist, antiquated professional thinking were explained by one professional with a cautionary tone: 'So what we want to do is beware of moral judgements and sometimes . . . we have to be careful we don't demonise a whole generation of young males and victimise a whole generation of young females. So I think it is problematic.'[45]

As also conveyed in the survey of the statistical data presented earlier, while 'females are more susceptible to coming forward for support',[46] a number of professionals in the study expressed the view that 'males are definitely underreported'[47] in terms of rates of victimisation. Earlier research has established marked gender differences in the

[42] Interview 3, 20 April 2016, Education Authority Professional.
[43] Interview 10, 25 May 2016, Youth Support Worker.
[44] Interview 23, 24 June 2016, Social Work Service Manager. [45] Ibid.
[46] Interview 28, 16 August 2016, Senior Voluntary Sector Interviewee (victim support).
[47] Interview 21, 23 June 2016, Social Work Practitioner.

victimisation patterns surrounding child sexual abuse in that victims are predominantly female (see e.g. Elliott et al., 1995; Grubin, 1998).[48] While on one level this might simply suggest higher levels of victimisation per se (as opposed to eventual reporting) among girls, older studies also attest that young males report less often than their female counterparts, which is often tied to broader male socialisation processes (Dimock, 1988; Crowder and Hawkings, 1995) which generally denounce the notion of male vulnerability (see further Chapter 3).[49]

Further reasons for the under-reporting by young males, however, were tied not only to broader cultural assumptions attached to gender, and masculinity in particular, but to the hegemonic sociopolitical context of Northern Ireland. Within the past few years in particular, there has been a high-profile public debate and the 'contours of a moral panic' about sex and sexuality stemming from a culturally conservative sociolegal discourse dominated by 'the Christian right' (see e.g. Ellison, 2016, 2017).[50] As a senior voluntary sector interviewee explained reflecting the view of several interviewees:

> I mean the whole thing in . . . particularly Northern Ireland with the homophobia and all the rest and the fear of coming out and all of that. Where do they go with this? How do they speak about it? But also there's the whole lack of disclosure . . . You know, why boys and young men are less likely to come forward about that. It is the shame and the guilt, and even though girls feel that too, there is that sense that men are men, I should have been able to fight him off. I should have been able to protect myself. What will people think of me? Will people think I'm gay when I'm not? Their own homophobia around all of that.[51]

48 See also Chapter 3, note 9 and accompanying text.

49 Baker and Duncan (1985), for example, found that 44 per cent of males reported being a victim of extrafamilial abuse compared to 30 per cent of girls, which may be indicative of under-reporting by boys. See also Mendel (1994) and Romano et al. (2001) who document contributory factors underlying male under-reporting including the stigma of homosexuality and the male ethic of self-reliance.

50 For example, homosexuality was not legalised in Northern Ireland until 1982 (via the Homosexual Offences (NI) Order 1982), some 15 years after England and Wales (see the Sexual Offences Act 1967). In 2011, the rest of the UK (England and Wales and Scotland) lifted the lifelong ban on gay men donating blood, but this did not occur in Northern Ireland until September 2016. While same-sex couples could adopt in England and Wales following the Adoption and Children Act 2002, this did not occur in Northern Ireland until 2013 when the UK Supreme Court refused the then NI health minister's (Edwin Poots, DUP) application for leave to appeal, thereby confirming the Court of Appeal ruling in *JR 65's Application* [2013] NIQB 101. In 2014, the Northern Ireland Assembly also voted not to implement legislation on equal marriage, allowing same-sex couples the right to marry which had been enacted in the Westminster parliament (see the Marriage (Same Sex Couples) Act 2013) making Northern Ireland out of line with the rest of the United Kingdom and the Republic of Ireland.

51 Interview 18, 14 June 2016, Senior Voluntary Sector Interviewee.

At the same time, however, there is also some evidence emerging from the primary data to suggest a recent increase in the reporting of sexual victimisation by males. One interviewee drew attention to the fact that of those coming forward as adults for counselling and support, 'the male figure has spiked in the last two years, so in 2014 when we last checked, it was 20 percent. So it is increasing.'[52] This was broadly attributed to what a number of interviewees referred to as the 'Savile effect', which 'has been helpful in that a lot of people have come out'[53] and in 'start[ing] a conversation in the last lot of years'.[54] As a victim support professional reflected:

> I think it is because, with the Savile inquiries[55] and the stuff that has been in the news, and I hope that the work that we are doing to try and be in the public realm more often ... that men feel now they can come forward and seek help, that it doesn't make you any less of a man if you want to seek help for something that happened. But there is a huge, still, difficulty around public perception of men and what they are supposed to be able to handle and their mental health. I know that we are not seeing all of the male victims. It is still difficult for them to come forward.[56]

As this interviewee also attests, however, there are residual difficulties for young males in their self-identification and societal acceptance of their status as victims of sexualised harm, particularly where the abuser might be female and of a similar or younger age. In this respect, there is also tentative evidence to suggest enhanced vulnerability of males as several interviewees explained in relation to young male perpetrators, 'most people that come in contact with police, most of the males have either got a diagnosis of ADHD or autism.'[57] Indeed, as this police officer suggested relating to the need for further specific research in this area: 'there is a huge piece of work that has to be done in and around boys and young men and their barriers of why they are not reporting.'[58]

[52] Interview 28, 16 August 2016, Victim Support Professional. The figure is currently 24 per cent for males.
[53] Interview 8, 23 May 2016, Rowan SARC Professional.
[54] Ibid. See also R. Ramesh, 'NSPCC Says Reports of Sexual Abuse Have Soared After Jimmy Savile Scandal', *The Guardian*, 31 August 2013.
[55] Jimmy Savile was a late British media personality whose prolific sexual offending has been traced back over a number of decades (Erooga, 2017). Following the initial report of the investigation into Operation Yewtree (Gray and Watt, 2013), there was an outpouring of further allegations by victims and the investigation was extended to a number of other high-profile British celebrities, with further investigations and public inquiries ongoing. See also Chapter 1, notes 24 and 25.
[56] Interview 28, 16 August 2016, Victim Support Professional.
[57] Interview 31, 17 October 2016, Police Officer. [58] Ibid.

The 'Dark Figure' of Peer-Based Abuse

Ministry of Justice (2013: 33) figures report that juveniles in England and Wales (those under age 18) account for 8.2 per cent of all convictions for sexual crimes. While the number of adults sentenced for sexual offences rose by 30.9 per cent in the six-year period between 2005 and 2011 (from 4,173 to 5,464), the number of juveniles sentenced for sexual offences within the same period fell by 11.9 per cent (from 556 to 491) (Ministry of Justice, 2013: 44). More recent internal figures compiled by the Youth Justice Board in England and Wales indicate similar percentages of children serving prison sentences for sexual offences (of around 8 per cent of all convictions for sexual crimes) for 2015 (Janes, 2016). However, between 2004 and 2012, on average 53 per cent of defendants proceeded against at a magistrates' court for rape of a child under age 13[59] (ranging from 58 per cent in 2004, peaking at 69 per cent in 2007 and declining to 37 per cent in 2012) were children ages 10 to 17.[60] On balance, therefore, when children are tried or convicted for sexual offences, it is typically for those at the higher end of the spectrum.

Indeed, as was noted in Chapter 3, the legislative and policy basis for the youth justice system was completely overhauled beginning in the late 1990s with a fundamental change of emphasis from custody to diversion.[61] In Northern Ireland, in terms of the volume of cases that ends up in the youth justice system, 'the numbers are quite small.'[62] Figures produced by the Youth Justice Agency (YJA) for 2013–2014 indicate that the YJA received 18 referrals relating to 17 children ages 10 to almost 18, 9 of which were court ordered; the remainder were diversionary. Three referrals came via the Probation Board for Northern Ireland (PBNI). For 2014–2015, the YJA received 14 referrals, 4 of which were court ordered, the remainder diversionary, with 3 referrals to PBNI.[63] For 2014–2015, these referrals were for a range of offences involving adult and child victims as well as animals: making/distributing indecent images of children[64] (which can include sexting

59 See the Sexual Offences Act 2003, section 5. See similarly, the Sexual Offences (NI) Order 2008, art 12.

60 See Jeremy Wright, *Hansard*, HC Debs, Col 818W (5 December 2013).

61 See the Youth Justice (NI) Act 2002, Part 4. See also Chapter 3, note 19.

62 Interview 17, 7 June 2016, Independent, former Youth Justice Professional.

63 Statistics supplied to the author during Interview 17, 7 June 2016, Independent, former Youth Justice Professional.

64 See the Protection of Children (NI) Order 1978, as amended (by the Sexual Offences (NI) Order 2008, art 42), which now extends protection against indecent photographs of children to those under 18.

or sending indecent images via social media) (three cases), sexual activity with a child under 13[65] (three cases), sexual assault of a child under 13[66] (three cases), indecent exposure[67] (to an adult woman) (two cases), engaging in sexual activity in the presence of a child[68] (one case), sexual assault[69] (one case) and intercourse with an animal[70] (one case). The majority of the victims, however, are children, with approximately 50 per cent under age 13.[71]

As might be expected then, there are low numbers of cases of sexual offences by children and young people coming through the criminal justice system for prosecution or sanctioning by the courts. One senior prosecutor explained of the 'tranche' of cases involving peer-based sexual behaviours coming through the Public Prosecution Service (PPS):

> It could be kids from 8 up, really . . . they would be between 12, 13 and could be up to 18 or older. But I am thinking in terms of that tranche of cases, they are usually in that age band . . . The children would tend to be maybe a year or two younger, or the same age. So when he would be 14 they would be 12. There could be then a younger one that would be 10 or would be 8 involved as well.[72]

Cases that end up in court, typically involve males in their mid-teens. A judge reflected: 'Most of the cases that I can actually think of having dealt with, we are talking about between 14 and 16.'[73] As indicated earlier, a range of studies have reported overall prevalence rates of between one-quarter and one-half of all known cases of child sexual abuse being committed by children and young people (Masson and Morrison, 1999; Taylor, 2003; Erooga and Masson, 2006; Vizard et al., 2007; Finkelhor et al., 2009). The pertinent question becomes, therefore, in the words of a youth justice professional, 'if there's only fourteen or seventeen coming through to the criminal justice system, what is happening to the rest?'[74]

Aside from fundamental changes to the youth justice system and the introduction of an ethos of diversion, the precise reasons underlying the drop in conviction rates for juveniles in England and Wales may be

[65] See the Sexual Offences (NI) Order 2008, art 15. [66] Ibid, art 14; see also arts 12–13.
[67] Ibid, art 70. [68] Ibid, art 18. [69] Ibid, art 7. [70] Ibid, art 73.
[71] Statistics supplied to the author during Interview 17, 7 June 2016, Independent, former Youth Justice Professional.
[72] Interview 30, 12 October 2016, Senior Prosecutor PPS.
[73] Interview 26, Interview 26, 1 August 2016, District Court Judge.
[74] Interview 17, 7 June 2016, Independent, former Youth Justice Professional.

difficult to ascertain. However, a number of broad assertions can be made. Official figures may omit the vast majority of HSB committed by children and young people especially where there has been no disclosure by the child or detection by others due to behaviours such as grooming (McAlinden, 2012a: 35–37) or the cultural normalisation of 'risky' sexual behaviour (see Chapters 4 and 5). As one professional involved in counselling and support for survivors of sexual abuse and violence explained in relation to the correlation between low levels of victim awareness and the under-reporting of HSB: 'I think that that is not because peer-to-peer abuse and exploitation isn't happening, I feel it is more to do with those victims having not identified us as a support mechanism yet.'[75] As discussed further in Chapter 7 in relation to legal responses, figures are also unlikely to be representative of the true number of offences due to a range of attrition factors, including victim withdrawal of the complaint and the police/prosecutorial decision not to proceed with the case (see generally, Gregory and Lees, 1996; Bunting, 2008).

Earlier research carried out in the context of Northern Ireland in relation to attrition rates with sexual offences against children has shown that those groups of child victims with lower 'formal sanction rates' included children under age 5, adolescents and those who experience abuse at the hands of peers (Bunting, 2008). Moreover, the data related to cases addressed by the criminal justice system does not include those who came to the notice of child protection services or those who were under age 10 as the age of criminal responsibility (Ashurst and McAlinden, 2015: 375). Indeed, referrals of youth displaying HSB via social media for treatment within HSB services (Hackett, 2014) also indicate that the combined figure of actual levels of HSB is potentially much higher. For example, the NSPCC's 'Turn the Page' programme which serves the Southern and Western HSC Trust, deals with approximately 40 children ages 5 to 18 per year.[76] As explored further, contemporary societal as well as professional uncertainty about the precise scope and parameters of some sexual behaviours among children and young people also has direct implications for engaging victim support mechanisms and for the criminalisation of peer-based sexual harm.

[75] Interview 28, 16 August 2016, Victim Support Professional.

[76] Data provided during Interview 5, 22 April 2016, NSPCC Professional.

A TAXONOMY OF PEER-TO-PEER ABUSE

Given the broad range of behaviours which may come under the umbrella of 'peer-to-peer abuse', a useful undertaking is to try to make sense of the various sexual behaviours among peers by offering a taxonomy based on the notion of 'harm'. The prevention of societal harm has long been the moral cornerstone of the criminal law (see generally, Williams, 1957; Hart, 1965; Feinberg, 1990) based on Mill's (1859) quintessential 'harm principle'. This holds that the only limiting principle on the freedom of action should be the prevention of harm to others.[77] The traditional focus of the substantive criminal law has been the harm *caused* by a defendant's conduct, as a necessary precondition of liability, as opposed to the harm merely 'intended or risked' (see e.g. Schulhofer, 1974; Robinson, 1975: 266; Ashworth and Zedner, 2012: 283).[78] Robinson (1975: 266), for example, has argued that the justification of the criminal law is 'to prevent harmful results rather than punish evil intent that produces no harm . . . or the mere possibility of harmful conduct'. Indeed, risk does not always equate with harm, in that not every perceived risk or intended harm will eventually manifest as actual harm. Such treatises, however, were written long before the advent of the 'precautionary principle' (Ewald, 2002; Ericson, 2007) and the 'pre-emptive turn' (Zedner, 2009) in contemporary criminal justice policy which seeks to capture future risk or 'pre-crime' (Zedner, 2007) before it occurs (see Chapter 3).

In addition, therefore, to helping clarify the threshold for where legal intervention *for past behaviour* ought to lie, a broad classification of peer-based sexual behaviours, based principally on the degree of harm, should also help to provide meaningful insights into where *future or potential risk* (in terms of the likelihood of harmful results) might manifest.[79] Within this broader context, the significance of harm may also be defined by its 'intensity, duration and frequency' and is measured

[77] As McGlynn and Ward (2014: 505) have acknowledged in the context of regulating pornography; Mill, however, provides no definition of harm but uses instead a wide variety of interchangeable terms such as 'injury', 'injurious', 'hurt' or 'hurtful' as well as words with more overtly moral undertones such as 'evil', 'mischief' and 'wrong'.

[78] See similarly the principles of causation in tort law in Finkelstein (2003). Note, however, the disagreement among moral philosophers in relation to whether resulting harm is necessary for criminal liability. See e.g. in the context of inchoate offences such as attempts to commit a crime (Robinson, 2008: 5).

[79] This broad distinction between the thresholds and justification for legal intervention also maps onto the divide between consequentialist and non-consequentialist rationales for punishment which are justified with reference to future or past behaviours respectively (see generally, Duff and Garland, 1994; Duff, 2001; Ristroph, 2009).

by the impact on not just the direct victim but in its widest extrinsic sense in terms of the consequences for the perpetrator as well as for others such as parents, family members and friends (Ashurst, 2015). It is for this reason, as noted in Chapter 1, that many practitioners and academics prefer the term 'harmful sexual behaviour', as opposed to the alternative 'sexually harmful behaviour', to denote the fact that the range of consequences proliferates beyond the sexual domain and the individual victim.[80]

Scholars and practitioners have generally distinguished the range of sexual behaviours presented by children and young people along a gamut of behaviours from the benign to the more serious. O'Callaghan and Print (1994: 146), for example, utilise the spectrum of 'normal, problematic, abusive' sexual behaviours to variously denote this range stemming from normative, age-appropriate, developmental behaviour which does not present any concerns, through to behaviour which is potentially concerning, to harmful or abusive behaviour. Similarly, Hackett (2010) prefers a more expansive continuum of 'normal', 'inappropriate', 'problematic', 'abusive' and 'violent', and Ashurst (2016: 3) the trichotomy 'experimental, exploitative and abusive' behaviour to describe the breadth or progression of sexual behaviours among peers. The salient point is that not all sexual behaviours displayed by children and young people are necessarily risky or ultimately harmful. The challenge again becomes, therefore, as highlighted at the outset of the book and throughout, one of being able to reliably differentiate and address normal/healthy/experimental sexual behaviours from behaviour which is potentially more problematic or exploitative at an early stage of concern before it becomes abusive or harmful. As one professional in the study succinctly expressed it, while 'most people are agreed with what the healthy and harmful are',[81] it is this middle category of 'the problematic' which is more difficult.[82] As I have argued previously, identifying harmful or potentially harmful sexual behaviour among peers involves recognising 'the range of harmful *consequences* and *factors* that determine the degree of harm' [emphasis added] (Ashurst and McAlinden, 2015: 376). What is harmful, however, ultimately depends upon conditions far more complex than

[80] See further Chapter 1, note 13 and accompanying text.

[81] In this respect, a range of proscribed behaviour relates to the 'healthy sexual development' of children in various age brackets: 0–4, 5–7, 8–12 and 13–18, relating to age and stage of development (see Carson, 2015).

[82] Interview 6, 25 April 2016, Independent Safeguarding Consultant.

simply the extrinsic behaviour itself or the intrinsic *motivations* of the perpetrator.

In relation to the outward consequences of the abuse or exploitation as experienced by the victim, as Wolak and Finkelhor (2011: 1) have helpfully delineated within the context of sexting, 'harm' can range from 'minor embarrassment to death', including the victim committing suicide.[83] By way of example, as one professional recounted:

> We had a victim who tried to kill herself because the perpetrator announced in school that she was all kinds of every slut under the sun and made a whole big drama out of this. And this kid went home, and she had had plenty of support, but that was just a step too far that she couldn't walk round the school and people believed this guy.[84]

Indeed, consistent with the generic literature on the long-term psychosocial effects of grooming and sexual abuse, the range of consequences may include psychological harms such as shame, guilt and fear (Finkelhor and Browne, 1985; La Fontaine, 1990; Ginzburg et al., 2009) as well as physical harm stemming from the sexual assault itself. Measuring harm, however, within this rather narrow framework of consequences for the victim may arguably be a rather subjective exercise as the extent to which an individual experiences the effects or consequences of abuse, to some degree at least, may be determined by the personal 'resilience'[85] or particular vulnerability of the victim.

As regards the motivation of the 'perpetrator', harm stemming from sexual behaviour among peers can encompass a range of 'motivations' from simple attention seeking to the intentional infliction of significant harm (Wolak and Finkehlor, 2011; Ashurst, 2015). As Ashurst (2015) contends, harmful motivations may be both 'intended' or 'unintended' where, for example, the former may relate to 'premeditated', 'malicious', 'callous' and 'persistent' conduct and the latter to more 'reckless' actions where the perpetrator takes advantage of a certain situation or 'opportunity' (see further Chapter 5). As discussed further in the next

[83] See e.g. the case of 15-year old Canadian teenager Amanda Todd who committed suicide in October 2012, following bullying and physical assault after exposing her breasts via a webcam. See M. Dean, 'The Story of Amanda Todd', *The New Yorker*, 18 October 2012. See also the infamous video which she posted on YouTube describing her ordeal by a series of flash cards: www.youtube.com/watch?v=ej7afkypUsc.

[84] Interview 1, 16 February 2016, Service Manager, HSS Trust.

[85] A number of studies have pinpointed factors underpinning the resilience of survivors of child sexual abuse, including positive self-image, strong emotional supports and external attributions of blame (see e.g. Valentine and Feinauer, 1993; Bouvier, 2003; Wilcox et al., 2004). See further discussion in Chapter 4.

chapter, 'intention' to cause harm within the context of HSB is not always easily captured within legal frameworks. Often the motivation derives from a desire to achieve something directly or trying to control others as a means of achieving something that is valued by themselves or others. An illustration may be provided within the context of gang culture, where such purposes may include 'sexual gratification, revenge, establishing or maintaining relationships or affiliations, or identification as an adult' (Ashurst and McAlinden, 2015: 376).

However, there may also be what could be termed 'a multiplicity of intentions' in which an initial and more benign motivation (e.g. establishing relationships or friendships) is superseded or replaced by another more sinister one (e.g. seeking sexual gratification or revenge). Moreover, as with pre-abuse behaviours such as grooming (McAlinden, 2012a: 213–21), harmful intent, particularly within the context of preexisting interpersonal relationships, is often very difficult to identify prior to the occurrence of actual harm. A simple reliance on motivation or intention alone, therefore, as the key determinant of harm is also unlikely to be adequate or reliable in accurately capturing risk or potential risk.

The arguments presented here point to the need to think more constructively about how we might conceive of harm within the broader context of sexualised behaviour among peers. In this respect, a range of *contextual factors* are thought to underpin the determination of 'harmful' sexual behaviour. Ashurst (2016: 4) provides a non-exhaustive list of factors including consent (incorporating age and level of understanding), equality of age and status between the parties, authority and control, cooperation, compliance and behaviour which amounts to criminal offending. To this list might be added the use of overt and deliberate grooming strategies among peers in the sense of 'direct compulsion' or manipulation to engage in sexual activity (see Chapter 5). In a somewhat narrower context, 'sexually abusive behaviour' among juveniles has also been defined as any sexual interaction that is perpetrated (i) against the victim's will; (ii) without consent; or (iii) as being carried out in an aggressive, exploitative, manipulative or threatening manner (Ryan et al., 2010: 3). The latter definition in particular places emphasis on the absence of consent and the coercive or exploitative context.

Indeed, following on from the analysis presented in the previous chapter in relation to the dynamics of peer-to-peer grooming, the two central underpinning variables which would appear to differentiate harmful sexual behaviour from that which is not and which can be distilled further from the previously described broad lists are power differentials and coercion – that is, the use of authority and control over another child or young person in a deliberately oppressive manner. It will also be remembered from the outset of the book that power is pivotal to the definition of HSB among peers – power which can be derived from imbalances in age, emotional maturity, gender, physical strength, intellect and a betrayal of trust (see Palmer, 1997: 11) or additionally, differences in social status or standing within peer groups.

Within the context of the present study, the majority of interviewees demonstrated a general consensus in articulating a broadly similar 'constellation of factors'[86] or 'indicators' underlying the categorisation of peer-based sexual behaviours as harmful or exploitative. Chief among these were power imbalances, age disparities and coercion or threats in the form of 'any element of force or psychological pressure'[87]; with the addition of 'deviant' sexual interests; repeated, rather than one-off, behaviour; and the use of 'secretive' or clandestine activities. As one professional articulated representing the views of many interviewees:

> The power difference . . . the age range between the children. The ability level of the child. Whether or not it was younger children, spontaneous, playful or whether or not it involves an element of secrecy, coercion, threats. That always starts to rack it up in terms of it being more harmful, and bringing it up into the amber, possibly into the red.[88]

The deliberate use of grooming strategies, in the sense of planned, secretive or forceful activities, was also identified by a small number of interviewees as an aggravating factor: 'certainly if you found that . . . you would be really concerned that that would be a risk factor . . . that would be something that would be suggesting a fairly deep-seated, deviant interest in either forcing somebody to have sex, or manipulating a much younger person.'[89]

Only a minority of interviewees, however, underlined the importance of contextual factors in the individual determination of 'harmfulness'. Primarily, these included the nature of the harm caused, the precise nature of the activity engaged in, whether it was relationship

[86] Interview 5, 22 April 2016, NSPCC Professional.
[87] Interview 24, 6 July 2016, Independent Treatment Professional.
[88] Interview 5, 22 April 2016, NSPCC Professional.
[89] Interview 24, 6 July 2016, Independent Treatment Professional.

based or age appropriate, where it took place and in particular the intention of the perpetrator. Such factors were deemed relevant to both risk assessment and the decision to prosecute:

> What was the type of the activity that they engaged in? . . . The type of the activity versus the age . . . where it took place. The context in which it took place. The experiences of both afterwards . . . W[ere] there then the threats and that sort of stuff afterwards? But also within that . . . even though they can't consent, was there a sense of them both saying . . . 'but that's how it started off' . . . I think we lose sight of context . . . Because we have to accept children experiment . . . We have to accept, children are being more and more given knowledge around sexual stuff . . . It still doesn't mean to say that it shouldn't have happened. But has it happened within a context?[90]
>
> Was there any coercion between the parties? Probably the intent. You know, is it a malicious intent? Is it an innocent intent? Is this a boyfriend/girlfriend send me a picture? . . . I am going to do something sinister with this? Or, I'll tell you what, I know we are finished, but I'll go away and leave you alone if you send me a picture. What is the intent and can you tell that there is something more in there?[91]

While the contextual nature of the sexual behaviour is undoubtedly important, these professional viewpoints, however, are somewhat circuitous and ultimately unhelpful in clarifying the threshold of harmfulness. In particular, they appear to suffer from the same core deficits which have been identified earlier: namely, difficulties in objectively quantifying the 'nature of harm' based on the 'type of activity' due to the subjective experience of victims; given the cultural normalisation of sexual behaviour among peers, it may be very difficult to pinpoint an unequivocal harmful intention on the part of the perpetrator prior to actual harm. As the opening quotation attests, there is an attendant lack of clarity in terms of the particular risk thresholds for triggering professional assessment, or therapeutic or justice interventions with children or young people. With these difficulties and challenges in mind, the remainder of this section attempts to delineate and make sense of the *contextual nature* of harmful sexual behaviour among children and young people along a continuum of healthy, problematic and harmful sexual behaviours, utilising a threefold typology of *peer-based relationships*, *peer-based recruitment* and *peer-based risk*.

[90] Interview 16, 6 June 2016, Social Work Consultant

[91] Interview 30, 12 October 2016, Senior Prosecutor PPS.

In brief, *peer-based relationships* are a useful shorthand reference which can be used to denote sexual behaviours among children and young people at the lower end of the spectrum which do not usually give cause for concern. Such behaviours are characterised by the presence of 'mutuality, consensuality and choice'[92] and tend to be of 'an exploratory nature, not exploitative in the sense that they may try out all sorts of different things, but . . . [where] there should be no sense that there's any intent to cause harm'.[93] This can include, for example, healthy, normative, developmental and experimental sexualised behaviours among peers such as those between teenagers in 'romantic' relationships including within the domains of sexting or partying/gang culture. Within the context of these normative behaviours, neither of the parties is being harmed, exploited or abused in the absence of power or coercion. Indeed, most forms of harmful sexual or exploitative behaviour emerge from within the context of preexisting normative relationships between peers (see further Chapter 5).

In the middle terrain lies *peer-based recruitment* which can be used to denote more problematic sexual behaviours between peers which may grow out of healthy or normative peer-based relationships but which potentially become harmful. This may include, for example, cases where a child or, more frequently, a young person may recruit another for the purposes of sexual exploitation or abuse by him- or herself or another, including by other children or adults. Indeed, in some cases, such as within the context of online grooming and abuse, CSE, as well as intra-familial abuse, the young person may be both a victim as well as a perpetrator as part of a 'continuum of offending' (McAlinden, 2014a: 186). It may also include cases of institutional child abuse where exploitation and abuse, derived principally from the abuse of power and authority, have become normalised as part of the organisational culture within a particular institutional setting.

At the opposite end of the spectrum lies *peer-based risk* which covers sexualised behaviours among children and young people which are overtly harmful, abusive or exploitative and may amount to criminal offending. I use this term to describe harmful sexual behaviour among peers which 'is at the high end'.[94] This may also include, for example, sexualised forms of cyberbullying and sexting in which sexualised images initially produced or sent on the basis of consensual activity are subsequently sent on to a third party without the subject's consent.

[92] Interview 6, 25 April 2016, Independent Safeguarding Consultant. [93] Ibid. [94] Ibid.

In this context, 'harmful' is generally defined as including more persistent, adult-type sexual behaviour which may involve aggression, coercion or force; causes distress in the child/other children; and has elements of secrecy and age or developmental inequality (Morrison, 2015).

Based on the foregoing analysis, the following sections seek to briefly illustrate this typology further within the context of a number of interpersonal, organisational and social settings where children and young people may display harmful sexual or exploitative behaviours. Although a comprehensive discussion of each of the main forms of peer-to-peer abuse is beyond the scope of this book, the analysis presented seeks to capture some of their salient features and complexities, drawing on the existing literature as well as the primary research.

SIBLING ABUSE

As discussed in Part I of the book, intra-familial and more intimate forms of abuse have generally lacked prominence within public and official discourses on sex offending concerning children. Even within this specific rubric, the traditional emphasis within academic discourses on 'incest' has overwhelmingly been on 'parent-child' incest (Medlicott, 1967; Justice and Justice, 1979; Groth, 1982; Russell, 1986) and father-daughter incest in particular (Giaretto, 1978; Herman, 1981; Christiansen and Blake, 1990; Phelan, 1995; Itzin, 2001). The term, however, also covers sexual activity between children and grandparents and, more pertinently for present purposes, between siblings (Adler and Schutz, 1995).

As noted in Chapter 2, 'sibling incest' (Adler and Schutz, 1995; Carlson et al., 2006) or 'sibling abuse' (Wiehe, 1997; Hoffman and Edwards, 2004; Caffaro, 2013) can include sexual abuse between older and younger children (Kaufman et al., 1996) or between adolescent siblings (Tidefors et al., 2010). Older studies estimate overall prevalence rates of sibling incest to be about five times more than that of parent-child incest (Finkelhor, 1980; Adler and Schutz, 1995). Harmful sexual behaviour among siblings is variously thought to account for between one-third (Hackett et al., 1998; Hackett, 2004) and one-half of overall levels of child-to-child sexual abuse (Beckett, 1996; Worling, 2001; Tidefors et al., 2010). Despite its statistical significance and relative prevalence, however, sibling incest remains somewhat understudied in comparison to parent-child incest and other forms of HSB among children and young people.

Sibling abuse clearly stems from within the context of sibling relationships which are said to be 'distinctive' in terms of their 'emotional power and intimacy' (Dunn, 1988: 119) and among the most formative and enduring influences on our lives (Dunn, 1988; Sanders, 2004). Interviewees in the study conveyed a range of examples of sexual behaviour among siblings ranging from sexual exploration in the form of sexual touching, the shared viewing of pornography or the 'acting out' of 'indecent images' they may have viewed on the Internet or their mobile phone, which were thought to be particularly prevalent with younger children, through to behaviour which involves coercive or aggressive sexual behaviour such as rape, including digital forms of penetration, which cause significant harm. In common with other forms of HSB, sibling abuse commonly takes place within the context of power differentials, typically derived from differences in age or physical strength, and the absence of consent (see e.g. Allardyce and Yates, 2013).

Interviewees drew on specific cases of sibling abuse which ranged from HSB by young adolescents, typically from ages 12 to 16, with a younger sibling of perhaps ages 8 to 10. While the most common form appeared to be 'an older brother abusing a younger sister',[95] cases also encompassed HSB within same-sex sibling relationships (typically between brothers) and between opposite sex preadolescent or adolescent 'siblings that are quite close in age'.[96] Moreover, although strictly speaking outside the confines of sibling abuse, abuse between opposite-sex cousins was another prevalent form of peer-to-peer abuse within families. Finally, as noted earlier, several professionals identified 'a lot of historic sibling abuse which people are only reporting now'.[97] In such familial contexts, the onset of abuse was generally ascribed to two principal factors: 'a degree of experimentation, of sexual curiosity, particularly in the family situation'[98] or as discussed in the previous chapter, to a range of environmental risk factors, including 'neglect ... a lack of supervision'[99] and 'a lack of education or ... openness in the

[95] Interview 4, 21 April 2016, Child Care Centre Professional.
[96] Interview 25, 25 July 2016, Consultant Paediatrician.
[97] Interview 30, 12 October 2016, Senior Prosecutor PPS.
[98] Interview 26, 1 August 2016, District Court Judge.
[99] Interview 24, 6 July 2016, Independent Treatment Professional.

home about your body and safety and boundaries and appropriateness and being able to talk about sexual matters in a healthy way'.[100]

Sibling abuse also emerged as one of the most significant and complex forms of HSB among children and young people. This complexity can be attributed to two main features: One is the fact that sibling abuse may take place against a backdrop of a wider spectrum of abuse which may be facilitative of sexual victimisation: 'where there is sibling abuse it is usually emotional, it is usually sexual and there is a bit of violence with it and coercion around it',[101] or there may have been 'transgenerational abuse coming down through the family'.[102] The other reason why such cases were often seen as being 'very complex'[103] is that they may involve an outward spiralling of risk beyond the immediate family, such as in cases of CSE:

> So I think then, if you thought you were going to get a way out, you would try it, and I think that's why intra-familial, in terms of bringing younger sisters or brothers along, so OK, you are taking the abuse maybe outside of the family . . . the abuse isn't necessarily happening within the family in terms of the act, but your groomer is maybe your sister or a brother.[104]
>
> In one of the cases, there's actually three brothers involved. So the younger brother has been referred to X . . . There's another one who is older, a cousin or a friend who got the three of these kids into watching pornography online. And then the three of them decided to try it out with each other in what they had watched . . . So the three of them, it has emerged, have been doing this for at least a year with each other. And sometimes it has been initiated by the 9-year old, sometimes by the 12-year-old, sometimes by the 13-year-old.[105]

Other scholars have deemed the range of contexts in which children may abuse, typically beginning within familial and extending to the community-based settings, as instances of 'victim crossover' (Yates et al., 2012; Allardyce and Yates, 2013). As the previous quotes attest, where victim recruitment takes place against a wider backdrop of abuse, it again becomes difficult at the level of praxis to clearly separate out where risk is thought to lie in terms of those who were the 'initiators' and those who have been victimised.

[100] Interview 16, 6 June 2016, Social Work Consultant.
[101] Interview 2,18 April 2016, Independent Forensic Psychologist. [102] Ibid.
[103] Interview 1, 16 February 2016, Service Manager, HSS Trust.
[104] Interview 11, 26 May 2016, Safeguarding Professional.
[105] Interview 1, 16 February 2016, Service Manager, HSS Trust.

The literature demonstrates that in comparison with other forms of sexual abuse, sibling abuse is often underreported to parents or teachers (see e.g. Laviola, 1992; Cafarro and Conn-Cafarro, 2005; Carlson et al., 2006). As discussed in the previous chapter, victims of peer-based abuse in general 'weigh up the risks' (Mishna and Alaggia, 2005: 217) and may delay disclosing for a range of reasons related to fear of the consequences, self-blame, reluctance to burden parents or worry about not being supported or believed (Sperry and Gilbert, 2005; Schönbucher et al., 2012). Such emotions are augmented within family settings, where there is the fear that 'you are going to destroy your whole family.'[106] In this respect, a further prominent theme from the interview narratives was the enhanced consequences for victims of sibling abuse in deciding whether to disclose, including the pivotal reaction of and impact upon their family:

> The thing that is most important for young people is that they get family support. They fear rejection most of all, I think, from family members. And if family members can accept . . . that the behaviour has taken place and not reject the young person that can be very powerful . . . because you need a very holistic approach to working with this situation.[107]
>
> The victims that have come to us would say that there are numerous barriers to them disclosing to anybody . . . They are afraid of what will happen when they disclose. Not only oftentimes to them but to the perpetrator. So if I tell my mother that my brother is abusing me, what will happen to him? I want the abuse to stop, but I still love my brother . . . what is going to happen to my family, because I still love my family and I don't want to break it up?[108]

Whether there is an 'accidental discovery' by a family member or 'purposeful disclosure' by the child, a customary reaction of the family, particularly emerging from non-recent cases of sibling abuse, is to keep the abuse quiet. To avoid 'the stigma of bringing in social services or the police into their personal life . . . they try to deal with it themselves until it escalates out of control'[109] with underlying potential lifelong consequences for the victim:

> And another aspect that is quite common is that the family were aware of it, and basically said we will deal with that, there is no need for police involvement. We will just monitor it and prevent contact and

[106] Interview 32, 2 November 2016, Police Officer.
[107] Interview 24, 6 July 2016, Independent Treatment Professional.
[108] Interview 28, 16 August 2016, Victim Support Professional.
[109] Interview 31, 17 October 2016, Police Officer.

> association ... But yet the victim has still had to live with that. They have never got support for it, they have never got any counselling for it, and I am sure it causes anger issues with them and some of them turn to substance abuse.[110]

There are also potential consequences for victims, however, even when abuse is reported to the authorities, as 'suddenly their whole family explode[s]'[111] and 'families have separated because of it.'[112] As discussed further in the next and final chapters, the complexity of sibling abuse, and the myriad challenges it raises, suggests the need for a more systemic and holistic approach to the risks presented by HSB among peers that seeks to engage children as well as their families. Indeed, sibling abuse, as a form of intra-familial abuse, is probably one of the most intractable forms of peer-based abuse in that it is harder to proactively target hidden sexual norms and behaviours as neither children nor their parents may perceive risk in such intimate terms.

PEER-TO-PEER FORMS OF INSTITUTIONAL ABUSE

As outlined in Part I of the book, instances of peer-to-peer forms of institutional child sexual abuse have predominantly emerged from within the confines of non-recent institutional child abuse by adults in a position of trust. There has been a plethora of high-profile public inquiries or official reviews worldwide relating to a range of childcare contexts in community (e.g. schools and nurseries) and particularly residential childcare contexts and including religious as well as secular settings.[113] These inquiries and subsequent academic analyses (see e.g. Gallagher, 1998; McAlinden, 2006; Erooga, 2009; Erooga et al., 2012) have collectively revealed that many of the systemic features of the institutional environment – such as the closed nature of childcare institutions, positions of trust and authority held by abusers, and the quasi-intra-familial features including proximity, unsupervised access and 'routine' interactions with children – are generally conducive to abuse of power and the 'corruption of care' (Erooga, 2009: 39–40; see further McAlinden, 2012a: Ch. 5). Against this broader backdrop, a small number of official inquiries have also established that some

[110] Interview 32, 2 November 2016, Police Officer.
[111] Interview 6, 25 April 2016, Independent Safeguarding Consultant.
[112] Interview 16, 6 June 2016, Social Work Consultant.
[113] See the detailed review in Chapter 1. For a critical overview, see Reder et al. (1993), Corby et al. (2001), Parton (2004).

victims were abused by their peers as well as adults where abuse became part of the organisational culture.[114] In such circumstances, children were not only victims but also 'insiders'/'bystanders' or active parties to the abusive process.

Moving from the historical to the contemporary context, peer-to-peer forms of institutional abuse again appear relationship based, stemming from close and constant personal interactions with other children and young people in quasi-intra-familial environments. Indeed, as discussed in the previous chapter, more recent research has also demonstrated that children and young people experience a higher volume of violence, sexual harassment and sexually abusive acts in organisational settings such as schools or residential care, where there is sustained exposure to social and behavioural norms related to 'gender, relationships and consent' (Firmin and Curtis, 2015: 4, citing Frosh et al., 2002; EVAW, 2010; see also House of Commons (HC) Women and Equalities Committee, 2016: 10–11). The preponderance of recent research on peer-abuse in organisational contexts, however, has tended to concentrate on bullying or physical violence in schools (see e.g. Olweus, 1995; Carney and Merrell, 2001; Schott and Søndergaard, 2014), including new forms of electronic or cyberbullying (Kowalski and Limber, 2007; Rivers and Noret, 2010; Kowalski et al., 2012; Völlink, 2016) which may involve verbal, emotional or psychological abuse.[115] To date, however, there is a dearth of research specifically focused on harmful *sexual* behaviour among peers within institutional childcare settings.

A number of examples of institutional child sexual abuse among children and young people, across both historic and contemporary contexts, emerged from the present study. Several legal professionals, including police and lawyers, spoke of 'the raft of referrals and cases . . . since the Savile inquiries'.[116] A senior prosecutor who professed to have dealt with a 'huge volume' of historic cases explained:

114 See e.g. Shaw (2007: 31–32) in the Scottish contest and the Commission to Inquire into Child Abuse (2009: Vol. 3, para 9.57) in the Irish context (the Ryan Report). The Ryan Report found, for example, that both males and females were abused by co-residents (Commission to Inquire into Child Abuse, 2009: Vol. 3, paras 7.138, 9.94).

115 Although traditional and cyber forms of bullying are closely related in terms, for example, of being acts of intentional aggression, based on power imbalances and which are repeated over time, the distinctiveness of the latter stems from the pervasive role of technology in children's and young people's lives, the often anonymous nature of cyberbullying, the breadth of the potential audience or number of 'bystanders' and the insidious and prolonged access to a victim at any time outside of school settings (see e.g. Shariff, 2008: Ch. 2; Li et al., 2012: 7–8; Menesini et al., 2012; Kim et al., 2016).

116 Interview 7, 13 May 2015, Former Police Officer. See note 55.

> Kids would have been saying, we were in the dormitory and the older boys abused the younger boys, or the older girls abused the younger girls. Or there would have been a girl in charge of the dormitory and she would have come over and done this. Or she would have got me and made me go over and do this. That happened all the time.[117]

As regards more contemporary examples of peer-based institutional sexual abuse, these related primarily to residential childcare contexts, such as care homes, but also community-based school settings. In relation to the latter, case examples within primary schools ranged from developmental/experimental behaviours such as 'inappropriate sexual comments' or 'inappropriate sexual behaviour' (e.g. children exposing themselves)[118] and sexual touching (including between girls) among children as young as age 5, aggressive sexual behaviours by boys towards girls to sexting and anal rape between adolescent boys post-primary school.[119] Many cases involved a range of contact and non-contact behaviours encompassing 'mutual masturbation' to the sharing of child abuse images via 'the dark web'.[120]

As regards residential contexts, the pervasiveness of peer-to-peer abuse in residential childcare settings was highlighted by several interviewees – social workers, police and prosecutors – relating to adolescent girls in particular:

> I have had a few cases where a girl in a care home . . . and she would say they were running the corridors at night and they were misbehaving and they were getting told off . . .. And then she would go to her room and then a couple of boys would come in and have sex with her . . . So for the troubled children who are in the care homes . . . there would be a lot of abuse towards staff, a lot of assaults, a lot of criminal damage. They would be breaking out at night, running out at night, drinking, being brought back by police. The behaviour would be on the extreme. So sexual behaviour would fall in with that as well . . . Those kids . . . would have had sexual relations with other kids in the home. And that may or may not have been consensual. But we have certainly had instances of complaints about it where they are saying I was raped when I was in

117 Interview 30, 12 October 2016, Senior Prosecutor PPS.

118 Interview 32, 2 November 2016, Police Officer.

119 Interview 3, 20 April 2016, Education Authority Professional.

120 Ibid. 'The dark web' is generally used to refer to a collection of websites which exist on an encrypted network and which cannot be accessed using traditional search engines or browsers. While there are many legitimate uses of the dark web, such as military intelligence and law enforcement, it can also be used to facilitate criminal activity including terrorism (see Chen et al., 2008), the drug trade (see Maddox et al., 2016) and the sharing of indecent images of children (see Gehl, 2016).

> that home. Those boys came into my room and one held me down and the other raped me.[121]

In other circumstances, however, even where someone has been 'coerced into having sex' and there is a notable age difference between the parties (e.g. a 17-year-old male and a 14-year-old female), the victim may be 'unwilling to make a statement because they say they agreed to it'.[122] This also reinforces a broader argument of this book, explored further in the next chapter, that where risky sexual behaviours have become normalised among children and young people, the dividing line between consent and coercion is often difficult to define.

A prominent theme pertaining to peer forms of institutional abuse was the significance of contextual factors which may increase the level of risk and allow abusive practices, and ultimately sexual victimisation, to flourish. As a form of quasi-intra-familial abuse, this was also related to the fact that many children 'grew up in an institution and ... didn't have any sexual boundaries'[123] or were absent protective factors or 'those significant adults'[124] (outside their residential social worker) to enforce those boundaries. The same senior prosecutor cited earlier likened the prevalence of institutional abuse to a 'sport' stemming from the normalisation and recreational nature of abusive practices:

> It was almost like sport. That is the only way I could describe some of the things ... Kids would have described things like you had to line up and go and see an older boy and you had to go into the room and you had to do what he told you. And that was pretty much like, well you had to go outside and play a game of rounders ... This was just something you had to do. And obviously the authority figures appeared to very much either turn a blind eye or, in certain cases, facilitate this going on.[125]

In a similar vein, several interviewees described the institutional environment as a veritable 'melting pot'[126] for harmful sexual or exploitative behaviour stemming from the traumatic histories or inherent vulnerabilities of children and young people. Such difficulties were compounded by the resource limitations of finding suitable placements:

121 Interview 30, 12 October 2016, Senior Prosecutor PPS.
122 Interview 1, 16 February 2016, Service Manager, HSS Trust.
123 Interview 30, 12 October 2016, Senior Prosecutor PPS.
124 Interview 23, 24 June 2016, Social Work Service Manager.
125 Interview 30, 12 October 2016, Senior Prosecutor PPS.
126 Interview 31, 17 October 2016, Police Officer.

> It is inevitable ... It is very difficult for six siblings to get on in the one house. When you put six people who aren't related, who have their own vulnerabilities and are going through all the trauma that they've been through, and they are going into a house with somebody else with all those traumas and maybe highly sexualised behaviour, where it is almost normalised sometimes ... So it is a big issue that we don't have enough places to protect people ... There have been times where a girl has been sexually assaulted by another resident and they have to remain living with each other ... But, social services have nowhere to move them to.[127]
>
> Young people go into a children's home, we know that the peer circle, your social field, poses the most risk ... There are care homes and they are just honey pots. And that's from older people looking in, but also amongst themselves as well ... they don't have any protective environment to go back into. Their social fields are all very dangerous ... And the reality is, especially for the young people in care, they sometimes have to leave care to realise that what they were involved in was so dangerous.[128]

Previous inquiries or research have noted that residential care settings provide a captive population of particularly vulnerable children (see e.g. Utting, 1997: 5; Powell, 2007: 39). The multiple or 'dual vulnerabilities' of children in residential settings, particularly adolescent females, many of whom have a 'substantiated history of sexual abuse' (van Vugt et al., 2016), may make them more susceptible to victimisation (see Chapter 5) and simultaneously impinge their credibility in the event of a disclosure of abuse (see further Chapter 7).

Reflecting the language of American legislative debates on sexual offending by adults, which focused on the 'boundary violations' by 'toxic' and 'polluted' sex offenders (Lynch, 2002: 545, 560) (see Chapter 3), other interviewees articulated a pathologising discourse in terms of the risk of 'contamination' where children and young people in care settings 'make links with each other'.[129] Central to this crucible of risk relating to HSB is the abusive or criminal histories of some of the young people. In relation to young males, for example, 'most of them have very extensive criminal backgrounds ... and then sticking a girl in the middle of them who is high risk CSE.'[130] Such cases which may involve 'group victimisation' and multiple perpetrators are particularly

[127] Ibid. [128] Interview 21, 23 June 2016, Social Work Practitioner.
[129] Interview 18, 14 June 2016, Senior Voluntary Sector Interviewee.
[130] Interview 31, 17 October 2016, Police Officer.

challenging for legal professionals essentially because 'if children have been abused more than once, it is difficult for them . . . as it is in a relatively short space of time . . . to know even who did what to whom.'[131]

A further noteworthy theme, in common with sibling abuse, was the potential crossover to other settings, including to other institutional contexts but particularly to community-based contexts involving CSE:

> It becomes almost a fraternity for want of a better word. This moving between homes. These young people who go into residential care . . . the way the system is now, they are moved about quite often, which is a vulnerability factor that we recognise when we are doing our risk assessment . . . So they may not have had any contact outside with anybody within it, but as soon as they go into that residential setting that's them . . . So the cross contamination is massive as well.[132]
>
> I think it becomes very blurred and complex. If you take just an example of a young person, say in a children's home, because there they have got other children and young people around them, and they are coerced and they are being sexually exploited. And the exploiter gets them to bring other, particularly young girls, maybe with them.[133]

As the same police officer cited earlier acknowledged, 'it is a very, very difficult thing to manage because they are still victims in essence, as well.'[134] Although CSE is by no means confined to this particular setting, there is a well-documented link between sexual exploitation and 'looked after children' (see e.g. Pearce, 2009; Beckett, 2011; Shuker, 2013). In such contexts, therefore, while peer-to-peer abuse may initially stem from immediate relational contexts, it may progress to recruiting victims for either themselves or others which augments the level of risk. As discussed further later, as with adult-child forms of institutional child abuse where the Internet may be used as an enabler to support offline or contact forms of sexual offending behaviour (see e.g. Elliott et al., 2013; McManus et al., 2015), there is also the potential for crossover between institutional and online contexts. These findings not only denote the intersection between different modes of HSB among children and young people but also the difficulties of neatly classifying such behaviours into neat categories.

[131] Interview 30, 12 October 2016, Senior Prosecutor PPS. [132] Ibid.
[133] Interview 18, 14 June 2016, Senior Voluntary Sector Interviewee.
[134] Interview 31, 17 October 2016, Police Officer.

PEER-TO-PEER ONLINE ABUSE: SEXTING AND CYBERBULLYING

Unlike the previous two settings which may be classified as private or pseudo-private in nature, sexting is a peer-based sexual behaviour which transverses the public-private divide in that it may begin within the confines of an interpersonal relationship and progress to third-party dissemination which is often played out in a public setting.[135] The literature establishes that a growing proportion of Internet-based sexual abuse or exploitation is committed by those under age 18 (Choo, 2009: xiii; Elliott et al., 2009; NSPCC, 2016).[136] This may take a number of forms, including the viewing or self-generation of child pornography (Flood, 2007, 2009; O'Leary et al., 2009; Lööf, 2012), unwanted sexual solicitation of others online (Finkelhor et al., 2000; Mitchell et al., 2008) and the 'recruitment' of other victims for adult offenders (O'Connell, 2003: 11) (see further Chapter 5).

More recently, sexting has emerged as a new form of online sexual exploitation committed predominantly, though not exclusively, by children and young people and which may constitute a form of sexualised cyberbullying (Ringrose and Barajas, 2011; Kofoed and Ringrose, 2012).[137] As noted at the outset of the book, this may take a number of forms including the sending of 'indecent' texts as well as images or videos, the consensual sharing of images between a girlfriend/boyfriend as well as the subsequent non-consensual dissemination of that image to someone else. As should become clear, of all the forms of potentially harmful or exploitative sexual behaviour among children and young people, considered within this chapter, and indeed throughout this book, sexting is perhaps the most theoretically and legally contentious in terms of establishing a clear threshold for risk and harm. From a broader social or cultural perspective, it also represents the latest 'panic' about sexualised forms of harm, not only relating to but also generated by children (Hasinoff, 2015) (see Chapter 2),

[135] The literature generally makes a broad distinction between 'primary' and 'secondary' sexting: see Wolalk and Finkehor (2011), Ringrose et al. (2012), Lievens (2014). See the recent example in Denmark where Facebook Messenger was used to share indecent video clips of two 15-year-olds having sex: 'Denmark Facebook Sex Video: More than 1,000 Young People Charged', *BBC News Online*, 15 January 2018.

[136] Although figures vary across studies, in relation to child pornography, for example, one in six of those reported to the police for possessing digital indecent images of children are under age 18 (NSPCC, 2016). See also Chapter 1, notes 3–5 and accompanying text.

[137] Among adults, coercive and non-consensual forms of sexting can be prosecuted under the offence colloquially known as 'revenge pornography': see the Justice (NI) Act 2016, art 51. See further Chapter 7.

providing a locus for contemporary concerns about 'the risks associated with childhood sexuality' (Lee et al., 2013: 35), as well as the 'technological risks' associated with 'new media' (Staksrud, 2013: 9, 59–61) (see further Chapters 3 and 4). As Lee et al. (2013: 35) have also contended, 'these broader social, cultural and moral anxieties have created an environment where rational debate . . . around teen sexting has been rendered almost impossible' and where 'any understanding about the differing behaviours and subsequent harms . . . has been lost.' This section of the chapter addresses this challenge by exploring the notions of 'risk' and 'harm' as related to sexting practices.

Studies on sexting have generally been confined to two broad groups: quantitative and qualitative analyses of its existence and prevalence among children and young people in predominantly British (see e.g. Phippen, 2012; Ringrose et al., 2012), American or Canadian (Davidson, 2014; Shariff, 2015) and Australian settings (Albury et al., 2013; Crofts et al., 2015) and its significance as a highly gendered phenomenon which differentially affects girls (see e.g. Rivers and Noret, 2010; Ringrose and Barajas, 2011; Salter et al., 2013) and which propagates culturally entrenched gendered double standards (Renold and Ringrose, 2011, 2013; Ringrose et al., 2013; Lee and Crofts, 2015: 458–59) (see further Chapter 4). In reality, however, rather than being pressurised into sending images as passive victims, many girls who engage in sexting are expressly motivated by 'pleasure and desire' (Lee and Crofts, 2015). Moreover, males may also send either explicit or posed naked images of themselves as well as request such images from females. The dominant protectionist risk discourse (Kitzinger, 1988: 81), however, tends to deny 'moral agency' (Dwyer, 2011; see also Gillespie, 2013: 642) and 'sexual citizenship' (Lee and Crofts, 2015: 467) to children and, in so doing, makes the framing of victimisation and thus the quantification of harm highly problematic.

A handful of studies have endeavoured to expound typologies of sexting based on the intrinsic motivations of the perpetrator (see e.g. Wolak and Finkelhor, 2011; Lee and Crofts, 2015). As noted earlier, Wolak and Finkelhor (2011), for example, in their study of more than 550 case reports of sexting within the United States, differentiate between 'experimentation' and 'aggravation' across a wide spectrum of motivations ranging from simple attention seeking or romantic purposes to the intentional infliction of significant harm, such as by someone seeking revenge or gang recognition. Although many young people see sexting as a form of sexual sharing that is 'mundane' and safer than face-to-face sexual intimacy (Wolak and Finkelhor, 2011: 8; see also Phippen, 2012: 10–11), the aggravating circumstances may include adult involvement, criminal or abusive behaviour (including extortion or threats), or the taking or sending of indecent images without the consent of the subject (Wolak and Finkehlor, 2011: 2–6).

On one level, sexting may be considered a modification of sexual expression in keeping with advancing technology (see e.g. Baym, 2010; Gillespie, 2013; Hasinoff, 2015; Albury, 2016) – as a form of 'flirty fun' rather than as cyberbullying or child pornography (Shariff, 2015: 8–11). On another level, however, the '*non-consensual* creation and/or distribution of private sexual images' (McGlynn and Rackley, 2017: 1, emphasis added), or what these authors conceptualise as 'image-based sexual abuse', may engender harm to both victims and wider society. These may relate to individual harms to the physical and mental well-being of victims or the infringement of their dignity, privacy and sexual autonomy, together with broader cultural harm which occurs through the normalisation or minimisation of such sexual activity.

The problems inherent, however, in a classification of harm based narrowly on either the outward consequences for the victim or the inward motivation of the perpetrator have been considered at length earlier. Indeed, what is notably absent from existing discourses, given the wide spectrum of behaviour which may come under the moniker of sexting, is how behaviour may be differentiated as normal, risky or harmful by children and young people themselves, as well as by professionals based on a more holistic assessment of contextual risk factors. In an age of 'digitally empowered kids' (Shariff, 2015), the determination of 'normal' is subject to a continuous process of social and cultural redefinition (see Chapters 3 and 4). Given that sexting for many young people 'is just a way of communicating',[138] it can be difficult in the minds of children and young people to differentiate 'between what is accepted as flirting and what is abusive'[139] (see also Lenhart, 2009: 10; Phippen, 2012: 10–11).

In this respect, there is a growing recognition that some of these complexities surrounding sexting cannot be captured by a simple check list of factors nor in absolute terms between, for example, consensual and non-consensual activity. Indeed, as also demonstrated in

[138] Interview 17, 7 June 2016, Independent, former Youth Justice Professional.
[139] Interview 11, 26 May 2016, Safeguarding Professional.

Chapter 4, much of children's and young people's engagement with sexual messages and imagery 'lies in the ambiguous and grey zone' (Ringrose et al., 2012: 7). Many professionals drew on examples of sexting which spanned an array of behaviours: 'for some young people it is that normalisation and that's OK. And then for other young people it is used to bully, so that they would be tricked into sending an image that then would be circulated.'[140] This same social work practitioner continued, giving case examples which covered both ends of the spectrum:

> It is the whole revenge porn thing as well. Even if an image was shared, as in boyfriend-girlfriend, the relationship breaks up and the image is circulated ... And then there's also ... when young people are off their heads, people record or take images of them and circulate them, of people having sex with them or doing sexual acts.[141]

Many other interviewees, however, emphasised the more insidious and covert nature of sexting and the underlying 'relational coercion' (Salter et al., 2013: 301) that this may involve:

> We had a young girl who had sent a sexualised image of herself to a male pupil, same age roughly. And police spoke to her and cautioned her about it . . . and what came out of it was, there was a degree of coercion there that unless certain questions are asked about what's going on here, you don't get to that. For example, he's saying, 'if I give you a kiss on the bus tomorrow, or if I put my arm around you at school or tell people I am going out with you, will you send me a sexy pic?' Now that level of coercion might not be classed as coercion by others. But where a young person's need is so great to be accepted, be loved and all of that.[142]

As others noted, in practice, this can often be very difficult to identify due to the daily cultural exposure to sexual norms (see Chapter 4): 'if there is any element of force or psychological pressure. Although it is very hard sometimes to actually discern that because there is pressure on young people to be using media . . . I think it is the exposure to sexual images generally now. That's been a creeping thing over a number of years.'[143] In this respect, as Crofts et al. (2015: 16–17) point out, there are three main sources of pressure: *individual pressure* (which operates within relationships between senders and receivers), *peer group pressure* (which relates to the social dynamics of particular groups and which are often gendered) and *sociocultural pressure* (stemming from the

[140] Interview 21, 23 June 2016, Social Work Practitioner. [141] Ibid.
[142] Interview 18, 14 June 2016, Senior Voluntary Sector Interviewee.
[143] Interview 24, 6 July 2016, Independent Treatment Professional.

normative expectations created by the contemporary sexualisation of popular culture). As argued in Chapter 4, it is the latter dynamic which tends to drive and reinforce the previous two.

Consistent with Wolak and Finkelhor's (2011: 8) typology, a number of factors can help in the determination of whether an image is harmful: (i) the ages of the parties and whether it was developmentally appropriate; (ii) their backgrounds, including whether there was a history of abuse or prior involvement with the criminal justice system; (iii) whether there was a coercive sexual or social relationship; (iv) the nature of the images; and (v) the extent of any dissemination. Police and social workers in particular generally acknowledged that 'not all sexting is unlawful. Some of it is within an intimate relationship . . . So, if you've got boyfriend and girlfriend, 15, 16, 17 . . . without realising that it is an indecent image.'[144] Moreover, the nature of that relationship is also pivotal in determining whether the sexting merits further investigation: 'Is it a healthy relationship? Is it sinister? Is it abusive? Is it exploitative?'[145] Sexting outside the bounds of a relationship, whether an opposite- or same-sex relationships, invites the questions of 'why the photograph was sent? . . . is there a history of sexual abuse? Is there alcohol? Are there behavioural problems? All the vulnerabilities.'[146]

In addition to the nature of the relationships and the age of the parties, some other core situational factors which were singled out as being indicative of risk and as taking the behaviour towards 'the abusive'[147] were 'obviously if an offence is committed'[148]; and 'looking at circumstances, situations, coercion and consent'[149]; and 'distribution of indecent images'.[150] As a police officer explained in relation to this latter element: 'if two children were having sex . . . one was 16 and one was 15, that will not be dealt with, but then if one person has taken a picture and put it online and distributed it to their friends, we will put a file in for that. For distribution of indecent images.'[151] Furthermore, the lasting impact on the victim, particularly when the image has been posted on social media, is also a relevant factor in determining harm: 'if we have got a victim who is extremely upset by this, we would prosecute it.'[152]

144 Interview 31, 17 October 2016, Police Officer. 145 Ibid. 146 Ibid.
147 Interview 27, 3 August 2016, Senior Social Work Practitioner. 148 Ibid.
149 Interview 11, 26 May 2016, Safeguarding Professional.
150 Interview 32, 2 November 2016, Police Officer. 151 Ibid.
152 Interview 30, 12 October 2016, Senior Prosecutor PPS.

In tandem with the research highlighted earlier demonstrating the augmented capacity for HSB in organisational and group settings (see e.g. Firmin and Curtis, 2015: 4; House of Commons (HC) Women and Equalities Committee, 2016: 10–11), the case examples provided by interviewees were primarily tied to two main settings: 'the whole sexting thing that's going on in school'[153] where the 'youngest sexting incident'[154] related to primary 5 (or children at ages 8–9) or 'the care homes, [where] it is just as prevalent. It is normalised, really.'[155] There was a broad acknowledgement among education and youth work professionals that sexting and the social pressures surrounding it are 'affecting younger people all the time',[156] and where a minority of primary school children were engaged in sending 'what children call "tit pics" and "dick pics"'.[157] The preponderance of sexting cases, however, which were investigated by police involved peers who 'tended to be of a similar age range . . . where we are talking about a 15-, 16-year-old boy, and where the girl is also aged in or about that'.[158]

At the lower end of the spectrum, identifying a harmful intention within the context of sexting can often be 'quite subjective'[159] and it is 'where it becomes exploitative that it's difficult'.[160] This was seen as relating not only to professional understanding but also to the perceptions of children and young people within the digital culture where the use of social media or mobile phones has become an 'emotional filter' in distorting any cognitions of potential harm (see Chapter 4) and where the online medium 'offers an added protection'[161] for the abuser: 'for a lot of kids, our experience is that it is almost like the online world and the real world are two parallel worlds and they never impact on each other'[162] and where 'children don't actually make those connections between the risks they face in the online world or walking down the street'.[163] For other interviewees, this separation of virtual and real-world contexts within the social identity and personal relationships of children was similarly related to the lack of visual (Short et al., 1976;

[153] Interview 18, 14 June 2016, Senior Voluntary Sector Interviewee.
[154] Interview 29, 10 October 2016, Police Officer.
[155] Interview 32, 2 November 2016, Police Officer.
[156] Interview 21, 23 June 2016, Social Work Practitioner.
[157] Interview 3, 20 April 2016, Education Authority Professional.
[158] Interview 26, 1 August 2016, District Court Judge.
[159] Interview 7, 13 May 2015, Former Police Officer.
[160] Interview 11, 26 May 2016, Safeguarding Professional.
[161] Interview 30, 12 October 2016, Senior Prosecutor PPS.
[162] Interview 29, 10 October 2016, Police Officer.
[163] Interview 15, 3 June 2016, NSPCC Worker.

Wells and Mitchell, 2007) or social cues (Kiesler et al., 1984; Sproull and Kiesler, 1986), which real-world contexts afford (see Chapter 4). In particular, 'sexting is a sort of form of dating process ... it is so accessible now just to talk and there is no face-to-face embarrassment of rejection ... [so] it also allows them then to get very sexualised very quickly without embarrassment'[164]:

> It is extraordinary to think how the whole social media has allowed, if you like, people being able to sit in front of their computer and to think that it's OK to write a message or send a message and then it's sort of forgotten about. They are not having to deal with that confrontation, that face-to-face aspect to it. And it is easier to do that and not appreciate or understand the impact it is going to have on that person who receives that.[165]
>
> There are very few of them that we actually come across that are using any coercion on the Internet. It is usually they have exchanged, and because it is such a flat medium and they don't have the same cues, they do all the stuff in their heads.[166]
>
> Social media enables people to commit offences because it is so widely used, particularly by young people, and there's so many different methods and modes that they can do it now. And it is instant, they can get in contact very easily, they can get in contact graphically with people now. It gives them the privacy that they think they have, which isn't reality. And it offers them a form of security.[167]

In some of the more serious cases, however, sexting was often 'part and parcel of something else'.[168] This also indicates once more the potential crossover between online and offline forms of HSB: 'sometimes it can be that [sexting] as well as contact abuse. So they are not mutually exclusive.'[169] This was particularly the case for the police working in the area of child abuse: 'it is massive and it has a massive impact on what we investigate as well ... And I would say nearly every investigation that comes through has an element of social media or sexting through it.'[170] For those involved in assessment and therapeutic work with perpetrators, there were clear examples of a crossover between contact and non-contact forms of HSB: 'some of the kids that we have

164 Interview 31, 17 October 2016, Police Officer.
165 Interview 7, 13 May 2015, Former Police Officer.
166 Interview 5, 22 April 2016, NSPCC Professional.
167 Interview 2, 18 April 2016, Independent Forensic Psychologist.
168 Interview 1, 16 February 2016, Service Manager, HSS Trust.
169 Interview 8, 23 May 2016, Rowan SARC Professional.
170 Interview 31, 17 October 2016, Police Officer.

worked with where sexting has been an issue . . . a few of them have actually been known to us at an earlier stage because of hands on or contact abuse . . . there would be that curious aspect to it that leads on to something that they can't really control.'[171] This potential crossover was most clearly related to cases of CSE which had an organised element or those stemming from a broader social scene or partying culture: 'phones have always been an issue, because that's how they're contacted. I think it's all intertwined. Drugs, phones, CSE, absconding'[172]:

> So a girl that meets a guy at a party but actually they form a relationship online loosely. Then they meet up and it is about sexting a little bit and using that power and control element of CSE, to then control that young person and to get things for it in exchange. And about then having sex with friends and that kind of thing.[173]

Indeed, notwithstanding the fact that sexting is an online form of peer-based sexual behaviour, the harms stemming from virtual contacts among peers can spill over into the real world, leading, for example, to sexual bullying in offline social networks such as physical attacks at school (see BASW, 2016).[174]

In this respect, a final prominent theme was the often deeply impactful consequences of sexting for victims in situations where sexting is coercive. While there was broad acknowledgement among professionals that sexting was 'part of young people growing up and finding out about their own sexual expression',[175] there was also a general consensus that sexting 'can be very harmful, particularly damaging'.[176] As this same forensic psychologist acknowledged: 'I think we need to be really careful about saying sexting is the norm. Because actually the damage caused, harm caused to a person, puts it well out of the norm. It puts it into something that all professionals should be bothered about.'[177] As noted earlier, the harm generated by sexting can range from 'emotional and reputational damage' (Lee and Crofts, 2015: 454) to self-harm, bullying and suicidal ideation and

171 Interview 4, 21 April 2016, Child Care Centre Professional.
172 Interview 9, 25 May 2016, Youth support worker.
173 Interview 14, 2 June 2016, Sexual Health Nurse.
174 See e.g. research by Milnes et al. (2015: 4) on sexual bullying among young people across five European countries (Bulgaria, Italy, Latvia, Slovenia and the UK) which found that nearly three-quarters of young people had been subject to one or more forms of sexual bullying behaviour on more than one occasion, a prevalence rate which was similar across all five countries.
175 Interview 2, 18 April 2016, Independent Forensic Psychologist. 176 Ibid. 177 Ibid.

behaviour (Nixon, 2014; Bottino et al., 2015). Crofts et al. (2015: 68–70) delineate this spectrum and the potential longevity of the consequences as 'direct harm' and 'haunting harm'. The 'risks' associated with sexting often stem from the young person's loss of control over the image and how it is shared, resulting in forms of blackmail or bullying and emotional harm. In this sense, sexting may also be said to be a form of what has been termed 'performance crime' in that the 'visual record of the initial victimisation' amplifies the harm via a 'perverse' social process of 'shaming-the-victim' (Surette, 2015: 6).

This may be particularly the case where either the image 'goes viral ... and it is very hard to quell'[178] when 'their life just falls to absolute pieces'[179] or alternatively, where there is a threat of extortion or blackmail that 'if they don't give money or they don't agree to do other things, they are going to send a copy of it to their parents'.[180] It is the sending of images as a result of coercion, as identified earlier, together with the verbal, emotional and even physical abuse of the subject which might accompany wider distribution of the image that make sexting a form of cyberbullying (Shariff, 2015) and which amplify the risk of harm: 'whether you refer to it as cyberbullying or sexting ... it is about people using their phone or Facebook or any of the forms of social media ... to bully or to groom'[181]; 'cyberbullying ... it is very bitchy-type bullying. It is like stuff that happens in the playground only it is aggravated by the amount of people that join in.'[182] In such instances, the motivation may not always be sexual, but rather 'spiteful ... or just to get back at them',[183] but the effects, however, are no less harmful.

Other long-term harmful consequences for victims relate to loss of reputation or future career prospects (Crofts et al., 2015: 39). Several interviewees underlined the enhanced harmful consequences for victims of online or cyber abuse stemming from either the permanent capture of the image or the fact that there may be no clear perpetrator to blame:

> There would be a view that online abuse is not as bad as actual contact abuse. But I think what the research says for kids is that it is worse ... in

[178] Interview 31, 17 October 2016, Police Officer.
[179] Interview 21, 23 June 2016, Social Work Practitioner.
[180] Interview 8, 23 May 2016, Rowan SARC Professional.
[181] Interview 3, 20 April 2016, Education Authority Professional.
[182] Interview 31, 17 October 2016, Police Officer.
[183] Interview 32, 2 November 2016, Police Officer.

> terms of the future consequences ... The fact that you can't delete anything off the Internet for some is secondary re-abuse and re-traumatisation. And stuff coming back at a future stage is just horrific.[184]
>
> If you are asking them, who has caused the harm to you? The online stuff has a deeper trauma than if it was somebody who did it to them in their room. So if the fella met them down the street and assaulted them, at least I can talk about him assaulting you. Him touching you ... You have none of that in the online stuff, because they are very clear, a machine doesn't touch them.[185]

Furthermore, the personal consequences tied to 'loss of reputation' also have a potential longer-term impact recognised by professionals, but usually not by children and young people: 'it's the inability to get a job, get a university place, because of what's put online. Because ... again they think the likes of some of these apps that they put photographs on ... oh well they are only on for five seconds and that's it. They genuinely don't understand that once you upload something, it is there.'[186]

Moreover, the further dissemination of images among peers, even if the initial image was sent on a seemingly consensual basis, may result in what one police officer termed a 'ripple effect'[187] and a wider proliferation of harmful consequences beyond the immediate victim. In this vein, as discussed further in the next chapter, children who produce, distribute or possess 'indecent' digital images may de facto infringe legal norms in the form of legislation governing child pornography (see generally, Karaian, 2012, 2014; Crofts and Lee, 2013). At the same time, however, sexting raises questions about privacy and consent in virtual settings (Gillespie, 2013; Hasinoff, 2015) where there may also be evidential difficulties related to the determination of harmful intent as well as a legitimate and unequivocal victim (see Chapter 7).

PEER-BASED CHILD SEXUAL EXPLOITATION: 'LINE UPS'

Moving from the private to the public domain, harmful sexual or exploitative behaviour also stems from peer-based relationships in localised, community settings. In common with institutional and Internet-based forms of peer-to-peer abuse, peer-based sexual

[184] Interview 15, 3 June 2016, NSPCC Worker.
[185] Interview 16, 6 June 2016, Social Work Consultant.
[186] Interview 31, 17 October 2016, Police Officer.
[187] Interview 29, 10 October 2016, Police Officer.

behaviour within the context of CSE is a derivative of the dominant adult-child paradigm. As outlined in the Chapter 1, there have been a number of high-profile cases and related inquiries in England and Wales (see e.g. Berelowitz, 2012, 2013, 2015) involving multiple perpetrators working in groups, grooming primarily female adolescents into a range of sexually exploitative situations from organised/networked exploitation to abuse through prostitution or pornography or 'internal' or 'domestic trafficking' (see generally, Chase and Statham, 2005; see also Barnardo's, 2009: 16, 2011: 6).

It was noted in Chapter 1 that the peer-based dimensions of such cases present as particularly complex and challenging for professionals along two core fronts: one is the perception of young girls as being in a 'relationship' with their abusers, who may only be a few years older than them (Montgomery-Devlin, 2008: 392; Barnardo's, 2011: 6; Beckett, 2011: 28), and the other is the role of young people, typically girls, in recruiting other young victims into exploitative networks or situations (Montgomery-Devlin, 2008: 393; CEOP, 2011: 11; Barnardo's, 2012: 71; Ost and Mooney, 2013: 432; Appleton, 2014: 156). In neither case do the female recruiters or those they recruit regard themselves as 'victims' or as having been 'victimised' (Melrose, 2013: 162). This is also referred to variously as 'survival consent' where consent is given in exchange for money or gifts or out of fear of the consequences or 'coerced consent' where the child or young person is manipulated into consenting to sexual activity (Pearce, 2013b: 53).

Previous empirical research (see especially, Beckett, 2011) and an independent inquiry into CSE in Northern Ireland (Marshall, 2014) has demonstrated the existence of these phenomena. Many of the interviewees in the present study confirmed the continued prevalence of these forms of peer-based sexual behaviours which often have an organised element linked to drugs and trafficking and involving individuals with ties to paramilitary organisations (see also Marshall, 2014: 11). While some professionals identified this as a continuing element of the legacy of the Northern Ireland conflict,[188] others were more reticent to pinpoint this as a specific issue and framed the problem within the broader context of powerful factions within local communities, which was not unique to Northern Ireland:

[188] For a contemporary critical overview of the historical, legal and cultural dimensions of the Northern Ireland conflict, see McAlinden and Dwyer (2015).

> There's still an element of it or people who would have been associated with paramilitaries. So I think it would be naïve of us not to recognise that that is still with us . . . So when people are being raped within their communities, it is very difficult for them to come forward. They might come forward for emergency contraception or to make sure they haven't got an STI. Those people will never come forward to make a complaint to the police, because they know that there is a group of people who are untouchable in our society. So I think that needs to be recognised.[189]
>
> People will use power over young people whether that is perceived or real power. You know you might have someone say, I am connected, I am in whatever group it is. You know, it is perceived power and control. I don't believe that that is unique to Northern Ireland or believe that it is unique to anywhere. There are always going to be people to take advantage of more vulnerable people, whether that is children or whether that is adults.[190]

For others, an added cultural dimension of CSE within Northern Ireland was Eastern European culture where 'sexual abuse and prostitution' are 'quite normalised'. A police officer explained in relation to their 'Master list' of confirmed or suspected cases of children and young people at risk of CSE:

> I think . . . when we talk about paramilitary, we also have to talk about the Eastern European culture of their expectations of what sex is. We have a few Eastern European girls on our list and there are a lot of links. And I think there is a lot more going on there than we know because of their cultural background.[191]

Indeed, ethnic minorities account for a growing proportion of the Northern Ireland population.[192] This brings with it added dimensions relating to differing social norms and cultural practices which may impact, for example, efforts to engage children and young people via schools and within local communities (see further Chapter 8).

As discussed earlier, within professional discourses, the term 'CSE' has often been associated with victimhood and predominantly female victims, whereas 'HSB' is typically seen as the preserve of 'offending'

189 Interview 8, 23 May 2016, Rowan SARC Professional.

190 Interview 27, 3 August 2016, Senior Social Work Practitioner.

191 Interview 31, 17 October 2016, Police Officer.

192 At the last census in 2011, 1.8 per cent (32,400) of the usually resident population of Northern Ireland belonged to minority ethnic groups, a figure which was more than double the proportion in 2001 (0.8 per cent): see 2011 Census available at www.nisra.gov.uk/Census/key_stats_bulletin_2011.pdf. Such figures are likely to have increased in the intervening six years with the free movement of persons within the European Union.

behaviour by males (see also Roesch-Marsh, 2014). The reality, however, is far more complex and enmeshed than some traditional policy and academic discourses might suggest. In this respect, unpublished and ongoing research by Carol Carson (2016)[193] has expounded a continuum of CSE which begins with 'poor relationship choices' and 'normative' peer behaviours (such as sexting); progressing to the 'exchange' of sexual behaviours among their immediate peer group; and then to more 'risky' sexual behaviours in groups, situations or relationships beyond their peer group where their ability to risk assess is lowered or compromised and which can lead in turn to more organised and systemic forms of CSE via networks and trafficking. In essence, therefore, peer-based forms of sexual exploitation which stem from normative peer relationships can be a catalyst for more serious and engrained forms of CSE involving adult perpetrators and may also cross the line into the commission of harmful sexual behaviours among peers. The significance of Carson's continuum and the blurring of the boundaries between CSE and HSB is that by 'changing the filter'[194] or with 'only a tiny tweak',[195] the sexualised behaviour of children and young people may be placed in either category.

As noted in Chapter 4, the literature establishes that the emergence of a gang (Beckett et al., 2012, 2013, 2014), or partying culture (Melrose, 2013) may encourage children and young people to exchange 'sex for popularity' (Melrose, 2013: 162; see generally, Pitts, 2008; Gover et al., 2009; Firmin, 2011; Beckett et al., 2013). This research, which was carried out predominantly within the context of England and Wales, has demonstrated the existence of CSE among peers against the backdrop of a formalised 'gang culture' where the sexual behaviours and acts were often part of a 'rite of passage' or gang rituals or initiation. One interviewee who had worked in both England and Wales and Northern Ireland explained as follows:

> As far as gang culture goes, [it] is more well known and practiced in England … the gangs would be the people who rule certain areas, where … there would be initiation ceremonies where young people would be recruited and have to perform sexual acts to actually be part of a gang. And then once they are in the gang, have to maintain those sexual acts to maintain their position within gangs.[196]

[193] Presented to the author for citation in the course of fieldwork for this study.

[194] Interview 6, 25 April 2016, Independent Safeguarding Consultant. [195] Ibid.

[196] Interview 2, 18 April 2016, Independent Forensic Psychologist. Note, this distinction maps broadly on to gang and group forms of CSE as set out by the Office of the Children's

Notwithstanding the fact that Northern Ireland does not have the same type of 'street gang culture' (Marshall, 2014: 11) as identified in the various reports by the Office of the Children's Commissioner in England (see Berelowitz, 2012, 2013, 2015), a new and emergent form of group-based CSE among peers was highlighted by a small number of interviewees in the form of 'line-ups'. Knowledge of this form of CSE was shared by those involved in youth work or therapeutic or intervention services with children and young people, particularly within the context of 'an assault of another young person in a peer-type situation in the community, maybe in a park . . . [where] usually that's boys against girls'[197] and where 'it's more multiple numbers . . . being abused at one time'[198]:

> There's loads of examples about young people just turning up, and the line ups that would take place. A girl is brought to give blow jobs to however many boys down the line. But then there's the kind of duality of perpetrator-victim, because some of those boys are standing in that line absolutely petrified, not wanting to be there, but have to kind of go through with letting someone give them a blow job, in case they will get beaten up by the leader or whoever has orchestrated the event.[199]
>
> Literally they are lined up in a park and so girls are either anally raped or boys are . . . and then the boy is told he is one of the perpetrators. So a young man can be equally as under pressure to be one of those perpetrators, because of the group that they are in . . . So not only do you get the girls who are being abused, but as a rite of passage and initiation that can also happen to a young man.[200]

Notwithstanding the fact that gang and group forms of CSE are usually differentiated, there is also a performative aspect to group-based CSE among adolescents, across both school settings as well as 'on the streets', as there is with gang-based contexts more broadly (see e.g. Garot, 2010). Within such contexts, there are also difficulties relating to children and young people recognising risks which stem from within their preexisting relationships and their immediate peer group (see further Chapter 4). Moreover, such instances of CSE involving multiple children and young people within a group setting cross the gender

Commissioner, where the former mode of association has a broader identity and underlying purpose beyond sexual activity (Berelowitz, 2012: 10).

197 Interview 24, 6 July 2016, Independent Treatment Professional.

198 Interview 16, 6 June 2016, Social Work Consultant.

199 Interview 21, 23 June 2016, Social Work Practitioner.

200 Interview 11, 26 May 2016, Safeguarding Professional.

divide and blur the lines between agency/responsibility and coercion and of victim and offender identities. As discussed further in the next chapter, however, legal and policy discourses on peer forms of abuse continue to be shaped by 'a coercive dyad' which 'juxtapose[s] an essentially passive victim with a predatory perpetrator' (Pitts, 2013: 25).

PARTYING CULTURE: 'CHEMSEX PARTIES'

A further exemplar of CSE in a group-based context is what has become known as the 'party house model' in which young people are provided with alcohol or drugs which must later 'be paid for' with sex, including with the initial 'partner's friends or associates' (Beckett, 2011: 2; Marshall, 2014: 11). In addition, however, to adult-child forms of CSE, harmful sexual or exploitative behaviour among peers also stems from twenty-first-century cultural norms and social practices (see e.g. Melrose, 2013) as a discrete form of peer-based exploitation or abuse among children and young people. Most notably perhaps, the phenomenon of sexual victimisation on college campuses, albeit with a slightly older population of young adults, also demonstrates the links between alcohol, drugs and 'party rape' (Armstrong et al., 2006; Daigle et al., 2015) or 'acquaintance rape' (Berkowitz, 1992). In this respect, the American fraternity culture in particular (Boswell and Spade, 1996; Schwartz and Nogrady, 1996) has become a focal point for male sexual aggression (Schwartz et al., 2001; Carr and Van Deusen, 2004) and instances of female sexual victimisation.[201]

It will be remembered from the discussion of gang or partying culture in Chapter 4 that this phenomenon is both a causative factor underlying the contemporary emergence of HSB by children and young people as well as a form of harmful sexual or exploitative behaviour in and of itself. Several interviewees recounted examples of potentially harmful sexual behaviour within the context of the risky environment of a party culture where sexualised risky behaviours are simply counted

[201] Over the period 1995–2013, American females ages 18 to 24 had higher rates of sexual victimisation compared to all other age groups with lower levels of reporting among college students (20 per cent) compared to non-students (32 per cent) (see Sinozich and Langton, 2014). See also more recently, a study based on a survey of 3,097 students at Queen's University Belfast (representing 12.5 per cent of the QUB student population) which found significant levels of non-consensual sexual experiences: e.g. 33.5 per cent experienced unwanted sexual touching and 5.5 per cent experienced at least one episode of non-consensual sexual penetration (SCORE, 2017).

as 'banter' among children and young people. One youth worker recalled the following:

> About six years ago I was working ... in a children's home and the young people were designing T-shirts and they wanted to write GHB on a T-shirt and I had no idea what that meant ... But it was 'Get Her Bucked'. And this was for their 14-year-old friend who was a virgin ... And they were planning to give her the date rape drug ... And go out for a night. And put this T-shirt on her, so basically she was live bait then, for anybody who wanted ... They were very clear they were doing it 'for the bant', was exactly what they said. It was all 'for the bant'.[202]

In this vein, one of the novel and emerging forms of potentially harmful sexual behaviour which takes place against the backdrop of the partying culture is the advent of what are known as 'chemsex parties', primarily involving young but also older gay men (see Wharton, 2017). These are defined as 'using chemical ... psychoactive drugs to enhance sexual experience. But they could be going on benders for 72 hours at the weekend with multiple sexual partners, whilst on these drugs. So the risks for STIs and HIV are huge ... [and] partner identification becomes very difficult.'[203] Not surprisingly, as the former quote attests, these sexualised risks were most pertinent for health professionals: 'Young people are taking highs on a Friday night and then coming into sexual health clinics on Monday morning with needles in their arm and saying, basically, I don't know where I was or what happened to me at the weekend.'[204] As another health professional explained, this form of peer-based sexual behaviour has potentially wide-reaching and harmful consequences for young people:

> The whole party scenario, like chemsex parties ... It's using drugs to be able to party longer, like for the whole weekend ... but that's within a party, friendship culture. And any of the young people that I have worked with that I would be worried about being at risk ... I don't know them, but yet what they are telling me this is a friend, this is consensual, all of those things. Yet I know that there are real concerns about their sexual health and about ... are they being manipulated.[205]

Such contexts also blur the boundaries around consent and coercion as well as risk of harm (see further Chapter 7). As noted in Chapter 4, in

[202] Interview 21, 23 June 2016, Social Work Practitioner. 'Bant' is short for 'banter', meaning the good-humoured exchange of playful or teasing remarks.
[203] Interview 12, 26 May 2016, Nurse Consultant in Sexual Health.
[204] Interview 31, 17 October 2016, Police Officer.
[205] Interview 14, 2 June 2016, Sexual Health Nurse.

such circumstances, young people may not consider themselves as being at risk or as a victim of sexual exploitation, but rather, from their perspective, they are 'just having a good time' (Melrose, 2013: 162).

Moreover, within such settings, young people appear to construct risk in terms of a very narrow range of potentially problematic or harmful consequences related principally to an unplanned pregnancy or contracting a sexually transmitted infection. This was evidenced in the views of professionals who relayed their experiences of directly engaging with young people in relation to sexual health and issues surrounding consent:

> The biggest risk for them is still really, teenage pregnancy ... And I mean even the young people's understanding of what sexual activity is. Because we had a whole school believe that the age of consent referred to intercourse, vaginal or anal, and everything else was good to go. So, you know, 14 and 15-year-olds saying to us, no, sexual activity, no, no. But I have given that boy three blow jobs at a party. Because in her head that was not sexual activity. That was just normal behaviour. Normal sexualised behaviour.[206]
>
> A lot of the young girls considered sex to be penis in the vagina. But if they were having anal sex, which they were doing quite a lot because you can't get pregnant, and because it looks really good and all the boys like it because they watch porn. Or oral sex, you can do that with anybody. But it is not sex ... So are they only going to be reporting things then that square with this very narrow sense of what sex is? And if that is not sex then, if they are queueing up and being told to give 10 boys in front of them a blow job or else something will happen or whatever it is, then do they do it and don't see that as abusive?[207]

A discernible tension, therefore, harks back to the traditional construction of the risks underpinning adolescent romantic relationships and the distinct nature of childhood and adulthood (Brownlie, 2001: 523–24; Oakley, 2015: 83) (Chapter 3) on the one hand, and the increasing pressure to behave in 'adultified ways' (Dines, 2008; Papadopoulos, 2010: 6) on the other. The latter factor is generated and sustained by the pervasive culture of 'transient sex' (Chapter 4), which brings with it a host of additional risks relating to the normalisation of potentially harmful sexual behaviour and the confusion between the bounds of childhood, agency and consent. These broad arguments also underscore the need to engage children and young

[206] Interview 29, 10 October 2016, Police Officer.
[207] Interview 8, 23 May 2016, Rowan SARC Professional.

people in educative discourses around the meaning of sexual consent (see further Chapter 8).

CONCLUSION

This chapter set out to critically examine the nature and extent of peer-to-peer harmful sexual and exploitative behaviours across a range of interpersonal and social contexts. In brief, the cases coming to the attention of the justice system or therapeutic intervention may involve younger children as well as adolescents and females as well as males as perpetrators and victims. The range of behaviours covers those at the most serious end of the spectrum such as rape and sexual activity with a child and which clearly constitute criminal offences. It also includes behaviours which may manifest as a result of wider social and sexual pressures such as sexual activity while under the influence of alcohol or drugs; pressure to have sex with multiple partners (line-ups); or to record, send or distribute sexual images or videos (sexting).

The picture which emerges of children and young people as potentially risky is multifarious and highly complex in which the victim-offender divide in terms of who may be considered at risk rather than being risky is not always an easy determination to make. As I have argued previously, 'what is harmful . . . is neither simple nor intuitive; nor is it strictly objective' (Ashurst and McAlinden, 2015: 376). Indeed, as one interviewee put it, 'harm is a lot more complex and wide ranging than we give credit for at the moment'[208] because in essence the legal system is looking for 'cause and effect'[209] in terms of establishing the motivations of the perpetrator and any injuries or consequences for the individual victim.

Based on these insights and to try to make sense of some of the complexities surrounding peer-based forms of harmful sexual or exploitative behaviours, the chapter expounded a taxonomy of peer-based abuse which differentiated types of sexual behaviour among peers along a continuum: peer-based relationships, peer-based recruitment and peer-based risk. While most forms of HSB or CSE begin from within the confines of an interpersonal relationship, a range of contextual risk factors can combine to change the initial motivation of the perpetrator leading to augmented risk and ultimately victimisation in a range of potentially harmful or sexually exploitative circumstances.

[208] Interview 2, 18 April 2016, Independent Forensic Psychologist. [209] Ibid.

Moreover, while this chapter has attempted to illustrate this typology via an analysis of the main forms of harmful sexual or exploitative behaviour among peers, neat categorisations are not always possible. In this vein, there are instances of potential crossover between the various forms of abuse, from interpersonal or private to more public, social or organisational settings as 'increasingly, youthful practices commute across online and offline borders' (Ringrose et al., 2012: 15) (see also Chapter 4). As I have argued previously, sexting, for example, 'can best be judged in light of its overall purpose in … facilitating abusive behaviour to determine whether or how it contributes to exploitation or harm' (Ashurst and McAlinden, 2015: 380). Sexting in this regard presents as one of the most complex and ambiguous forms of CSE in essence because of the variety of forms it may take, encompassing normative as well as potentially harmful sexual behaviour, and consensual as well as non-consensual activity.

Moving to the next and penultimate chapter, the nuances and complexities surrounding peer-based sexual behaviours are no less complex when extended into legal and societal domains. In the main, some of the principal difficulties and ambiguities underlying the precise scope of peer-based abuse as highlighted in this chapter – in terms of identifying harmful *intention* on the part of abusers, evidencing harmful *consequences* and impact on individual victims, separating out victims from perpetrators in complex forms of HSB or CSE and establishing a clear threshold for risk – also pervade legal, societal and professional responses to risk.

7

LEGAL AND SOCIETAL RESPONSES TO 'RISK'

> It is legislation written by adults for adults. And you have to think, what consideration when writing that legislation has there been in terms of how children are so different now to perhaps we were twenty, thirty years ago? The influences that children experience … And you know, were they consulted, by the way, when we developed this legislation? For all intents and purposes, we could actually find ourselves in a situation where we are criminalising 11-, 12- and 13-year-olds for behaviour that would otherwise be seen as them experimenting.[1]

This chapter aims to examine legal and societal responses to risk concerning harmful sexual or exploitative behaviour by children and young people. It was noted in the previous chapter that a small number of cases of harmful sexual behaviour (HSB) by children and young people enter the youth justice system annually and that 'not that many cases have actually gone through court'.[2] As might be expected, those that do are typically at the higher end of the spectrum such as sexual assault of a child under age 13,[3] sexual activity with a child under age 13[4] and making/distributing indecent images of children.[5] It is not the intention of this chapter to focus on those cases or behaviours which clearly constitute a sexual offence against children under the substantive criminal

[1] Interview 7, 13 May 2015, Former Police Officer.

[2] Interview 32, 2 November 2016, Police Officer.

[3] See the Sexual Offences (NI) Order 2008, art 14; see also arts 12–13. [4] Ibid., art 15.

[5] See the Protection of Children (NI) Order 1978, art 3(1), as amended by the Sexual Offences (NI) Order 2008, art 42, which now extends protection to those under age 18. The term 'photograph' was later extended to include 'pseudo-photographs' (see s84(2)(a)(ii) of the Criminal Justice and Public Order Act 1994).

law. Rather, in keeping with the overall purpose of this book and the overarching rubric of 'risk', the emphasis is predominantly on the more legally and socially contentious aspects of potentially harmful sexual or exploitative behaviour among peers, such as sexting or allegations of a contact sexual offence within preexisting adolescent relationships. Within this broader context, the chapter considers the normative difficulties and pragmatic challenges which are intrinsic to legal and societal responses to capturing and managing peer-based sexual risks among peers.

Many of the principal themes and debates concerning children who display HSB, as highlighted in the earlier chapters, also appear to pervade public and official discourses on risk at the level of praxis. These relate to a 'deep' professional and societal 'ambivalence' (Brooks, 2006: 16, citing Professor Al-Aynsley Green, 2005) towards children who display HSB which is underpinned by an ideological construction of children and childhood as inviolable and inherently innocent (Kitzinger, 1988: 79; Zelizer, 1994; Furedi, 2013: 45); a 'child panic' (Brooks, 2006: 16) around practices such as sexting where responses are characterised by 'extreme positions' (Conte, 1994: 224), oscillating between 'cultural disassociation' (Olafson et al., 1993: 7) or 'denial' (Summit, 1988; see generally, Cohen, 2001) to abhorrence; the 'culture of confusion' surrounding the demarcation of normative and harmful sexual behaviour among children and young people, and in particular the obfuscation of coercion and consent in a culturally sexualised and digital age which has been scaffolded by legal and policy frameworks; and the difficulties which the criminal justice system, professionals as well as the wider society, face in apportioning 'blame' and in accommodating 'deviant' children or 'victims' who are not 'completely innocent' (Von Hentig, 1948; Mendelsohn, 1956) within their often antiquated normative frameworks. The chapter is divided into two broad parts which consider these themes primarily in relation to legislative and policy responses, as well as societal and familial responses to peer-based risks.

LEGISLATIVE AND POLICY RESPONSES

A number of core themes emerged from the primary data. These relate to the (de)criminalisation of sexting, age-based anomalies within legislative frameworks, evidential and practical difficulties in investigating and prosecuting cases and system tensions which impact expediency and parity within the legal process.

The (De)Criminalisation of Sexting

England and Wales[6] and, more recently, Northern Ireland[7] have introduced the offence of 'disclosing private sexual photographs or films with the intent to cause distress'. This offence, known colloquially as 'revenge pornography', effectively criminalises the disclosure of indecent images without the subject's consent. Although the introduction of this legislation has been welcomed as protecting victims from 'imaged-based sexual abuse' (McGlynn and Rackley, 2017; see also Gillespie, 2015), it has been criticised as 'prurient' in 'fusing … the erotic and the punitive' (Dymock, 2016: 209). The age of the parties is not specified, which means that a young person disclosing a picture of a similarly aged 'partner' to a friend of a similar age may also be committing an offence. Sexting is also potentially caught by legislation governing child pornography which criminalises the creation, possession and distribution of indecent images of children under age 18.[8]

In Canada, the police have utilised a discretionary approach to sexting, or non-consensual intimate image sharing among youth which also incorporates 'scare tactics' and educative responses (Dodge and Spencer, 2017). Within other jurisdictions, however, including Australia[9] (Albury et al., 2013; Lee et al., 2013; Salter, 2013; Crofts et al., 2015) and especially the United States[10] (Karaian, 2012; Thompson, 2014; Hasinoff, 2015), there has been an overzealous approach by law enforcement to prosecuting teen sexting under federal

[6] See the Criminal Justice and Courts Act 2015, s 33.

[7] See the Justice (NI) Act 2016, art 51.

[8] See note 5. Following international instruments on child pornography and child sexual exploitation (e.g. Council of Europe Convention on the Protection of Children against Sexual Exploitation and Abuse (the 'Lanzarote Convention'), 25 October 2007, CETS No 201; The United Nations Convention on the Rights of the Child, Optional Protocol on the Rights of the Child on the Sale of Children, Child Prostitution and Child Pornography, A/RES/54/263, 25 May 2000), many countries have enacted laws criminalising sexual images of a child as child pornography.

[9] See e.g. federal legislation governing 'telecommunications offences': Criminal Code Act 1995 (Cth), Ch. 10 – Division 474 – Subdivision D – 'Offences relating to Use of Carriage Service for Child Pornography Material or Child Abuse Material'. See also *DPP* v. *Eades* [2009] NSWC 1352. The Parliament of Victoria Law Reform Committee *Inquiry into Sexting* recommended that minors and young adults should have a defence to child pornography offences, provided that they are able to engage in lawful sexual activity with the person depicted in an image, and that they are not more than two years older than any minor depicted in that image (Law Reform Committee, 2013: 145). This was later enacted within the Crimes Amendment (Sexual Offences and Other Matters) Act 2014 (Vic), s 8, inserting s 70AAA into the Crimes Act 1958 (Vic).

[10] See e.g. 18 U.S.C.A. § 2251. See also *A.H.* v. *State*, 949 So. 2d 234, 235 (Fla. Dist. Ct. App. 2007); *State* v. *Canal*, 773 N.W.2d 528, 532 (Iowa 2009). For a detailed discussion, see Shariff (2015: 75–102).

and state legislation governing child pornography until relatively recently. In some states, such as Florida,[11] Utah[12] and Georgia,[13] this can also be treated as a felony offence rather than a misdemeanour. For example, in North Carolina, a 17-year-old high school quarterback and his 16-year-old girlfriend faced felony charges as adults for sending sexually explicit photos of minors after exchanging naked images of each other.[14] As some commentators have argued, adolescent sexting provokes 'panic' and 'is often seen as a technological, legal, sexual, and moral crisis' (Hasinoff, 2015: 1) which conflates consensual sexual behaviours among adolescent peers with sexual harm. Such responses, however, vary across states. A 2013 US study on sexting and the decision to prosecute found that 36 per cent of state prosecutors who had handled a teen sexting case had filed charges where most were for felonies of producing child pornography (Walsh et al., 2013). Similar concerns about variations in state practices have also been raised in Australia (Tyson et al., 2012). Indeed, such criticisms are perhaps symptomatic of broader structuralist concerns, voiced by several interviewees in the present study which point to arbitrary and inconsistent decision-making by police and prosecutors in cases of HSB: 'it is very inconsistent and with no rhyme or reason'[15]; 'there is nothing scientific about it'[16]; 'there is no equity in the systems that young people go into'[17]; and where 'the distinction between people who didn't get convictions and somebody that did get convictions seemed very mercurial.'[18]

Similarly, in England and Wales, until relatively recently, police have gone down the route of criminalising children and young people for sexting as 'self-produced child pornography' (Becker and Marcum, 2015: 142).[19] Following the Bichard Inquiry,[20] Home Office counting

[11] Fla. Stat. Ann. § 847.0141. [12] Utah Code Ann. § 76–10-1206.

[13] Ga. Code Ann. § 16–12-100.

[14] K. McLaughlin, 'High School Quarterback and His Girlfriend Both CHARGED by Cops for Privately Sharing Nude Photos of Themselves', *Mail Online*, 5 September 2015. Note that the age of consent varies across the United States where it is 16 in 29 states, 17 in 7 states and 18 in 14 states (see Koon-Magnin, 2015).

[15] Interview 1, 16 February 2016, Service Manager, HSS Trust.

[16] Interview 17, 7 June 2016, Independent, former Youth Justice Professional.

[17] Interview 2, 18 April 2016, Independent Forensic Psychologist.

[18] Interview 15, 3 June 2016, NSPCC Worker.

[19] See the Protection of Children Act 1978, s1(1), as amended by the Sexual Offences Act 2003, s 45.

[20] The Bichard Inquiry, into the 'Soham murders' of Holly Wells and Jessica Chapman by Ian Huntley in 2002, found 'systemic and corporate failures' (Bichard, 2004: para 8) in the management of police intelligence systems which led to Huntley being cleared to work in Soham Primary School.

rules require police to record such incidents as a 'crime' once they are reported even if the decision is eventually taken for non-prosecution.[21] Figures from South Wales Police for 2015, for example, showed that 65 children under age 18 were investigated over the past two years, 40 girls and 25 boys, with ages ranging from 8 to 17 and a median age of 14. Most children investigated were simply 'advised accordingly', some were referred to social services or made to complete a restorative youth conference,[22] with only three children receiving a youth caution after admitting a criminal offence.[23] Northumbria Police held 18 investigations into sexting during 2014 where two pre-teen boys, ages 10 and 12, were cautioned for sending explicit pictures of themselves to 11-year-old girls.[24] A boy age 14 was added to the Greater Manchester Police intelligence database for the crime of 'making and distributing an indecent image of a child' after sexting a female classmate a naked image of himself via Snapchat who then shared it with others.[25] Although the boy was not charged with any crime, the file remains active for a minimum of 10 years and may be disclosed under an advanced Disclosure and Barring Service (DBS) check in the event he applies to work with children.[26] Moreover, if he were an adult, he would have been afforded the status of being a 'victim' of 'revenge pornography'[27] rather than a perpetrator of 'child pornography' as the indecent images of him were shared without his consent. Those cases which are recorded as a 'crime' also carry with them further legal

[21] See now 'Outcome 21': Home Office Counting Rules, issued January 2016, which allows the police to record a crime as having happened but for no formal criminal justice action to be taken if it is not considered to be in the public interest: www.gov.uk/government/publications/counting-rules-for-recorded-crime. See also the guidance issued by the Association of Chief Police Officers of England and Wales and Northern Ireland on 'Young People Who Post Self-Taken Indecent Images' which advocates broadly non-prosecution or non-criminalisation within an overall approach of safeguarding: www.ceop.police.uk/Documents/ceopdocs/externaldocs/ACPO_Lead_position_on_Self_Taken_Images.pdf.

[22] See Chapter 3, note 19, for details on the restorative reforms to the legal framework governing youth justice.

[23] See e.g. M. Fricker, 'Police Reveal Children as Young as EIGHT are "Sexting" Explicit Images to Each Other', *Mirror*, 30 August 2015.

[24] A. Martin, 'Sexting Could Give You Police Record for Life, Children Warned', *Daily Mail*, 5 September 2015.

[25] See note 19. See H. Lewis, 'Why a Police Record for Sexting Teen?' *The Guardian*, 6 September 2015.

[26] See the Protection of Freedoms Act 2012, Part 5, Ch. 3 which establishes the DBS for England and Wales. In Northern Ireland, such criminal record checks are undertaken by AccessNI under the Safeguarding Vulnerable Groups Order (NI) 2007 as amended by the Protection of Freedoms Act 2012, sched 7.

[27] See note 6.

consequences for those deemed 'offenders' in terms of the possibility of being subject to the sex offender notification requirements ('the sex offenders' register') (see Wolak and Finkelhor, 2011: 2; Crofts et al., 2015: 39).[28] Police figures are likely to only be the 'tip of the iceberg' given the normalisation of sexting within adolescent relationships and the inadvertent and ongoing risks which children may take in virtual contexts in particular (see Chapter 4).

As documented in Part I of the book, the criminalisation of sexting 'emanates from a specific value base' encompassing 'the abhorrence of child pornography, the threat of the paedophile, and the angers of unregulated sexuality' (Lee et al., 2013: 44). More specifically, several noteworthy paradoxes underlie this approach. The first is that legislation designed to protect children from 'an offender who is often imagined to be a predatory, middle-aged white man' (Hasinoff, 2015: 149) (see Chapter 2) is used to frame the legal response to children and young people who display potentially harmful sexual behaviour. The second relates to the 'pre-existing conceptualisations of abuse' (Firmin, 2013: 38) underlying child protection frameworks within the United Kingdom and internationally which have centred on the protection of younger children in familial or quasi-intra-familial contexts (see also Chapter 2), but which are ill suited as protection strategies for adolescents negotiating emerging adulthood and experiencing exploitation or abuse outside the home (see generally, Pearce, 2017: 171–72). Third, a criminal response to consensual forms of sexting is counter-intuitive to managing risk, detracting attention and resources from more serious forms of HSB among children and young people, as well as risks posed by adults to children in both real-world and virtual settings. Fourth, the line between victim and perpetrator becomes blurred as technically the subject of the image may be both a victim and a creator, possessor or distributor of child pornography. In this respect, the application of the indecent images legislation to sexting scenarios, and the irony of criminalising children via laws designed to protect them, has aptly been described as putting 'a square peg in a round hole' (Shariff, 2015: 19).

[28] Originally enacted by the Sex Offenders Act 1997, Part I, and subsequently replaced by an enhanced framework under the Sexual Offences Act 2003, Part 2. For those under age 18, the duration of the notification requirement is generally halved unless the notification period is indefinite: see the Sexual Offences Act 2003, s 82. These provisions also extend to Northern Ireland.

In Northern Ireland, however, a punitive stance has not found the same traction.[29] Instead, there has been a conscious 'tilt towards not criminalising children who are experimenting when there's nothing else'[30] within the context of consenting, albeit under-age, romantic or sexual relationships: 'it used to be the case where it was very black and white. You have made, processed and sent an indecent image and we are going to interview you and all these huge consequences'[31]; and 'there was a huge rash of cases' where two young people were exchanging indecent images 'in a relationship, where there was no coercion and anything like that . . . I don't think police are actually submitting as many of them now.'[32] This is also borne out by Public Prosecution Service (PPS) data on sexting cases. During the approximately two-year period between 1 March 2013 and 31 March 2015, of the 75 case decisions made on prosecution, 66 (88 per cent) were for non-prosecution with only one prosecution (1 per cent) and 8 (11 per cent) for diversionary or youth caution.[33]

Several police officers and legal professionals explained how 'there are very few prosecutions of sexting'[34] in the absence of potentially aggravating factors including the commission of a more serious contact sexual offence or the wider distribution of the image[35]:

> We don't become involved, particularly if it is known that they are both children . . . If there is a small age gap, essentially two years, they don't tend to prosecute . . . By the letter of the law, the person sending the message is also committing a criminal offence. Really the law is there to protect them, so we recognise that and we don't deal with them as suspects . . . I think we are all in agreement upstairs. How can you criminalise the person? Both parties really.[36]

29 The Safeguarding Board for Northern Ireland (SBNI) and the Police Service of Northern Ireland (PSNI) issued a guide for practitioners and the public on 'Sexting and the Law' in 2015 which differentiates a range of scenarios governing sexually explicit text/chat or pictures/images between children, between adults and children and between adults: www.psni.police.uk/contentassets/fae34aff4af6409e9ad393130043ec55/sexting__the_law_leaflet_trifold.pdf. Similarly, the National Police Chiefs Council (NPCC) in 2016 produced a briefing note on 'Police Action in Response to Youth Produced Sexual Imagery (Sexting)': www.college.police.uk/News/College-news/Documents/Police_action_in_response_to_sexting__briefing_(003).pdf.

30 Interview 30, 12 October 2016, Senior Prosecutor PPS.

31 Interview 31, 17 October 2016, Police Officer.

32 Interview 30, 12 October 2016, Senior Prosecutor PPS.

33 See 'NI: Child Protection Expert Backs Change in Indecent Images Law', *Irish Legal News*, 19 January 2016.

34 Interview 30, 12 October 2016, Senior Prosecutor PPS.

35 See the Protection of Children (NI) Order 1978, art 3(1)(b).

36 Interview 32, 2 November 2016, Police Officer.

> I can think of two cases ... It's not something that we see often ... And as I say, it's not because I believe it is not happening. It is just whether it has been reported or what's happening there ... I'm not quite sure. But we only get a very small number coming through.[37]
>
> What we will encourage is that you act appropriately. And the built-in defence in the legislation talks about acting appropriately and that's about getting it to someone who is in a position to do something about it. Or delete it off your phone ... Sometimes if it is contained within a class ... we endeavour just to have the image deleted from the source and let sleeping dogs lie, because how far do you go? Do you end up bringing in a whole classroom or a whole year group or a whole school?[38]

As the latter quote attests, resource implications and the sheer volume of potential cases of sexting which might amount to technical infringement of the Protection of Children (NI) Order 1978 are pertinent factors which mitigate against a criminal response: 'I do think that the police and Public Prosecution Service have made significant inroads into the sexting issue ... and I think that they are really making a proportionate decision on those. But there is a thing about volume. And that's always going to be a really big issue.'[39] As the analysis of the international studies on the prevalence of sexting in the previous chapter demonstrates, however, retrenchment on a criminal response does not mean that it is not happening.

The law also leaves open the possibility of prosecution for sending indecent images of children among peers under various other legal frameworks, including the offences of harassment[40] and malicious communication (Gillespie, 2006: 126–32).[41] Several interviewees reflected on the legal framework governing child pornography in

[37] Interview 26, 1 August 2016, District Court Judge.

[38] Interview 29, 10 October 2016, Police Officer.

[39] Interview 11, 26 May 2016, Safeguarding Professional.

[40] See e.g. the offence of harassment under the Protection from Harassment (NI) Order 1997, art 3, which prohibits the causing of 'harassment, alarm or distress by a course of conduct'. See similarly in England and Wales, the Protection from Harassment Act 1997, s 1.

[41] See the Malicious Communications (NI) Order 1988, art 3, which makes it an offence to send an indecent, grossly offensive or threatening communication with intent to cause distress or anxiety. See the equivalent in England and Wales, the Malicious Communications Act 1988 (as amended). Section 127 of the Communications Act 2003, which also extends to Northern Ireland, introduced the offence of 'improper use of public electronic communications networks' and also makes it an offence to send a message or other matter that is 'grossly offensive or of an indecent, obscene or menacing character' (s 127(1)(a)). A minority of commentators have also argued that cyberbullying or sexting may also be actionable in civil law such as via the tort of libel in posting defamatory comments: see e.g. Gillespie, 2006: 132–35; Shariff, 2008: 194–221, 2015: 103–40; Crofts et al., 2015: 196–98.

terms of its being outdated for twenty-first century modes of communication (see further Chapter 4):

> Maybe the law is wrong in that regard ... The legislation that covers it predates everyone having a smart phone at the end of their hands, so it is probably a bit dated and there should be a few caveats in it to reduce the circumstances where technically it meets the criminal offence criteria.[42]
>
> Our legislation isn't equipped for it. I mean I am talking to you about communications offences, about sending malicious communications and offensive messages. It is not equipped for it. Indecent image legislation, that's not equipped for this ... And harassment legislation is not the way to go either ... But then is it right to criminalise children for this ... People have been doing it for years ... indecent images is not the place for this sort of stuff.[43]

This legislative deficit was also related to the difficulties of judging 'indecency' by contemporary social and cultural standards 'as the legislators in 1978 and what they would have been exposed to is so far beyond the pale of what a twenty-first-century legislator will be exposed to'[44]:

> If you look at the term 'indecent' from a legislative point of view ... not decent to me is different from not decent to you and it is different from someone of an older generation ... as a 15-year-old, your concept of what is decent and not decent is so far off the scale to what mine would be, or my mother's would be. But bearing in mind the age of the judiciary who will ultimately be deciding whether something is decent or not, they will be the age of your grannies and grandads. So what we would say to them is ... what you think about it, or what your peer thinks about it, is neither here nor there. Because if it comes into the realms of an investigation and your phone gets seized, it won't be somebody your age that's judging whether it's indecent or not.[45]

Unlike the other jurisdictions cited earlier, such as Australia and the United States, there is no statutory definition of 'indecent' in England and Wales or Northern Ireland. The jury makes this objective determination with reference to the ordinary standards of 'decency',[46] which, as Gillespie (2005) notes, potentially makes the definition of indecency extremely wide. As the latter and also the opening quotation to the

[42] Interview 32, 2 November 2016, Police Officer.
[43] Interview 30, 2 October 2016, Senior Prosecutor PPS.
[44] Interview 29, 10 October 2016, Police Officer. [45] Ibid.
[46] See *R* v. *Stanford* [1972] QB 391. The motivation of the person making or viewing the image is irrelevant: see also *R* v. *Graham-Kerr* [1988] 1 WLR 1098. See further Chapter 1, note 14.

chapter attest, judging indecency is inherently problematic due to the gulf between not only adults and children but also legal and normative frameworks related to the contemporary social practices and sexual identities of children and young people (see Chapter 4).

While there was broad recognition among professionals of the need for police discretion and to 'take a much more pragmatic view',[47] there was an underlying emphasis on the importance of a proportionate criminal response which seeks to balance the possible consequences of sexting for the subject of the image as well as those who might distribute it:

> In terms of the electronic world and the world we are now in . . . I think we have to be alive to the fact that, you know, a child who takes a naked picture and sends it to her boyfriend and then it is round the whole world and then she commits suicide and that's a life gone. Maybe we do have to criminalise that sort of behaviour and say you can't do that . . . I mean I am not on for criminalisation of bullying but there has to be a level where it becomes harmful . . . I think our legislation should move forward as we move forward in the world. Why are we not having a new piece of legislation for that?[48]
>
> What about the girl who is interested in a boy who takes her top off and sends him a picture of her chest? Do we really want to criminalise her? Do we really want to stop her having a future, getting the job that she wants, because she has a criminal record? Do we have any right to do that for one mistake? . . . No. She did it for a purpose in a situation and it was attention-seeking behaviour. And the harm is to her, because the consequences for her are far greater than the consequences for the person receiving it. Because she will be seen by her peers, by society, as somebody who has committed a sexual offence. And I don't agree with that at all. I don't think it is in her interest or society's interest to criminalise children like that.[49]

In tandem with this approach, the majority of interviewees advocated an educative rather than a punitive response to sexting: 'we need to do a lot more about that and the decriminalisation of activities where young people are involved without intent needs to be looked at and changed'[50]; 'I don't think they should be criminalised, but I don't think they should just leave it either. We as agencies need to be doing something. But criminalisation isn't the right way to tackle it.'[51]

[47] Interview 15, 3 June 2016, NSPCC Worker.
[48] Interview 30, 2 October 2016, Senior Prosecutor PPS.
[49] Interview 2, 18 April 2016, Independent Forensic Psychologist. [50] Ibid.
[51] Interview 18, 14 June 2016, Senior Voluntary Sector Interviewee.

Indeed, as a counter to the 'moral panic' about sexting evidenced in some jurisdictional responses, several scholars have noted that sexting, as a form of expression of sexual identity, 'raises key questions about privacy and consent in networked digital social environments' (Hasinoff, 2015: 1; see also e.g. Baym, 2010; Simpson, 2013; Albury, 2016).[52] Gillespie (2013) argues that sexting should be considered a legitimate form of sexual expression when carried out on a consensual basis in pursuance of human rights under Articles 8 and 10 of the European Convention on Human Rights which govern the right to respect for private life and freedom of expression respectively.[53] While this argument has merit, and certainly accords with the perception of sexting as 'mundane' or 'routine' and as a form of 'flirting' among children and young people (see also Lenhart, 2009: 10; Wolak and Finkelhor, 2011: 8; Phippen, 2012: 10–11) (see Chapter 6), it does not take account of the difficulties of distinguishing between consensual and non-consensual forms of sexting and the complexities of current social contexts and practices among adolescents (see Chapter 4). Taken as a whole, these arguments underline the need to move 'beyond criminalisation' (Salter et al., 2013; see also Thomas and Cauffman, 2014) and 'take a much more educative response',[54] which seeks to balance 'risk' with children's 'rights' to negotiate their emerging sexual identities (see Chapter 8).

The 'Confusion of Years': Age-Based Anomalies Within Legislative Frameworks

As noted at the outset of the book, there are significant variations in terms of age-based thresholds across a range of legal contexts within Northern Ireland and the United Kingdom more broadly where, in the words of a judge in the present study, 'there is confusion of years.'[55] Most notable among these for present purposes are the tensions between the age of criminal responsibility (10)[56] and the age of consent

[52] In the United States, for example, in *Miller* v. *Mitchell* 598 F.3d 139 (3d Cir. 2010), three girls in Wyoming County, Pennsylvania, challenged the constitutionality of prosecuting them for digital sexual expression under the First Amendment after they refused to attend an educative programme.

[53] See also corresponding rights in the United Nations Convention on the Rights of the Child (1989), arts 12 and 13: the rights to freedom of expression and information, and art 16: the right to privacy.

[54] Interview 15, 3 June 2016, NSPCC Worker.

[55] Interview 26, 1 August 2016, District Court Judge.

[56] The rebuttable presumption of 'doli incapax', that children ages 10–14 were incapable of committing a criminal offence, was abolished by the Crime and Disorder Act 1998, s 34, in

in relation to sexual activity (16)[57] and creating, possessing or distributing 'indecent' photographs or pseudo-photographs of children (where protection is extended up to 18).[58] Several interviewees advocated the need to raise the age of criminal responsibility[59] and the fact that this is often at odds with the age of consent in relation to sexual offences (see generally, Herring, 2016). In essence, a child or young person can be held criminally responsible for committing sexual (and other) offences from age 10 but cannot legally consent to sexual intercourse until age 16[60]:

> I think it is horrific, it should be much higher. Twelve at the minimum. And what we would find is that the younger kids, they are questioned by the police and they admit everything. Not all the time, but you know . . . I think younger kids haven't the ability to respond . . . or deny their offences.[61]
>
> There appears little flexibility and this whole consent aspect also is troubling in terms of prosecution. Legislation is quite clear in terms of, if a child is under 13 then it is rape regardless. Yet it's still an offence if the child is 13 but under 16. So you will have a 14-year-old who thinks they consent. And that then becomes a challenge for policing in terms of wanting to seek prosecution.[62]

There is also a related 'confusion of years' within policymaking and professional discourses around therapeutic service provision (Hackett, 2014). A small number of interviewees articulated the scope of this problem, including the following:

England and Wales, and by art 3 of the Criminal Justice (Northern Ireland) Order 1998. For a critical overview, see Arthur (2016); Fitz-Gibbon (2016).

57 See the Sexual Offences (NI) Order 2008, Part 3 (or the equivalent Sexual Offences Act 2003, Part 1 in England and Wales) for the substantive criminal law on sexual offences against children. Note, however, that the law generally distinguishes offences and related penalties for sexual offences against children under 13 and those under 16 where the former are subject to aggravated penalties.

58 See notes 5 and 19.

59 Northern Ireland and England and Wales have one of the lowest ages of criminal responsibility in the world at age 10, but higher than Scotland where the current age of criminal responsibility is 12 for prosecution, though children as young as 8 can have a criminal record: see the Criminal Justice and Licensing (Scotland) Act 2010, s 52. The United Nations Committee on the Rights of the Child (CRC General Comment No. 10 (2007): *Children's Rights in Juvenile Justice*, CRC/C/GC/10, 25 April 2007) recommends 12 as the minimum age of criminal responsibility (MACR). There have been various calls to raise the MACR across the United Kingdom and elsewhere to at least 12: see e.g. Delmage (2013); Goldson (2013); Sutherland (2016); Dwyer and McAlister (2017).

60 There are also huge variations and discrepancies in the ages of consent and the ages of criminal responsibility across the world. For a critical overview, see Waites (2005).

61 Interview 4, 21 April 2016, Child Care Centre Professional.

62 Interview 7, 13 May 2015, Former Police Officer.

> I think that we need to be better on the age of criminal responsibility . . . I don't think that's helpful . . . I think because we haven't had clarity around ages, then what has happened is we go 10 and under. And then we go 12–18, because most adolescent services start at 14. But what about those 10- to 12-year-olds? I don't think we deal with that well. I don't think we are clear around that. And I think that people start to have issues around labelling the behaviour and how we deal with it . . . I think we should be consistent, and if that's 10, then we need to make it 10 to 18.[63]

Legislation to fix an age of consent 'ostensibly' seeks to protect children, yet in practice it also deems those below that threshold as 'lacking in sexual agency' (Jackson, 2006: 235). Indeed, although the age of consent to lawfully engage in sexual intercourse is 16, children under that may also legally obtain contraceptive advice or treatment without parental consent under the '*Gillick* competency test' and associated 'Fraser guidelines' for health practitioners.[64] As Pearce (2017: 172–73) argues, however, this guidance for determining whether a child is capable of consenting 'is inappropriately based on the individual, rather than the social conditions' surrounding them. This argument is particularly pertinent given a contemporary cultural environment which prematurely sexualises children against a backdrop of ever evolving social and sexual norms surrounding what is 'normal' or 'risky' peer-based sexual behaviour (see Chapter 4). The result is that 'there are lots of mixed messages'[65] for parents and professionals, as well as children, in terms of the competency of children, their capacity to consent and when they are to be held legally responsible for their actions in varying social settings.

[63] Interview 2, 18 April 2016, Independent Forensic Psychologist.

[64] In *Gillick* v. *West Norfolk and Wisbech AHA* [1986] AC 112, the majority of the House of Lords set down what has become known as '*Gillick* Competency': 'as a matter of law the parental right to determine whether or not their minor child below the age of 16 will have medical treatment terminates if and when the child achieves a sufficient understanding and intelligence to enable him or her to understand fully what is proposed', per Lord Scarman at 188–89. Lord Fraser set out criteria which must be satisfied before a doctor or nurse can proceed to give contraceptive advice or treatment: (i) that the girl will understand the advice; (ii) he cannot persuade her to inform her parents or to allow him to inform the parents that she is seeking contraceptive advice; (iii) that she is very likely to begin or continue having sexual intercourse with or without contraceptive treatment; (iv) unless she receives contraceptive advice or treatment her physical or mental health or both are likely to suffer; and (v) her best interests require him to give her contraceptive advice, treatment or both without the parental consent, per Lord Fraser at 174. This landmark decision effectively requires professionals to perform a delicate balancing exercise between children's rights and the need to safeguard children from potential harm. For a critical review, see Wheeler (2006); Gilmore and Herring (2011); Cave (2014).

[65] Interview 24, 6 July 2016, Independent Treatment Professional.

A more pressing concern is the differing ages of consent in relation to engaging in sexual activity and creating, possessing or distributing indecent images, whether there is a reliance on age rather than consent as the basis of criminal activity. Several police officers reflected on this absurdity and the difficulties which it poses for children and young people and their parents:

> It does seem to be a big anomaly that ... if I am a 17- or 18-year-old boy I can have sex with my 16-year-old girlfriend, but I can't get a picture of her, even though I have obviously seen her naked. It is also very, very wrong that it is technically wrong for a girl to have a picture of herself on her phone, when clearly she can see it [her body] every single day when she gets a shower. I don't understand why there is any need for the criminal justice system to get involved in that at all ... We all have difficulties with this in our unit.[66]
>
> It is farcical. And I think sometimes parents ... adults and children alike, struggle to understand how can the age of consent be 16, and I can physically engage in sexual intercourse at 16, but can't take a picture of my bits until I am 18. It is that two-year gap which is such a grey area ... I think the natural course of things would be to bring the indecent image legislation down from 18 to 16 ... to stop that sort of 16- to 18-year-old bracket getting into bother when they are engaging legitimately and offence free at 16, 17 ... I think there is still protection from the point of view of revenge porn and things like that, there is still legislative protection for anybody who abuses that sort of intimate relationship.[67]

These anomalies within and across existing legal frameworks are testament to the systemic nature of the culture of confusion concerning the sexual identity of youth stemming from a blurred demarcation of childhood and adulthood (Dines, 2008; Papadopoulos, 2010: 6) and the ambiguous parameters of victimisation within contemporary popular culture (Chapters 3 and 4). Moreover, as Gillespie argues (2013: 637), such anomalies also lie at the heart of the questions of 'necessity and proportionality' in criminalising sexting.

As the police officer cited earlier argues, given the normalisation of practices such as sexting among children and young people (see Chapters 4 and 6), a logical and easy-fix solution to this incongruity would be 'to bring the indecent image legislation down from 18 to 16'.[68] An alternative, however, would be to introduce a special provision within the legislation relating to 16- and 17-years-olds as Scotland has

[66] Interview 32, 2 November 2016, Police Officer.
[67] Interview 29, 10 October 2016, Police Officer. [68] Ibid.

done. While both England and Wales and Northern Ireland have also introduced clauses relating to 'indecent photographs of persons aged 16 and 17' where the photograph was taken on a consensual basis, exceptions which negate liability for the offence are couched in much narrower legal terms relating, for example, to 'marriage and other relationships', where the latter is further defined as 'living together as partners in an enduring family relationship'.[69] The construction of this defence, therefore, while it acknowledges that children and young people may engage in sexual relationships, does not take account of the transient nature of postmodern sexual and romantic relationships among adolescents (see Chapter 4) and so will not apply in most cases.

In Scotland, however, section 16 of the Protection of Children and Prevention of Sexual Offences (Scotland) Act 2005 creates a series of exceptions to the indecent photographs of children offences insofar as they relate to photographs of 16 and 17 year olds. These exceptions include that 'the photograph was of the child aged 16 or over' or 'the accused reasonably believed that to be so'; 'the accused and the child were married or civil partners' or 'partners in an established relationship'; and either 'the child consented to the photograph being taken or made' or 'the accused reasonably believed that to be so.'[70] In essence, this legal compromise effects a delicate and important balance between 'protectionist' or 'paternalistic' (Kitzinger, 1988: 81; Faulkner, 2010: 108) discourses about risk on the one hand and rights-based/'participatory' discourses (Gillespie, 2013: 641–42; see also Alderson, 2008: 17) on the other (see Chapter 3). That is, it recognises that children and young people are still vulnerable to those who would wish to exploit or abuse them. At the same time, however, it also acknowledges experimentation as a natural and essential part of child and adolescent development, as well as the need to support the emerging agentic capacity of children and young people as competent social and sexual actors against a backdrop of rapidly evolving contemporary cultural norms and social practices.

[69] See respectively, s 1A of the Protection of Children Act 1978, as amended by the Sexual Offences Act 2003, s 45, and art 3B of the Protection of Children (NI) Order 1978, as amended by the Sexual Offences (NI) Order 2008, art 42.

[70] See s 52B of the Civic Government (Scotland) Act 1982, as amended by the Protection of Children and Prevention of Sexual Offences (Scotland) Act 2005, s 16.

Evidential and Practical Difficulties in Investigating and Prosecuting HSB: Intention and Consent

While there is a growing body of international literature on the factors underlying attrition in cases of sexual assault involving adult victims and perpetrators, including the existence of 'rape myths', which is drawn on later, there is comparatively little existing scholarship on the investigation or prosecution of children and young people for harmful sexual behaviour. In this respect, analysis of the primary data revealed a number of significant themes which were prevalent across the interview narratives. These relate to the difficulties of proving harmful intent on the part of the 'perpetrator' and the lack of consent on the part of the 'victim', particularly in cases where there is a preexisting relationship, as well as factors underpinning the credibility of adolescents as victims/witnesses. Many of these problems can be distilled to a single factor which has been a central theme of this book – the normalisation of risky if not harmful sexual behaviour among peers.

As discussed in Chapter 4, one of the further consequences stemming from the normative and cultural obfuscation around the dividing line between coercion and consent is the inadvertent infringement of legal norms. That is, while there may have been 'technical infringement of the law',[71] there is often 'a lack of intent to cause harm'[72] in terms of an overtly harmful motivation on behalf of the perpetrator. Several interviewees explained this issue in relation to what one police officer termed 'peer-on-peer consent'[73]: 'a lot of it is to do with ... well everybody does it. And it is almost this peer-on-peer consent. Well everybody's doing it so it's OK. And it is just a serious lack of understanding'[74]; 'It's maybe from probably quite an innocent angle or not realising the consequences of it.'[75]

However, while this may be the case where, for example, sexting occurs within the confines of 'an exchange' within an adolescent 'relationship', it is argued that the wider sharing and dissemination of that image moves sexting into the realms of intentionality where it may be possible to *infer* a motivation to cause harm. A police officer reflected on this potential to infer knowledge of wrongdoing:

[71] Interview 7, 13 May 2015, Former Police Officer.
[72] Interview 6, 25 April 2016, Independent Safeguarding Consultant.
[73] Interview 31, 17 October 2016, Police Officer. [74] Ibid.
[75] Interview 14, 2 June 2016, Sexual Health Nurse.

> In terms of children who then distribute those images . . . I think they know it is wrong but possibly not that it is criminally wrong . . . It is obvious you can't steal, it is obvious you can't hit someone . . . but maybe not just as obvious is you can't put a picture up and share it with your friends as a laugh.[76]

In this respect, as Smith et al. (2013: 29) note within the context of cyberbullying or sexting, 'a common defense of . . . [a] bullying person is that no harm was intended, and "it was just for fun"' (see also Shariff, 2015: 55–60, 76–77). However, an independent forensic psychologist who had worked with both victims and perpetrators of HSB argued as follows:

> If they are experimenting, nobody gets hurt. And then there's this aggravated category. And that is where we look at the intent to harm. And I think it is that bit that concerns me. The intent to harm. It is very difficult to prove in some cases, but once somebody puts pictures of another person out into the public arena, then there has to be an intent to harm there. And I think those cognitions are what need dealing with in the person who is perpetrating that activity.[77]

This 'intent to harm', which may be inferred from the reasonably foreseeable harmful consequences of 'putting pictures of another person out into the public arena', also accords with the 'aggravated' type of sexting cases, as opposed to 'experimental' adolescent sexual behaviour, as identified by Wolak and Finkelhor (2011: 2–6) and outlined in the previous chapter.

In a generalist sense, proving criminal intent, or that the perpetrator knew it was 'morally wrong', is central to the moral designation of blame and the formal attribution of criminal responsibility which lies at the heart of the criminal justice system (Dingwall and Hillier, 2015). Proving mens rea, however, is traditionally one of the most contentious and problematic areas of the criminal law (see Duff, 1990; Chan and Simester, 2011; Norrie, 2014: Ch. 3). The offence of 'indecent photographs of children'[78] is one of strict liability for which a specific mens rea does not have to be proven, subject only to the statutory defences of distributing, showing or possessing the photographs for a legitimate reason,[79] or not having seen the photographs or known or suspected

[76] Interview 32, 2 November 2016, Police Officer.

[77] Interview 2, 18 April 2016, Independent Forensic Psychologist.

[78] Protection of Children (NI) Order 1978, art 3(1), as amended. [79] Ibid., art 3(3)(a).

them to be indecent.[80] It is for this reason, as noted earlier, that the police stress to children and young people the importance of 'acting appropriately . . . about getting it to someone who is in a position to do something about it . . . or delet[ing] it off your phone'.[81]

However, the preponderance of alternative legislative frameworks under which third party and non-consensual sexting may be prosecuted as outlined earlier (e.g. 'revenge pornography', 'harassment' or 'malicious prosecution')[82] refer to the intent to cause anxiety or distress. As outlined in the previous chapter, sexting can have harmful and long-lasting consequences for the subject of the photograph, ranging from 'minor embarrassment to death' (Wolak and Finkelhor, 2011: 1), where the image is perhaps initially sent consensually to one person but then distributed by that person or others on a non-consensual basis. It is this indirect or oblique attention – where the harmful effect on the subject was not the person's primary purpose or aim (which, for example, may have been to seek revenge or gain status among their peers (Ashurst and McAlinden, 2015: 376)) but something that occurred as a foreseeable adverse effect of the their actions – which is arguably inherent to third-party, non-consensual sexting.[83] In this respect, and as argued in the previous chapter, the determination of harm, or the intent to cause harm, within the context of HSB among peers is far more complex than simply the outward impact on the victim, or the inward motivation of the perpetrator but must also take account of a range of objective contextual factors (such as the nature of the images, any age differentials between the parties and the presence of power or coercion).

The actual determination of criminal intent, however, is not always an easy one to make. In many cases, for example, much depends on the victims' capacity to see themselves as victims and their willingness to make an initial complaint to police where 'it is a big ask to ask a child . . . I want you to tell me everything'[84]:

[80] Ibid., art 3(3)(b). [81] Interview 29, 10 October 2016, Police Officer.
[82] See notes 6–7 and 40–41.
[83] The criminal law distinguishes between 'direct' and 'indirect' or 'oblique' intention. The modern authority for the latter is contained in the case of *R* v. *Woolin* [1998] 4 All ER 103, where the House of Lords held that the jury should be directed that (in a case of murder) if a consequence of a defendant's action was a 'virtual certainty', and they foresaw it as such, then that result may be found to be intended. For a critical overview see Wilson (1999); Coffey (2009).
[84] Interview 31, 17 October 2016, Police Officer.

> They [victims] are often very reluctant to speak to us . . . Try as we might, and as great as evidence that we get from the phone, they just won't give us a complaint and they are quite confident that is going to have to be a no prosecution. Even though there is no doubt this boy has had sex with her. You can see it. But how can you prove it?[85]
>
> That's the biggest one. They don't see themselves as a victim. You've got teenagers who want to be adults ... these kids don't comprehend that they are being abused . . . Some of them are . . . I want to have sex. I am 15 but I like sex . . . They love being older. They look older. I mean sure if you look at some of the profiles, they are all like little clones . . . They've all got the hair and the makeup and the pout. And they all dress the same . . . they also become quite defensive of whoever it is that they are partying with or being abused by ... they either see them as a boyfriend or their mate or . . . I am having a great time, so why would I tell you? . . . Child abuser officers . . . rely on the statement. They rely on the child telling them, unless there is video evidence or unless there is something else there and they can go along with it.[86]

In practice, this is also very pertinent at the decision-to-prosecute stage when the actual charges are being selected: 'where you've got two very young people, and one person is saying it was rape and one person is saying it wasn't; well then we are looking for "first complaint."'[87] Indeed, where the victim refuses to make a statement and the perpetrator alleges that the sex was consensual, this can often result in the downgrading of a charge from rape[88] to one of the other sexual offences against a child under 16,[89] where it fails the evidential threshold for prosecution because 'they maybe just couldn't get the absolute proof.'[90]

From a forensic point of view, the centrality of smart phones to the twenty-first-century lives of children and their staunch sense of ownership and privacy in relation to their mobile phones (see Chapter 4) also present as challenging for police and prosecutors:

> The difficulty we have is getting the phone off the child ... And if someone is taking their £600 iPhone off them, is it really proportionate?

[85] Interview 32, 2 November 2016, Police Officer.
[86] Interview 31, 17 October 2016, Police Officer.
[87] Interview 30, 12 October 2016, Senior Prosecutor PPS. 'First complaint' evidence is the testimony of the person to whom the complainant first reported the alleged sexual assault.
[88] Sexual Offences (NI) Order 2003, art 5.
[89] Ibid., arts 16–19, e.g. sexual activity with a child (art 16) or causing or inciting a child to engage in sexual activity (art 17). Note that when a child or young person commits one of these particular offences, the term of imprisonment is restricted to five years (see art 20). See also the Sexual Offences Act 2003 in England and Wales, ss 9–12 and s 13 respectively.
[90] Interview 17, 7 June 2016, Independent, former Youth Justice Professional.

> And that's where it can cause a lot of angst with families, and they obviously are saying, my son has done nothing wrong. His girlfriend sent him a picture and you took his phone off him. We are out of pocket here quite a bit. And yes, there is a recognition that we shouldn't be criminalising them ... but there is also the difficulty of, well your son has a picture of an underage child on his phone, so we can't give it back.[91]
>
> I have had other cases where people do not want to hand over their phones. And the fact that it takes a year, maybe more, to get your phone back. You are not handing over your phone. I've had sex cases where victims won't hand over their phones because they can't be without it . . . it is the best evidence. It is what they are sent from, that's what they want. And people don't want to give it.[92]

The possible repercussions for victims and the fear of being 'punished' in some form (BASW, 2016: 11) also impact potentially on children and young people in making initial disclosures of abuse if they know that a consequence will be the long term and perhaps permanent relinquishing of their mobile phone: 'I think that is a big problem for the victims and how they deal with it, because then the onus is on them to go without rather than the bully, by having the phone taken off them'[93] and 'young people don't report for fear of losing their phone . . . It is months later before a young person would get their phone back. So they would go to extreme lengths to avoid that.'[94]

In terms of the giving of evidence if the case reaches court, cultural stereotypes relating to victim and offender hierarchies and the related bifurcated processes of blame allocation surrounding child victims who are both 'innocent/evil' (see Brown, 2011; Barter, 2013) also come into play. Several interviewees articulated the fact 'that we are still in a culture of victim blaming'[95]which tends to 'stigmatiz[e] the knowing child' (Kitzinger, 1988: 80) and which differentiates between 'worthy sufferers and the unworthy remainder' (Tilly, 2008: 9). This was thought to be the case with children more generally, as well as in relation to 'looked after children' within the residential care system specifically:

> The problem then, if you've got a young person who has been a victim and they are also seen as a perpetrator, then that's a minefield for the defence, which really just throws the whole character of that young

[91] Interview 32, 2 November 2016, Police Officer.
[92] Interview 30, 12 October 2016, Senior Prosecutor PPS.
[93] Interview 31, 17 October 2016, Police Officer.
[94] Interview 21, 23 June 2016, Social Work Practitioner. [95] Ibid.

> person ... If they are suddenly made out to be a perpetrator it undermines their credibility and that makes it really difficult and challenging for court purposes.[96]
>
> The truth of the matter is, whenever they are getting cross examined, they will be ... hauled over the coals. If there is stuff there, the defence barrister will use it. A lot of our children in the care system will have been arrested by police for being drunk and disorderly or stealing ... once they have been questioned by police they will lie and this is used against them because you have lied before and you are a liar ... And I think children are aware of that. So some of our more vulnerable victims are actually even more vulnerable by the fact that they know, if they come forward, all their history and all their past is going to be dragged up against them.[97]

The failure of the justice system to take account of what Renold and Ringrose (2011: 292) refer to as 'the messy realities of lived sexual subjectivities' of some victims also accords with the notion of 'normalised consent' (Pearce, 2013b: 53) where through societal attitudes or peer pressure, the child assumes sexual violence to be normal or expected.

Historically, and prior to the late 1990s, child witnesses were seen as inherently unreliable in evidential terms (Dent and Finn, 1992; Cashmore and Bussey, 1996).[98] Moreover, such perceptions about unreliability, based in essence on a perception of their high suggestibility, were often compounded in cases of child sexual abuse (see e.g. Birch, 2000; Jackson, 2000: Ch. 5; Chetti, 2005). Legislative reforms designed to protect 'vulnerable witnesses', including children under age 18, were intended to ease the ordeal of giving evidence in court and help 'achieve best evidence'.[99] Indeed, the overall ethos of this 'new' statutory framework was heralded at the time as effecting 'a better deal for vulnerable witnesses' (Birch, 2000) in changing the focus from the unreliability of the evidence of children and other witnesses to one of protection (see also Hoyano, 2001). However, as the earlier interview

[96] Interview 7, 13 May 2015, Former Police Officer.

[97] Interview 32, 2 November 2016, Police Officer.

[98] See e.g. the old corroboration warning which judges had to give to juries (now abrogated by Criminal Justice (Evidence, etc.) (NI) Order 1988, art 13) about the dangers of relying on the uncorroborated evidence of child witnesses. See also the Criminal Justice Act 1988, s 34 in England and Wales.

[99] See the Criminal Evidence (NI) Order 1999, Part II, which introduced a number of 'special measures' for children and other categories of 'vulnerable witness' such as evidence by live link (art 12) and video-recorded evidence in chief (art 15). See the equivalent in England and Wales as the Youth Justice and Criminal Evidence Act 1999, Part II.

excerpts attest, 'there is a lot for any young person in going to court'[100] as either a victim or a perpetrator. Professionals in the present study thought that this was particularly the case for victims where 'they have a lot of responsibility to tell their story evidentially, rather than just how it happened and their experience of it.'[101] Moreover, as discussed further later, in terms of broader supports for victims, 'a lot of families don't want to believe it.'[102]

However, given the vulnerabilities in the backgrounds of many children who commit harmful sexual behaviour (see Chapter 5), child 'defendants' may also be in need of protection during the giving and testing of their evidence, yet they have not traditionally been afforded the same level of legislative protection as 'vulnerable witnesses'.[103] In brief, vulnerable defendants under age 18 are not automatically eligible for 'special measures' unlike all other child witnesses, the availability of which remains at the discretion of the trial judge (see especially Hoyano, 2010, 2015; McEwan, 2013).[104] At the same time, historical and socially constructed cultural stereotypes relating to the innate sexual innocence of children (Kitzinger, 1988: 79; Zelizer, 1994; Furedi, 2013: 45) also appear to work to the benefit of child defendants at the expense of effective risk identification and management:

> At the minute, you know, it is very hard to get a lot of rapes through court, because a lot of people in juries are going, I can't believe he would have done that ... That can't be right. That's too farcical or fantastical ... So the young person comes out, having admitted nothing, having stepped back for about a year, year and a half, and they have got away effectively with a rape. And so they are high risk and they have gone away with the idea that you don't have to admit to anything. You just say nothing. That's not helpful to them and it's not helpful to those people who are going to come into contact in the sphere of that young person in the future.[105]

100 Interview 3, 20 April 2016, Education Authority Professional.
101 Interview 2, 18 April 2016, Independent Forensic Psychologist.
102 Interview 3, 20 April 2016, Education Authority Professional.
103 The courts have consistently refused the use of live link and pre-recorded evidence for child defendants stating that it was parliament's intention that defendants should be excluded from the remit of the Youth Justice and Criminal Evidence Act 1999: see *R (S)* v. *Waltham Forest Youth Court* [2004] 2 Cr App R 21 and *R* v. *Camberwell Green Youth Court ex p D a minor* [2005] UKHL 4.
104 See the Court of Appeal decision in *R* v. *Anthony Cox* [2012] EWCA Crim 549. See note 99.
105 Interview 8, 23 May 2016, Rowan SARC Professional.

The upshot is a complex and conflicting assortment of views about risk vulnerability and protection which are systemic to legal constructions of child victims and perpetrators of harmful sexual behaviour.

Indeed, related complexities surrounding the cultural construction of victim and offender identities emerge further in the legal sphere in relation to proving lack of consent or reasonable belief in consent where such intricacies impact child victims as witnesses. Although there is no requirement for the prosecution to prove absence of consent for offences against children under age 13 as a strict liability offence,[106] this is a core element of other sexual offences, such as rape or sexual assault where the victim may be over age 16.[107] In these circumstances, however, as Koon-Magnin (2015: 104) has argued in the American context, 'there is a very fine line between consensual relationships among adolescents and the crime of statutory rape.' As noted in Chapter 4, there are cultural pressures on young girls in particular to dress and act in 'sexualised' or 'adultified' ways (Dines, 2008; Papadopoulos, 2010: 6) or older than they are. This may also be pivotal in sexual offences cases involving peers in terms of impinging upon 'reasonable belief' that the alleged victim is age 16 or over. As a senior prosecutor explained:

> One difficulty is this thing about if this person is between 13 and 16 and you believe that they were over 16. You reasonably believed ... And that's very hard, because 13 and 16, that's a big span. ... a girl for example who is little more than a baby at age 13, but who looks like a 20 year old at 16. So those things are sometimes difficult to get round. And that's where a jury or judge would perhaps be influenced by how someone presents, how they actually looked. That they looked a lot older ... And those factors could come into play there. I hate that gap in the law ... oh well, you might reasonably have believed they were over the age.[108]

The law defines 'consent' in broad terms as 'a person consents if he agrees by choice, and has the freedom and capacity to make that choice.'[109] As one assessment and treatment professional put it:

[106] See the Sexual Offences (NI) Order 2008, Part 3. See also the Sexual Offences Act 2003, Part 1 in England and Wales.

[107] See the Sexual Offences (NI) Order 2008, arts 5–8 or the Sexual Offences Act 2003, ss 1–4.

[108] Interview 30, 12 October 2016, Senior Prosecutor PPS. Note that cases involving children under age 17 are tried in the Youth Court usually by a District Court judge or magistrates, although serious offences such as rape can be referred to the Crown Court for trial with a jury.

[109] Sexual Offences (NI) Order 2008, art 3. See the equivalent in England and Wales: Sexual Offences Act 2003, s 74.

'consent implies that it is informed consent, that there is the absence of coercion, manipulation, trickery, the absence of power differentials whether they are very grand or very subtle.'[110] In line with this statutory definition, while the consumption of alcohol by a 'drunken victim' (Firth, 2011) may undermine the capacity to give true consent, it has been held by the courts that 'drunken consent is still consent' (Wallerstein, 2009) in the circumstances where the victim voluntarily consumes substantial quantities of alcohol but nonetheless remains capable of choosing whether or not to have intercourse.[111] In terms of the perception of professionals in such circumstances, there was also evidence of what one police officer termed 'condoned consent' which she explained as follows: 'it is people's attitudes as well . . . professional consent, or condoned consent . . . it is about our attitudes to it as well and what we accept as consent . . . And there are professionals who say . . . "sure she's nearly 18. Sure what about it, she is streetwise." And they apply their own personal judgement or their own moral judgement to it, and that means then it is not dealt with as it should be'[112] (see also Pearce, 2013b: 53).

This also accords with two of the core rape myths and constructs of victim blaming, namely that the victims are blamed for putting themselves in circumstances in which 'rape happens' and that consent is mistakenly interpreted as having been given in circumstances where the victim lacked the freedom to do so (Gurnham, 2016). Moreover, an 'attributional double standard in favour of the perpetrator' (Qi et al., 2016: 20) has also been found to be prevalent among young people, irrespective of gender, who generally ascribe less blame or responsibility to the perpetrator and more to the victim in acquaintance rape scenarios where either the perpetrator or the victim is intoxicated or under the influence of drugs.

It has been a central argument of this book, however, that the cultural pressures on children and young people to engage in risky sexual behaviours and the constant proliferation of contemporary norms related to sexual and social identity distort the boundaries of coercion and consent and thus undermine the capacity of young girls to say 'no' to unwanted sexual activity. Such concerns about 'the freedom and capacity to choose', as stipulated by the legislation,[113] are particularly important in relation to sexual activity among peers within the

[110] Interview 23, 24 June 2016, Social Work Service Manager.
[111] See *R* v. *Bree* [2007] EWCA Crim 256. [112] Interview 31, 17 October 2016, Police Officer.
[113] See note 109.

context of the gang (Gover, 2009; Beckett et al., 2012, 2013; Pitts, 2013) and partying cultures (Melrose, 2013) (see Chapters 4 and 6). This normalisation factor not only makes sexual activity in such contexts more likely but may also impede the effective prosecution of harmful sexual or exploitative behaviour among peers. The same prosecutor cited earlier recounted a particularly pertinent example of a sexual offences case and the reflexive and 'routine' nature of sexting practices among young people, often devoid of emotion (see Chapters 4 and 6), which aptly illustrates the difficulties of 'configuring consent' in the digital age (see generally Powell, 2010b):

> I had a case and I could have cried for the young girl . . . she alleged that fellas had abused her in a car . . . one fella sent her a text when he got home. And she sent him a text back . . . At the end of the text she put LOL. And I had to bring her in and say, 'what did you mean?' . . . And she said, 'I don't know. I just did. And I just can't explain it.' And it blew the case out of the water. Because half the jury would have thought it meant 'lots of love'. Half the jury would have thought it meant 'laugh out loud'. We couldn't say what it meant and she didn't really even know what she meant when she sent it. Why did she send that to somebody who had just abused her? But children . . . they put Xs [kisses] on everything. So there are difficulties with that.[114]

As this prosecutor explained, in some cases, 'once you start trying to unravel the whole electronic mess of . . . what did you send to him? It all just starts usually to get very messy in the middle somewhere.'[115] Victims' feelings of complicity in such circumstances may also make them unwilling to proceed with the case as 'the victim is usually mortified and doesn't want any prosecution . . . they are not really wanting all that dragged through.'[116] While this will not always be a barrier to prosecution in every case, it would undoubtedly make the process of giving evidence much more uncomfortable for the victim and, in tandem with this, make it more difficult perhaps for judges and juries to recognise them as such.

Indeed, in addition to accepted behavioural norms, the broader literature on cultural rape myths and the impact of extralegal factors on attrition in cases of sexual assault also establishes, in the words of one prosecutor, that 'the jury have a very clear preconception of what a victim should look like'[117] (Olsen-Fulero and Fulero, 1997; Temkin and Krahé, 2008: Ch. 3; Ellison and Munro, 2009). Consistent with the

[114] Interview 30, 12 October 2016, Senior Prosecutor PPS. [115] Ibid. [116] Ibid. [117] Ibid.

literature on the 'ideal victim' (Christie, 1986: 18) and the 'real child abuse' stereotype (McAlinden, 2014a: 184) (see Chapter 3), there is also some evidence to suggest that younger children have more credibility in the minds of judges or juries than older children or adolescents (see e.g. Regan and Baker, 1998) who may be 'disputed victims' (Reid, 2015). As a police officer explained:

> For the younger children, particularly under 16 ... sort of 15-, 14-, 13-year-olds, I think juries would be more inclined to believe them and less inclined to think they were making it up ... and maybe as a child you would be more inclined to just say it as it happened. A bit more factually. So I think ... juries would be a bit more inclined to believe younger children.[118]

The 'ambivalent' and 'conflicting' legal construction of the 'child victim' of sexual abuse, and indeed of children's developing sexuality, is not a modern phenomenon (Smart, 1999; Jackson, 2000). Jackson's (2000: 90–106) analysis of children as witnesses in the Victorian court room, for example, demonstrates that attitudes towards child victims and defendants were interpreted with regards to age and gender where cases involving children under age 9 and male victims were more likely to end in conviction. As she argues, 'the confusion as to whether abused children were victims or threats, morally innocent or guilty of delinquency, affected the way they were dealt with in court' (Jackson, 2000: 96). Being afforded the label of 'victim', however, is not a purely objective occurrence. Rather, structural and experiential factors are thought to underpin the social construction of the 'imagined victim' (Walklate, 2007). As Nils Christie (1986: 18) put it, 'it will not be the same to all people in situations externally described as being the "same". *It has to do with the participants' definitions of the situation*' [emphasis in original].

Moreover, this often highly moralistic process and the competing tension between being judged 'at risk' or as 'potentially threatening' (Scott et al., 1998: 689; see also Stainton Rogers and Stainton Rogers, 1992) (see Chapter 3) may also pertain to professional decision-making as a whole. As a former police officer explained: 'the professional dangerousness in terms of professionals who are engaging with young people in these cases is how they behave and not allowing their own personal views, judgements, emotional feelings at that moment in time,

[118] Interview 32, 2 November 2016, Police Officer.

to influence their decision-making.'[119] This important sub-theme which reflects the need to bridge the gap between children and adults surrounding sexual norms and behaviours among children and adolescents in contemporary society and embrace 'the messy realities' of victims' lives (Renold and Ringrose, 2011: 292) will be addressed further in the final chapter.

System Tensions

Besides the tensions within the substantive legal and policy frameworks governing the commission of harmful sexual or exploitative behaviours among peers, there are also the procedural aspects of law which impact the progress of a case and militate the response to risk within the criminal process. In this respect, there were two principal structural or procedural issues relating to the criminal justice management of risk posed by children and young people who display harmful sexual or exploitative behaviour which were raised by a preponderance of interviewees. The first of these related to the impact of delays.

Several professionals commented that 'the court process in itself is very drawn out in Northern Ireland'[120] and described cases taking from 18 months to two to three years to come to court which had consequences for the perpetrator, the victim, as well as their families. In relation to the young perpetrator, for example:

> Quite often they are held in queues, either to get into a service or even within the criminal justice system. It can be a year to two years before their offence is heard, therefore before they get treatment. So it is really difficult for young people to access the right service at the right time and the right place in their lives … I think that is really important, in particular for high-risk groups.[121]
>
> That's one of the things that bothers me is that there can be a very long delay … he [the young person] admitted it … And then it took maybe a year and a half to get to court. So he had no input. Whereas I think when the situation comes to light, that really you need therapeutic input straight away.[122]

Such difficulties are particularly pertinent in cases of sibling abuse where effectively lives 'are put on hold' or families are 'split down the

[119] Interview 7, 13 May 2015, Former Police Officer.
[120] Interview 31, 17 October 2016, Police Officer.
[121] Interview 2, 18 April 2016, Independent Forensic Psychologist.
[122] Interview 4, 21 April 2016, Child Care Centre Professional.

middle' until the resolution of the court case as explained by a senior medical professional and a judge:

> I know from going to case conferences that everything will be frozen until that decision is made. They may be working with the perpetrator, but in terms of that family's life moving forward ... that is a long, long time ... Sometimes, the children are put on the child protection register, but often by that time they have come to some sort of arrangement where the victim is with the mum and dad and the perpetrator is with their granny or uncle or something ... But emotionally for that family to be sitting like that for two or three, goodness knows how long, years, with no clear idea of what is going to happen to their son or their daughter ... they are left in limbo and they are wondering what's going on ... They can't move on ... you just feel for the parent in the middle of it.[123]
>
> I had a couple of cases where families were just totally riven ... where basically mum has had to live with the victim; it is usually that way. Mum with the victim and dad has had to go off somewhere else with the perpetrator, as it were. And unfortunately some of these cases don't move that fast, and it can take a long time. So any hope of a healing process is just delayed by so long ... Two years is not unusual, by the time we have actually finished with the case, but quite often we are talking about something that has been running 12, 15 months before I have ever seen it.[124]

Moreover, aside from the emotional impact, delays can also have a potential practical effect on the quality of the evidence, particularly for younger victims: 'Like how on earth are they going to remember a thing about that?'[125]; 'the fact that a child's memory, or anybody's memory even a year later isn't as good. Children move on quicker'[126]; or 'when they are ready to prosecute ... the victim has moved on ... They don't want to go ahead at that stage.'[127] Indeed, this is also indicative of a broader tension within the child protection and criminal justice systems in relation to pre-cautionary responses to risk (Ewald, 2002; Ericson, 2007) and attempts to govern pre-crime (Zedner, 2007 (see Chapter 3) – whereas social services operate on the *risk* of significant harm as 'the new order' of child protection (Ferguson, 1997, 2004; Wattam et al., 1997; Brandon and Thoburn, 2008), the criminal

[123] Interview 25, 25 July 2016, Consultant Paediatrician.
[124] Interview 26, 1 August 2016, District Court Judge.
[125] Interview 25, 25 July 2016, Consultant Paediatrician.
[126] Interview 30, 12 October 2016, Senior Prosecutor PPS. [127] Ibid.

court operates on the presumption of innocence and the need to *prove actual harm* (see further Chapter 6) beyond reasonable doubt. The same judge cited earlier explained this friction and the possible reasons behind the delays:

> Everything is going on outside of the court because you've got social services involvement and their natural thing is, we need to protect. In law you are seen as innocent until proven guilty. In social service terms they have to move in on the assumption this is right . . . It is a different way of looking at it. But from my point of view, I have to start . . . he is innocent until he is proven guilty. And you know, obviously we want to get that decision made as quickly as possible . . . I am fighting all the time to get things pushed on, because . . . everyone is ultra-sensitive about these things to the point, you know, we want to get expert reports on everything. I think there is a very cautious approach to things. I don't mean that I want everyone to be gung-ho, but it just means I think sometimes you can have too many reports. And the reports that we get, it takes too long to get them, simply because we can't identify the experts we want. We have to go across to England and Wales to get those . . . It means that time is just moving on and it becomes more difficult to deal with the problem.[128]

A second theme was a manifestation of the long-established tension between welfare and justice imperatives, which has been a mainstay of youth justice discourses (see e.g. Gelsthorpe and Morris, 2002; McAra, 2006; Muncie and Goldson, 2006), and which impacted in two principal ways: the lack of access to therapeutic services for children and young people displaying HSB following a 'no comment' interview on legal advice and the lack of specialist facilities and treatment for child or juvenile perpetrators. In relation to the former, many interviewees across both therapeutic and justice contexts articulated concern that 'if a young person said yes, I did that, it means at the minute they face a custodial sentence. So of course their legal representation is . . . say nothing and then hopefully you will get off'[129]; 'sometimes kids are told to do no comment interviews by their solicitors. And that prohibits any work'[130]; and 'it becomes a real issue with a young person denying . . . the alleged abuse . . . the solicitors can be quite black and white. Why would you admit it? . . . They don't take it from a welfare perspective . . . why would you engage in harmful sexual behaviour treatment if you

[128] Interview 26, 1 August 2016, District Court Judge.
[129] Interview 8, 23 May 2016, Rowan SARC Professional.
[130] Interview 4, 21 April 2016, Child Care Centre Professional.

haven't done anything?'[131] A police officer explained more fully and how this factor may also impede effective investigation and the probing of risk:

> If we are involved with a suspect through these types of things, without contact offences, maybe receiving images or sexting, then they have a solicitor there and they are very afraid to say why they are engaging in this behaviour because it would just be an admission of it. And the solicitor's advice quite often is not to admit to it, if I am honest with you. Even where the likes of . . . the more serious offence, the contact offences where it is children on children, again when a solicitor becomes involved and it is a criminal interview after a caution, I don't feel we get to the bottom of it.[132]

In essence, 'justice' concerns and a focus on 'due process' (Packer, 1969) within legal processes may obstruct or impede therapeutic intervention and effectively undermine the ultimate 'welfare' of the child in terms of addressing the future potential for HSB.

As regards therapeutic service provision, in the words of a medical professional: 'all the focus is on the victims.'[133] This deficit was believed to be particularly acute at the investigation or evidence-gathering stage. Whereas victims in Northern Ireland have access to the Rowan Sexual Assault Referral Centre which offers a 'one-stop shop' for victims, including forensic medical examination, emotional and follow-up support and contraceptive advice or screening for sexually transmitted infections, there is no dedicated facility for young perpetrators. Another medical professional explained the implications of this victim-centric approach as follows:

> It is usually a boy [who] has committed an offence . . . we will have the victim here and he will be in a police station having his intimate areas swabbed for evidence. So that's difficult, and it is very difficult for families. Forensically we can't have them both here . . . Certainly for the examinations of 12-year-olds who are committing sexual offences shouldn't be in police stations having their bits swabbed. And that whole message that that conveys . . . So whether it should happen in a hospital setting or whether there is a better way of doing that, because as you know the perpetrator has often been a victim. . . . children who sexually harm, quite often will have underlying difficulties, whether it is

[131] Interview 5, 22 April 2016, NSPCC Professional.
[132] Interview 32, 2 November 2016, Police Officer.
[133] Interview 25, 25 July 2016, Consultant Paediatrician.

a learning difficulty or Asperger's or whether they have been neglected or have been sexually abused themselves ... How much harm you do them by taking them down to a police station ... but maybe that's something that we can look at.[134]

Further, the provision of treatment or intervention was described by several interviewees as being 'a patchwork'[135] or 'a postcode lottery'[136] in terms of whether 'there is a service that's available to them'.[137] For example, while there are a range of different specialist therapeutic services for adolescents and children across the five Heath and Social Care Trust (HSCT) areas in Northern Ireland, 'there's lots of people doing different things, but there is no universal kind of service where every young person is getting the same.'[138] These factors are also broadly illustrative of system bias in favour of victims of peer-based abuse and the institutional and policy embodiment of victim and offender hierarchies as highlighted earlier.

SOCIETAL AND FAMILIAL RESPONSES TO RISK

In addition to legal and policy frameworks, the responses of individual families and the community more broadly are also pivotal to the perception and management of risks related to harmful sexual or exploitative behaviour by peers. These relate to cultural dimensions pertaining to Northern Ireland as a post-conflict conservative society and the difficulties for families in coming to terms with HSB in such a context. Although some of these are congruent with the existing literature and indeed professional discourses as outlined earlier, others suggest the need to be cognisant of the underlying and often more complex societal factors which may ultimately have a bearing on the construction and management of risk in localised contexts.

Cultural Dimensions of HSB

As discussed in Chapter 2, a history of cyclical concerns with the eponymous predatory paedophile has effectively obscured the notion

134 Interview 20, 20 June 2016, Rowan SARC Professional.
135 Interview 2, 18 April 2016, Independent Forensic Psychologist.
136 Interview 18, Senior Voluntary Sector Interviewee.
137 Interview 2, 18 April 2016, Independent Forensic Psychologist.
138 Interview 18, Senior Voluntary Sector Interviewee. See for example, the NSPCC 'Turn the Page' programme within the Western and Southern HSCT, 'Making Changes' within the Northern HSCT and 'Aim to Change' within the Belfast and South Eastern HSCTs. See generally Bunting et al. (2009).

of risk as stemming from children and young people themselves. The community reaction to known or suspected adult sex offenders who prey on young children has largely been to cast them as 'monstrous' (Simon, 1998) or 'the ultimate demon' (McAlinden, 2005: 288) resulting in labelling, stigmatisation and their symbolic and literal expulsion from the community (Spencer, 2009: 219–20; see also Edwards and Hensley, 2001; McAlinden, 2007a; Lacombe, 2008) (see further Chapter 3). Research in the context of Northern Ireland has also shown that public attitudes to sex offenders against children are considerably less tolerant and more severe than those who sexually offend against adults (McAlinden, 2007b). In relation to young sexual offenders, predominantly American research has shown that community reactions to young people who sexually offend are often as negative and severe as those for adult sex offenders (Comartin et al., 2009; Kernsmith et al., 2009). The 'collateral consequences of juvenile sex offender registration and notification' can include impact on mental health, harassment, problems at school and living instability (Harris et al., 2016: 770). Within the context of the United Kingdom, Hackett et al. (2015) found a wide range of community responses including stigmatisation, social exclusion and 'collateral damage'. This 'contagion effect' typically took the form of labelling, physical attacks and vigilante action which tended to spread and snowball throughout the community, including to the local school (Hackett et al., 2015: 247–48).

More specifically, however, a number of cultural factors relate to Northern Ireland as a deeply conservative Christian society transitioning from political conflict (see e.g. Ellison, 2016, 2017) (see also Chapter 6): the presence of paramilitaries and the culture of 'shame' surrounding sex and sexuality. As regards the first of these, several interviewees referenced the legacy of 'the conflict' in Northern Ireland in terms of the continued presence of paramilitaries and mistrust or fear of the authorities in some communities, as well as the parochial nature of Northern Irish society (see generally Knox, 2002; Haydon and Scraton, 2008):

> There is also the cultural history still that certain parts of the community, on both sides of the political divide, have certain views about the police and may not want to advise them. And the other thing is that social services have a really negative image within the community. I am not sure whether we score lower in acceptability than the police. So a lot

> of people may not want to go, because they wouldn't want social services at their door.[139]
>
> It is communities dealing with these matters themselves . . . We have had families have had to move out of areas because of the threats to young people . . . You know there's still a thing about communities dealing with issues themselves more effectively, and a lack of trust in the police, or in the effectiveness of the judicial system . . . So there is definitely I think, in the North, an attitude of, we will sort it . . . And that would be a huge fear of the families that any of this gets out . . . because they know they would be run out of the house, or the child would be beaten up.[140]
>
> Whilst within my court . . . names of youngsters are not to be published and anything that leads to their identification; that's a totally false situation because within a community everyone knows . . . That's where we get big problems of families being forced out or split up. So and so cannot come back. And that is where I think the biggest danger lies with people who cannot resume a normal relationship. And after a while the danger is, they start to feel that they are the victims as opposed to recognising that what they have done is wrong.[141]

As the latter quote from a judge attests, the upshot of community responses to peer forms of sexual abuse may well lead to latent reinforcement of victim status among young perpetrators which may undermine their capacity to accept responsibility for their actions. Indeed, as is well documented for adult sex offenders, negative community reactions to sex offenders can increase the risk of reoffending (McAlinden, 2005, 2007a; Tewksbury and Lees, 2006; Willis et al., 2010), whereas positive social responses may actually enhance the chances of rehabilitation, reintegration and desistance (Kruttschnitt et al., 2000; Laws and Ward, 2011; McAlinden et al., 2016). The generally smaller corresponding literature on young people who sexually abuse has also found that public misperceptions about young people who sexually abuse are based on conceptualisations of risk as 'high', 'intransigent', 'special' and 'homogeneous' (Chaffin, 2008). Moreover, these conceptions are often derived from negatives views related to the archetypal 'dangerous' adult sex offender (Sahlstrom and Jeglic, 2008; Salerno et al., 2010) and are usually at odds with the realities of HSB and the goals of rehabilitation and longer-term management of risk (Hackett et al., 2015). Indeed, children given the label 'HSB' may have longer-

139 Interview 23, 24 June 2016, Social Work Service Manager.
140 Interview 1, 16 February 2016, Service Manager, HSS Trust.
141 Interview 26, 1 August 2016, District Court Judge.

term difficulties in accessing mainstream education and employment opportunities because of ingrained public, and even professional, perceptions about the immutability of risk. As Hackett et al. (2015: 249) caution, negative community reactions may also cause young people to withdraw socially, 'thereby cutting off potential sources of emotional and practical support'. This may in turn restrict their life chances and reinforce rather than challenge their self-identification as a 'sex offender'.

Beyond community reactions in individual cases, however, there are also more systemic and far-reaching consequences stemming from the 'societal taboos' in Northern Ireland around sex. Many interviewees in the study highlighted this factor:

> It is part of our culture and we are not very open to talking about it ... We have a fear that if we talk about it, they will be doing it. And so it is like, so don't talk about it and keep them away from it ... But I think there is a sort of an acceptance that young people are going to have sex. There is more of an acceptance of that now. But we don't prepare them for it.[142]
>
> I think as well, Northern Ireland has quite a fear culture and in terms of RSE [Relationships and Sexuality Education] we are quite behind ... I think church and religion [have] a big part to play in terms of shaming people and not letting them talk about stuff. And I think that's dreadful ... I think that in Northern Ireland we have a very religious sort of background that has a huge part to play in it as well.[143]
>
> There are still societal taboos around that subject ... So there's little to no public discussion about it. And the fact that there's no discussion means that the crimes go underground. And the fact that they are underground makes it even harder for a victim to come forward, because nobody is talking about these things happening. So it creates more barriers than we need. And certainly if there's no public discussion about it, there are very few and limited educational discussions about it.[144]

Other professionals framed this slightly differently in terms of 'I think there's denial, hidden issues in the family, but I think there is also a lack of knowledge about HSB as well as what's normal and not normal sexual development.'[145] Both of these viewpoints also underscore the

[142] Interview 12, 26 May 2016, Nurse Consultant in Sexual Health.
[143] Interview 14, 2 June 2016, Sexual Health Nurse.
[144] Interview 28, 16 August 2016, Senior Voluntary Sector Interviewee (victim support).
[145] Interview 1, 16 February 2016, Service Manager, HSS Trust.

need for 'openness' about sex and sexuality among children and young people and 'to get away from the language of shaming'.[146] As argued further in the next chapter, this could take the form of informed discussion and engagement programmes within the local community, and in particular schools, which 'break the taboos of childhood' (Brownlie, 2001: 526) and recognise the developing sexual agency of children.

Familial Responses

Whereas there is a broader and abundant literature on community responses to adult sex offenders who abuse children, there is a dearth of corresponding empirical research on familial responses to adult sex offenders (see e.g. Levenson and Tewksbury, 2009; McAlinden et al., 2016) or to children and young people who display HSB (see e.g. Pithers et al., 1998; Hackett et al., 2006, 2014). Research in the former category has found that loss of family relationships is one of the 'collateral consequences' of being named or registered as a sex offender (Tewksbury and Lees, 2006; Levenson, 2008) and that family members also experience high levels of social isolation, fear, shame, property damage and forced relocation (Tewksbury and Levenson, 2009).

One notable exception in the latter category is research by Simon Hackett and colleagues based on data related to 117 British young people who had sexually abused peers (Hackett et al., 2014). This research found that parental responses were 'complex and varied' (Hackett et al., 2014: 136), ranging from being 'supportive' of the child (25 per cent), through to 'ambivalence' (28 per cent) and 'negative' responses in the form of 'outright rejection' (7 per cent) or 'disintegrative shaming' (Braithwaite, 1989; McAlinden, 2005, 2007a). Moreover, as might be expected, parents were more likely to be supportive when the abuse was extrafamilial and condemnatory when the abuse was intra-familial. In this respect, the consequences for families have been likened to a 'shot gun blast' that 'frequently take[s] in not only sex offenders but everyone around them' (Hackett et al., 2015: 245). Goffman (1963: 30) also refers to this extension of stigmatisation beyond the individual as 'courtesy stigma' (or 'stigma by association') which families can experience whether or not they reject or support the offender. In practice, this can mean that not only the young person, but also his or her family, can be attacked or forced out of their home.

[146] Interview 19, 16 June 2016, Youth Worker, Family Planning Association.

Indeed, in cases of sibling abuse in particular, there is a difficult balance between individual safety and the well-being of all family members (Keane et al., 2013).

Consistent with this previous research, professionals recounted the difficulties of engaging families, particularly in cases of sibling abuse where 'it is a massive head mess for parents'[147] and 'it is difficult if you have a child who is removed from the family ... because you love the person but not what they have done.'[148] Professionals generally highlighted the divergent responses of families, the labelling of children and young people and the divisive effect on the family which is particularly pertinent in therapeutic contexts:

> They can either go one of two ways ... they can either be completely shocked and they don't know what to do. But a lot of them do react – my child has done this. It doesn't matter what ... he has done this to my little girl. And they get very upset and usually the boys are put to another family member or even outside of the area. So they are put into foster care or ... usually there is some family member who will look after them. And they are viewed as a perpetrator ... But they are not; they are children.[149]
>
> If a parent is supportive of the child coming in, often the parent would see the child as the problem. Whenever we try to look at it more holistically, that's generally what can throw up a lot of resistance ... And for us to push to try and understand it holistically and historically ... we can encounter a lot of resistance there from families, and that's understandable ... And there is a guilt then, because we are looking at the background and we are explaining why. We are not saying this is your fault, we are saying there are factors.[150]

Previous research on parental experiences of the child protection system has found that many parents report feeling fearful or intimidated (see e.g. Dale, 2004; Dumbrill, 2006; Buckley et al., 2011) and experience a range of reactions such as shock, self-blame and guilt (Duane et al., 2002). Such issues around familial and parental engagement are arguably augmented within a transitional society such as Northern Ireland, as noted earlier, due to the residual threat of responses from paramilitary groups.

147 Interview 7, 13 May 2015, Former Police Officer.
148 Interview 20, 20 June 2016, Rowan SARC Professional.
149 Interview 25, 25 July 2016, Consultant Paediatrician.
150 Interview 5, 22 April 2016, NSPCC Professional.

The small but growing body of empirical studies on the reintegration and desistance of adult sex offenders reinforces the importance of social supports such as familial and intimate relationships which underlie 'trajectories of change' (Laub et al., 1998); see in particular Farmer et al., 2015; McAlinden et al., 2016). A cautionary tale was presented by a judge in the current study who recalled one case example documenting the effects of labelling (Becker, 1963) and 'disintegrative shaming' (Braiwthwaite, 1989):

> I can think of one wee fella who is very, very bright. That was a familial case where the victim in that was his sister. And that's just a very, very sad case where it was the parents who reported, but he has been cut off entirely . . . his family have just basically pulled down the shutters. They don't want to know. And I now see him not coming back as a sexual offender, but just as someone who is lashing out . . . it is interesting that the youngsters that he runs round with, they are not sex offenders or anything like that, but they all have a similar . . . for one reason or another their family don't want to know them. So it is a bit like the three musketeers, they see a common theme. So I see more of him now and the others just simply . . . because I think they see themselves as outcasts and they are just in their own wee gang.[151]

In essence, in much the same way as negative community responses, familial rejection may ultimately result in what has become known as 'secondary deviation' (Lemert, 1951) or the 'pygmalion' or 'looking glass effect' (Maruna et al., 2004) wherein deviance becomes integral to personal identity or 'incorporated as part of the "me" of the individual' (Lemert, 1951: 7). In many ways, this issue is even more pertinent for children and young people whose patterns of 'offending' may not yet be entrenched (see generally Craisatti et al., 2002; Taylor, 2003; Lussier and Davies, 2011; Van den Berg et al., 2017). The present research, therefore, also supports the professional and academic consensus that working with families and incorporating systemic support systems are pivotal to successful intervention with young people who display HSB (see e.g. Pithers et al., 1998; Hackett et al., 2006; Letourneau et al., 2009). Although family environments and demographic characteristics are generally thought to be risk factors which are pivotal to the onset of HSB (Bischof et al., 1995; Graves et al., 1996; Taylor, 2003; Vizard et al., 2007) (see Chapter 5), the present findings also underline the need to further develop 'strengths-based' approaches (Ayland and

[151] Interview 26, 1 August 2016, District Court Judge.

West, 2006; Pratt, 2014) which focus on supporting children and their families in the aftermath of the abuse and helping families and children overcome the stigma of sexual offending (Yoder and Ruch, 2016) (See Chapter 8). In brief, as one professional put it: 'parents are a vital part of the assessment in trying to understand why the behaviour occurred in the first place. And they are also a vital part of the intervention . . . but people have to be helped through that process.'[152]

CONCLUSION

This chapter has demonstrated that societal responses and legal frameworks in particular governing the risks posed by children and young people who display harmful sexual or exploitative behaviour act as an 'echo chamber for conversations about credit and blame' (Tilly, 2008: 35) both reverberating as well as enshrining broader cultural constructions of risk. In this respect, there is a deep cultural ambivalence to countenancing peer-based forms of potential sexual harm among peers which is often characterised by extreme positions, ranging from outright 'denial' to abject 'horror' or 'panic'. This is evidenced most clearly in the pendulous police and prosecutorial responses to criminalising sexting. The outmoded nature of some legal responses, effectively utilising legislation to criminalise children which was originally designed to protect them, demonstrates that 'we are living in the law'[153] rather than acknowledging the contemporary realities of the lives of children and young people.

Such reactionary viewpoints appear to stem from a nexus of 'cultural and moral anxieties' (Lee et al., 2013: 2–13: 35; see also Holloway and Jefferson, 1997: 255) surrounding childhood and adolescence; the 'confusion of years' surrounding the dividing line between childhood and adulthood and the associated thresholds for child protection; the 'lack of understanding of the complexity of peer to peer relationships'[154]; and the differences between 'normal', 'risky' or 'harmful' sexual behaviours among peers. There are also inherent difficulties in countenancing what I have previously termed '"deviant" victims' or '"vulnerable" offenders' (McAlinden, 2014a: 182) whose behaviour may lie in the middle ground between the schism of putative victim and offender status.

[152] Interview 24, 6 July 2016, Independent Treatment Professional.
[153] Interview 19, 16 June 2016, Youth Worker, Family Planning Association.
[154] Interview 11, 26 May 2016, Safeguarding Professional.

These cultural factors have a practical bearing for the trier of fact on the factual questions of 'reasonable belief in consent' and whether there was 'intent' to cause harm as well as the credibility of adolescents as victims/witnesses. The consequences of this series of befuddled legal responses to peer-based sexual behaviours, often devoid of contextual factors and the lived experiences of victims, is to limit not only the understanding of the problem but also effective responses to addressing risk. Moreover, cultural stereotypes also resonate as social and personal consequences for young people and their families, who are impacted by system delays and access to support and therapeutic services, in coming to terms with the aftermath of the abuse.

At the policy level, the arguments presented in the course of this chapter present further challenges for traditional 'protectionist' discourses on risk (Kitzinger, 1988: 81; Faulkner, 2010: 108). In so doing, they point towards the need to incorporate rights-based, participatory discourses (Alderson, 2008: 17; Gillespie, 2013: 641–42) which take fuller account of the prevailing 'new' cultural and behavioural norms among children and young people, the sexual agency of children and their developing capacity for decision-making and the need to counter-balance victim-centric approaches with the needs of young perpetrators and address the concerns about dual vulnerability and protection (see Chapter 5).

At a broader societal level, this also means engaging parents and professionals, as well as children and young people themselves, in mainstream educative responses which seek to strike a more effective balance between recognising the vulnerability of children and young people and the need to build in protective factors. As discussed in the next and final chapter, such an approach would encompass 'contextual understandings' of risk, including vulnerability and consent (Munro, 2017) and, more specifically, helping the child to navigate his or her rights and responsibilities as a 'citizen' growing up within a highly sexualised cultural landscape and a digital world.

PART III

FUTURE APPROACHES

8

CONCLUSION: REIMAGINING 'RISK'

> Risk tends to be quite a negative discourse ... Risk is always seen as negative and something intolerable. So I think once you are talking to professionals or laypeople or parents about 'this person is a risk', they will always immediately assume the worst, and immediately assume it is unmanageable. Whereas a lot of the work I do is about ... yes, it's a risk, but let's put it in perspective. A risk to whom? A risk how? A risk when? A risk where? So actually about how you manage the risk within that particular context.[1]

This book has charted the contemporary emergence of harmful sexual or exploitative behaviours by children and young people as a distinct societal problem and the various complexities they pose for legal, policy and societal discourses on 'risk'. It has been argued that the cyclical nature of public and official 'panics' (Cohen, 1972) about the risks posed by predatory adult strangers in a range of intra-familial and extrafamilial settings has produced a narrow and homogenous version of sexualised risks to children (see Chapter 2). Recurring historical concerns about the perilous state of childhood are exacerbated by contemporary cultural concerns about the risks posed by sex, technology, consumerism and new media. At the same time, 'paternalistic' (Kitzinger, 1988: 81) discourses on childhood deny the sexuality and sexual agency of children and subjugate an acknowledged understanding of children as constituting a risk to others in sexual terms. The result is the cultural construction and reproduction of dyadic and highly gendered stereotypes wherein risk is disconnected from domestic or

[1] Interview 6, 25 April 2016, Independent Safeguarding Consultant.

private spaces and the child is constructed as 'victim' or as 'at risk' *from* sexual offending (see Chapter 3).

Harmful sexual behaviour (HSB) by children and young people has emerged against the backdrop of the contemporary cultural sexualisation of children which has impacted the social and sexual identities of adolescents in particular (see Chapter 4). 'The messy realities' of children's lives (Renold and Ringrose, 2011: 292), however, means that they may be both passive objects shaped by social and cultural experiences as well as autonomous or 'savvy' consumers (Ringrose et al., 2012: 17). Indeed, as well as *accessing* pornography, children and young people can also *produce* their own sexualised media via practices such as sexting (see Chapter 6). This broadens our understanding of sexualised risks to children to include not only 'contact' risks but also 'conduct' risks created by children (see e.g. Staksrud, 2013: 150).

The normalisation of risky sexual behaviours among peers has dual consequences. Primarily, the culture of confusion concerning the boundaries of 'normal' or 'risky' sexual behaviours may affect how children and young people negotiate their social and sexual identities, undermining their capacity to say 'no' to unwanted sexual behaviours or to see themselves as 'victims'. In turn, the blurred lines between coercion and consent may result in the advertent infringement of legal norms (Chapter 4). Normalisation processes also present significant normative and practical challenges for legal and policy frameworks in responding to what may be the 'new normal' for children and young people. There is a discernible tension, for example, in the over-criminalisation of sexting and the under-criminalisation of other potentially more serious and complex forms of HSB where there is often a failure to identify and manage 'risk' (see Chapters 6 and 7). This tension is also symptomatic of the systemic nature of broader cultural discourses on victim hierarchies and 'blame' concerning child sexual abuse (McAlinden, 2014a) which often cannot countenance fluid understandings of harmful sexual behaviour or child sexual exploitation (CSE) and the 'dual vulnerabilities' of victims and perpetrators (see Chapter 5).

Based on these insights, this closing chapter offers some thoughts on how we might reframe the current regulatory agenda to better capture the complexity of sexualised risks posed *by* and *among* as well as *to* children and young people. In presenting these arguments and in light of the literature and primary data examined in the course of this book, three residual issues fall to be addressed: (i) how we can move beyond risk within social and policy discourses on HSB; (ii) how we may recognise the agency, resilience and citizenship potential of children and young people; and finally (iii) how to bridge what may be termed the 'normalisation gap' between adults and children in relation to what constitutes normal, risky or harmful sexual behaviour.

MOVING BEYOND 'RISK'

While the ubiquitous nature of risk was evident throughout the professional narratives, only a minority of interviewees recognised the complexity of risk as a nebulous concept, variously noting that there are 'layers of risk'[2] and questioning whether 'we are focusing too much on risk':[3]

> Risk is a moving target. Risk is not static. It doesn't stay the same. So one young person can be less risky one day and more so the next . . . Which is why, if you become totally risk averse you put young people into boxes, and that it is not helpful. It is about managing risk and identifying it and looking at the triggers.[4]
>
> We are totally reliant as a group of professionals on risk frameworks in which to work . . . Because actually when you look at somebody, you are looking for a lot more than just those risk factors. And if we just keep ourselves to those risk factors, then we will never find the causes of what has happened. Therefore we won't effectively stop, or intervene, at the right place.[5]

As discussed later, the importance of this paradigm shift was related to a number of imperatives stemming from the gulf between adults and children regarding sexual norms: engaging children in meaningful discourse around healthy and risky sexual behaviours and increasing adult and professional understanding of the causes and impact of HSB on children and young people. As Donoghue (2013: 805) argues, a key criticism of the 'new penology' (Feeley and Simon, 1992) is that it has produced over 'simplistic accounts of . . . risk as a largely homogeneous and unifying process'. In this vein, it is argued that this reimagined version of risk presents challenges to current criminal justice orthodoxies along three primary fronts: in extending 'responsibilisation' beyond core statutory and voluntary agencies, in broadening

[2] Interview 29, 10 October 2016, Police Officer.
[3] Interview 18, 14 June 2016, Senior Voluntary Sector Interviewee.
[4] Interview 9, 25 May 2016, Youth Support Worker.
[5] Interview 2, 18 April 2016, Independent Forensic Psychologist.

technocratic understandings of risk, and in re-examining who society classes as 'victims'.

In this vein, moving beyond 'risk' as the paradigm response to HSB entails four essential components. The first requires greater professional and societal recognition of the complexity of cases which may transverse the victim-offender divide and the need to move away from 'what is quite a blame culture'[6] and the 'moral and emotive' dimensions of 'risk' (Sparks, 2001: 169; see also Rose, 2000). Central to this process is the need to change binary and rigid categorisations of 'victims' and 'perpetrators' and, in particular, the use of the language of moral governance that usually attaches to particular child victims:

> We are so good at victim blaming . . . a lot of professionals even would do that as well . . . It is still 'so and so continues to put themselves at risk.' You know, you are only ever at risk if someone seeks to exploit your vulnerability. . . . It doesn't matter how drunk you are, how out if it you are, you are only ever at risk if someone seeks to abuse or exploit you.[7]

Those professionals working in the criminal justice system, such as police, noted that the primary concern was that of dealing with the young person as 'a suspect', irrespective of a history of victimisation, where 'it is then left to the courts to decide what degree of mitigation to factor in.'[8] Several professionals, however, recognised that 'there is a need to really look holistically at what is going on in this child's life'[9]; 'there has to be a way of working with it, kind of holding both those concepts in your head'[10] and where 'people start realising that they are young people and that they could be either or both.'[11] In addition, as noted in Chapter 4, such polarised categorisations of children and young people who display HSB as either victims or perpetrators were also firmly embedded in cultural constructions of gender and in particular in 'not seeing girls in their own right as sexual aggressors'.[12] There is also a related need, therefore, to address professional and societal understanding of reified dyadic gendered stereotypes as 'something we have to shift'[13]; otherwise, 'we might demonise

[6] Interview 11, 26 May 2016, Safeguarding Professional.
[7] Interview 18, 14 June 2016, Senior Voluntary Sector Interviewee.
[8] Interview 32, 2 November 2016, Police Officer.
[9] Interview 7, 13 May 2015, Former Police Officer.
[10] Interview 6, 25 April 2016, Independent Safeguarding Consultant.
[11] Interview 10, 25 May 2016, Youth Support Worker.
[12] Interview 16, 6 June 2016, Social Work Consultant.
[13] Interview 18, 14 June 2016, Senior Voluntary Sector Interviewee.

a whole generation of young males and victimise a whole generation of young females'.[14] Indeed, as discussed further later, and as a safeguarding professional admitted, 'the element of agency with regard to peer-to-peer abuse is really not understood by professionals'.[15]

At the level of praxis, balancing concerns about 'at risk victims' (Donoghue, 2013: 807) with 'risky individuals' (O'Malley, 2004a: 318–19) requires a fundamental reconceptualisation of traditional accounts of 'childhood', and of children's sexuality, which entails recognising a new account of the child as 'individual' rather than as 'threat' or 'victim'. A forensic mental health practitioner explained: 'I do think these children are victims themselves. They are not born predators and they are not born criminals, they become like that because life and society and their upbringing and what they are exposed to makes them like this.'[16] Moreover, addressing these complexities and the underlying causes of HSB also involves the development of a greater range of therapeutic services for young perpetrators:

> There are people who are perpetrators of these crimes who are also victims. And we also need a coordinated response to perpetrators ... We need proper investment and services. And it is not there for them ... And a lot of people think, oh but if you are investing in perpetrators you are taking away from victims. But if we invest in services to deal with perpetrators, the hope is that there will be less victims into the future. So we need to think about how we fund both sides of the house for the future.[17]

In addition, overcoming binary distinctions between victims and perpetrators of HSB within front-line service provision also means educating legal and other professionals about the normalising effect of contemporary popular culture and the harmful effects of grooming, which may affect the victims' own self-identification as well as how they are perceived by others.

The second element is the requirement for, what several interviewees termed, 'professional curiosity'. This was framed in terms of 'digging a bit deeper', 'the need to be asking more questions',[18] 'constantly having it on your radar',[19] 'pick[ing] up on very much on the red flags',[20]

[14] Interview 23, 24 June 2016, Social Work Service Manager.
[15] Interview 11, 26 May 2016, Safeguarding Professional.
[16] Interview 22, 10 June 2016, Forensic CAMHS Professional.
[17] Interview 8, 23 May 2016, Rowan SARC Professional.
[18] Interview 31, 17 October 2016, Police Officer.
[19] Interview 14, 2 June 2016, Sexual Health Nurse.
[20] Interview 21, 23 June 2016, Social Work Practitioner.

and 'go[ing] with your gut feeling'.[21] This was explained more fully by a senior voluntary sector interviewee: 'it is not just about the law . . . you can have all the legislation in the world, but it may not be used in the right way either, to protect young people.'[22] These viewpoints also underscore the limitations of 'actuarial justice' (Feely and Simon, 1994) which relies on scientific and expert assessments of risk often based on risk-assessment scales and check lists of factors. Furthermore, it also underlines the importance of balancing the technocratic or, what Sparks (2001: 169) terms, the 'calculative', dimensions of risk, with experiential and intuitive assessments concerning children and young people involved in HSB or CSE. The contemporary political and policy ethos of risk as social control has tended to overtake the provision of social care with an emphasis on responsibility, accountability and the need for caution (Webb, 2006; Kemshall, 2010). Other research, however, has also shown that social workers are 'active and purposive . . . moral agents' in responding to risk within morally conservative societies (Stanford, 2011: 1514). The challenges of navigating current risk orthodoxies and the consequences for professionals of 'getting it wrong', however, are arguably greater within the field of HSB because it intersects two culturally and politically sensitive domains: sexual offending involving children and the state of modern childhood.

The third element is the further development of 'strengths-based approaches' and holistic methods of working with the young person and his or her family. Recognition is growing internationally that strengths-based approaches are crucial to intervention with young people who display HSB (see e.g. Pratt, 2014). Whereas risk-based approaches are centred on public protection and social control, strengths-based approaches are premised on systemic understandings of risks as well as needs and aim to support individual resilience and promote positive decision-making (Hackett, 2014). The 'Good Lives' model, for example, which originated in New Zealand, focuses on 'narrative therapy' and relapse prevention, on helping young persons to understand the consequences and impact of their abusive behaviour and develop their ability to choose the 'good way' (Ayland and West, 2006; Collie et al., 2007).

As highlighted in the previous chapter, there is a broad understanding in the field that proactive and positive 'working with families is

[21] Interview 13, 31 May 2016, Public Health Nurse.
[22] Interview 18, 14 June 2016, Senior Voluntary Sector Interviewee.

absolutely key'[23] as part of the assessment and intervention processes because 'children live in systems and families'[24] (see e.g. Pithers et al., 1998; Hackett et al., 2006; Letourneau et al., 2009; Yoder and Ruch, 2016). There is little specific provision, however, dedicated to supporting families and engaging parents in their own right in the aftermath of the abuse to help them 'face the future' (see e.g. Hackett, 2001). This concern was shared by many interviewees:

> There is more that we could do with families of victims, but there is also a huge amount of work to do with the families of perpetrators. Because they are victims ... Oftentimes ... there is not a history of sexual abuse in a family and someone just becomes a perpetrator. And that family is devastated and I am not aware of any support that they can get. So I think that there's a job of work to do for them in terms of offering a support service ... allowing them a safe place to come and talk about how these sexual offences have impacted on them as a family.[25]
>
> If you have played 'Kerplunk' you know that sometimes if you take a straw out and it all stays up. Sometimes you take it out and it all collapses. What we want to do with families is be the straw you take out and it stays up, not the straw that the only reason the whole thing stays up is because you are there.[26]

As the latter quotation makes clear, moving beyond risk also means supporting families in the aftermath of the abuse so that families affected by HSB, as well as the children living within them, are sustainable once the formal structural supports are removed. Such imperatives are particularly acute within the context of intra-familial forms of peer abuse.

At the broader societal level, a final element of reimagining risk is engaging communities via schools. In the words of an independent forensic psychologist, 'we need to engage every situation and context that child is going to be in, for the future safety of the child.'[27] It has been argued that the negative consequences of hostile community reactions to young people who display HSB are exacerbated in a post-conflict society such as Northern Ireland with vestiges of paramilitary 'policing' (see Chapter 7). Several professionals recounted stories of primary school children being returned to the local school following an

[23] Interview 6, 25 April 2016, Independent Safeguarding Consultant.
[24] Interview 2, 18 April 2016, Independent Forensic Psychologist.
[25] Interview 28, 16 August 2016, Senior Voluntary Sector Interviewee (victim support).
[26] Interview 6, 25 April 2016, Independent Safeguarding Consultant.
[27] Interview 2, 18 April 2016, Independent Forensic Psychologist.

investigation of HSB often to an extremely hostile reaction. As one former police officer explained, the response of schools to incidents of HSB is often variable:

> I think a big thing is not shaming children and trying to ensure that you work in that kind of way with them. I suppose it is also ensuring that other organisations don't shame them … At some of the case conferences, I have been aware of kids that have had to use different toilets in school, who are educated isolated from other children. And again there is that kind of range of responses where some schools are fantastic and really come on board and try to help the young person. Others just isolate them and even expel them.[28]

For children and young people under age 16 who display HSB, the school is the fulcrum of early identification of, or changes to, concerning sexual behaviour (Hackett and Taylor, 2008; Hackett et al., 2016). Indeed, as discussed further, engaging schools also involves the development of preventative work, not just with children who have displayed harmful sexual or exploitative behaviour but also children and young people more broadly.

AGENCY, RESILIENCE AND CITIZENSHIP

Academic discourses have long recognised the agency of children as autonomous and competent social beings (Alderson, 1995, 2000; Farrell, 2005; Lundy and McEvoy, 2012), capable of making decisions and contributing to their own development and well-being (see e.g. Hallett and Prout, 2003; Hill et al., 2004; Matthews, 2007). Such concerns are particularly pertinent in relation to the developing sexuality of adolescents where they have the right to age-appropriate information to support this development. For the most part, however, matters relating to sex and sexuality have been governed by 'a "both" approach' (Graham, 2011: 1540) in which it is recognised that 'a child may need protection in one context and rights of self-determination in another' (Thorne, 2002: 437).

In an age of cultural premature sexualisation in which children appear to be 'growing up' at a younger age, there has never been a more pressing need to re-evaluate how we perceive children and young people as competent social actors in matters which impact their daily lives. Recognising the agentic capacity of children also

[28] Interview 4, 21 April 2016, Child Care Centre Professional.

invites consideration of the *individual* 'resilience' of children (Pearce, 2009: 95–99) and how we may bolster their personal and social skills by providing 'protective knowledge' (Craven et al., 2007: 70) which 'ameliorate[s] risk' (Doll et al., 1998: 348). Indeed, in tandem with managing or addressing risk factors, promoting resilience is also a feature of modern health and social care practice in terms of reducing vulnerability (see e.g. Fraser et al., 1999; Pollard et al., 1999; Gilligan, 2004; Jenson and Fraser, 2015). Resilience in youth, however, is also thought to be culturally and contextually embedded (Ungar, 2008). That is, despite significant social and contextual risk factors, stemming from the proliferation of cultural norms about sex and/or experiential norms arising from a history of sexual victimisation, not all children are adversely impacted and go on to display HSB (see Chapters 4 and 5). Schools in particular are 'sources of resilience' (Aisenberg and Herrenkohl, 2008: 296) and represent an important resource for 'maximising opportunities' to strengthen resilience (Brooks, 2006).

Recognising the agency of children and young people also invokes questions of their rights and responsibilities as 'sexual' and 'digital' 'citizens'. Notwithstanding the fact that harmful sexual or exploitative behaviour among peers can take place in both online as well as offline settings, social media and smart phones are often central to such cases. This view was supported by a police officer, cited in Chapter 7, who explained: 'it is massive and it has a massive impact on what we investigate as well. And I would say nearly every investigation that comes through has an element of social media/sexting through it.'[29] Central to the use of the Internet as a 'deviant and democratizing space' (Wykes, 2017) are the responsibilities and rights that attach to being a citizen in the digital age (Mossberger et al., 2007; Bennett et al., 2009; Lenhart et al., 2011; Henry and Powell, 2016). As Mossberger et al. (2007: x) acknowledge, 'digital citizenship requires educational competencies as well as technology access and skills.' While the majority of youth adopt what Bennett et al. (2009) term 'self-actualizing styles' of digital citizenship as adept 'digital natives', there is also a requirement for schools to promote 'dutiful citizenship' as part of learning about civic participation. This should include, for example, lessons on how to navigate instances of 'challenging behaviours' online such as cyberbullying (see generally Lenhart et al., 2011) as well as how to intervene positively as 'on lookers' or 'by standers'.

[29] Interview 32, 2 November 2016, Police Officer.

Moreover, contemporary sexual and social norms among children and young people which cross digital and real-world contexts also invoke the rights and responsibilities of 'sexual citizenship' (Bell, 1995; Richardson, 2000; Evans, 2013). This polarised discourse reflects the importance of informing children and young people about what Bell (1995) terms the 'paradoxical spaces of sexual citizenship' as 'pleasure and the dangers' or the 'power and peril' of the child citizen (Staksrud, 2013: 163–65). In this vein, research on sexual readiness has shown that adolescents may not view the initiation of sex as 'problematic' but focus instead on the 'rewards' of sex rather than health concerns (Templeton et al., 2016). Given the range of nontraditional sexual identities among youth, as also highlighted by this study, in which 'gender' and sexuality are understood in far broader terms than masculinity and femininity, there is also a related need to disassociate developing sexuality with 'masculine hetero-sexual privilege' (Richardson, 2000) and take account of the plurality of youth sexual identities (see generally Evans, 2013). Northern Ireland–based research, for example, has shown that even where children and young people had received 'relationships and sex education' (RSE) at school, only 39 per cent had received information on LGB issues and only 17 per cent on transgender issues.[30] Framed within such narrow parameters, 'sex education' is seemingly used to 'regulate' rather than inform (Haydon and Scraton, 2002).

Risk and risk governance are traditionally reactive frameworks which are only invoked once there is a clear risk of harm. Given the prevalence of risky or harmful sexual behaviours by children and young people, such behaviours are rapidly becoming a public health problem which necessitate a more wide-ranging preventative and proactive response (see generally Laws, 1996). Central to 'classic public health approaches' to societal problems are public education and awareness programmes at the primary level of prevention (Laws, 2000: 31). In this respect, a number of education initiatives run by statutory and voluntary agencies in Northern Ireland are aimed at providing children with age-appropriate information about factors which might underpin decision-making in potentially risky circumstances and which 'create a culture for them [children] to be able to talk about such things'.[31] This includes a range of preventative programmes on e-safety and child

[30] See the Young Life and Times Survey 2014: www.ark.ac.uk/ylt/2014/index.html.
[31] Interview 14, 2 June 2016, Sexual Health Nurse.

sexual exploitation delivered in schools and other community-based youth settings.[32] A youth worker articulated the importance of a child-centric approach for engaging children and young people: 'through case studies, through animations, it is simpler and it is easier to understand. Whereas if you jargonise it, overcomplicate it and if it is all about triggers and risk . . . it sort of becomes removed, doesn't it.'[33]

Collectively, such programmes are aimed at what Brookfield (2013) terms 'culture jamming' – at addressing a broad range of cultural norms about sexual and social identity and promoting social skills among children and adolescents to 'push back' against such norms. Topics include healthy relationships, emotional well-being, empowering decision-making, seeking help and support and the legal meaning of consent in a range of contexts and the fact that 'they have the right to say no.'[34] As Straksrud (2013: 12) argues, managing risk in this context is 'about setting boundaries and limits'. Supporting values which underpin such work were explained by several professionals as 'old fashioned social values like showing respect for yourself, respect for your peers and learning how to be socially adept and to be able to engage and have relationships with people'[35] and building 'empathy, confidence, self-esteem'.[36] The Police Service of Northern Ireland's (PSNI) 'Chat, Share, Think' programme in particular encompasses the consequences of harmful sexual or exploitative behaviour by children and adolescents as 'victims' but also the long-term reputational and legal consequences for them as 'perpetrators'.

International approaches to educating youth on sexting, cyberbullying or youth sexual health, however, have been criticised as 'confusing and disengaging' (Shariff, 2008: 114–16) and in promoting an adult-centric view of risk which emphasises negative outcomes and the need for abstinence rather than harm reduction (Shoveller and Johnson, 2006; Salter et al., 2013; Crofts et al., 2015: 76–90; Hasinoff, 2015: 88–91). As outlined in Chapter 3, this is also broadly in keeping with penal and social policies within the 'risk society' which are focused on being 'risk averse' (Gill, 2007), rather than simply 'risk aware'. Indeed,

[32] See e.g. primary school programmes such as the NSPCC's 'Keeping Safe' and 'Share Aware'; and post-primary programmes such as the CEOP's 'Think You Know' and 'Nude Selfies'; the PSNI's award-winning 'Chat, Share, Think'; and Barnardo's 'The Real Story' and 'False Freedom'.

[33] Interview 9, 25 May 2016, Youth Support Worker.

[34] Interview 8, 23 May 2016, Rowan SARC Professional.

[35] Interview 12, 26 May 2016, Nurse Consultant in Sexual Health.

[36] Interview 14, 2 June 2016, Sexual Health Nurse.

by focusing on the negative aspects of children's sexuality, their vulnerability and the risks of victimisation or adverse consequences, we essentially reinforce binary gendered and cultural stereotypes and further limit their capacity for agency and informed decision-making. As Coy (2013: 157) argues, in empowering children in 'media literacy' we need to guard against the assumption that this will 'cancel out' other responses to sexualisation, such as 'fun, desire or humour'.

Indeed, several professionals acknowledged gaps in the current school provision relating to 'the emotional aspects of sex',[37] 'the normalisation of sexual language and images',[38] 'reinforcement of gender stereotypes'[39] and 'the nature of masculinity and femininity'.[40] In this respect, such 'gendered communication' (Marston, 2004) tends to shift the blame to girls (Hasinoff, 2015: 78) rather than utilise 'masculinity' as a possible site of 'disrupting' and 'contesting' sexual violence prevention (Carline, 2017). A minority of interviewees also articulated concern with the particular deficit within faith-based schools where 'a lot of it is wrong and poor information'.[41] Indeed, there was broad consensus among interviewees that 'more education in schools is necessary'[42]; 'schools are in the vanguard in all of this'[43]; 'we need to go back to basics . . . there isn't a high tech solution to the problem'[44]; and 'it has to be embedded in the curriculum.'[45] Moreover, in addition to addressing gendered norms, such programmes should also take account of cultural sensitivities surrounding public discourses on child sexual abuse in localised contexts including those related to ethnic minority groups (see e.g. Gilligan and Akhtar, 2006; Cowburn et al., 2015).

While there were 'pockets of really good practice' and 'different groups are doing different little things',[46] professionals also acknowledged that 'it is just not a standard or rolled out as a standard part of educational provision.'[47] Schools, in the opinions of many professionals in the study 'can do a lot more [and] have really got to step up to the mark here . . . and accept some responsibility around educating on

[37] Interview 9, 25 May 2016, Youth Support Worker.
[38] Interview 2, 18 April 2016, Independent Forensic Psychologist. [39] Ibid.
[40] Interview 23, 24 June 2016, Social Work Service Manager.
[41] Interview 19, 16 June 2016, Youth Worker, FPA.
[42] Interview 32, 2 November 2016, Police Officer.
[43] Interview 15, 3 June 2016, NSPCC Worker.
[44] Interview 11, 26 May 2016, Safeguarding Professional.
[45] Interview 15, 3 June 2016, NSPCC Worker.
[46] Interview 8, 23 May 2016, Rowan SARC Professional.
[47] Interview 9, 25 May 2016, Youth Support Worker.

sexual norms'.[48] The lack of province-wide provision was attributed to two factors – lack of resources and professionals and schools in particular which 'are frightened to deal with the issues'.[49]

Advocating the promotion of children's agency, resilience and digital and sexual citizenship is not to suggest overburdening children or young people with the sole responsibility for their safety and well-being. Rather than imposing further legal constraints on behaviours, however, it entails recognising the value of age-appropriate sex education as an important tool for facilitating discussions around responsibility and accountability, as well as risks tied to sexual behaviours. It also concerns giving children the trust and autonomy to make meaningful decisions for themselves and empowering them to navigate the myriad contemporary cultural challenges stemming from their developing sexuality and early romantic or sexual relationships. Indeed, as discussed further, this also points to the necessity of engaging parents and professionals more generally in discourses around contemporary sexual norms among children and adolescents.

BRIDGING THE 'NORMALISATION GAP'

As acknowledged earlier, one of the underlying premises of the risk paradigm is responsiblisation and the requirement for different constituencies, including schools and children and young people, to play their part in addressing potential risk. This task of engaging with contemporary cultural norms related to sex and sexuality among children and adolescents also extends to parents and other professionals who have an important role to play as part of the contextual strengthening of resilience (Aisenberg and Herrenkohl, 2008; Ungar, 2008) and addressing environmental protective factors (Pearce, 2009: 93–95). Indeed, more generally, emerging youth sexual identities are also embedded within community and family as well as peer or broader social contexts (Shoveller et al., 2004).

It has been argued, however, that the social and cultural understanding of risk-taking behaviour among children and young people often differs markedly from that of the adult world (see Chapter 4). This 'normalisation gap' between children and adults in terms of what constitutes normal, harmful or risky sexual behaviour has been

[48] Interview 24, 6 July 2016, Independent Treatment Professional.
[49] Interview 2, 18 April 2016, Independent Forensic Psychologist.

attributed to two competing factors – the failure or unwillingness of children and young people to regard sexual behaviour among peers as unwelcome, risky or potentially harmful and the deep-seated reticence of parents to countenance the 'being child' (Brownlie, 2001: 523–24) – what they are now rather that what they will become – in sexual terms, rooted in a paternalistic, romantic and 'golden' view (Pearson, 1984) of childhood.

Several interviewees spoke of the need for adults to engage with a broader range of risks to children and young people and come to terms with contemporary sexual norms as the 'new normal'. This priority was related to 'understanding it more and not labelling it . . . by having the knowledge of what young people are saying about it',[50] 'to get into the psyche of adolescence'[51] and 'to reframe where do they see sex'.[52] This was explained more fully by several professionals:

> Normality I think is a huge, huge comment. What does that mean to young people? And how do we react to their norm? And how do we manage them and then in terms of their risk . . . because are we still trying to manage their risk in relation to what general society perceives as normal? And I don't think we are geared up really, to deal with that.[53]
>
> What we mean by 'risk' young people don't mean the same thing . . . Risk to us is completely different, usually, from what a young person is talking about . . . Because if you are talking abstractly about risk, it just doesn't work . . . they don't see any risk there and they don't see themselves as being at risk or anything wrong with what's happening, at all.[54]

At a practical level, a key element of 'parental education' is addressing 'the digital disconnect' (Shariff, 2008: 124–30) between adults and children and 'upskilling' parents in digital literacy (Shariff, 2015: 154): 'parents haven't got the capacity or . . . the knowledge to be able to understand the impact of giving their child a phone that gives them access to the World Wide Web. Parents not knowing how to put parental controls on.'[55] Many interviewees also further related this to the importance of vocational training on HSB as a standard part of the university curriculum for those destined for future front-line service provision with children such as teachers, doctors and nurses.

[50] Ibid. [51] Interview 16, 6 June 2016, Social Work Consultant. [52] Ibid.
[53] Interview 11, 26 May 2016, Safeguarding Professional.
[54] Interview 18, 14 June 2016, Senior Voluntary Sector Interviewee.
[55] Interview 3, 20 April 2016, Education Authority Professional.

Engaging professionals and parents in discourses around HSB, however, invokes three principal challenges. The first relates to promoting a culture of 'openness' around children's sexuality. 'Sex-based shame' (Shoveller et al., 2004), premised on the view of sex as 'wrong and dirty',[56] silences meaningful discussion about sex and is particularly acute in Northern Ireland (see Chapter 7): 'it just having to have those uncomfortable conversations'[57]; 'we need to talk about that to say, there is no shame on us ... if we can reduce that stigma and have a conversation where people feel more freed up to talk about it, I think that's the best way to tackle some of the issues'[58]; 'making it normal ... it is being open to answering their questions at an age-appropriate level ... not hiding it ... not making it something shameful, I think is the bottom line.'[59] Indeed, as one safeguarding professional explained in relation to the issue of e-safety: 'it is not just about being technically savvy ... it is about communication.'[60] This issue of openness was also seen as being relevant to the capacity building of some professionals, 'who would be well aware of the issue [but] just don't have the confidence to deal with it'.[61] There is a delicate balance to be struck here, however, in terms of empowering children and young people around exploring their sexuality and their developing sexual identity and encouraging a culture of permissiveness and further experimentation around promiscuous or risky sexual behaviour.

The second relates to the need for parents and professionals to embrace or 'legitimise the fear' around children's sexuality where 'people are scared of opening Pandora's Box.'[62] A youth worker explained this factor as the 'transactional analysis' between parents and children in terms of understanding the other's perception of risk:

> It is about getting parents to actually realise who owns those fears ... We say well how do we work it to the middle? The transactional analysis. The parent/adult/child. How do you work it that way where you are giving your son or daughter the ability to make the informed choices? Because you own the fear ... It is about getting parents to accept the fear ... So it is fine to be frightened ... If you are not, there is something wrong ... But how I can overcome my fears is by giving my son or

56 Interview 19, 16 June 2016, Youth Worker, FPA.
57 Interview 28, 16 August 2016, Senior Voluntary Sector Interviewee (victim support).
58 Interview 8, 23 May 2016, Rowan SARC Professional.
59 Interview 12, 26 May 2016, Nurse Consultant in Sexual Health.
60 Interview 11, 26 May 2016, Safeguarding Professional.
61 Interview 21, 23 June 2016, Social Work Practitioner.
62 Interview 15, 3 June 2016, NSPCC Worker.

> daughter the best factual information that I can, and then allowing them to go.[63]

While schools and families have traditionally been the 'primary sites' of children's 'social experiences and socialization', they have also 'limit[ed] and confin[ed] children's knowledge and understanding' (Scraton, 1997b: 185). Sex education, for example, particularly in schools, has always been engulfed in a 'climate of fear' (Corteen and Scraton, 1997: 91). This is in large part due to the legal ambiguity surrounding the sexual competence of children and, as acknowledged earlier, broader social anxieties about regulating children's sexual activity. In this respect, embracing our fear as adults concerning children's sexuality challenges us to accept that 'the "crisis" is not one of "childhood" but of adultism' (Scraton, 1997b: 186).

A final challenge in engaging parents is the necessity for consistency of message. The rationale for this was related in particular to the difficulties for parents in 'trying to keep up to date with it . . . when everything is always moving on'[64]:

> Society changes and what becomes normal within age groups will change along with that. It always will. But it is what underlies that behaviour, those new actions, those new methods that they use. Fundamentally it is still the same. So we don't need to change the fundamentals of what causes harmful sexual behaviour .... We just need to be better at understanding people, society and communities.[65]

A small number of interviewees highlighted the difficulties around the lack of 'privacy around your image' where 'loads of parents put pictures of their children up on Facebook and they are not closed down'[66] and where children may follow the learned example of parents. A police officer explained the impact of this practice, which has become known as 'sharenting',[67] on perceptions of the digital self (see generally Blum-Ross and Livingstone, 2017):

> There was an expectation of privacy around your image. And I think that is lost. And I think that parents are contributory to that, because as a proud parent you may want to put your wee Johnny's First Holy

[63] Interview 19, 16 June 2016, Youth Worker, FPA.
[64] Interview 4, 21 April 2016, Child Care Centre Professional.
[65] Interview 2, 18 April 2016, Independent Forensic Psychologist.
[66] Interview 11, 26 May 2016, Safeguarding Professional.
[67] 'Sharenting' is a term used to describe the overuse of social media by parents in posting content or photos about their children.

> Communion picture up, or his first fall in a puddle, or first slobbery kiss by nanny. But you bring your children up having no expectation of privacy around their images. So it is no surprise that at 14 or 15, when they get control of their own image, that they don't know how to keep it private. And they have no expectation of keeping it private.[68]

Other interviewees related this issue to parental responsibility in offline contexts more broadly: 'there needs to be a better education of parents and making parents stop growing their children up older . . . I think we need parents to start parenting properly with clothes, with fashion, with computer games . . . there needs to be much more of a parent management and control of it that is not fed into it.'[69]

One of the consequences of the widespread availability of public health messages about e-safety in particular is that 'the message becomes very diluted . . . parents' heads are spinning because they do not know which is the right piece of information to look at. So they get confused. Professionals get confused.'[70] This book has documented the existence of the culture of confusion among children and young people around sexual norms and what constitutes risky or harmful sexual behaviour which has also become embedded within legal and policy frameworks governing sexual offences. A core goal of educative responses in engaging both adults and children should be to remove the 'isolation, fear and confusion' (Sanders and Spraggs, 1989: 17) surrounding sexual behaviours by children and young people. There is, therefore, a related need for consistency of message across organisational responses at a strategic policy level.

In sum, more effective policy or social responses to the problem of harmful sexual or exploitative behaviours by children and young people requires multilayered prevention involving children, parents, professionals and schools. It entails shared responsibility and 'participatory' social responses, rather than purely 'elitist' legal or policy responses (Johnstone, 2000), proactively managing potential risk, and incorporating children's views and voices. As one former police officer stated:

68 Interview 29, 10 October 2016, Police Officer. See e.g. the case of the Austrian teenager who sued her parents for posting childhood pictures on Facebook without permission: J. Huggler, 'Austrian Teenager Sues Parents for "Violating Privacy" with Childhood Facebook Pictures', *The Telegraph*, 24 September 2016. See also in the Italian context: L. Smith, 'Woman Faces £9,000 Fine if She Posts Pictures of Her Son on Facebook', *The Independent*, 12 January 2018.

69 Interview 16, 6 June 2016, Social Work Consultant.

70 Interview 27, 3 August 2016, Senior Social Work Practitioner.

> You can't criminalise everyone. So I think society has to take some responsibility, as do schools ... I think the media have to take some responsibility. Parents have to take some responsibility. There's a shared responsibility to send the right messages in terms of what may be seen as appropriate, what is definitely not appropriate, or what is not appropriate. There has to be some ownership right across communities but also across media in terms of how this is dealt with.[71]

Across cultures and over time, there will always be 'a new normal' and an ever evolving set of cultural and social risks to children and young people, stemming from consumer culture or technological advances, which existing legal and policy frameworks may struggle to capture or address. Moreover, as children change and develop psychologically, socially, cognitively and emotionally, so too does the world around them. At the same time, however, there are enduring basic human needs, shared by adults and children, for 'communication, intimacy, and interaction' (Davidson, 2014: 115) which, in line with children's broader social and emotional development, gradually extend outside the bounds of their immediate family environment. It is, therefore, the core cultural messages that we give to children and young people concerning navigating risky situations and the potential personal, social and legal consequences of peer-based sexual behaviours that need to be constant and consistent.

[71] Interview 7, 13 May 2015, Former Police Officer.

APPENDIX: RESEARCH METHODOLOGY

SAMPLING

Interviewees were initially selected on the basis of 'purposeful sampling' using a range of criteria including knowledge and experience of working on cases of harmful sexual behaviour or child sexual exploitation concerning children and young people and included those at the 'elite' managerial or policy level as well as those directly involved in front-line provision. Initial contacts were known professional associates of the author. Further participants were identified and recruited in two main ways. The first was on a 'snowballing' basis using professional referrals to other colleagues. Additionally, where research permissions were sought formally from the research governance department at a central agency level, the author was provided by the agency with the names and contact details of participants selected by them who had agreed to be interviewed and who matched the sampling criteria. The primary data was not intended to be representative but is used as an illustration of the difficulties concerning legal and policy constructions of 'risk' relating to children and young people who display harmful sexual or exploitative behaviours.

The author did not interview children or their families. There is no ethical justification for research that would risk further traumatisation of child victims and their families. Further, previous studies have examined the experiences of children and young people of online forms of offending using a quantitative methodology. This study presents a comprehensive and systematic review of these relevant literatures. A unique contribution of the study is an examination of the risks concerning child sexual exploitation and abuse committed by children and young people from an institutional perspective. As such, the perspectives of children and their families concerning broad experiences within these types of cases were examined through the prism of professional agencies as well as advocacy groups.

INTERVIEW SCHEDULE AND PROCEDURE

Thirty-two face-to-face, semi-structured in-depth interviews were conducted on a one-to-one basis, lasting between 60 and 90 minutes. Interview questions were framed around the key themes from the secondary literature on harmful sexual and exploitative behaviours by children and young people, as well as sexual offending more generally. Participants, however, were encouraged to go beyond these questions to address other issues which they believed were important to tackling such behaviours. These included broader reflections on the legal and policy frameworks, and wider professional challenges in this area of work. Brief notes were taken by the author during the interview. All interviews were taped and fully transcribed. The transcripts were analysed by the author in conjunction with similarities or departures from the key themes arising from the secondary literature.

BIBLIOGRAPHY

Adler, N. A. and Schutz, J. (1995), 'Sibling Incest Offenders', *Child Abuse & Neglect* 19(7): 811–19.

Aisenberg, E. and Herrenkohl, T. (2008), 'Community Violence in Context: Risk and Resilience in Children and Families', *Journal of Interpersonal Violence* 23(3): 296–315.

Akdeniz, Y. (2008), *Internet Child Pornography and the Law* (Aldershot: Ashgate).

Alao, A. A. and Molojwane, M. B. (2008), 'Childhood Sexual Abuse: The Botswana Perspectives', in M. J. Smith (ed.), *Child Sexual Abuse: Issues and Challenges* (New York: Nova Science Publishers).

Albrecht, H.-J. (1997), 'Dangerous Criminal Offenders in the German Criminal Justice System', *Federal Sentencing Reporter* 10(2): 69–73.

Albury, K., Crawford, K., Byron, P. and Mathews, B. (2013), *Young People and Sexting in Australia: Ethics, Representation, and the Law*, ARC Centre for Creative Industries and Innovation, University of New South Wales, Australia, www.cci.edu.au/sites/default/files/Young_People_And_Sexting_Final.pdf.

Albury K. M. (2016), 'Politics of Sexting Revisited', in A. McCosker, S. Vivienne and A. Johns (eds), *Negotiating Digital Citizenship: Control, Contest and Culture* (London: Rowman and Littlefield International).

Alderson, P. (1995), *Listening to Children: Children, Social Research and Ethics* (London: Barnardo's).

(2000), 'Children as Researchers: The Effects of Participation Rights on Research Methodology', in P. Christensen and A. James (eds), *Research with Children: Perspectives and Practices* (London: Falmer Press).

(2008), *Young Children's Rights: Exploring Beliefs, Principles and Practice* (2d edn) (London and Philadelphia: Jessica Kingsley Publishers).

Allardyce, S. and Yates, P. M. (2013), 'Assessing Risk of Victim Crossover with Children and Young People Who Display Harmful Sexual Behaviours', *Child Abuse Review* 22(4): 255–67.

Allen, M., Emmers, T., Genhardt, L. and Giery, M. A. (2006), 'Exposure to Pornography and Acceptance of Rape Myths', *Journal of Communication* 45 (1): 5–26.

Allnock, D. (2010), *Children and Young People Disclosing Abuse: A Research Briefing* (London: NSPCC).

Almeida, A., Correia, I., Marinho, S. and Garcia, D. (2012), 'Virtual But Not Less Real', in Q. Li, D. Cross and P. K. Smith (eds), *Cyberbullying in the Global Playground: Research from International Perspectives* (Chichester: Wiley-Blackwell).

Ambert, A. M. (1994), 'A Qualitative Study of Peer Abuse and Its Effects: Theoretical and Empirical Implications', *Journal of Marriage and the Family* 56(1): 119–30.

Ambler, W. (1987), 'Aristotle on Nature and Politics: The Case of Slavery', *Political Theory* 15(3): 390–410.

American Psychiatric Association (APA) (2013), *Diagnostic and Statistical Manual of Mental Disorders DSM-5* (5th edn) (Arlington, VA: American Psychiatric Publishing).

Ames, M. A. and Houston, D. A. (1990), 'Legal, Social, and Biological Definitions of Pedophilia', *Archives of Sexual Behavior* 19(4): 333–42.

Anderson, C. A., Shibuya, A., Ihori, N., Swing, E. L., Bushman, B. J., Brad, J., Sakamoto, A., Rithstein, H. and Saleem, M. (2010), 'Violent Video Game Effects on Aggression, Empathy, and Prosocial Behavior in Eastern and Western Countries: A Meta-Analytic Review', *Psychological Bulletin* 136(2): 151–73.

Appleton, J. V. (2014), 'Child Sexual Exploitation, Victimisation and Vulnerability', *Child Abuse Review* 23(3): 155–58.

Aries, P. (1962), *Centuries of Childhood; a Social History of Family Life*. Translated from the French by Robert Baldick (New York: Knopf).

Armstrong, D. (2004), 'A Risky Business? Research, Policy, Governmentality and Youth Offending', *Youth Justice* 4(2): 100–16.

Armstrong, E. A., Hamilton, L. and Sweeney, B. (2006), 'Sexual Assault on Campus: A Multilevel, Integrative Approach to Party Rape', *Social Problems* 53(4): 483–99.

Arnold, B. (2009), *The Irish Gulag: How the State Betrayed Its Innocent Children* (Dublin: Gill and Macmillan).

Arthur, R. (2016), 'Exploring Childhood, Criminal Responsibility and the Evolving Capacities of the Child: The Age of Criminal Responsibility in England and Wales', *Northern Ireland Legal Quarterly* 67(3): 269–82.

Ashe, F. (2014), '"All About Eve": Mothers, Masculinities and the 2011 UK Riots', *Political Studies* 62(3): 652–68.

Ashenden, A. (2002), 'Policing Perversion: The Contemporary Governance of Paedophilia', *Cultural Values* 6(1–2): 197–222.

Ashfield, S., Brotherston, S., Eldridge, H. and Elliott, I. (2010), 'Working with Female Sexual Offenders: Therapeutic Process Issues', in T. A. Gannon and F. Cortoni (eds), *Female Sexual Offenders: Theory, Assessment and Treatment* (Chichester: Wiley-Blackwell).

Ashurst, L. (2013), 'Social Media; Their Impact on Sexual Norms', paper presented at NOTA (National Organisation for the Treatment of Abusers) Northern Ireland Conference, New-forge, Belfast, 28 May 2013.

(2014), 'CSE', paper presented at an Include Youth Seminar, Belfast, 18 December 2014 (copy supplied to the author).

(2015), 'HSB: Causal Assumptions', paper presented at the NOTA Northern Ireland Seminar, 25 November 2015.

(2016), 'Children and Young People with Harmful Sexual Behaviour', policy paper prepared for NOTA (copy supplied to the author).

Ashurst, L. and McAlinden, A. (2015), 'Young People, Peer-to-Peer Grooming and Sexual Offending: Understanding and Responding to Harmful Sexual Behaviour Within a Social Media Society', *Probation Journal* 62(4): 374–88.

Ashworth, A. and Zedner, L. (2012), 'Prevention and Criminalization: Justification and Limits', *New Criminal Law Review* 15(4): 542–71.

Atkinson, R. and Rodgers, T. (2016), 'Pleasure Zones and Murder Boxes: Online Pornography and Violent Video Games as Cultural Zones of Exception', *British Journal of Criminology* 56(6): 1291–307.

Attwood, F. (2017), *Sex Media* (Oxford: Polity Press).

Australian Human Rights Commission. (1997), *Bringing Them Home*. Report of the National Inquiry into the Separation of Aboriginal and Torres Strait Islander Children from Their Families (Australia: Australian Human Rights Commission).

Ayland, L. and West, B. (2006), 'The Good Way Model: A Strengths-Based Approach for Working with Young People, Especially Those with Intellectual Difficulties, Who Have Sexually Abusive Behaviour', *Journal of Sexual Aggression* 12(2): 189–201.

Bagley, C. and King, K. (1990), *Child Sexual Abuse: The Search for Healing* (London and New York: Tavistock, Routledge).

Bailey, R. (2011), *Letting Children Be Children*. Report of an Independent Review of the Commercialisation and Sexualisation of Childhood (London: Department for Education).

Baker, A. W. and Duncan, S. P. (1985), 'Child Sexual Abuse: A Study of Prevalence in Great Britain', *Child Abuse and Neglect* 9(4): 457–67.

Ball, C. (2000), The Youth Justice and Criminal Evidence Act 1999 Part I: A Significant Move Towards Restorative Justice, or a Recipe for Unintended Consequences? *Criminal Law Review*, 211–22.

Ballet, J., Biggeri, M. and Comim, F. (2011), 'Children's Agency and the Capability Approach: A Conceptual Framework', in M. Biggeri, J. Ballet and F. Comin (eds), *Children and the Capability Approach* (Basingstoke: Palgrave Macmillan).

Bancroft, J. (2009), *Human Sexuality and Its Problems* (London: Elsevier Health Sciences).

Barbaree, H. E. and Marshall, W. L. (eds) (2008), *The Juvenile Sex Offender* (New York: Guilford Press).

Barnardo's (2009), *Whose Child Now? Fifteen Years of Working to Prevent Sexual Exploitation of Children in the UK*, www.barnardos.org.uk/whose_child_now.pdf.

(2011), *Puppet on a String: The Urgent Need to Cut Children Free from Sexual Exploitation*, www.barnardos.org.uk/ctf_puppetonastring_report_final.pdf.

(2012), *Cutting Them Free: How Is the UK Progressing in Protecting Its Children from Sexual Exploitation*, www.barnardos.org.uk/cuttingthemfree.pdf.

(2014,) *Research on the Sexual Exploitation of Boys and Young Men: A UK Scoping Study, Summary of Findings* (Barkingside: Barnardo's).

Baron, S. W. (2003), 'Street Youth Violence and Victimization', *Trauma, Violence, & Abuse* 4(1): 22–44.

Barrett, D. (ed.) (1997), *Child Prostitution in Britain: Dilemmas and Practical Responses* (London: Children's Society).

Barter, C. (2011), 'A Thoroughly Gendered Affair: Teenage Partner Violence and Exploitation', in C. Barter and D. Berridge (eds), *Children Behaving Badly? Peer Violence Between Children and Young People* (West Sussex: John Wiley & Sons Ltd).

(2013), 'Children and Young People Who Harm Others', *Child Abuse Review* 22(4): 227–31.

(2015), *Briefing Paper 2: Incidence Rates and Impact of Experiencing Interpersonal Violence and Abuse in Young People's Relationships*, www.stiritup.eu/wp-content/uploads/2015/02/STIRBriefing-Paper-21.pdf.

Barter, C. and Berridge, D. (eds) (2011), *Children Behaving Badly?: Peer Violence Between Children and Young People* (Chichester: John Wiley & Sons).

Barter, C., McCarry, M., Berridge, D. and Evans, K. (2009), *Partner Exploitation and Violence in Teenage Intimate Relationships* (London: NSPCC).

Baumeiser, R. F. (1996), *Evil: Inside Human Violence and Cruelty* (New York: W. H. Freeman).

Baym, N. K. (2010), *Personal Connections in the Digital Age* (Cambridge: Polity Press).

Beck, U. (1992), *Risk Society: Towards a New Modernity* (London: Sage).

(1999), *World Risk Society* (Cambridge: Polity Press).

(2002), 'The Terrorist Threat: World Risk Society Revisited', *Theory, Culture & Society* 19(4): 39–55.

(2009), *World at Risk* (Cambridge: Polity Press).

Becker, H. (1963), *Outsiders: Studies in the Sociology of Deviance* (New York: The Free Press of Glencoe).

Becker, J. V. and Hicks, S. J. (2003), 'Juvenile Sexual Offenders', *Annals of the New York Academy of Sciences* 989(1): 397–410.

Becker, K. and Marcum, C. D. (2015), 'Sexual Victimization Online', in T. R. Richards and C. D. Marcum (eds), *Sexual Victimization: Then and Now* (Thousand Oaks, CA: Sage Publications).

Beckett, H. (2011), *Not a World Away: The Sexual Exploitation of Children and Young People in Northern Ireland* (Barnardo's Northern Ireland), www.barnardos.org.uk/13932_not_a_world_away_full_report.pdf.

Beckett, H., with Brodie, I., Factor, F., Melrose, M., Pearce, J. Pitts, J. and Warrington, C. (2012), *Research into Gang-Associated Sexual Exploitation and Sexual Violence: Interim Report*, University of Bedfordshire, www.beds.ac.uk/__data/assets/pdf_file/0008/215873/GASV_Interim.pdf.

(2013), *'It's Wrong – But You Get Used to It': A Qualitative Study of Gang-Associated Sexual Violence Towards, and Exploitation of, Young People in England.* A Report commissioned by the Office of the Children's Commissioner's Inquiry into Child Sexual Exploitation in Gangs and Groups, www.beds.ac.uk/__data/assets/pdf_file/0005/293234/Gangs-Report-final.pdf.

Beckett, H., Firmin, C., Hynes, P. and Pearce, J. (2014), *Tackling Child Sexual Exploitation: A Study of Current Practice in London* (London: London Councils and The London Safeguarding Children Board).

Beckett, R. (1996), 'Risk Prediction, Decision Making and Evaluation of Adolescent Sexual Abusers', in M. Erooga and H. Masson (eds), *Children and Young People Who Sexually Abuse Others: Current Developments and Practice Responses* (2d edn) (Abingdon: Routledge).

Behlmer, G. K. (1982), *Child Abuse and Moral Reform in England 1870–1980* (Stanford, CA: Stanford University Press).

Bell, D. (1995), 'Pleasure and Danger: The Paradoxical Spaces of Sexual Citizenship', *Political Geography* 14(2): 139–53.

Bem, S. L. (1993), *The Lenses of Gender: Transforming the Debate on Sexual Inequality* (New Haven, CT: Yale University Press).

Ben-Amos, I. K. (1995), 'Adolescence as a Cultural Invention: Philippe Ariès and the Sociology of Youth', *History of the Human Sciences* 8(2): 69–89.

Bennett, W. L., Wells, C. and Rank, A. (2009), 'Young Citizens and Civic Learning: Two Paradigms of Citizenship in the Digital Age', *Citizenship Studies* 13(2): 105–20.

Bentovim, A. (2002), 'Research on the Development of Sexually Abusive Behaviour in Sexually Abused Males: The Implications for Clinical Practice', in M. C. Calder (ed.), *Young People Who Sexually Abuse: Building the Evidence for Your Practice* (Lyme Regis: Russell House Publishing).

Ben-Yehuda, N. (2001), *Betrayal and Treason: Violations of Trust and Loyalty* (Boulder, CO: Westview).

Berelowitz, S., Clifton, J., Firmin, C., Gulyurtlu, S. and Edwards, G. (2013), *'If Only Someone Had Listened'*, Office of the Children's Commissioner's Inquiry into Child Sexual Exploitation in Gangs and Groups: Final Report, www.thebromleytrust.org.uk/files/chidrens-commission.pdf.

Berelowitz, S., Firmin, C., Edwards, G. and Gulyurtlu, S. (2012), *'I Thought I Was the Only One. The Only One in the World'*, The Office of the Children's Commissioner's Inquiry into Child Sexual Exploitation in Gangs and Groups: Interim Report, www.dera.ioe.ac.uk/16067/1/FINAL_REPORT_FOR_WEBSITE_Child_Sexual_Exploitation_in_Gangs_and_Groups_Inquiry_Interim_Report__21_11_12.pdf.

Berelowitz, S., Ritchie, G., Edwards, G., Gulyurtlu, S. and Clifton, J. (2015), *'If It's Not Better It's Not the End'*, Inquiry into Child Sexual Exploitation in Gangs and Groups: One Year On, www.childrenscommissioner.gov.uk/sites/default/files/publications/If%20its%20not%20better%20its%20not%20the%20end_web%20copy.pdf.

Berkowitz, A. (1992), 'College Men as Perpetrators of Acquaintance Rape and Sexual Assault: A Review of Recent Research', *Journal of American College Health* 40(4): 175–81.

Berliner, L. and Conte, J. R. (1995), 'The Effects of Disclosure and Intervention on Sexually Abused Children', *Child Abuse & Neglect* 19(3): 371–84.

Bernstein, D. P., Fink, L., Handelsman, L., Foote, J., Lovejoy, M., Wenzel, K. Sapareto, E. and Ruggiero, J. (1994), 'Initial Reliability and Validity of a New Retrospective Measure of Child Abuse and Neglect', *The American Journal of Psychiatry* 151(8): 1132–36.

Berry, J. (1992), *Lead Us Not Into Temptation: Catholic Priests and the Sexual Abuse of Children* (New York: Doubleday).

Berry, M., Philo, G., Tiripelli, G., Docherty, S., and Macpherson, C. (2012), 'Media Coverage and Public Understanding of Sentencing Policy in Relation to Crimes Against Children', *Criminology and Criminal Justice* 12 (5): 567–91.

Berscheid, E. and Walster, E. (1974), 'Physical Attractiveness', in L. Berkowitz (ed.), *Advances in Experimental Social Psychology*, Vol. 7: 157–215.

Best, J. (1993), *Threatened Children: Rhetoric and Concern About Child-Victims* (Chicago: University of Chicago Press).

Bichard, Sir M. (2004), *The Bichard Inquiry Report* (London: Home Office).

Birch, D. (2000), 'A Better Deal for Vulnerable Witnesses?' *Criminal Law Review* 223–49.

Birmingham Safeguarding Children Board (BSCB) (2010), *Serious Case Review Under Chapter VII, 'Working Together to Safeguard Children' in Respect of the Death of a Child Case Number 14*, www.northshropshe.wordpress.com/scr-khyra-ishaq/.

Bischof, G. P., Stith, S. M. and Whitney, M. L. (1995), 'Family Environments of Adolescent Sex Offenders and Other Juvenile Delinquents', *Adolescence*, 30(117): 157–71.

Blum-Ross, A. and Livingstone, S. (2017), '"Sharenting," Parent Blogging, and the Boundaries of the Digital Self', *Popular Communication* 15(2): 110–25.

Boer, D. P., Eher, R., Craig, L. A., Miner, M. H. and Pfäfflin, F. (2011), *International Perspectives on the Assessment and Treatment of Sexual Offenders: Theory, Practice and Research* (Chichester: Wiley-Blackwell).

Bok, S. (1983), *Secrets: On the Ethics of Concealment and Revelation* (New York: Vintage Books).

Booth, A., Crouter, A. C. and Snyder, A. (eds) (2015), *Romance and Sex in Adolescence and Emerging Adulthood: Risks and Opportunities* (Mahwah, NJ: Lawrence Erlbaum Associates).

Boswell, A. A. and Spade, J. Z. (1996), 'Fraternities and Collegiate Rape Culture: Why Are Some Fraternities More Dangerous Places for Women?' *Gender & Society* 10(2): 133–47.

Bottino, S. M.B., Bottino, C., Regina, C. G., Correia, A. V. L. and Ribeiro, W. S. (2015), 'Cyberbullying and Adolescent Mental Health: Systematic Review', *Cadernos de Saude Publica* 31(3): 463–75.

Bouvier, P. (2003), 'Child Sexual Abuse: Vicious Circles of Fate or Paths to Resilience?' *The Lancet* 361(9356): 446–47.

Boyd, D. (2014), *It's Complicated: The Social Lives of Networked Teens* (New Haven, CT: Yale University Press).

Braithwaite, J. (1989), *Crime, Shame and Reintegration* (Cambridge: Cambridge University Press).

(2000), 'The New Regulatory State and the Transformation of Criminology', *British Journal of Criminology* 40(2): 222–38.

(2003), 'Principles of Restorative Justice', in A. von Hirsch, J. V. Roberts, A. E. Bottoms, K. Roach and M. Schiff (eds), *Restorative Justice and Criminal Justice: Competing or Irreconcilable Paradigms* (Oxford: Hart Publishing).

Brandon, M. and Thoburn, J. (2008), 'Safeguarding Children in the UK: A Longitudinal Study of Services to Children Suffering or Likely to Suffer Significant Harm', *Child & Family Social Work* 13(4): 365–77.

Bray, A. (2008), 'The Question of Intolerance: "Corporate Paedophilia" and Child Sexual Abuse Moral Panics', *Australian Feminist Studies* 23 (57): 323–41.

Brennan, C. (2008), 'Facing What Cannot Be Changed: The Irish Experience of Confronting Institutional Child Abuse', *Journal of Social Welfare & Family Law* 29(3–4): 245–63.

Brent Borough Council (BBC) and Brent Health Authority (BHA) (1985), *A Child in Trust: The Report of the Panel of Inquiry into the Circumstances*

Surrounding the Death of Jasmine Beckford (London: London Borough of Brent).

British Association of Social Workers (BASW) (2016), *Fixers Investigates: The Trouble with . . . Sex in Schools.* Report in Support of the Sexual Harassment and Violence in Schools Inquiry (HC, the Women and Equalities Committee), www.parliament.uk/documents/commons-committees/women-and-equalities/FixersSS.pdf.

Brodie, I. and Pearce, J. (2012), *Exploring the Scale and Nature of Child Sexual Exploitation in Scotland,* Scottish Government and Social Research, www.gov.scot/Resource/0040/00404853.pdf.

Brookfield, S. D. (2013), 'Helping Children to Stand Up to Society: Critical Challenges and Culture Jamming', in J. Wild (ed.), *Exploiting Childhood: How Fast Food, Material Obsession and Porn Culture Are Creating New Forms of Child Abuse* (London: Jessica Kingsley Publishers).

Brooks, J. E. (2006), 'Strengthening Resilience in Children and Youths: Maximizing Opportunities through the Schools', *Children & Schools* 28(2): 69–76.

Brooks, L. (2006), *The Story of Childhood: Growing up in Modern Britain* (London: Bloomsbury Publishing).

Brown, A. (2011), 'Relationships, Community, and Identity in the New Virtual Society', *The Futurist* 45(2): 29–31.

Brown, J. D. (2002), 'Mass Media Influences on Sexuality', *Journal of Sex Research* 39(1): 42–45.

(2011), 'Understanding Dimensions of "Peer Violence" in Preschool Settings: An Exploration of Key Issues and Questions', in C. Barter and D. Berridge (eds), *Children Behaving Badly* (Chichester: Wiley-Blackwell).

Brown, J. D., L'Engle, K. L., Pardun, C. J., Guo, G., Kenneavy, K. and Jackson, C. (2006), 'Sexy Media Matter: Exposure to Sexual Content in Music, Movies, Television, and Magazines Predicts Black and White Adolescents' Sexual Behavior', *Pediatrics* 117(4): 1018–27.

Brown, J. D., Halpern, C. T. and L'Engle, K. L. (2005), 'Mass Media as a Sexual Super Peer for Early Maturing Girls', *Journal of Adolescent Health* 36(5): 420–27.

Brown, J. D. and Strasburger, V. C. (2007), 'From Calvin Klein to Paris Hilton and MySpace: Adolescents, Sex, and the Media', *Adolescent Medicine: State of the Art Reviews* 18(3): 484–507.

Brown, S. (2005), *Understanding Youth and Crime: Listening to Youth?* (Maidenhead: McGraw-Hill Education).

Brownlie, J. (2001), 'The "Being-Risky" Child: Governing Childhood and Sexual Risk', *Sociology* 35(2): 519–37.

Bryant, J. (1985), *Frequency of Exposure, Age of Initial Exposure and Reactions to Initial Exposure to Pornography*. Report presented to Attorney General's Commission on Pornography (Houston, TX).

Bryce, J. O. and Rutter, J. (2003), 'Gender Dynamics and the Social and Spatial Organization of Computer Gaming', *Leisure Studies* 22(1): 1–15.

Buckingham, D. and Bragg, S. (2003), *Young People, Media and Personal Relationships* (London: Research Project funded by the Advertising Standards Authority, the British Board of Film Classification, the BBC, the Broadcasting Standards Commission and the Independent Television Commission).

Buckingham, D., Bragg, S., Russell, R. and Willett, R. (2010), *Sexualised Goods aimed at Children*. Research Report (Edinburgh: Scottish Parliament).

Buckley, H., Carr, N. and Whelan, S. (2011), 'Like Walking on Eggshells': Service User Views and Expectations of the Child Protection System', *Child & Family Social Work* 16(1): 101–10.

Buckley, H., Skehill, C. and O'Sullivan, E. (1997), *Child Protection Practices in Ireland* (Dublin: Oak Tree Press).

Buckley, O. (2016), 'Sexual Violence in Pre-pubertal Children', paper presented at the NOTA Northern Ireland Seminar, 25 November 2015.

Bunting, L. (2008), 'Sexual Offences Against Children: An Exploration of Attrition in the Northern Ireland Criminal Justice System', *Child Abuse & Neglect* 32(12): 1109–18.

Bunting, L., Anderson, P. and Allnock, D. (2009), *Sexual Abuse and Therapeutic Services for Children and Young People in Northern Ireland* (London: NSPCC).

Burton, D. L., Nesmith, A. A., and Badten, L. (1997), 'Clinician's Views on Sexually Aggressive Children and Their Families: A Theoretical Exploration', *Child Abuse & Neglect* 21(2): 157–70.

Butler, J. (1990), *Gender Trouble: Feminism and the Subversion of Identity* (London: Routledge).

(1993), *Bodies That Matter: On the Discursive Limits of 'Sex'* (New York: Routledge).

Button, D. M., O'Connell, D. J. and Gealt, R. (2012), 'Sexual Minority Youth Victimization and Social Support: The Intersection of Sexuality, Gender, Race, and Victimization', *Journal of Homosexuality* 59(1): 18–43.

Caffaro, J. V. (2013), *Sibling Abuse Trauma: Assessment and Intervention Strategies for Children, Families, and Adults* (2d edn) (Hove, East Sussex and New York: Routledge).

Caffaro, J. V. and Conn-Caffaro, A. (2005), 'Treating Sibling Abuse Families', *Aggression and Violent Behavior* 10(5): 604–23.

Calder, M. C. (2002), 'A Framework for Conducting Risk Assessment', *Child Care in Practice* 8(1): 7–18.

Calder, M. C., Epps, K. J. and Hanks, H. G. (1997), *Juveniles and Children Who Sexually Abuse: A Guide to Risk Assessment* (Dorset: Russell House).

Carline, A., Gunby, C. and Taylor, S. (2017), 'Too Drunk to Consent? Exploring the Contestations and Disruptions in Male-Focused Sexual

Violence Prevention Interventions', *Social & Legal Studies*, online first version, doi:0964663917713346.

Carlson, B. E., Maciol, K. and Schneider, J. (2006), 'Sibling Incest: Reports from Forty-one Survivors', *Journal of Child Sexual Abuse* 15(4): 19–34.

Carney, A. G. and Merrell, K. W. (2001), 'Bullying in Schools: Perspectives on Understanding and Preventing an International Problem', *School Psychology International* 22(3): 364–82.

Carr, J. L. and VanDeusen, K. M. (2004), 'Risk Factors for Male Sexual Aggression on College Campuses', *Journal of Family Violence* 19(5): 279–89.

Carr, N. and McAlister, S. (2014), 'Youth Justice in Ireland North and South: Legacies of the Past, Influences on the Present', *Youth Justice* 14(3): 207–11.

Carrabine, E. (2012), 'Just Images Aesthetics, Ethics and Visual Criminology', *British Journal of Criminology* 52(3): 463–89.

Carrabine, E., Inganski, P., Lee, M., Plummer, K. and South, N. (2004), *Criminology: A Sociological Introduction* (London: Routledge).

Carrington, K. (1993), *Offending Girls: Sex, Youth and Justice* (Sydney: Allen and Unwin).

Carroll, J. S., Padilla-Walker, L. M., Nelson, L. J., Olson, C. D., Barry, C. M. and Madsen, S. D. (2008), 'Generation XXX: Pornography Acceptance and Use Among Emerging Adults', *Journal of Adolescent Research* 23(1): 6–30.

Carson, C. (2015), 'Understanding and Working with Children Under 12 and Their Families', paper presented at the NOTA Northern Ireland Seminar, 25 November 2015.

(2016), 'CSE Continuum', unpublished, presented to the author for citation in the course of fieldwork for this study.

Casey, L. (2015), *Report of Inspection of Rotherham Metropolitan Borough Council*, HC 1050, www.gov.uk/government/uploads/system/uploads/attachment_data/file/401119/46966_Rotherham_Report_PRINT.pdf.

Cashmore, J. and Bussey, K. (1996), 'Judicial Perceptions of Child Witness Competence', *Law and Human Behavior* 20(3): 313–34.

Castel, R. (1991), 'From Dangerousness to Risk', in G. Burchell, C. Gordon and P. Miller (eds), *The Foucault Effect: Studies in Govermentality* (Chicago: University of Chicago Press).

Cavadino, M. and Dignan, J. (2006), 'Penal Policy and Political Economy', *Criminology and Criminal Justice* 6(4): 435–56.

Cave, E. (2014), 'Goodbye *Gillick*? Identifying and Resolving Problems with the Concept of Child Competence', *Legal Studies* 34(1): 103–22.

Cawson, P, Wattam, C, Brooker, S. and Kelly, G. (2000), *Child Maltreatment in the United Kingdom* (London: NSPCC).

Chaffin, M. (2008), 'Our Minds Are Made Up – Don't Confuse Us with the Facts: Commentary on Policies Concerning Children with Sexual Behavior Problems and Juvenile Sex Offenders', *Child Maltreatment* 13(2): 110–21.

Chan, W. and Simester, A. P. (2011), 'Four Functions of Mens Rea', *The Cambridge Law Journal* 70(2): 381–96.

Chase, E, and Statham, J. (2005), 'Commercial and Sexual Exploitation of Children and Young People in the UK: A Review', *Child Abuse Review* 14 (1): 4–25.

Chen, H., Chung, W., Qin, J., Reid, E., Sageman, M. and Weimann, G. (2008), 'Uncovering the Dark Web: A Case Study of Jihad on the Web', *Journal of the American Society for Information Science and Technology* 59(8): 1347–59.

Chesnais, J. C. (1981), *History of Violence in the West* (Paris: University of Paris).

Chetti, S. (2005), 'Effects of Interview Style and Witness Age on Perceptions of Children's Credibility in Sexual Abuse Cases', *Journal of Applied Social Psychology* 35(2): 297–319.

Child Exploitation and Online Protection Centre (CEOP) (2010), *Strategic Overview 2009–2010* (London: CEOP), www.ceop.police.uk/Documents/Strategic_Overview_2009-10_(Unclassified).pdf.

(2011), *Out of Mind, Out of Sight. Breaking Down the Barriers to Understanding Child Sexual Exploitation*, www.ceop.police.uk/Documents/ceopdocs/ceop_thematic_assessment_executive_summary.pdf

(2012), *Threat Assessment of Child Sexual Exploitation and Abuse*, www.ceop.police.uk/Documents/ceopdocs/CEOP_TACSEA2013_240613%20FINAL.pdf

Choi, E. P. H., Wong, J. Y. H., Lo, H. H. M., Wong, W., Chio, J. H. M. and Fong, D. Y. T. (2016), 'The Impacts of Using Smartphone Dating Applications on Sexual Risk Behaviours in College Students in Hong Kong', *PLoS one*, 11(11), early online version: e0165394. doi:10.1371/journal.pone.0165394.

Choo, K.-K. R. (2009), *Online Child Grooming: A Literature Review on the Misuse of Social Networking Sites for Grooming Children for Sexual Offences*, AIC Reports Research and Public Policy Series 103 (Canberra: Australian Institute of Criminology).

Christiansen, J. and Blake, R. (1990), 'The Grooming Process in Father-Daughter Incest', in A. Horton, B. Johnson, L. Roundy and D. Williams (eds), *The Incest Perpetrator: A Family Member No One Wants to Treat* (Newbury Park, CA: Sage).

Christie, C. (1986), 'The Ideal Victim', in E. Fattah (ed.), *From Crime Policy to Victim Policy* (Basingstoke: Macmillan).

Chung, D. (2005), 'Violence, Control, Romance and Gender Equality: Young Women and Heterosexual Relationships', *Women's Studies International Forum* 28(6): 445–55.

Clapton, G., Cree, V. E. and Smith, M. (2013), 'Moral Panics and Social Work: Towards a Sceptical View of UK Child Protection', *Critical Social Policy* 33(2): 197–217.

Clutton, S. and Coles, J. (2007), *Sexual Exploitation Risk Assessment Framework: A Pilot Study* (Cardiff: Barnardo's Cymru).

Cockbain, E. (2013), 'Grooming and the "Asian Sex Gang Predator": The Construction of a Racial Crime Threat', *Race & Class* 54(4): 22–32.

Coffey, G. (2009), 'Codifying the Meaning of "Intention" in the Criminal Law', *The Journal of Criminal Law* 73(5): 394–413.

Cohen, L. E. and Felson, M. (1979), 'Social Change and Crime Rate Trends: A Routine Activity Approach', *American Sociological Review* 44(4): 588–608.

Cohen, S. (1972), *Folk Devils and Moral Panics* (London: Paladin).

(2001), *States of Denial: Knowing About Atrocities and Suffering* (Cambridge: Polity Press).

Coleman, J. S. (1990), *Foundations of Social Theory* (Cambridge, MA: Harvard University Press).

Collie, R., Ward, T., Ayland, L. and West, B. (2007), 'The Good Lives Model of Rehabilitation: Reducing Risks and Promoting Strengths with Adolescent Sexual Offenders', in M. C. Calder (ed.), *Working with Children and Young People Who Sexually Abuse: Taking the Field Forward* (Lyme Regis: Russell House).

Collison, M. (1996), 'In Search of the High Life: Drugs, Crime, Masculinities and Consumption', *British Journal of Criminology* 36(3): 428–44.

Colton, M. (2002), 'Factors Associated with Abuse in Residential Child Care Institutions', *Children and Society* 16(1): 33–44.

Colton, M., Vanstone, M. and Walby, C. (2002), 'Victimization, Care and Justice: Reflections on the Experience of Victims/Survivors involved in Large-scale Historical Investigations of Child Sexual Abuse in Residential Institutions', *British Journal of Social Work* 32(5): 541–51.

Comartin, E. B. Kernsmith, P. D. and Kernsmith, R. M. (2009), 'Sanctions for Sex Offenders: Fear and Public Policy', *Journal of Offender Rehabilitation* 48 (7): 605–19.

Commission of Inquiry (2011), *Sexual Abuse of Minors in the Roman Catholic Church*, Summary of the report in English: www.onderzoekrk.nl/fileadmin /commissiedeetman/data/downloads/eindrapport/20111216/Samenvatting _eindrapport_Engelstalig.pdf.

Commission of Investigation (2009), *Report into the Catholic Archdiocese of Dublin* (Chair: Judge Yvonne Murphy) (November 2009) (Dublin: Department of Justice and Law Reform), also available at www.dacoi.ie.

(2011), *Report into the Catholic Archdiocese of Cloyne* (Chair: Judge Yvonne Murphy) (July, 2011) (Dublin: Department of Justice and Law Reform), also available at www.dacoi.ie.

Commission to Inquire into Child Abuse (2009), *Report of the Commission to Inquire Into Child Abuse* (Chair: Judge Séan Ryan) (May 2009), www .childabusecommission.ie.

Connell, R. W. and Messerschmidt, J. W. (2005). 'Hegemonic Masculinity Rethinking the Concept', *Gender & Society* 19(6): 829–59.

Conte, J. R. (1994), 'Child Sexual Abuse: Awareness and Backlash', *The Future of Children* 4(2): 224–32.

Conte, J. R., Wolf, S. and Smith, T. (1989), 'What Sexual Offenders Tell Us About Prevention Strategies', *Child Abuse and Neglect* 13(2): 293–301.

Coppock, V. (1997), '"Families" in "Crisis"', in P. Scraton (ed.), *'Childhood' in 'Crisis'* (London: Routledge).

Coppock, V., Haydon, D. and Richter, I. (1995), *The Illusions of Post-feminism: New Women, Old Myths* (London: Routledge).

Corby, B. (1987), *Working with Child Abuse: Social Work Practice and the Child Abuse System* (Milton Keynes and Philadelphia: Open University Press).

(ed.) (2012), *Child Abuse: An Evidence Base for Confident Practice* (Maidenhead: Open University Press).

Corby, B., Doig, A. and Roberts, V. (2001), *Public Inquiries into Abuse of Children in Residential Care* (London: Jessica Kingsley).

Corteen, K. and Scraton, P. (1997), 'Prolonging "Childhood", Manufacturing "Innocence" and Regulating Sexuality', in P. Scraton (ed.), *'Childhood' in 'Crisis'* (London: UCL Press).

Cortoni, F. and Hanson, R. K. (2005), *A Review of the Recidivism Rates of Adult Female Sexual Offenders*. Research Report No R-169 (Ottawa, ONT: Correctional Service of Canada).

Costin, L. B. (1992), 'Cruelty to Children: A Dormant Issue and Its Rediscovery, 1920–1960', *Social Service Review* 66(2): 177–98.

Cottle, T. J. (1980), *Children's Secrets* (Reading, MA: Addison-Wesley).

Cougar Hall, P., West, J. and Hill, S. (2012), 'Sexualization in Lyrics of Popular Music from 1959 to 2009: Implications for Sexuality Educators', *Sexuality & Culture* 16(2): 103–17.

Coventry Safeguarding Children Board (CSCB) (2013), *Serious Case Review Re Daniel Pelka*, www.coventrylscb.org.uk/files/SCR/FINAL%20Overview%20Report%20%20DP%20130913%20Publication%20version.pdf.

Cowburn, M. and Dominelli, L. (2001), 'Making Hegemonic Masculinity: Reconstructing the Paedophile as the Dangerous Stranger', *British Journal of Social Work* 31(3): 399–415.

Cowburn, M., Gill, A. K. and Harrison, K. (2015), 'Speaking About Sexual Abuse in British South Asian Communities: Offenders, Victims and the Challenges of Shame and Reintegration', *Journal of Sexual Aggression* 21(1): 4–15.

Coy, M. (2009), 'Milkshakes, Lady Lumps and Growing Up to Want Boobies: How the Sexualisation of Popular Culture Limits Girls' Horizons', *Child Abuse Review* 18(6): 372–83.

(2013), 'Children, Childhood and Sexualised Popular Culture', in J. Wild (ed.), *Exploiting Childhood: How Fast Food, Material Obsession and Porn*

Culture are Creating New Forms of Child Abuse (London: Jessica Kingsley Publishers).

Coy, M. and Garner, M. (2012), 'Definitions, Discourses and Dilemmas: Policy and Academic Engagement with the Sexualisation of Popular Culture', *Gender and Education* 24(3): 285–301.

Coy, M. and Horvath, M. A. (2011), 'Lads Mags, Young Men's Attitudes Towards Women and Acceptance of Myths About Sexual Aggression', *Feminism & Psychology* 21(1): 144–50.

Coy, M., Kelly, L., Elvines, F., Garner, M. and Kanyeredzi, A. (2013), '"Sex Without Consent, I Suppose That Is Rape": How Young People in England Understand Sexual Consent', *Office of the Children's Commissioner*, www.childrenscommissioner.gov.uk/sites/default/files/publications/Sex_without_consent_I_suppose_that_is_rape_newprint.pdf.

Craissati, J., McClurg, G. and Browne, K. (2002), 'Characteristics of Perpetrators of Child Sexual Abuse Who Have Been Sexually Victimized as Children', *Sexual Abuse: A Journal of Research and Treatment* 14(3): 21–35.

Craven, S., Brown, S. and Gilchrist, E. (2006), 'Sexual Grooming of Children: Review of the Literature and Theoretical Considerations', *Journal of Sexual Aggression* 12(3): 287–99.

(2007), 'Current Responses to Sexual Grooming: Implication for Prevention', *The Howard Journal of Crime and Justice* 46(1): 60–71.

Crawford, A. (2006), 'Networked Governance and the Post-Regulatory State? Steering, Rowing and Anchoring the Provision of Policing and Security', *Theoretical Criminology* 10(4): 449–79.

Cree, V. E., Clapton, G. and Smith, M. (2014), 'The Presentation of Child Trafficking in the UK: An Old and New Moral Panic?' *British Journal of Social Work*, 44(2): 418–33.

Critcher, C. (2003), *Moral Panics and the Media* (Buckingham and Philadelphia: Open University Press).

Crofts, T. and Lee, M. (2013), 'Sexting, Children and Child Pornography', *Sydney Law Review* 35(5): 85–106.

Crofts, T., Lee, M., McGovern, A. and Milivojevic, S. (2015), *Sexting and Young People* (Basingstoke: Palgrave Macmillan).

Crowder, A. and Hawkings, R. (1995), *Opening the Door: A Treatment Model for Therapy with Male Survivors of Sexual Abuse* (New York: Brunner/Mazel).

Cunningham, H. (1998), 'Histories of Childhood', *American Historical Review* 103(4): 1195–208.

(2006), *The Invention of Childhood* (London: BBC Books).

(2014), *Children and Childhood in Western Societies Since 1500* (3d edn) (Abingdon, Oxon and New York: Routledge).

Daigle, L. E., Mummert, S., Fisher, B. S. and Scherer, H. L. (2015), 'Sexual Victimization on College Campuses', in T. N. Richards and C. D. Marcum (eds), *Sexual Victimization: Then and Now* (Thousand Oaks, CA: Sage Publications).

Dale, P. (2004), '"Like a Fish in a Bowl": Parents' Perceptions of Child Protection Services', *Child Abuse Review* 13(2):137–57.

Daley, A., Solomon, S., Newman, P. A. and Mishna, F. (2007), 'Traversing the Margins: Intersectionalities in the Bullying of Lesbian, Gay, Bisexual and Transgender Youth', *Journal of Gay & Lesbian Social Services* 19(3–4): 9–29.

Davidson, A. I. (1987), 'How to Do the History of Psychoanalysis: A Reading of Freud's "Three Essays on the Theory of Sexuality"', *Critical Inquiry* 13(2): 252–77.

Davidson, J. (2014), *Sexting: Gender and Teens* (Rotterdam, The Netherlands: Sense Publishers).

Davidson, J. and Gottschalk, P. (2010), *Online Groomers: Profiling, Policing and Prevention* (Dorset: Russell House Publishing).

(2011), *Internet Child Abuse: Current Research and Policy* (London: Routledge).

Davidson, J. C. and Martellozzo, E. (2005), 'Policing the Internet and Protecting Children from Sex Offenders Online: When Strangers Become "Virtual Friends"', paper presented at the Cybersafety Conference, University of Oxford, 8–10 September, www.childcentre.info/robert/extensions/robert/doc/c346d88f5786691dbb85040d651e8255.pdf.

(2008a), 'Protecting Vulnerable Young People in Cyberspace from Sexual Abuse: Raising Awareness and Responding Globally', *Police Practice and Research* 9(4): 277–89.

(2008b), 'Protecting Children Online Towards a Safer Internet', in G. Letherby, K. Williams, P. Birch and M. Cain (eds), *Sex as Crime?* (Cullompton, Devon: Willan Publishing).

Davidson, J., Quayle, E., Morgenbesser, L. and Brown, S. (2010), 'Editorial: Special Issue on Child Sexual Abuse and the Internet: Offenders, Victims and Managing the Risk', *Journal of Sexual Aggression* 16(1): 1–4.

Davis, E. C. and Friel, L. V. (2001), 'Adolescent Sexuality: Disentangling the Effects of Family Structure and Family Context', *Journal of Marriage and Family* 63(3): 669–81.

Davis, H. and Bourhill, M. (1997), '"Crisis": The Demonization of Children and Young People', in P. Scraton (ed.), *'Childhood' in 'Crisis'* (London: Routledge).

De Haan, W. and Loader, I. (2002), 'On the Emotions of Crime, Punishment and Social Control', *Theoretical Criminology*, 6(3): 243–54.

DeHart, G. B., Sroufe, L. A. and Cooper, R. G. (2000), *Child Development: Its Nature and Course* (4th edn) (New York: McGraw-Hill).

DeLamater, J. D. and Hyde, J. S. (1998), 'Essentialism vs Social Constructionism in the Study of Human Sexuality', *Journal of Sex Research* 35(1): 10–18.

Delmage, E. (2013), 'The Minimum Age of Criminal Responsibility: A Medico-legal Perspective', *Youth Justice* 13(2): 102–10.

De Melo-Martín, I. (2003), 'When Is Biology Destiny? Biological Determinism and Social Responsibility', *Philosophy of Science*, 70(5): 1184–94.

Denov, M. S. (2003), 'The Myth of Innocence: Sexual Scripts and the Recognition of Child Sexual Abuse by Female Perpetrators', *Journal of Sex Research* 40(3): 303–14.

(2004), *Perspectives on Female Sex Offending: A Culture of Denial* (Hampshire: Ashgate Publishing).

Dent, H. E. and Flin, R. E. (1992), *Children as Witnesses* (Chichester: John Wiley & Sons).

Denzin, N. (2010), *Childhood Socialization* (2d edn) (New Brunswick, NJ: Transaction Publishers).

Department of Health and Social Services (DHSS) (1974), *Report of the Inquiry into the Child Care and Supervision Provided in Relation to Maria Colwell* (London: HMSO).

(1988), *Report of the Inquiry into Child Abuse in Cleveland* (The Butler-Sloss Report), Cmnd 412 (London: HMSO).

Derby Safeguarding Children Board (DSCB) (2010), *Derby Safeguarding Children Board Serious Case Review BD09*, Executive Summary July 2010, www.derbyscb.org.uk/docs/BD09SCRExecutiveSummary.pdf.

Dessecker, A. (2008), *Dangerousness, Long Prison Terms, and Preventive Measures in Germany*, Séminaire GERN. Longues Peines et Peines Indéfinies. Punir la dangerosité. Paris, 21 March 2008, www.champpenal.revues.org/document7169.html.

De Vries, R. (2000), 'Vygotsky, Piaget, and Education: A Reciprocal Assimilation of Theories and Educational Practices', *New Ideas in Psychology* 18(2): 187–213.

De Young, M. (2004), *The Day Care Ritual Abuse Moral Panic* (Jefferson, NC: McFarland & Co).

Dhawan, S. and Marshall, W. L. (1996), 'Sexual Abuse Histories of Sexual Offenders', *Sexual Abuse: A Journal of Research and Treatment* 8(1): 7–15.

Dimock, P. T. (1988), 'Adult Males Sexually Abused as Children: Characteristics and Implications for Treatment', *Journal of Interpersonal Violence* 3(2): 203–21.

Dines, G. (2008), 'Childified Women', in S. Olfman (ed.), *The Sexualization of Childhood* (Westport, CT: Praeger Publishers).

Dingwall, G. and Hillier, T. (2015), *Blamestorming, Blamemongers and Scapegoats: Allocating Blame in the Criminal Justice Process* (Bristol: Policy Press).

Delmage, E. (2013), 'The Minimum Age of Criminal Responsibility: A Medico-legal Perspective', *Youth Justice* 13(2): 102–110.

Dodge, A. and Spencer, D. C. (2017), 'Online Sexual Violence, Child Pornography or Something Else Entirely? Police Responses to Non-

Consensual Intimate Image Sharing Among Youth', *Social & Legal Studies*, 0964663917724866.

Doll, B. and Lyon, M. A. (1998), 'Risk and Resilience: Implications for the Delivery of Educational and Mental Health Services in Schools', *School Psychology Review* 27(3): 348–63.

Donoghue, J. (2013), 'Reflection on Risk, Anti-Social Behaviour and Vulnerable/Repeat Victim', *British Journal of Criminology* 53(5): 805–23.

Donzelot, J. D. (1979), *The Policing of Families* (London: Hutchinson).

Döring, N. A. (2000), 'Feminist Views of Cybersex: Victimisation, Liberation and Empowerment', *Cyber Psychology* 3(5): 863–84.

Doshay, L. J. (1943), *The Boy Sex Offender and His Later Career* (Montclair, NJ: Patterson Smith).

Driscoll, C. (2002), *Girls: Feminine Adolescence in Popular Culture and Cultural Theory* (New York: Columbia University Press).

(2013), *Girls: Feminine Adolescence in Popular Culture and Cultural Theory* (New York: Columbia University Press.

Duane, Y., Carr, A., Cherry, J., McGrath, K. and O'Shea, D. (2002), 'Experiences of Parents Attending A Programme for Families of Adolescent Child Sexual Abuse Perpetrators in Ireland', *Child Care in Practice* 8(1): 46–57.

Dubber, M. D. (2006), *Victims in the War on Crime: The Use and Abuse of Victims' Rights* (New York: New York University Press).

Duff, A. (2001), *Punishment, Communication, and Community* (New York: Oxford University Press).

Duff, R. A. (1990), *Intention, Agency and Criminal Liability: Philosophy of Action and the Criminal Law* (Chichester: Wiley-Blackwell).

Duff, R. A. and Garland, D. (eds) (1994), *A Reader on Punishment* (New York: Oxford University Press).

Duggan, L. (2000), *Sapphic Slashers: Sex, Violence, and American Modernity* (Durham, NC: Duke University Press).

Dumbrill, G. C. (2006), 'Parental Experience of Child Protection Intervention: A Qualitative Study', *Child Abuse & Neglect* 30(1): 27–37.

Dunn, J. (1988), 'Sibling Influences on Childhood Development', *Journal of Child Psychology and Psychiatry* 29(2): 119–27.

Durham, M. G. (2009), *The Lolita Effect: The Media Sexualization of Young Girls and What We Can Do About It* (London/New York: Duckworth Overlook).

Durkin, K. (1997), 'Misuse of the Internet by Pedophiles: Implications for Law Enforcement and Probation Practice', *Federal Probation* 61(3): 14–18.

Duschinsky, R. (2012), 'The 2010 UK Home Office "Sexualisation of Young People" Review: A Discursive Policy Analysis', *Journal of Social Policy* 41(4): 715–31.

(2013), 'What Does Sexualisation Mean?' *Feminist Theory* 14(3): 255–64.

Dymock, A. (2016), 'Prurience, Punishment and the Image: Reading "Law-and-order Pornography"', *Theoretical Criminology*, 21(2): 209–24.

Dwyer, C. and McAlister, S. (2017), 'Raising the Age of Criminal Responsibility: Endless Debate, Limited Progress', *ARK Feature*, No. 3, December.

Dwyer, J. G. (2011), *Moral Status and Human Life: The Case for Children's Superiority* (Cambridge: Cambridge University Press).

Edwards, W. and Hensley, C. (2001), 'Contextualizing Sex Offender Management Legislation and Policy: Evaluating the Problem of Latent Consequences in Community Notification Laws', *International Journal of Offender Therapy and Comparative Criminology* 45(1): 83–101.

Egan, R. D. (2013), *Becoming Sexual: A Critical Appraisal of the Sexualization of Girls* (Cambridge: John Wiley & Sons).

Egan, R. D. and Hawkes, G. L. (2008a), 'Endangered Girls and Incendiary Objects: Unpacking the Discourse on Sexualization', *Sexuality & Culture* 12 (4): 291–311.

(2008b), 'Girls, Sexuality and the Strange Carnalities of Advertisements: Deconstructing the Discourse of Corporate Paedophilia', *Australian Feminist Studies* 23(57): 307–22.

(2009), 'The Problem with Protection: Or, Why We Need to Move Towards Recognition and the Sexual Agency of Children', *Continuum: Journal of Media & Cultural Studies* 23(3): 389–400.

(2012), 'Sexuality, Youth and the Perils of Endangered Innocence: How History Can Help Us Get Past the Panic', *Gender and Education* 24(3): 269–84.

Elias, R. (1993), *Victims Still: The Political Manipulation of Crime Victims* (London: Sage).

Elliott, I. A., Beech, A. R. and Mandeville-Norden, R. (2013), 'The Psychological Profiles of Internet, Contact, and Mixed Internet/ Contact Sex Offenders', *Sexual Abuse* 25(1): 3–20.

Elliott, I. A., Beech, A. R., Mandeville-Norden, R. and Hayes, E. (2009), 'Psychological Profiles of Internet Sexual Offenders: Comparisons with Contact Sexual Offenders', *Journal of Research and Treatment* 21(1): 76–92.

Elliott, I. A., Eldridge, H. J., Ashfield, S. and Beech, A.R. (2010), 'Exploring Risk: Potential Static, Dynamic, Protective and Treatment factors in the Clinical Histories of Female Sex Offenders', *Journal of Family Violence* 25(6): 595–602.

Elliott, M., Browne, K. and Kilcoyne, J. (1995), 'Child Abuse Prevention: What Offenders Tell Us', *Child Abuse and Neglect* 19(5): 579–94.

Ellison, G. (2016), 'Who Needs Evidence? Radical Feminism, The Christian Right and Sex Work Research in Northern Ireland', in S. Armstrong, J. Blaustein and H. Alistair (eds), *Reflexivity and Criminal Justice:*

Intersections of Policy, Practice and Research (Basingstoke: *Palgrave Macmillan)*.

(2017), 'Criminalizing the Payment for Sex in Northern Ireland: Sketching the Contours of a Moral Panic', *British Journal of Criminology*, 57(1): 194–214.

Ellison, L. and Munro, V. E. (2009), 'Reacting to Rape: Exploring Mock Jurors' Assessments of Complainant Credibility', *British Journal of Criminology* 49 (2): 202–19.

End Violence Against Women (EVAW) (2010), 'Almost a Third of Girls Experience Unwanted Sexual Touching in UK Schools – New YouGov Poll', www.endviolenceagainstwomen.org.uk/2010-poll-on-sexual-harassment-in-schools.

Epstein, M. and Ward, L. M. (2008), '"Always use protection": Communication Boys Receive About Sex from Parents, Peers, and the Media', *Journal of Youth and Adolescence* 37(2): 113–26.

Ericson, R. V. (1994), 'The Division of Expert Knowledge in Policing and Security', *British Journal of Sociology* 45(2): 149–75.

(2007), *Crime in an Insecure World* (Cambridge: Polity Press).

Haggerty, K. D. (1997), *Policing the Risk Society* (Oxford: Clarendon Press).

Erikson, E. H. (1950), *Childhood and Society* (New York: W. W. Norton & Co.).

Erooga, M. (2009), *Towards Safer Organisations: Adults Who Pose a Risk to Children in the Workplace and Implications for Recruitment and Selection*, www.nspcc.org.uk/globalassets/documents/research-reports/towards-safer-organisations-2009-report.pdf.

(2017), *After Savile: What Do We Know, What Do We Need To Do?* (London: Jessica Kingsley).

Erooga, M., Allnock, D. and Telford, P. (2012), *Towards Safer Organisations II: Using the Perspectives of Convicted Sex Offenders to Inform Organisational Safeguarding of Children* (London: NSPCC).

Erooga, M. and Masson, H. (2006), *Children and Young People Who Sexually Abuse Others: Current Developments and Practice Responses* (2d edn) (London: Routledge).

Evans, D. (2013), *Sexual Citizenship: The Material Construction of Sexualities* (London: Routledge).

Ewald, F. (2002), 'The Return of Descartes' Malicious Demon: An Outline of a Philosophy of Pre-caution', in T. Baker and J. Simon (eds), *Embracing Risk: The Changing Culture of Insurance and Responsibility* (Chicago: University of Chicago Press).

Family and Community Development Committee Victoria (2013), *Betrayal of Trust: Inquiry into the Handling of Child Abuse by Religious and Other Non-government Organisations*. Parliamentary Paper No. 275, Session 2010–13 (Melbourne: Parliament of Victoria).

Farmer, M., McAlinden, A.-M. and Maruna, S. (2015), 'Understanding Desistance from Sexual Offending: A Thematic Review of Research Findings', *Probation Journal* 62(4): 320–35.

Farrell, A. (2005), *Ethical Research with Children* (Maidenhead: McGraw-Hill Education).

Faulkner, J. (2010), 'The Innocence Fetish: The Commodification and Sexualisation of Children in the Media and Popular Culture', *Media International Australia Incorporating Culture and Policy* 135(1): 106–17.

Feeley, M. and Simon, J. (1992), 'The New Penology: Notes on the Emerging Strategy of Corrections and Its Implications', *Criminology* 30(4): 449–74.

(1994), 'Actuarial Justice: The Emerging New Criminal Law', in D. Nelken (ed.), *The Futures of Criminology* (London: Sage).

Feelgood, S. and Hoyer, J. (2008), 'Child Molester or Paedophile? Sociolegal Versus Psychopathological Classification of Sexual Offenders Against Children', *Journal of Sexual Aggression* 14(1): 33–43.

Fehrenbach, P. A. and Monastersky, C. (1988), 'Characteristics of Female Adolescent Sexual Offenders', *American Journal of Orthopsychiatry* 58(1): 148–51.

Fehrenbach, P. A., Smith, W., Monastersky, C. and Deisher, R. W. (1986), 'Adolescent Sexual Offenders: Offender and Offense Characteristics', *American Journal of Orthopsychiatry* 56(2): 225–33.

Feinberg, J. (1990), *The Moral Limits of the Criminal Law*, Vol. 4: *Harmless Wrongdoing* (New York: Oxford University Press).

Ferguson, C. J. and Hartley, R. D. (2009), 'The Pleasure Is Momentary . . . the Expense Damnable? The Influence of Pornography on Rape and Sexual Assault', *Aggression and Violent Behavior* 14(5): 323–29.

Ferguson, H. (1990), 'Rethinking Child Protection Practices: A Case for History', in *The Violence Against Children Study Group: Taking Child Abuse Seriously*, *Taking Child Abuse Seriously* (London: Unwin Hyman).

(1997), 'Protecting Children in New Times: Child Protection and the Risk Society', *Child & Family Social Work* 2(4): 221–34.

(2004), *Protecting Children in Time: Child Abuse, Child Protection and the Consequences of Modernity* (Basingstoke: Palgrave Macmillan).

Fernandez, Y. M. (2006), 'Focusing on the Positive and Avoiding Negativity in Sexual Offender Treatment', in W. L. Marshall, Y. M. Fernandez, L. E. Marshall and G. A. Serran (eds), *Sexual Offender Treatment: Controversial Issues* (West Sussex: John Wiley and Sons, Ltd).

Finkelhor, D. (1979), *Sexually Victimized Children* (New York: Sage Publications).

(1980), 'Sex Among Siblings: A Survey on Prevalence, Variety, and Effects', *Archives of Sexual Behavior* 9(3): 171–94.

(1984), *Child Sexual Abuse: New Theory and Research* (New York: The Free Press).

(1990), 'Early and Long-term Effects of Child Sexual Abuse: An Update', *Professional Psychology: Research and Practice* 21(5): 325–30.

(1991), 'Child Sexual Abuse', in M. L. Rosenberg and M. A. Fenley (eds), *Violence in America: A Public Health Approach* (New York: Oxford University Press).

(1994a), 'The "Backlash" and the Future of Child Abuse Advocacy: Insights from the Study of Social Issues', in J. E. B. Myers (ed.), *The Backlash: Child Protection Under Fire* (Newbury Park, CA: Sage).

(1994b), 'Current Information on the Scope and Nature of Child Sexual Abuse', *The Future of Children* 4(2): 31–53.

(2014), *Childhood Victimization: Violence, Crime, and Abuse in the Lives of Young People* (New York: Oxford University Press).

Finkelhor, D. and Browne, A. (1985), 'The Traumatic Impact of Child Sexual Abuse: A Conceptualization', *American Journal of Orthopsychiatry* 55(4): 530–41.

Finkelhor, D., Mitchell, K. J. and Wolak, J. (2000), *Online Victimization: A Report on the Nation's Youth* (Alexandria, VA: National Center for Missing and Exploited Children), www.unh.edu/ccrc/pdf/jvq/CV38.pdf.

Finkelhor, D., Ormrod, R. and Chaffin, M. (2009), 'Juveniles Who Commit Sex Offenses Against Minors', *Juvenile Justice Bulletin*, National Criminal Justice Reference Service, www.ncjrs.gov/pdffiles1/ojjdp/227763.pdf.

Finkelhor, D., Ormrod, R., Turner, H., & Hamby, S. L. (2005), 'The Victimization of Children and Youth: A Comprehensive, National Survey', *Child Maltreatment*, 10(1): 5–25.

Finkelstein, C. (2003), 'Is Risk a Harm?' *University of Pennsylvania Law Review* 151(3): 963–1001.

Fionda, J. (2005), *Devils and Angels: Youth, Policy and Crime* (Oxford: Hart Publishing).

Firmin, C. (2011), *This Is It. This Is My Life: Female Voice in Violence*, Final Report (London, Race on the Agenda (ROTA)).

(2013), 'Something Old or Something New: Do Pre-existing Conceptualisations of Abuse Enable a Sufficient Response to Abuse in Young People's Relationships and Peer Groups', in M. Melrose and J. Pearce (eds), *Critical Perspectives on Child Sexual Exploitation and Related Trafficking* (Basingstoke: Palgrave Macmillan).

Firmin, C. and Beckett, H. (2014), 'Child Sexual Exploitation', in M. Dalton (ed.), *Forensic Gynaecology* (Cambridge: Cambridge University Press).

Firmin, C. and Curtis, G. (2015), *Practitioner Briefing #1: What Is Peer-on-Peer Abuse?* (London: MsUnderstood Partnership).

Firth, G. (2011), 'Not An Invitation to Rape: The Sexual Offences Act 2003, Consent and the Case of the "Drunken" Victim', *Northern Ireland Legal Quarterly* 62(1): 99–118.

Fitz-Gibbon, K. (2016), 'Protections for Children Before the Law: An Empirical Analysis of the Age of Criminal Responsibility, the Abolition of Doli Incapax and the Merits of a Developmental Immaturity Defence in England and Wales', *Criminology & Criminal Justice* 16(4): 391–409.

Fitzgibbon, W. (2011), *Probation and Social Work on Trial: Violent Offenders and Child Abusers* (Basingstoke: Palgrave Macmillan).

Flannery, T. (ed.) (2009), *Responding to the Ryan Report* (Dublin: The Columba Press).

Flood, F. and Hamilton, C. (2003), *Regulating Youth Access to Pornography*. Discussion Paper Number 53 (Canberra: The Australia Institute).

Flood, M. (2007), 'Exposure to Pornography Among Youth in Australia', *Journal of Sociology* 43(1): 45–60.

(2009), 'The Harms of Pornography Exposure Among Children and Young People', *Child Abuse Review* 18(6): 384–400.

Foucault, M. (1978), *The History of Sexuality*. Vol. 1:*An Introduction*, translated by R. Hurley (New York: Vintage Books).

Francis, P. and Turner, N. (1995), 'Sexual Misconduct Within the Christian Church: Who Are the Perpetrators and Those They Abuse?' *Counselling and Values* 39(3): 218–27.

Franklin, B. and Parton, N. (1991), 'Media Reporting of Social Work: A Framework for Analysis', in B. Franklin and N. Parton (eds), *Social Work, the Media and Public Relations* (London: Routledge).

Fraser, M. W., Galinsky, M. J. and Richman, J. M. (1999), 'Risk, Protection, and Resilience: Toward a Conceptual Framework for Social Work Practice', *Social Work Research* 23(3): 131–43.

Freedman, E. B. (1987), '"Uncontrolled Desires": The Response to the Sexual Psychopath, 1920–1960', *The Journal of American History* 74(1): 83–106.

Freud, S. (1896), 'The Aetiology of Hysteria', in *The Standard Edition of the Complete Psychological Works of Freud*, Vol. 3 (London: Hogarth Press).

(1975), *Three Essays on the Theory of Sexuality* (originally published in 1905) (New York: Basic Books).

Friedrichs, D. O. (1996), *Trusted Criminals: White-Collar Crime in Contemporary Society* (New York: Wadsworth Publishing Company).

Frosh, S., Phoenix, A. and Pattman, R. (2002), *Young Masculinities: Understanding Boys in Contemporary Society* (Basingstoke: Palgrave).

Furedi, F. (2013), *Moral Crusades in an Age of Mistrust: The Jimmy Savile Scandal* (Basingstoke: Palgrave Macmillan).

Furlong, A. and Cartmel, F. (2007), *Young People and Social Change: New Perspectives* (2d edn) (Maidenhead: Open University Press, McGraw-Hill).

Gagnon, J. H. and Simon, W. (1987), 'The Sexual Scripting of Oral Genital Contacts', *Archives of Sexual Behaviour* 16(1): 1–25.

Gallagher, B. (1998), *Grappling with Smoke: Investigating and Managing Organised Abuse – A Good Practice Guide* (London: NSPCC).

(2000), 'The Extent and Nature of Known Cases of Institutional Child Sexual Abuse', *British Journal of Social Work* 30(6): 795–817.

Gallagher, B., Christmann, K., Fraser, C. and Hodgson, B. (2003), 'International and Internet Child Sexual Abuse and Exploitation: Issues Emerging From Research', *Child and Family Law Quarterly* 15(4): 353–70.

(2006), *International and Internet Child Sexual Abuse and Exploitation*, research report (Huddersfield: University of Huddersfield, Centre for Applied Childhood Studies).

Galley, J. (2010), 'Derby Safeguarding Children Board Serious Case Review BD09', Executive Summary July 2010, www.derbyscb.org.uk/docs/BD09SCRExecutiveSummary.pdf.

Gannon, T. . and Cortoni, F. (eds), (2010), *Female Sexual Offenders: Theory, Assessment and Treatment* (Chichester: Wiley-Blackwell).

Garbarino, J. and Gilliam, G. (1980), *Understanding Abusive Families* (Lexington, MA: Lexington Books).

Gardner, R. A. (1991), *Sex Abuse Hysteria: Salem Witch Trials Revisited* (Cresskill, NJ: Creative Therapeutics).

Garland, D. (2001), *The Culture of Control: Crime and Social Order in Contemporary Society* (Oxford: Oxford University Press).

(2008), 'On the Concept of Moral Panic', *Crime, Media, Culture* 4(1): 9–30.

Garot, R. (2010), *Who You Claim: Performing Gang Identity in School and On the Streets* (New York: New York University Press).

Gehl, R. W. (2016), 'Power/Freedom on the Dark Web: A Digital Ethnography of the Dark Web Social Network', *New Media & Society* 18(7): 1219–35.

Gelman, S. A. (2003), *The Essential Child: Origins of Essentialism in Everyday Thought* (New York: Oxford University Press).

Gelsthorpe, L. and Morris, A. (2002), 'Restorative Justice: The Last Vestiges of Welfare?' in J. Muncie, G. Hughes and E. McLaughlin (eds), *Youth Justice: Critical Readings* (London: Sage).

Giarretto, H. (1978), 'Humanistic Treatment of Father-Daughter Incest', *Journal of Humanistic Psychology* 18(4): 59–76.

Giddens, A. (1984), *The Constitution of Society* (Cambridge: Polity Press).

(1990), *The Consequences of Modernity* (Cambridge: Polity Press).

(1991), *Modernity and Self Identity: Self and Society in the Late Modern Age* (Cambridge: Polity Press).

(1999), 'Risk and Responsibility', *The Modern Law Review* 62(1): 1–10.

Giddens, A. and Pierson, C. (1998), *Conversations with Anthony Giddens: Making Sense of Modernity* (Redwood City, CA: Stanford University Press).

Giles, J. (2006), 'Social Constructionism and Sexual Desire', *Journal for the Theory of Social Behaviour* 36(3): 225–38.

Gill, A. K. and Harrison, K. (2015), 'Child Grooming and Sexual Exploitation: Are South Asian Men the UK Media's New Folk Devils?' *International Journal for Crime, Justice & Social Democracy* 4(2): 34–49.

Gill, E. and Johnson, T. C. (1993), *Sexualized Children: Assessment and Treatment of Sexualized Children and Children Who Molest* (Rockville, MD: Launch Press).

Gill, T. (2007), *No Fear: Growing Up in a Risk Averse Society* (London: Calouste Gulbenkian Foundation).

Gillespie, A. A. (2001), 'Children, Chatrooms and the Law', *Criminal Law Review* 8: 435–46.

(2004), '"Grooming": Definitions and the Law', *New Law Journal* 154 (7124): 586–87.

(2005), 'Indecent Images of Children: The Ever-changing Law', *Child Abuse Review* 14(6): 430–43.

(2006), 'Cyber-bullying and Harassment of Teenagers: The Legal Response', *Journal of Social Welfare & Family Law* 28(2): 123–36.

(2007), 'The Future of Child Protection and the Criminal Law', *Irish Criminal Law Journal* 17(3): 2–8.

(2008), 'Cyber-Stings: Policing Sex Offences on the Internet', *Police Journal* 81(3): 196–208.

(2010), 'Defining Child Pornography: Challenges for the Law', *Child and Family Law Quarterly* 22(2): 200–22.

(2013), 'Adolescents, Sexting and Human Rights', *Human Rights Law Review* 13(4): 623–43.

(2015), '"Trust Me, It's Only For Me": "Revenge Porn" and the Criminal Law', *Criminal Law Review* (11): 866–80.

Gilligan, P., and Akhtar, S. (2006), 'Cultural Barriers to the Disclosure of Child Sexual Abuse in Asian Communities: Listening to What Women Say', *British Journal of Social Work* 36(8): 1361–77.

Gilligan, R. (2004), 'Promoting Resilience in Child and Family Social Work: Issues for Social Work Practice, Education and Policy', *Social Work Education* 23(1): 93–104.

Gilmore, S. and Herring, J. (2011), '"No" Is the Hardest Word: Consent and Children's Autonomy', *Child and Family Law Quarterly* 23(1): 3–25.

Ginzburg, K., Butler, L. D., Giese-Davis, J., Cavanaugh, C. E., Neri, E., Koopman, C., Classen, C. C. and Spiegel, D. (2009), 'Shame, Guilt, and Posttraumatic Stress Disorder in Adult Survivors of Childhood Sexual Abuse at Risk for Human Immunodeficiency Virus: Outcomes of a Randomized Clinical Trial of Group Psychotherapy Treatment', *The Journal of Nervous and Mental Disease* 197(7): 536–42.

Giordano, P. C., Manning, W. D. and Longmore, M. A. (2006), 'Adolescent Romantic Relationships: An Emerging Portrait of their Nature and Developmental Significance', in A. C. Crouter and A. Booth (eds),

Romance and Sex in Adolescence and Emerging Adulthood: Risks and Opportunities (Mahwah, NJ: Lawrence Elrbaum Associates).

Girard, R. (1989), *The Scapegoat* (repr) (Baltimore, MD: John Hopkins University Press).

Gittins, D. (1998), *The Child in Question* (Basingstoke: Macmillan).

Glaser, B. and Straus, A. (1967), *The Discovery of Grounded Theory: Strategies for Qualitative Research* (New York: Aldine Publishing Company).

Goffman, E. (1959), *The Presentation of Self in Everyday Life* (Garden City, NY: Anchor).

(1963), *Stigma: Notes on the Management of Spoiled Identity* (Englewood Cliffs. NJ: Prentice-Hall).

(1971), *Relations in Public* (London: Pelican).

(1979), *Gender Advertisements* (New York: Harper and Row Publishers).

Gohir, S. (2013), *Unheard Voices: The Sexual Exploitation of Asian Girls and Young Women* (London: Muslim Women's Network UK).

Goldman, R. and Goldman, J. (1982), *Children's Sexual Thinking: A Comparative Study of Children Aged 5 to 15 Years in Australia, North America, Britain and Sweden* (London: Routledge & Kegan Paul).

Goldson, B. (1997a), '"Crisis": The Demonization of Children and Young People', in P. Scraton (ed.), *'Childhood' in 'Crisis'* (London: Routledge).

(1997b), 'Children in Trouble: State Response to Juvenile Crime', in P. Scraton (ed.), *'Childhood' in 'Crisis'* (London: Routledge).

(ed.) (2011), *Youth in Crisis?: 'Gangs', Territoriality and Violence* (London: Routledge).

(2013), '"Unsafe, Unjust and Harmful to Wider Society": Grounds for Raising the Minimum Age of Criminal Responsibility in England and Wales', *Youth Justice*, 13(2): 111–30.

Goldson, B. and Muncie, J. (2006), 'Rethinking Youth Justice: Comparative Analysis, International Human Rights and Research Evidence', *Youth Justice* 6(2): 91–106.

Goode, E. and Ben-Yehuda, N. (1994), *Moral Panics: The Social Construction of Deviance* (Oxford: Blackwell).

Gordon, L. (1988), *Heroes in Their Own Lives: The Politics and History of Family Violence* (New York: Viking Penguin).

Gordon, M. and Miller, R. L. (1984), 'Going Steady in the 1980s: Exclusive Relationships in Six Connecticut High Schools', *Sociology & Social Research* 68: 462–79.

Gover, A. R., Jennings, W. G. and Tewksbury, R. (2009), 'Adolescent Male and Female Gang Members' Experiences with Violent Victimization, Dating Violence, and Sexual Assault', *American Journal of Criminal Justice* 34(1–2): 103–15.

Grabosky, P. N. (2001), 'Virtual Criminality: Old Wine in New Bottles?' *Social & Legal Studies* 10(2): 243–49.

Graham, M. (2011), 'Changing Paradigms and Conditions of Childhood: Implications for the Social Professions and Social Work', *British Journal of Social Work* 41(8): 1532–47.

Graves, R. B., Openshaw, D. K., Ascione, F. R. and Ericksen, S. L. (1996), 'Demographic and Parental Characteristics of Youthful Sexual Offenders', *International Journal of Offender Therapy and Comparative Criminology* 40(4): 300–317.

Gray, D. and Watt, P. (2013), *Giving Victims A Voice:* A Joint MPS and NSPCC Report into Allegations of Sexual Abuse Made Against Jimmy Savile Under Operation Yewtree, www.nspcc.org.uk/globalassets/documents/research-reports/yewtree-report-giving-victims-voice-jimmy-savile.pdf.

Greer, C. (2003), *Sex Crime and the Media: Sex Offending and the Press in a Divided Society* (Cullompton, Devon: Willan Publishing).

(2007), 'News Media, Victims and Crime', in P. Davies, P. Francis and C. Greer (eds), *Victims, Crime and Society* (London: Sage).

Gregory, J. and Lees, S. (1996), 'Attrition in Rape and Sexual Assault Cases', *British Journal of Criminology*, 36(1): 1–17.

Griffin, H. and Beech, A. (2004), *Evaluation of the AIM framework for the Assessment of Adolescents Who Display Sexually Harmful Behaviour, A Report for the Youth Justice Board*, www.yjbpublications.justice.gov.uk/Resources/Downloads/AIM%20Full%20Report.pdf.

Groth, A. N. (1982), 'The Incest Offender', in S. M. Sgroi (ed.), *Handbook of Clinical Intervention in Child Sexual Abuse* (Lexington, MA: Lexington Books).

Grubin, D. (1998), *Sex Offending Against Children: Understanding the Risk.* Police Research Series Paper 99 (London: Home Office).

Guilliatt, R. (1996), *Talk of the Devil* (Melbourne: Text Publishing).

Gunter, B. (2014), *Media and the Sexualization of Childhood* (London: Routledge).

Gurnham, D. (2016), 'Victim-Blame as a Symptom of Rape Myth Acceptance? Another Look at How Young People in England and Wales Understand Sexual Consent', *Legal Studies* 36(2): 258–78.

Gwynne, J. (2013), 'Japan, Postfeminism and the Consumption of Sexual(ised) Schoolgirls in Male-Authored Contemporary Manga', *Feminist Theory* 14(3): 325–43.

Hackett, S. (2001), *Facing the Future: A Guide for Parents of Young People Who Have Sexually Abused* (Lyme Regis: Russell House Publishing).

(2002), 'Abused and Abusing: Work with Young People Who Have a Dual Sexual Abuse Experience', in M. C. Calder (ed.), *Young People Who Sexually Abuse: Building the Evidence Base for Your Practice* (Lyme Regis: Russell House Publishing).

(2004), *What Works for Children and Young People with Harmful Sexual Behaviours?* (Ilford: Barnardo's).

(2010), 'Children, Young People and Sexual Violence', in C. Barter and D. Berridge (eds), *Children Behaving Badly? Exploring Peer Violence Between Children and Young People* (London: Blackwell Wiley).

(2014), *Children and Young People with Harmful Sexual Behaviours: Research Review* (London: Research in Practice).

Hackett, S., Balfe, M., Masson, H. and Phillips, J. (2014), 'Family Responses to Young People Who Have Sexually Abused: Anger, Ambivalence and Acceptance', *Children & Society* 28(2): 128–39.

Hackett, S., Holmes, D. and Branigan, P. (2016), *Operational Framework for Children and Young People Displaying Harmful Sexual Behaviours* (London: NSPCC).

Hackett, S., Masson, H. Balfe, M. and Phillips, J. (2015), 'Community Reactions to Young People Who Have Sexually Abused and Their Families: A Shotgun Blast, Not a Rifle Shot', *Children & Society* 29(4): 243–54.

Hackett, S., Masson, H. and Phillips, S. (2006), 'Exploring Consensus in Practice with Youth Who Are Sexually Abusive: Findings from a Delphi Study of Practitioner Views in the United Kingdom and the Republic of Ireland', *Child Maltreatment* 11(2): 146–56.

Hackett, S., Phillips, J., Masson, H. and Balfe, M. (2013), 'Individual, Family and Abuse Characteristics of 700 British Child and Adolescent Sexual Abusers', *Child Abuse Review* 22(4): 232–45.

Hackett, S., Print, B. and Dey, C. (1998), 'Brother Nature? Therapeutic Intervention with Young Men Who Sexually Abuse Their Siblings', in A. Bannister (ed.), *From Hearing to Healing: Working with the Aftermath of Child Sexual Abuse* (2d edn) (Chichester: Wiley).

Hackett, S. and Taylor, A. (2008), 'School Responses to Children with Harmful Sexual Behaviours', in M. Baginsky (ed.), *Safeguarding Children and Schools* (London: Jessica Kingsley).

Hacking, I. (2003), 'Risk and Dirty', in R. Ericson and A. Doyle (eds), *Risk and Morality* (Toronto: University of Toronto Press).

Hall, M. (2000), 'After Waterhouse: Vicarious Liability and the Tort of Institutional Abuse', *Journal of Social Welfare and Family Law* 22(2): 159–73.

Hall, S., Critcher, C., Jefferson, T., Clarke, J. and Roberts, B. (1978), *Policing the Crisis: Mugging, the State, and Law and Order* (London and Basingstoke: The Macmillan Press).

Hallett, C. and Prout, A. (eds) (2003), *Hearing the Voices of Children: Social Policy for a New Century* (London: Routledge).

Hansen, W. B. and Graham, J. W. (1991), 'Preventing Alcohol, Marijuana, and Cigarette Use Among Adolescents: Peer Pressure Resistance Training Versus Establishing Conservative Norms', *Preventive Medicine* 20(3): 414–30.

Hanson, R. K. and Slater, S. (1988), 'Sexual Victimization in the History of Sexual Abusers: A Review', *Annals of Sex Research* 1(4): 485–99.

Harden, J. (2000), 'There's No Place Like Home: The Public/Private Distinction in Children's Theorizing of Risk and Security', *Childhood* 7(1): 43–59.

Harris, A. J., Walfield, S. M., Shields, R. T. and Letourneau, E. J. (2016), 'Collateral Consequences of Juvenile Sex Offender Registration and Notification: Results from a Survey of Treatment Providers', *Sexual Abuse*, 28(8): 770–90.

Harrison, K., Manning, R. and McCartan, K. F. (2010), 'Current Multidisciplinary Definitions and Understandings of "Paedophilia"', *Social and Legal Studies* 19(4): 481–96.

Harrison, K. and Rainey, B. (eds) (2013), *The Wiley-Blackwell Handbook of Legal and Ethical Aspects of Sex Offender Treatment and Management* (Chichester: John Wiley & Sons).

Hart, Sir A., Lane, D. and Doherty, G. (2017), *Report of the Historical Institutional Abuse Inquiry* (United Kingdom: The Inquiry into Historical Institutional Abuse 1922 to 1995 and The Executive Office), www.hiainquiry.org/historical-institutional-abuse-inquiry-report-chapters.

Hart, H. L. A. (1965), *The Morality of the Criminal Law* (London: Oxford University Press).

Harvey, L., Ringrose, J. and Gill, R. (2013), 'Swagger, Ratings and Masculinity: Theorising the Circulation of Social and Cultural Value in Teenage Boys' Digital Peer Networks', *Sociological Research Online* 18(4): Article No 9.

Hasinoff, A. A. (2015), *Sexting Panic: Rethinking Criminalization, Privacy, and Consent* (Chicago: University of Illinois Press).

Haugaard, J. J. (2000), 'The Challenge of Defining Child Sexual Abuse', *American Psychologist* 55(9): 1036–39.

Haydon, D. and Scraton, P. (2000), '"Condemn a Little More, Understand a Little Less": The Political Context and Rights' Implications of the Domestic and European Rulings in the Venables-Thompson Case', *Journal of Law and Society* 27(3): 416–48.

(2002), 'Sex Education as Regulation', in B. Goldson, M. Lavalette and J. McKechnie (eds), *Children, Welfare and the State* (London: Sage Publications).

(2008), 'Conflict, Regulation and Marginalisation in the North of Ireland: The Experiences of Children and Young People', *Current Issues Criminal Justice* 20(1): 59–78.

(2016), 'Childhood, Rights and Justice in Northern Ireland', in D. Healy, C. Hamilton C. Y. Daly and M. Butler (eds), *The Routledge International*

Handbook of Criminology and Human Rights (Abingdon, Oxon and New York: Routledge).
Hayward, K. (2009), 'Visual Criminology: Cultural Criminology-Style: Keith Hayward Makes the Case for "Visual Criminology"', *Criminal Justice Matters* 78(1): 12–14.
Haywood, T., Kravitz, H., Grossman, L., Wasyliw, O. and Hardy, D. (1996), 'Psychological Aspects of Sexual Functioning Among Cleric and Noncleric Alleged Sex Offenders', *Child Abuse and Neglect* 20(6): 527–36.
Hebenton, B. and Seddon, T. (2009), 'From Dangerousness to Precaution: Managing Sexual and Violent Offenders in an Insecure and Uncertain Age', *British Journal of Criminology* 49(3): 343–62.
Hendrick, H. (1997), 'Constructions and Reconstructions of British Childhood: An Interpretative Survey, 1800 to the Present', in A. James and A. Prout (eds), *Constructing and Reconstructing Childhood: Contemporary Issues in the Sociological Study of Childhood* (London: Routledge).
(2005), *Child Welfare and Social Policy: An Essential Reader* (Cambridge, MA: MIT Press).
Henry, N. and Powell, A. (2016), 'Sexual Violence in the Digital Age: The Scope and Limits of Criminal Law', *Social & Legal Studies* 25(4): 397–418.
Her Majesty's (HM) Government (2010), *Call to End Violence Against Women and Girls* (London: Home Office).
Herman, J. (1981), *Father-Daughter Incest* (Cambridge, MA: Harvard University Press).
Herman, R. D. (1955), 'The "Going Steady" Complex: A Re-Examination', *Marriage and Family Living* 17(1): 36–40.
Herring, J. (2016), 'The Age of Criminal Responsibility and the Age of Consent: Should They Be Any Different?' *Northern Ireland Legal Quarterly* 67(3): 343–56.
Hester, H. (2014), *Beyond Explicit: Pornography and the Displacement of Sex* (Albany: State University of New York Press).
Hetherton, J. (1999), 'The Idealisation of Women: Its Role in the Minimisation of Child Sexual Abuse by Females', *Child Abuse and Neglect* 23(2): 161–74.
Heywood, C. (2013), *A History of Childhood: Children and Childhood in the West from Medieval to Modern Times* (Chichester, UK and New York: John Wiley & Sons).
Hickey, N., McCrory, E., Farmer, E. and Vizard, E. (2008), 'Comparing the Developmental and Behavioural Characteristics of Female and Male Juveniles Who Present with Sexually Abusive Behaviour', *Journal of Sexual Aggression* 14(3): 241–52.

Hier, S. P. (2003), 'Risk and Panic in Late Modernity: Implications of the Converging Sites of Social Anxiety', *The British journal of Sociology* 54(1): 3–20.

(2008), 'Thinking Beyond Moral Panic: Risk, Responsibility, and the Politics of Moralization', *Theoretical Criminology* 12(2): 173–90.

Hier, S. P., Lett, D., Walby, K. and Smith, A. (2011), 'Beyond Folk Devil Resistance: Linking Moral Panic and Moral Regulation', *Criminology and Criminal Justice* 11(3): 259–76.

Hill, M. (1990), 'The Manifest and Latent Lessons of Child Abuse Inquiries', *British Journal of Social Work* 20(3): 197–213.

Hill, M., Davis, J., Prout, A. and Tisdall, K. (2004), 'Moving the Participation Agenda Forward', *Children & Society* 18(2): 77–96.

Hillier, L. and Harrison, L. (2007), 'Building Realities Less Limited Than Their Own: Young People Practising Same-Sex Attraction on the Internet', *Sexualities* 10(1): 82–100.

Hoffman, K. L., and Edwards, J. N. (2004), 'An Integrated Theoretical Model of Sibling Violence and Abuse', *Journal of Family Violence* 19(3): 185–200.

Holland, S., Renold, E., Ross, N. and Hillman, A. (2008), 'The Everyday Lives of Children in Care: Using a Sociological Perspective to Inform Social Work Practice', ESRC National Centre for Research Methods (NCRM) Working Paper Series 1/08, www.eprints.ncrm.ac.uk/466/1/0108%2520everyday%2520lives%2520of%2520children.pdf.

Holloway, W. and Jefferson T. (1997), 'The Risk Society in an Age of Anxiety', *British Journal of Sociology* 48(2): 255–66.

Holt, T., Blevins, K. and Burkert, N. (2010), 'Considering the Pedophile Subculture Online', *Sexual Abuse: A Journal of Research and Treatment* 22 (1): 3–24.

Hood, L. (2001), *A City Possessed: The Christchurch Civic Creche Case* (Dunedin: Longacre Press).

Home Affairs Committee (2013), *Child Sexual Exploitation and the Response to Localised Grooming*, Second Report of Session 2013–14, HC 68-I (London: The Stationery Office).

(2014), *Child Sexual Exploitation and the Response to Localised Grooming: Follow-up*, Sixth Report of Session 2014–15, HC 203 (London: The Stationery Office).

Hörnle, J. (2011), 'Countering the Dangers of Online Pornography – Shrewd Regulation of Lewd Content', *European Journal of Law and Technology* 2(1): 1–26.

Horvath, M. A., Alys, L., Massey, K., Pina, A., Scally, M. and Adler, J. R. (2013), *Basically . . . Porn Is Everywhere. A Rapid Evidence Assessment on the Effects That Access and Exposure to Pornography Has on Children and Young People* (London: Office for the Children's Commissioner).

House of Commons (HC) Women and Equalities Committee (2016), *Sexual Harassment and Sexual Violence in Schools*, Third Report of Session 2016–17, HC 91, https//publications.parliament.uk/pa/cm201617/cmselect/cmwomeq/91/91.pdf.

Howitt, D. (1995), *Paedophiles and Sexual Offences Against Children* (Oxford: John Wiley and Sons).

Hoyano, L. C. (2001), 'Striking a Balance Between the Rights of Defendants and Vulnerable Witnesses: Will Special Measures Directions Contravene Guarantees of a Fair Trial?' *Criminal Law Review* 948–69.

(2010), 'Coroners and Justice Act 2009 (3) – Special Measures Directions Take Two: Entrenching Unequal Access to Justice', *Criminal Law Review* 345–68.

(2015), 'Reforming the Adversarial Trial for Vulnerable Witnesses and Defendants', *Criminal Law Review* 107–29.

Hoyle, C., Bosworth, M. and Dempsey, M. (2011), 'Labelling the Victims of Sex Trafficking: Exploring the Borderland Between Rhetoric and Reality', *Social and Legal Studies*, 20(3): 313–29.

Hudson, B. (2001), 'Human Rights, Public Safety and the Probation Service: Defending Justice in the Risk Society', *Howard Journal of Criminal Justice* 40 (2): 103–13.

Huitema, A. and Vanwesenbeeck, I. (2016), 'Attitudes of Dutch Citizens Towards Male Victims of Sexual Coercion by a Female Perpetrator', *Journal of Sexual Aggression* 22(3): 308–22.

Hunt, A. (1997), '"Moral Panic" and Moral Language in the Media', *British Journal of Sociology*, 48(4): 629–48.

(2011), 'Moral Panics and Moral Regulation', in S. Hier (ed.), *Moral Panic and the Politics of Anxiety* (London: Routledge).

Hunter, J. A., Goodwin, D. W. and Wilson, R. J. (1992), 'Attributions of Blame in Child Sexual Abuse Victims: An Analysis of Age and Gender Influences', *Journal of Child Sexual Abuse* 1(3): 75–89.

Hutchison, R. (1986), 'Effect of Inquiries into Cases of Child Abuse upon the Social Work Profession', *The British Journal of Criminology* 26(2): 178–82.

Ignatieff, M. (2004), *The Lesser Evil: Political Ethics in an Age of Terror* (Edinburgh: Edinburgh University Press).

Innes, M. (2004), 'Signal Crimes and Signal Disorders: Notes on Deviance as Communicative Action', *British Journal of Sociology* 55(3): 335–55.

Itzin, C. (2001), 'Incest, Paedophila, Pornography and Prostitution: Making Familial Males More Visible as the Abusers', *Child as the Abusers* 10(1): 35–48.

Jackson, L. A. (2000), *Child Sexual Abuse in Victorian England* (London: Routledge).

(2006), 'Childhood and Youth', in H. G. Cocks and M. Houlbrook (eds), *The Modern History of Sexuality* (Basingstoke: Palgrave Macmillan).

Jackson, S. (1982), *Childhood and Sexuality* (Oxford: Blackwells).

Jackson, S. and Scott, S. (1999), 'Risk Anxiety and the Social Construction of Childhood', in D. Lupton (ed.), *Risk and Socio-cultural Theory: New Directions and Perspectives* (Cambridge: Cambridge University Press).

Jacobs, J. E. and Klaczynski, P. A. (eds) (2006), *The Development of Judgment and Decision Making in Children and Adolescents* (New York: Psychology Press).

Jago, S., Arocha, L., Brodie, I., Melrose, M., Pearce, J. and Warrington, C. (2011), What's Going on to Safeguard Children and Young People from Sexual Exploitation? How Local Partnerships Respond to Child Sexual Exploitation, www.beds.ac.uk/__data/assets/pdf_file/0004/121873/wgoreport2011-121011.pdf.

James, A. and James, A. (2004), *Constructing Childhood: Theory, Policy and Social Practice* (Basingstoke: Palgrave Macmillan).

James, A. and Jenks, C. (1996), 'Public Perceptions of Childhood Criminality', *British Journal of Sociology* 47(2): 315–31.

James, A., Jenks, C. and Prout, A. (1998), *Theorizing Childhood* (New York: Teachers College Press).

James, A.C. and Neil, P. (1996), 'Juvenile Sexual Offending: One-year Period Prevalence Study Within Oxfordshire', *Child Abuse & Neglect* 20 (6): 477–85.

James, A. and Prout, A. (eds) (2015), *Constructing and Reconstructing Childhood: Contemporary Issues in the Sociological Study of Childhood* (London: Routledge).

James, E. L. (2012), *Fifty Shades of Grey* (London: Arrow Books).

Janes, L. (2016), 'Young People, Sex and the Law', paper presented at the NOTA Conference (National Organisation for the Treatment of Abusers) Northern Ireland Conference, 'Sexual Offending, 18–25: Young People or Risky Adults', 9 November 2016.

Jay, A. (2014), Independent Inquiry into Child Sexual Exploitation in Rotherham 1997–2013, www.rotherham.gov.uk/downloads/file/1407/independent_inquiry_cse_in_rotherham.

Jay, A., Evans, M., Frank, I. and Sharpling, D. (2018), *Interim Report of the Independent Inquiry into Child Sexual Abuse*, HC 954-I (London: HMSO).

Jenks, C. (1996), 'The Postmodern Child', in J. Brannen and M. O'Brien (ed.), *Children in Families: Research and Policy* (London: Falmer Press).

Jenkins, P. (1992), *Intimate Enemies: Moral Panics in Contemporary Great Britain* (New York: Aldine de Gruyter).

(2004), *Moral Panic: Changing Concepts of the Child Molester in Modern America* (New Haven, CT: Yale University Press).

Jennings, W. G. and Meade, C. (2017), 'Victim-Offender Overlap Among Sex Offenders', in T. Sanders (ed.), *The Oxford Handbook of Sex Offences and Sex Offending* (New York: Oxford University Press).

Jenson, J. M. and Fraser, M. W. (eds) (2015), *Social Policy for Children and Families: A Risk and Resilience Perspective* (London: Sage Publications).

Jewkes, Y. (2010), 'Much Ado About Nothing? Representations and Realities of Online Soliciting of Children', *Journal of Sexual Aggression*, 16(1): 5–18.

Jewkes, Y. and Sharp, K. (2003), 'Crime, Deviance and the Disembodied Self: Transcending the Dangers of Corporeality', in Y. Jewkes (ed.), *Dot. Coms: Crime, Deviance and Identity on the Internet* (Cullompton: Willan).

John Jay College (2004), *The Nature and Scope of Sexual Abuse of Minors by Catholic Priests and Deacons in the United States, 1950–2002* (Washington, DC: United States Conference of Catholic Bishops).

(2011), *The Causes and Context of Sexual Abuse of Minors by Catholic Priests in the United States, 1950–2010, A Report Presented to the United States Conference of Catholic Bishops by the John Jay College Research Team* (Washington, DC: United States Conference of Catholic Bishops).

Johnson, J., Honnol, J. and Stevens, F.P. (2010), 'Using Social Network Analysis to Enhance Nonprofit Organizational Research Capacity: A Case Study', *Journal of Community Practice* 18(4): 493–512.

Johnson, T. C. (1988), 'Child Perpetrators – Children Who Molest Other Children: Preliminary Findings', *Child Abuse & Neglect* 12(2): 219–29.

(1989), 'Female Child Perpetrators: Children Who Molest Other Children', *Child Abuse & Neglect* 13(4): 571–85.

Johnson-George, C. and Swap, W. (1982), 'Measurement of Specific Inter-personal Trust: Construction and Validation of a Scale to Assess Trust in a Specific Other', *Journal of Personality and Social Psychology* 43(6): 1306–17.

Johnston, L. (2000), *Policing Britain: Risk, Security and Governance* (Essex: Longman Publishing).

Johnstone, A. and Dent, C. (2015), *Investigation into the Association of Jimmy Savile with Stoke Mandeville Hospital: A Report for Buckinghamshire Healthcare NHS Trust* (Amersham: Buckinghamshire Healthcare NHS Trust).

Johnstone, G. (2000), 'Penal Policy Making: Elitist, Populist or Participatory?' *Punishment and Society* 2(2): 161–80.

Jones, D. M., Pickett, J., Oates, M. R. and Barbor, P. (eds) (1987), *Understanding Child Abuse* (2d edn) (London: Macmillan Education Ltd).

Jonker, F. and Jonker-Bakker, I. (1997), 'Effects of Ritual Abuse: The Results of Three Surveys in the Netherlands', *Child Abuse & Neglect* 21(6): 541–56.

Justice, B. and Justice, R. (1979), *The Broken Taboo: Sex in the Family* (New York: Human Sciences Press).

Kahn, T. J. and Chambers, H. J. (1991), 'Assessing Reoffense Risk with Juvenile Sexual Offenders', *Child Welfare: Journal of Policy, Practice, and Program* 70(3): 333–44.

Kalisch, B. J. (1978), *Child Abuse and Neglect: An Annotated Bibliography* (Westport, CT: Greenwood).

Kan, M. L. and Cares, A. C. (2006), 'From "Friends with Benefits" to "Going Steady": New Directions in Understanding Romance and Sex in Adolescence and Emerging Adulthood', in A. C. Crouter and A. Booth (eds), *Romance and Sex in Adolescence and Emerging Adulthood: Risks and Opportunities* (Mahwah, NJ: Lawrence Elrbaum Associates).

Karaian, L. (2012), 'Lolita Speaks: "Sexting", Teenage Girls and the Law', *Crime, Media, Culture* 8(1): 57–83.

(2014), 'Policing "Sexting": Responsibilization, Respectability and Sexual Subjectivity in Child Protection/Crime Prevention Responses to Teenagers' Digital Sexual Expression', *Theoretical Criminology* 18(3): 282–99.

Karmen, A. (1983), 'Introduction: Deviance and Victimology', in D. MacNamara and A. Karmen (eds), *Deviants: Victims or Victimizers* (Beverly Hills, CA: Sage).

Kaufman, J. and Zigler, E. (1989), 'The Intergenerational Transmission of Child Abuse', in D. Cicchetti and V. Carlson (eds), *Child Maltreatment: Theory and Research on the Causes and Consequences of Child Abuse and Neglect* (New York: Cambridge University Press).

Kaufman, K. L., Hilliker, D. R., and Daleiden, E. L. (1996), 'Sub Group Differences in the Modus Operandi of Adolescent Sexual Offenders', *Child Maltreatment* 1(1): 17–24.

Kaufman, K. L., Holmberg, J. K., Orts, K. A., McCrady, F. E., Rotzien, A. L., Daleiden, E. L. and Hilliker, D. R. (1998), 'Factors Influencing Sexual Offenders' Modus Operandi: An Examination of Victim-Offender Relatedness and Age', *Child Maltreatment* 3(4): 349–61.

Keane, M., Guest, A. and Padbury, J. (2013), 'A Balancing Act: A Family Perspective to Sibling Sexual Abuse', *Child Abuse Review* 22(4): 246–54.

Keenan, M. (2011), *Child Sexual Abuse and the Catholic Church: Gender, Power and Organizational Culture* (New York: Oxford University Press).

Kelley, A. E., Schochet, T. and Landry, C. F. (2004), 'Risk Taking and Novelty Seeking in Adolescence: Introduction to Part I', *Annals of the New York Academy of Sciences* 1021(1): 27–32.

Kelly, L. (2013), *Surviving Sexual Violence* (Chichester: John Wiley & Sons).

Kelly, P. (2000), 'The Dangerousness of Youth-At-Risk: The Possibilities of Surveillance and Intervention in Uncertain Times', *Journal of Adolescence* 23(4): 463–76.

Kempe, H. (1978), 'Sexual Abuse: Another Hidden Pediatric Problem', *Pediatrics* 62(3): 382–89.

Kempe, H., Silverman, F. N., Steele, B. F., Droegemueller, W. and Silver, M. K. (1962), 'The Battered Child Syndrome', *Journal of the American Medical Association* 181(1): 17–24.

Kemshall, H. (2010), 'Risk Rationalities in Contemporary Social Work Policy and Practice', *British Journal of Social Work* 40(4): 1247–62.

Kemshall, H., Kelly, G. and Wilkinson, B. (2012), 'Child Sex Offender Public Disclosure Scheme: The View of Applicants Using the English Pilot Disclosure Scheme', *Journal of Sexual Aggression* 18(2): 164–78.

Kemshall, H. and Maguire, M. (2001), 'Public Protection, Partnership and Risk Penalty: The Multi-agency Risk Management of Sexual and Violent Offenders', *Punishment and Society* 3(2): 237–64.

Kemshall, H., Parton, N., Walsh, M. and Waterson, J. (1997), 'Concepts of Risk in Relation to the Organisational Structure and Functioning Within the Personal Social Services and Probation', *Social Policy and Administration* 31(3): 213–32.

Kennedy, M. T., Manwell, M. K. C., Mackenzie, G., Blaney, R., Chivers, A. T. and May, I. (1990), *Child Sexual Abuse in Northern Ireland: A Research Study of Incidence* (Antrim: Greystone Books).

Kernsmith, P. D., Comartin, E., Craun, S. W. and Kernsmith, R. M. (2009), 'The Relationship Between Sex Offender Registry Utilization and Awareness', *Sexual Abuse: A Journal of Research and Treatment* 21(2): 181–93.

Kierkegaard, S. (2008), 'Cybering, Online Grooming and Ageplay', *Computer Law & Security Report* 24(1): 41–45.

Kiesler, S. J., Siegel, J. and McGuire, T. W. (1984), 'Social Psychological Aspects of Computer-mediated Communications', *American Psychologist* 39 (10): 1123–34.

Kim, J., Song, H. and Jennings, W. G. (2016), 'A Distinct Form of Deviance or a Variation of Bullying? Examining the Developmental Pathways and Motives of Cyberbullying Compared with Traditional Bullying in South Korea', *Crime & Delinquency*, early on-line version, doi:0011128716675358.

Kincaid, J. R. (1998), *Erotic Innocence. The Culture of Child Molesting* (Durham, NC and London: Duke University Press).

Kirkup, B. and Marshall, P. (2014), *Jimmy Savile Investigation: Broadmoor Hospital: Report to the West London Mental Health NHS Trust and the Department of Health* (London: West London Mental Health NHS Trust).

Kirkwood, A. (1993), The Report of the Inquiry into Aspects of the Management of Children's Homes in *Leicestershire Between 1973 and 1986* (Leicester: Leicestershire County Council).

Kitzinger, J. (1988), 'Defending Innocence: Ideologies of Childhood', *Feminist Review* 28: 77–87.

1996), 'Media Representations of Sexual Abuse Risks', *Child Abuse Review* 5 (5): 319–33.

(1997), 'Who Are You Kidding? Children, Power, and the Struggle Against Sexual Abuse', in A. James and A. Prout (eds), *Constructing and*

Reconstructing Childhood: Contemporary Issues in the Sociological Study of Childhood (London: Falmer Press).

(1999a), 'The Ultimate Neighbour from Hell: Media Framing of Paedophiles', in B. Franklin (ed.), *Social Policy, the Media and Misrepresentation* (London: Routledge).

(1999b), 'Researching Risk and the Media', *Health, Risk & Society* 1(1): 55–69.

(2004), *Framing Abuse: Media Influence and Public Understandings of Sexual Violence Against Children* (New York: Pluto).

Knox, C. (2002), 'See No Evil, Hear No Evil: Insidious Paramilitary Violence in Northern Ireland', *British Journal of Criminology* 42(1): 164–85.

Kofoed, J. and Ringrose, J. (2012), 'Travelling and Sticky Affects: Exploring Teens and Sexualized Cyberbullying through a Butlerian-Deleuzian-Guattarian Lens', *Discourse* 33(1): 5–20.

Koon-Magnin, S. (2015), 'The Fine Line Between Statutory Rape and Consensual Relationships', in T. N. Richards and C. D. Marcum (eds), *Sexual Victimization: Then and Now* (Thousand Oaks, CA: Sage Publications).

Kosaraju, A. (2008), 'Grooming: The Myth and Reality of Child Sexual Exploitation', *Childright* 246: 14–17.

Kowalski, R. M. and Limber, S. P. (2007). 'Electronic Bullying Among Middle School Students', *Journal of Adolescent Health* 41(6): S22–S30.

Kowalski, R. M., Limber, S. P. and Agatson, P. W. (2012), *Cyberbullying: Bullying in the Digital Age* (Oxford: Blackwell Publishing).

Krafft-Ebing, R. von (1914), *Psychopathia Sexualis*, 14th edn (Stuttgart: Enke).

Kramer, R. M., Brewer, M. B. and Hanna B. (1996), 'Collective Trust and Collective Action: Trust as a Social Decision', in R. Kramer and T. Tyler (eds), *Trust in Organisations* (Thousand Oaks, CA: Sage Publications).

Kruttschnitt, C., Uggen, C. and Shelton, K. (2000), 'Predictors of Desistance Among Sex Offenders: The Interaction of Formal and Informal Social Controls', *Justice Quarterly* 17(1): 61–87.

Kubik, E. K., Hecker, J. E. and Righthand, S. (2003), 'Adolescent Females Who Have Sexually Offended: Comparisons with Delinquent Adolescent Female Offenders and Adolescent Males Who Sexually Offend', *Journal of Child Sexual Abuse* 11(3): 63–83.

Kutchinsky, B. (1991), 'Pornography and Rape: Theory and Practice? Evidence from Crime Data in Four Countries Where Pornography Is Easily Available', *International Journal of Law and Psychiatry* 14 (1–2): 47–64.

Kytle, B. and Ruggie, J. G. (2005), 'Corporate Social Responsibility as Risk Management: A Model for Multinationals', *Corporate Social Responsibility Working Paper Initiative Working Paper* No. 10. (Cambridge, MA: John F. Kennedy School of Government, Harvard University).

Lacombe, D. (2008), 'Consumed with Sex: The Treatment of Sex Offenders in Risk Society', *British Journal of Criminology* 48(1): 55–74.

La Fontaine, J. S. (1990), *Child Sexual Abuse* (Cambridge: Polity Press).

(1998), *Speak of the Devil: Tales of Satanic Abuse in Contemporary England* (Cambridge: Cambridge University Press).

Lagus, K. A., Bernat, D. H., Bearinger, L. H., Resnick, M. D. and Eisenberg, M. E. (2011), 'Parental Perspectives on Sources of Sex Information for Young People', *Journal of Adolescent Health* 49(1): 87–89.

Lalumière, M. L., Harris, G. T., Quinsey, V. L. and Rice, M. E. (2005), *The Causes of Rape: Understanding Individual Differences in the Male Propensity for Sexual Aggression* (Washington: American Psychological Association).

Lamb, S. (1996), *The Trouble with Blame: Victims, Perpetrators and Responsibility* (Cambridge, MA: Harvard University Press).

Lambie, I. and Johnston, E. (2016), '"I Couldn't Do It to a Kid Knowing What It Did to Me": The Narratives of Male Sexual Abuse Victims' Resiliency to Sexually Offending', *International Journal of Offender Therapy and Comparative Criminology* 60(8): 897–918.

Laming, Lord, H. (2003), *The Victoria Climbié Inquiry* (London: The Stationery Office).

(2009), *The Protection of Children in England: A Progress Report*, HC 330 (London: The Stationery Office).

Lane, S. and Lobanov-Rostovsky, C. (1997), 'Special Populations: Children, Females, the Developmentally Disabled, and Violent Youth', in G. Ryan and S. Lane (ed.), *Juvenile Sexual Offending – Causes, Consequences, and Corrections* (2d edn) (San Francisco: Jossey-Bass).

Lanning, K. V. (1992), *Child Molesters: A Behavioral Analysis* (Washington, DC: National Center for Missing and Exploited Children).

(2005), 'Compliant Child Victims: Confronting an Uncomfortable Reality', in E. Quayle and M. Taylor (eds), *Viewing Child Pornography on the Internet* (Lyme Regis: Russell House Publishing).

Lash, S., Szerszynski, B. and Wynne, B. (eds) (1996), *Risk, Environment and Modernity: Towards a New Ecology* (London: Sage Publications).

Laub, J. H., Nagin, D. S. and Sampson, R. J. (1998), 'Trajectories of Change in Criminal Offending: Good Marriages and the Desistance Process', *American Sociological Review* 63(2): 225–38.

Lavalette, M. and Cunningham, S. (2002), 'The Sociology of Childhood', in B. Goldson, M. Lavalette and J. McKecnhie (eds), *Children, Welfare and the State* (London: Sage).

Laviola, M. (1992), 'Effects of Older Brother-Younger Sister Incest: A Study of the Dynamics of 17 Cases', *Child Abuse & Neglect* 16(3): 409–21.

Law Commission of Canada (2000), *Restoring Dignity: Responding to Child Abuse in Canadian Institutions* (Ontario, Canada: Law Commission of Canada).

Law Reform Committee (2013), *Report of the Law Reform Committee for the Inquiry into Sexting*, Parliamentary Paper No. 230, Session 2010–2013 (Melbourne: Parliament of Victoria).

Lawrence, D. H. (1969), *Lady Chatterley's Lover* (Harmondsworth: Penguin Books) [originally published in Italy in 1928].

Laws, D. R. (1996), 'Relapse Prevention or Harm Reduction?' *Sexual Abuse: A Journal of Research and Treatment* 8(3): 243–47.

(2000), 'Sexual Offending as a Public Health Problem: A North American Perspective', *Journal of Sexual Aggression* 5(1): 30–44.

Laws, D. R. and Ward, T. (2011), *Desistance from Sex Offending: Alternatives to Throwing Away the Keys* (New York: Guilford Press).

Leclerc, B., Beauregard, E., and Proulx, J. (2008), 'Modus Operandi and Situational Aspects in Adolescent Sexual Offenses Against Children: A Further Examination', *International Journal of Offender Therapy and Comparative Criminology* 52(1): 46–61.

Leclerc, B. and Felson, M. (2016), 'Routine Activities Preceding Adolescent Sexual Abuse of Younger Children', *Sexual Abuse* 28(2): 116–31.

Leclerc, B., Wortley, R. and Smallbone, S. (2011), 'Getting into the Script of Adult Child Sex Offenders and Mapping Out Situational Prevention Measures', *Journal of Research in Crime and Delinquency* 48(2): 209–37.

Lee, M. and Crofts, T. (2015), 'Gender, Pressure, Coercion and Pleasure: Untangling Motivations for Sexting Between Young People', *British Journal of Criminology* 55(3): 454–73.

Lee, M., Crofts, T., Salter, M., Milivojevic, S. and McGovern, A. (2013), '"Let's Get Sexting": Risk, Power, Sex and Criminalisation in the Moral Domain', *International Journal for Crime, Justice and Social Democracy* 2 (1): 35–49.

Lee, M. and O'Brien, R. (1995), *The Game's Up: Redefining Child Prostitution* (London: The Children's Society).

Lemert, E. M. (1951), *Social Pathology: Systematic Approaches to the Study of Sociopathic Behaviour* (New York: McGraw-Hill).

L'Engle, K. L., Brown, J. D. and Kenneavy, K. (2006), 'The Mass Media Are an Important Context for Adolescents' Sexual Behavior', *Journal of Adolescent Health* 38(3): 186–92.

Lenhart, A. (2009), 'Teens and Sexting', Pew Internet & American Life Project, www.ncdsv.org/images/PewInternet_TeensAndSexting_12-2009 .pdf.

Lenhart, A., Madden, M., Smith, A., Purcell, K., Zickuhr, K. and Rainie, L. (2011), *Teens, Kindness and Cruelty on Social Network Sites: How American*

Teens Navigate the New World of 'Digital Citizenship' (Washington, DC: Pew Research Center's Internet & American Life Project).

Lerpiniere, J., Hawthorn, M., Smith, I., Connelly, G., Kendrick, A. and Welch, V. (2013), 'The Sexual Exploitation of Looked After Children in Scotland: A Scoping Study to Inform Methodology for Inspection'. Research Report RR-2013-05, www.celcis.org/media/resources/publications/Sexual-Exploitation-of-Looked-After-Children.pdf.

Letourneau, E. J., Henggeler, S. W., Borduin, C. M., Schewe, P. A., McCart, M. R., Chapman, J. E. and Saldana, L. (2009), 'Multisystemic Therapy for Juvenile Sexual Offenders: 1-year Results from a Randomized Effectiveness Trial', *Journal of Family Psychology* 23(1): 89–102.

Levenson, J. (2008), 'Collateral Consequences of Sex Offender Residence Restrictions', *Criminal Justice Studies* 21(2): 153–66.

Levenson, J. and Tewksbury, R. (2009), 'Collateral Damage: Family Members of Registered Sex Offenders', *American Journal of Criminal Justice* 34 (1–2): 54–68.

Levenson, J. S., Willis, G. M. and Prescott, D. S. (2016), 'Adverse Childhood Experiences in the Lives of Male Sex Offenders: Implications for Trauma-informed Care', *Sexual Abuse* 28(4): 340–59.

Levin, D. E. and Kilbourne, J. (2009), *So Sexy So Soon: The New Sexualized Childhood and What Parents Can do to Protect their Kids* (New York: Ballantine Books).

Levy, A. (2006), *Female Chauvinist Pigs: Women and the Rise of Raunch Culture* (New York: Simon & Schuster).

Lewis, P. and Mullis, A. (1999), 'Delayed Prosecution for Childhood Sexual Abuse', *Law Quarterly Review* 115(2): 265–95.

Li, Q., Cross, D. and Smith, P.K. (eds) (2012), *Cyberbullying in the Global Playground: Research from International Perspectives* (Chichester: Wiley-Blackwell).

Lieb, R. (2003), 'Joined-up Worrying: the Multi-Agency Public Protection Panels', in A. Matravers (ed.), *Sex Offenders in the Community: Managing and Reducing the Risks* (Cullompton, Devon: Willan Publishing, Cambridge Criminal Justice Series).

Lieb, R., Kemshall, H. and Thomas, T. (2011), 'Post-release Controls for Sex Offenders in the US and UK', *International Journal of Law and Psychiatry* 34 (3): 226–32.

Lievens, E. (2014), 'Bullying and Sexting in Social Networks: Protecting Minors from Criminal Acts or Empowering Minors to Cope with Risky Behaviour?' *International Journal of Law, Crime and Justice* 42(3): 251–70.

Livingstone, S. (2009), *Children and the Internet: Great Expectations and Challenging Realities* (Cambridge: Polity).

Livingstone, S. and Bober, M. (2004), *UK Children Go Online: Surveying the Experiences of Young People and Their Parents* (London: London School of Economics).

(2005), *Internet Literacy Among Children and Young People* (London: London School of Economics).

Local Safeguarding Children Board (LSCB) Haringey (2009), 'Serious Case Review: Baby Peter', www.haringeylscb.org/sites/haringeylscb/files/executive_summary_peter_final.pdf.

Locke, J. (1812), *Some Thoughts Concerning Education* [originally published in 1693] (Cambridge: Cambridge University Press).

Loftus, J. and Camargo, R. (1993), 'Treating the Clergy', *Annals of Sex Research* 6: 287–303.

London Borough of Lambeth (LBL) (1987), *The Report of the Panel of Inquiry into the Death of Tyra Henry* (London: London Borough of Lambeth).

Lööf, L. (2012), 'Sexual Behaviour, Adolescents and Problematic Content', in E. Quayle and K. Ribisl (eds), *Understanding and Preventing Online Sexual Exploitation of Children* (Abingdon: Routledge).

Luhmann, N. (1988), 'Family, Confidence, Trust: Problems and Alternatives', in D. Gambetta (ed.), *Trust: Making and Breaking Co-operative Relations* (Oxford: Basil Blackwell).

Lundy, L. and McEvoy, L. (2012), 'Children's Rights and Research Processes: Assisting Children to (In)formed Views', *Childhood* 19(1): 129–44.

Lussier, P. and Davies, G., (2011), 'A Person-Oriented Perspective on Sexual Offenders, Offending Trajectories, and Risk of Recidivism: A New Challenge for Policymakers, Risk Assessors, and Actuarial Prediction?' *Psychology, Public Policy, and Law* 17(4): 530–61.

Lynch, M. (2002), 'Pedophiles and Cyber-Predators as Contaminating Forces: The Language of Disgust, Pollution, and Boundary Invasions in Federal Debates on Sex Offender Legislation', *Law & Social Inquiry* 27 (3): 529–66.

Maddox, A., Barratt, M. J., Allen, M. and Lenton, S. (2016), 'Constructive Activism in the Dark Web: Cryptomarkets and Illicit Drugs in the Digital "Demimonde"', *Information, Communication & Society* 19(1): 111–26.

Madlingozi, T. (2007), 'Good Victims, Bad Victims: Apartheid's Beneficiaries, Victims and the Struggle for Social Justice', in W. Le Roux and L Van Maerle (eds), *Memory and the Legacy of Apartheid* (Pretoria: Pretoria University Press).

Maisch, H. (1973), *Incest* (London: Andre Deutsch).

Malinowski, B. (1932), *The Sexual Life of Savages in North-Western Melanesia: An Ethnographic Account of Courtship, Marriage, and Family Life Among the Natives of the Trobriand Islands, British New Guinea* (London: Routledge).

Mann, L., Harmoni, R. and Power, C. (1989), 'Adolescent Decision-Making: The Development of Competence', *Journal of Adolescence* 12(3): 265–78.

Manning, W. D., Longmore, M. A. and Giordano, P. C. (2005), 'Adolescents' Involvement in Non-Romantic Sexual Activity', *Social Science Research* 34 (2): 384–407.

Mantovani, F. (2001), 'Networked Seduction: A Test-bed for the Study of Strategic Communication on the Internet', *Cyber Psychology & Behaviour* 4 (1): 147–54.

Marron, K. (1988), *Ritual Abuse: Canada's Most Infamous Trial on Child Abuse* (Toronto: Seal Books).

Marshall, K. (2014), 'Child Sexual Exploitation in Northern Ireland: Report of the Independent Inquiry', www.cjini.org/getattachment/f094f421-6ae0-4ebd-9cd7-aec04a2cbafa/Child-Sexual-Exploitationin-Northern-Ireland.aspx.

Marshall, W. L. (2010), 'The Role of Attachments, Intimacy, and Loneliness in the Etiology and Maintenance of Sexual Offending', *Sexual and Relationship Therapy* 25(1): 73–85.

Marston, C. (2004), 'Gendered Communication Among Young People in Mexico: Implications for Sexual Health Interventions', *Social Science & Medicine* 59(3): 445–56.

Martellozzo, E. (2012), *Online Child Sexual Abuse: Grooming, Policing and Child Protection in a Multi-Media World* (London and New York: Routledge).

Martellozzo, E., Monaghan, A., Adler, J. R., Davidson, J., Leyva, R. and Horvath, M. A. (2016), '*... I Wasn't Sure It Was Normal to Watch It...*' (London: NSPCC).

Martino, S. C., Collins, R. L., Elliott, M. N., Strachman, A., Kanouse, D. E. and Berry, S. H. (2006), 'Exposure to Degrading Versus Non-degrading Music Lyrics and Sexual Behavior Among Youth', *Pediatrics* 118(2): 430–41.

Martinson, F. M. (1994), *The Sexual Life of Children* (Westport, CT: Greenwood Publishing Group).

Maruna, S., Lebel, T. P., Mitchell, N. and Naples, M. (2004), 'Pygmalion in the Reintegration Process: Desistance from Crime through the Looking Glass', *Psychology, Crime & Law* 10(3): 271–81.

Mason, J. and Urquhart, R. (2001), 'Developing a Model for Participation by Children in Research on Decision Making', *Children Australia* 26(4): 16–21.

Masson, H., Hackett, S., Phillips, J. and Balfe, M. (2015), 'Developmental Markers of Risk or Vulnerability? Young Females Who Sexually Abuse: Characteristics, Backgrounds, Behaviours and Outcomes', *Child and Family Social Work* 20(1): 19–29.

Masson, H. and Morrison, T. (1999), 'Young Sexual Abusers: Conceptual Frameworks, Issues and Imperatives', *Children and Society* 13(3): 203–15.

Matravers, A. (ed.) (2003), *Sex Offenders in the Community: Managing and Reducing the Risks* (Cullompton, Devon: Willan Publishing, Cambridge Criminal Justice Series).

Matthews, H. (2003), 'Children and Regeneration: Setting an Agenda for Community Participation and Integration', *Children & Society* 17(4): 264–76.

Matthews, J. K. (1998), 'An 11-year Perspective of Working with Female Sexual Offenders', in W. L. Marshall, T. Ward and S. M. Hudson (eds), *Sourcebook of Treatment Programs for Sexual Offenders*' (New York: Plenum Press).

Matthews, J. K., Mathews, R. and Speltz, K. (1991), 'Female Sexual Offenders. A Typology', in M. Q. Patton (ed.), *Family Sexual Abuse: Frontline Research and Evaluation* (London: Sage Publications).

Mathews, R., Hunter, J. A., and Vuz, J. (1997), 'Juvenile Female Sexual Offenders: Clinical Characteristics and Treatment Issue', *Sexual Abuse: A Journal of Research and Treatment* 9(3): 187–99.

Matthews, S. (2007), 'A Window on the "New" Sociology of Childhood', *Sociology Compass* 1(1): 322–34.

Matusov, E. and Hayes, R. (2000), 'Sociocultural Critique of Piaget and Vygotsky', *New Ideas in Psychology* 18(2): 215–39.

Mawby, R. and Walklate, S. (1994), *Critical Victimology: International Perspectives* (London: Sage Publications Ltd).

McAlinden, A.-M. (2005), 'The Use of "Shame" with Sexual Offenders', *British Journal of Criminology* 45(3): 373–94.

(2006), '"Setting 'Em Up": Personal, Familial and Institutional Grooming in the Sexual Abuse of Children', *Social & Legal Studies* 15(3): 339–62.

(2007a), *The Shaming of Sexual Offenders: Risk, Retribution and Reintegration* (Oxford: Hart Publishing).

(2007b), 'Public Attitudes Towards Sex Offenders in Northern Ireland', *Research and Statistical Bulletin 6/2007* (Belfast: Northern Ireland Office, Statistics and Research Branch).

(2010), 'Vetting Sexual Offenders: State Over-extension, the Punishment Deficit and the Failure to Manage Risk', *Social & Legal Studies* 19(1): 25–48.

(2012a), *'Grooming' and the Sexual Abuse of Children: Internet, Institutional and Familial Dimensions*, Clarendon Studies in Criminology (Oxford: Oxford University Press).

(2012b), 'The Governance of Sexual Offending Across Europe: Penal Policies, Political Economies and the Institutionalisation of Risk', *Punishment and Society* 14(2): 166–92.

(2013), 'An Inconvenient Truth: Barriers to Truth Recovery in the Aftermath of Institutional Child Abuse in Ireland', *Legal Studies* 33(2): 189–214.

(2014a), 'Deconstructing Victim and Offender Identities in Discourses on Child Sexual Abuse: Hierarchies, Blame and the Good/Evil Dialetic', *British Journal of Criminology*, 54(2): 180–98.

(2014b) 'Sexting and Cyberbullying', in R. Atksinon (ed.), *Shades of Deviance: A Primer on Crime, Deviance and Social Harm* (London and New York: Routledge).

(2015), 'Sexual Abuse Within Institutional Contexts', in A. Ackerman and R. Furman (eds), *Sexual Crimes: Transnational Crimes and Global Perspectives* (New York: Columbia University Press).

McAlinden, A. M. and Dwyer, C. (eds) (2015), *Criminal Justice in Transition: The Northern Ireland Context* (Oxford: Hart Publishing).

McAlinden, A. M., Farmer, M. and Maruna, S. (2016), 'Desistance from Sexual Offending: Do the Mainstream Theories Apply?' *Criminology and Criminal Justice* 17(3): 266–83.

McAlinden, A. M. and Naylor, B. (2016), 'Reframing Public Inquiries as "Procedural Justice" for Victims of Institutional Child Abuse: Towards a Hybrid Model of Justice', *Sydney Law Review* 38(3): 277–309.

McAra, L. (2006), 'Welfare in Crisis? Key Developments in Scottish Youth Justice', in J. Muncie and B. Goldson (eds), *Comparative Youth Justice* (London: Sage).

McCartan, F. M., Law, H., Murphy, M. and Bailey, S. (2011), 'Child and Adolescent Females Who Present with Sexually Abusive Behaviours: A 10-year UK Prevalence Study', *Journal of Sexual Aggression* 17(1): 4–14.

McCartan, K. F. (2004), '"Here There Be Monsters": The Public's Perception of Paedophiles with Particular Reference to Belfast and Leicester', *Medicine, Science and the Law* 44(4): 327–42.

(2008), 'Current Understandings of Paedophilia and the Resulting Crisis in Modern Society', in J. M. Caroll and M. K. Alena (eds), *Psychological Sexual Dysfunctions* (New York: Nova Biomedical).

(2010), 'Media Constructions and Reactions to Paedophilia in Modern Society', in K. Harrison (ed.), *Dealing with High-risk Sex offenders in the Community: Risk Management, Treatment and Social Responsibilities* (Cullompton: Willan).

McCrory, E., Hickey, N., Farmer, E. and Vizard, E. (2008), 'Early-onset Sexually Harmful Behaviour in Childhood: A Marker for Life-course Persistent Antisocial Behaviour?' *The Journal of Forensic Psychiatry & Psychology* 19(3): 382–95.

McEvoy, K. and McConnachie, K. (2012), 'Victimology in Transitional Justice: Victimhood, Innocence and Hierarchy', *European Journal of Criminology* 9(5): 527–38.

McEwan, J. (2013), 'Vulnerable Defendants and the Fairness of Trials', *Criminal Law Review* 100–113.

McGee, H., Garavan, R., de Barra, M., Byrne, J. and Conroy, R. (2002), *The SAVI Report: Sexual Abuse and Violence in Ireland* (Dublin: The Liffey Press in Association with the Dublin Rape Crisis Centre).

McGlynn, C. and Rackley, E. (2017), 'Image-Based Sexual Abuse', *Oxford Journal of Legal Studies*, online advance publication, 31 January 2017, doi: www.doi.org/10.1093/ojls/gqw033.

McGlynn, C. and Ward, I. (2014), 'Would John Stuart Mill Have Regulated Pornography?' *Journal of Law and Society*, 41(4): 500–522.

McIvor, G. (2017), 'Female Sex Offenders', in T. Sanders (ed.), *The Oxford Handbook of Sex Offences and Sex Offending* (New York: Oxford University Press).

McLaughlin, J. H. (2012), 'Exploring the First Amendment Rights of Teens in Relationships to *Sexting* and Censorship', *University of Michigan Journal of Law Reform* 45: 315–50.

McLaughlin, S. (2009), 'Online Sexual Grooming of Children and the Law', *Communications Law* 14(1): 8–19.

McManus, M. A., Long, M. L., Alison, L. and Almond, L. (2015), 'Factors Associated with Contact Child Sexual Abuse in a Sample of Indecent Image Offenders', *Journal of Sexual Aggression* 21(3): 368–84.

McNeely, C. and Blanchard, J. (2010), *The Teen Years Explained: A Guide to Healthy Adolescent Development* (Baltimore, MD: Johns Hopkins University Press).

McRobbie, A. (2004), 'Post-feminism and Popular Culture', *Feminist Media Studies* 4(3): 255–64.

(2009), *The Aftermath of Feminism: Gender, Culture and Social Change* (London: Sage).

Measor, L. (2004), 'Young People's Views of Sex Education: Gender, Information and Knowledge', *Sex Education* 4(2): 153–66.

Medlicott, R. W. (1967), 'Parent-Child Incest', *Australian and New Zealand Journal of Psychiatry* 1(4): 180–87.

Melossi, D. (2001), 'The Cultural Embeddedness of Social Control: Reflections on the Comparison of Italian and North-American Cultures Concerning Punishment', *Punishment and Society* 5(4): 403–24.

Melrose, M. (2013), 'Twenty-First Century Party People: Young People and Sexual Exploitation in the New Millennium', *Child Abuse Review* 22(3): 155–68.

Melrose, M., Barrett, D. and Brodie, I. (1999), *One Way Street: Retrospectives on Childhood Prostitution* (London: The Children's Society).

Melrose, M. and Pearce, J. (eds) (2013), *Critical Perspectives on Child Sexual Exploitation and Related Trafficking* (London: Palgrave Macmillan).

Menaker, T. A. and Miller, A. K. (2013), 'Culpability Attributions Towards Juvenile Female Prostitutes', *Child Abuse Review* 22(3): 169–81.

Mendel, M. P. (1994), *The Male Survivor: The Impact of Sexual Abuse* (Thousand Oaks, CA: Sage Publications).

Mendelsohn, B. (1956), 'Une Nouvelle Branche de La Science Bio-Psycho-Sociale: Victimologie', *Revue Internationale de Criminologie et de Police Technique*' 10: 782–89.

Menesini, E., Calussi, P. and Nocentini, A. (2012), 'Cyberbullying and Traditional Bullying', in Q. Li, D. Cross and P. K. Smith (eds) *Cyberbullying in the Global Playground: Research from International Perspectives* (Chichester: Wiley-Blackwell).

Merleau-Ponty, M. (1973), *The Prose of the World* (Evanston: Northwestern University Press).

Messerschmidt, J. W. (1993), *Masculinities and Crime: Critique and Reconceptualization of Theory* (Lanham, MD: Rowman & Littlefield Publishers).

Middleton, D., Elliott, I. A., Mandeville-Norden, R. and Beech, A. (2006), 'An Investigation into the Applicability of the Ward and Siegert Pathways Model of Child Sexual Abuse with Internet Offenders', *Psychology, Crime and Law* 12(6): 589–603.

Miers, D. (1990), 'Positivist Victimology: A Critique Part 2: Critical Victimology', *International Review of Victimology* 1(3): 219–30.

Mill, J. S. (1859), *On Liberty* (London: J. W. Parker and Son).

Miller, B. and Morris, R. G. (2016), 'Virtual Peer Effects in Social Learning Theory', *Crime & Delinquency* 62(12): 1543–69.

Miller, E. M. and Costello, C. Y. (2001), 'The Limits of Biological Determinism', *American Sociological Review* 66(4): 592–98.

Milnes, K., Turner-Moore, T., Gough, B., Denison, J., Gatere, L., Haslam, C., Videva, D., Zajesk, T. and Zoppi, I. (2015), 'Sexual Bullying in Young People Across Five European Countries'. A Research Report for the Addressing Sexual Bullying Across Europe (ASBAE) Project, www.papilot.si/f/docs/ASBAE-Daphne_III/Research_report_final.pdf.

Ministry of Justice (2013), *An Overview of Sexual Offending in England and Wales* (London: Ministry of Justice, Home Office and Office for National Statistics).

Mirkin, H. (1999), 'The Pattern of Sexual Politics: Feminism, Homosexuality and Pedophilia', *Journal of Homosexuality* 37(2): 1–24.

Mishna, F. and Alaggia, R. (2005), 'Weighing the Risks: A Child's Decision to Disclose Peer Victimization', *Children & Schools* 27(4): 217–26.

Mitchell, K. J., Finkelhor, D. and Wolak, J. (2001), 'Risk Factors for and Impact of Online Sexual Solicitation of Youth', *Journal of the American Medical Association* 285(23): 3011–14.

(2007), 'Youth Internet Users at Risk for the Most Serious Online Sexual Solicitations', *American Journal of Preventive Medicine* 32(6): 532–37.

Mitchell, K. J., Wolak, J. and Finkelhor, D. (2008), 'Are Blogs Putting Youth at Risk for Online Sexual Solicitation or Harassment?' *Child Abuse & Neglect* 32(2): 277–94.

Moghal, N. E., Nota, I. K., and Hobbs, C. J. (1995), 'A Study of Sexual Abuse in an Asian Community', *Archives of Disease in Childhood* 72(4): 346–47.

Montgomery-Devlin, J. (2008), 'The Sexual Exploitation of Children and Young People in Northern Ireland: Overview from the Barnardo's Beyond the Shadows Service', *Child Care in Practice* 14 (4): 381–400.

Moore, S. and Rosenthal, D. (2006), *Sexuality in Adolescence: Current Trends* (New York: Routledge).

Morrison, A. (2015), 'Understanding Sexual Behaviour in the Under 12s', paper presented at the NOTA Northern Ireland Seminar, 25 November 2015.

Morrison, T. and Henniker, J. (2006), *Building a Comprehensive Inter-agency Assessment and Intervention System for Young People Who Sexually Harm: The AIM Project* (London: Routledge).

Mort, F. (2000), *Dangerous Sexualities: Medico-Moral Politics in England Since 1830* (London: Taylor & Francis).

Mossberger, K., Tolbert, C. J. and McNeal, R. S. (2007), *Digital Citizenship: The Internet, Society, and Participation* (Cambridge, MA: MIT Press).

Mottier, V. (2008), *Sexuality: A Very Short Introduction* (Oxford: Oxford University Press).

Mrazek, P. B., Lynch, M. and Bentovim, A. (1981), 'A Recognition of Child Sexual Abuse in the United Kingdom', in P. B. Mrazek and C. Kempe (eds), *Sexually Abused Children and Their Families* (Oxford: Pergamon).

Muncie, J. (1984), *'The Trouble with Kids Today': Youth and Crime in Post-war Britain* (London: Hutchinson).

(2005), 'The Globalization of Crime Control: The Case of Youth and Juvenile Justice Neo-Liberalism, Policy Convergence and International Conventions', *Theoretical Criminology* 9(1): 35–64.

Muncie, J. and Goldson, B. (eds) (2006), *Comparative Youth Justice* (London: Sage).

Munro, V. E. (2017), 'Shifting Sands? Consent, Context and Vulnerability in Contemporary Sexual Offences Policy in England and Wales', *Social & Legal Studies*, 26(4): 417–40.

Murphy, F. D., Buckley, H. and Joyce, L. (2005), *The Ferns Report*, presented by the Ferns Inquiry to the Minister for Health and Children (Dublin: Government Publications).

Murphy, M. (1995), *Working Together in Child Protection: An Exploration of the Multi-Disciplinary Task and System* (Aldershot: Arena).

Myers, J. E. B. (1994), 'Definitions and Origins of the Backlash Against Child Protection', in J. E. B. Myers (ed.), *The Backlash: Child Protection Under Fire* (Newbury Park, CA: Sage).

Nagy, R. and Kaur-Sehdev, R. (2012), 'Introduction: Residential Schools and Decolonization', *Canadian Journal of Law and Society* 27(1): 67–73.

Nair, A. (2006), 'Mobile Phones and the Internet: Legal Issues in the Protection of Children', *International Review of Law and Computers* 20(1–2): 177–85.

Näsi, M., Räsänen, P., Kaakinen, M., Keipi, T. and Oksanen, A. (2017), 'Do Routine Activities Help Predict Young Adults' Online Harassment: A Multi-nation Study', *Criminology & Criminal Justice* 17(4): 418–32.

Nathan, D. and Snedeker, M. (1995), *Satan's Silence: Ritual Abuse and the Making of a Modern American Witch Hunt* (Boston: Basic Books).

Nathan, P. and Ward, T. (2002), 'Female Sex Offenders: Clinical and Demographic Features', *The Journal of Sexual Aggression* 8(1): 5–21.

National Children's Home (NCH) (1992), *The Report of the Committee of Enquiry into Children and Young People Who Sexually Abuse Other Children* (London: National Children's Home).

National Society for Prevention of Cruelty to Children (NSPCC) (2013), 'Statistics on Bullying', March 2013, www.nspcc.org.uk.

(2016), '1 in 6 of Reported to Police for Indecent Images Are Under 18', *NSPCC News*, 1 September 2016, www.nspcc.org.uk/what-we-do/news-opinion/1-6-reported-police-child-sexual-images-under-18/.

Nava, M. (1988), 'Cleveland and the Press: Outrage and Anxiety in the Reporting of Child Sexual Abuse', *Feminist Review* 28: 103–21.

Nayak, A. and Kehily, M. J. (2013), *Gender, Youth and Culture: Young Masculinities and Femininities* (Basingstoke: Palgrave Macmillan).

Newburn, T. (2012), 'Counterblast: Young People and the August 2011 Riots', *The Howard Journal of Criminal Justice*, 51(3): 331–35.

(2015), 'The 2011 England Riots in Recent Historical Perspective', *British Journal of Criminology*, 55(1): 39–64.

Newburn, T. and Stanko, E. A. (eds) (1994), *Just Boys Doing Business? Men, Masculinities and Crime* (London: Routledge).

Nisbet, I. A., Wilson, P. H. and Smallbone, S. W. (2004), 'A Prospective Longitudinal Study of Sexual Recidivism Among Adolescent Sex Offenders', *Sexual Abuse: A Journal of Research and Treatment* 16(3): 223–34.

Nixon, C. L. (2014), 'Current Perspectives: The Impact of Cyberbullying on Adolescent Health', *Adolescent Health, Medicine and Therapeutics* (5): 143–58.

Nolan, L. (2001), 'Report of the Review on Child Protection in the Catholic Church in England and Wales: A Programme for Action', www.cathcom.org/mysharedaccounts/cumberlege/finalnolan1.htm.

Norrie, A. (2014), *Crime, Reason and History: A Critical Introduction to Criminal Law* (Cambridge: Cambridge University Press).

Oakley, A. (2015), *Sex, Gender and Society* (Surrey and Burlington, VT: Ashgate Publishing, Ltd).

O'Callaghan, D. and Print, B. (1994), 'Adolescent Sexual Abusers: Research, Assessment, and Treatment', in T. Morrison, M. Erooga, and R. Beckett (eds), *Sexual Offenders Against Children: Practice, Management, and Policy* (London: Routledge).

O'Connell, R. (2001), 'Paedophiles Networking on the Internet', in C. A. Arnaldo (ed.), *Child Abuse on the Internet: Ending the Silence* (Paris: UNESCO Publishing/Berghahn Books).

(2003), 'A Typology of Child Cybersexploitation and Online Grooming Practices', www.netsafe.org.nz/Doc_Library/racheloconnell1.pdf.

O'Donnell, I. and Milner, C. (2007), *Child Pornography: Crime, Computer and Society* (Cullompton, Devon: Willan Publishing).

O'Higgins Norman, J. and McGuire, L. (2016), *Cyberbullying in Ireland: A Survey of Parents Internet Usage and Knowledge* (Dublin: Dublin City University, ABC, National Anti-Bullying Research and Resource Centre).

Okami, P. (1992), '"Child Perpetrators of Sexual Abuse": The Emergence of a Problematic Deviant Category', *Journal of Sex Research* 29(1): 109–30.

Olafson, E., Corwin, D. L. and Summit, R. C. (1993), 'Modern History of Child Sexual Abuse Awareness: Cycles of Discovery and Suppression', *Child Abuse and Neglect* 17(1): 7–24.

O'Leary, N. P. M. and Caretti, K. M. (2009), 'When Clean Kids Take Dirty Pictures: The Sexting Phenomenon and Its Impact on American Teenagers, the Criminal Justice System, and Parental Responsibility', *Children's Legal Rights Journal* 29(4): 65–81.

Olfman, S. (ed.) (2008), *The Sexualization of Childhood* (Westport, CT: Praeger Publishers).

Oliver, A. L. (1997), 'On the Nexus of Organizations and Professions: Networking through Trust', *Sociological Inquiry* 67(2): 227–45.

Olsen-Fulero, L. and Fulero, S. M. (1997), 'Commonsense Rape Judgments: An Empathy–Complexity Theory of Rape Juror Story Making', *Psychology, Public Policy, and Law* 3(2–3): 402–27.

Olweus, D. (1995), 'Bullying or Peer Abuse in School: Intervention and Prevention', in G. Davies, S. Lloyd-Bostock, M. McMurran and C. Wilson (eds), *Psychology, Law, and Criminal Justice: International Developments in Research and Practice* (Berlin: Walter de Gruyter).

O'Malley, P. (1998), *Crime and Risk* (London: Sage Publications Ltd).

(1999), 'Volatile Punishments: Contemporary Penalty and the Neo-Liberal Government', *Theoretical Criminology* 3(2): 175–96.

(2004a), *Risk, Uncertainty and Government* (London: The Glasshouse Press).

(2004b), 'The Uncertain Promise of Risk', *Australian & New Zealand Journal of Criminology* 37(3): 323–43.

(2010), *Crime and Risk* (London: Sage Publications).

O'Neill, B. and Dinh, T. (2015), 'Net Children Go Mobile: Full Findings from Ireland', www.arrow.dit.ie/cserrep/55/.

Opie, I. (1993), *The People in the Playground* (New York: Oxford University Press).

Orwell, G. (1949), *1984* (New York: Harcourt Publishing).

Ost, S. (2009), *Child Pornography and Sexual Grooming: Legal and Societal Responses* (Cambridge: Cambridge University Press).

Ost, S. and Mooney, J.-L. (2013), 'Group Localised Grooming: What Is It and What Challenges Does It Pose for Society and Law?' *Child and Family Law Quarterly* 25(4): 425–50.

Oxfordshire Safeguarding Children Board (OSCB) (2015), 'Serious Case Review into Child Sexual Exploitation in Oxfordshire: From the experiences of Children A, B, C, D, E, and F', www.oscb.org.uk/wp-content/uploads/SCR-into-CSE-in-Oxfordshire-FINAL.pdf.

Packer, H. (1969), *The Limits of the Penal Sanction* (Stanford, CA: Stanford University Press).

Paolucci, E. O., Genuis, M. L., and Violato, C. (2001), 'A Meta-analysis of the Published Research on the Effects of Child Sexual Abuse', *The Journal of Psychology* 135(1): 17–36.

Palmer, S. (2007), *Toxic Childhood: How the Modern World Is Damaging Our Children and What We Can Do About It* (London: Orion).

Palmer, S. and Pitts, J. (2006), '"Othering" the Brothers: Black Youth, Racial Solidarity and Gun Crime', *Youth and Policy* 91: 5–22.

Palmer, T. (1997), 'Young People Who Sexually Abuse', in M. Calder, S. Goulding, H. Hanks, K. Rose, J. Skinner and J. Wynne (eds), *Juveniles and Children Who Sexually Abuse. A Guide to Risk Assessment* (Lyme Regis, Dorset: Russell House Publishing).

(2001), *No Son of Mine! Children Abused Through Prostitution* (Barkingside, UK: Barnardo's).

Palmer, S. and Stacey, L. (2004), *Just One Click: Sexual Abuse of Children and Young People through the Internet and Mobile Phone Technology* (Barkingside, UK: Barnardo's).

Papadopoulos, L. (2010), 'Sexualisation of Young People Review', www.webarchive.nationalarchives.gov.uk/20100418065544/http:/homeoffice.gov.uk/documents/Sexualisation-of-young-people.html.

Parke, R. D. and Collmer, C. W. (1975), 'Child Abuse: An Inter-disciplinary Analysis', in E. M. Hetherington (ed.), *Review of Child Development Research*, Vol. 5 (Chicago: University of Chicago Press).

Parker, H., Measham, F. and Aldridge, J. (1995), *Drugs Futures: Changing Patterns of Drug Use Amongst English Youth* (London: Institute for the Study of Drug Dependence).

Parker, H., Williams, L. and Aldridge, J. (2002), 'The Normalization of "Sensible" Recreational Drug Use: Further Evidence from the North West England Longitudinal Study', *Sociology* 36(4): 941–64.

Parker, R. G., and Aggleton, P. (eds) (1999), *Culture, Society and Sexuality: A Reader* (London and Philadelphia: UCL Press).

Parsons, T. and Bales, R. F. (1955), *Family, Socialization and Interaction Process* (Glencoe, IL: Free Press).

Parton, N. (1981), 'Child Abuse, Social Anxiety and Welfare', *British Journal of Social Work* 11(1): 391–414.

(1985), *The Politics of Child Abuse* (Basingstoke: Macmillan).

(1998), 'Risk, Advanced Liberalism and Child Welfare: The Need to Rediscover Uncertainty and Ambiguity', *British Journal of Social Work* 28 (1): 5–27.

(ed.) (1997), *Child Protection and Family Support: Tensions, Contradictions and Possibilities* (Hove, East Sussex: Psychology Press).

(2004), 'From Maria Colwell to Victoria Climbié: Reflections on Public Inquiries into Child Abuse a Generation Apart', *Child Abuse Review* 13(2): 80–94.

Parton, N., Thorpe, D. and Wattam, C. (1997), *Child Protection: Risk and the Moral Order* (Hampshire: Macmillan).

Patchin, J. W. and Hinduja, S. (eds) (2012), *Cyberbullying Prevention and Response: Expert Perspectives* (Abingdon, Oxon: Routledge).

Paul, P. (2005), *Pornified: How Pornography Is Transforming Our Lives, Our Relationships, and Our Families* (New York: Henry Holy & Company).

Pearce, J. J. (2009), *Young People and Sexual Exploitation: It's Not Hidden You Just Aren't Looking* (Abingdon, Oxon: Routledge).

(2011), 'Working with Trafficked Children and Young People: Complexities in Practice', *British Journal of Social Work* 41(8): 1424–41.

(2013a), 'What's Going On to Safeguard Children and Young People from Child Sexual Exploitation: A Review of Local Safeguarding Children Boards' Work to Protect Children from Sexual Exploitation', *Child Abuse Review* 23(3): 159–70.

(2013b), 'A Social Model of "Abused Consent"', in M. Melrose and J. Pearce (eds), *Critical Perspectives on Child Sexual Exploitation and Related Trafficking* (Basingstoke: Palgrave Macmillan).

(2017), 'Commercial Sexual Exploitation of Children', in T. Sanders (ed.), *The Oxford Handbook of Sex Offences and Sex Offending* (New York: Oxford University Press).

Pearce, J. J., Hynes, P. and Bovarnick, S. (2013), *Trafficked Young People: Breaking the Wall of Silence* (London: Routledge Falmer).

Pearson, G. (1984), *Hooligan: A History of Respectable Fears* (New York: Schocken Books).

Perren, S. and Gutzwiller-Helfenfinger, E. (2012), 'Cyberbullying and Traditional Bullying in Adolescence: Differential Roles of Moral Disengagement, Moral Emotions, and Moral Values', *European Journal of Developmental Psychology* 9(2): 195–209.

Peterson, K. L. (2011), *Corporate Risk and National Security Redefined* (London and New York: Routledge).
Pfohl, S. J. (1977), 'The Discovery of Child Abuse', *Social Problems* 24(3): 310–23.
Phelan, P. (1995), 'Incest and Its Meaning: The Perspectives of Fathers and Daughters', *Child Abuse and Neglect* 19(1): 7–24.
Phippen, A. (2012), *Sexting: An Exploration of Practices, Attitudes and Influences* (London: NSPCC).
Piaget, J. (1929), *The Child's Conception of the World* (London: Routledge and Kegan Paul).
Piaget, J. and Duckworth, E. (1970), 'Genetic Epistemology', *American Behavioral Scientist* 13(3): 459–80.
Pilcher, J. (1996) 'Gillick and After: Children and Sex in the 1980s and 1990s', in J. Pilcher and S. Wagg (eds), *Thatcher's Children? Politics, Childhood and Society in the 1980s and 1990s* (London: Falmer Press).
Pithers, W. D., Gray, A., Busconi, A. and Houchens, P. (1998), 'Caregivers of Children with Sexual Behavior Problems: Psychological and Familial Functioning', *Child Abuse & Neglect* 22(2): 129–41.
Pitts, J. (2008), *Reluctant Gangsters: The Changing Face of Youth Crime* (Cullompton: Willan Publishing).
(2013), 'Drifting into Trouble: Sexual Exploitation and Gang Affiliation', in M. Melrose and J. Pearce (eds), *Critical Perspectives on Child Sexual Exploitation and Related Trafficking* (Basingstoke: Palgrave Macmillan).
Plummer, K. (1982), 'Symbolic Interactionism and Sexual Conduct: An Emergent Perspective', in M. Brake (ed.), *Human Sexual Relations: Towards a Redefinition of Sexual Politics* (New York: Pantheon Books).
(2003), 'Queers, Bodies and Postmodern Sexualities: A Note on Revisiting the "Sexual" in Symbolic Interactionism', *Qualitative Sociology* 26(4): 515–30.
Pollard, J. A., Hawkins, J. D. and Arthur, M. W. (1999), 'Risk and Protection: Are Both Necessary to Understand Diverse Behavioral Outcomes in Adolescence?' *Social Work Research* 23(3): 145–58.
Postman, N. (1994), *The Disappearance of Childhood* (New York: Vintage Books).
Potter, T. and Reeves, S. (2015), 'Sexually Harmful Behaviour', in A. Rogers, J. Harvey and H. Law (eds), *Young People in Forensic Mental Health Settings: Psychological Thinking and Practice* (Basingstoke: Palgrave, Macmillan).
Powell, A. (2007), *Paedophiles, Child Abuse and the Internet* (Oxford: Radcliffe Publishing).
(2010a), *Sex, Power and Consent: Youth Culture and the Unwritten Rules* (Cambridge: Cambridge University Press).
(2010b), 'Configuring Consent: Emerging Technologies, Unauthorized Sexual Images and Sexual Assault', *Australian & New Zealand Journal of Criminology* 43(1): 76–90.

Pratt, J. (2005), 'Child Sexual Abuse: Purity and Danger in an Age of Anxiety', *Crime Law & Social Change* 43(4): 263–87.

(2014), 'A Therapeutic Treatment Model for Sexually Abusive Behaviours in Victoria Australia: What Does Treatment Look Like?' *Sexual Abuse in Australia and New Zealand* 6(1): 20–30.

Priebe, G. and Svedin, C. G. (2008), 'Child Sexual Abuse Is Largely Hidden from the Adult Society: An Epidemiological Study of Adolescents' Disclosures', *Child Abuse & Neglect* 32(12): 1095–108.

Proctor, S., Galloway, R., Chaloner, R., Jones, C. and Thompson, D. (2014) *The Report of the Investigation into Matters relating to Savile at Leeds Teaching Hospitals NHS Trust* (Leeds: Leeds Teaching Hospitals NHS Trust).

Prout, A. and James, A. (1997), 'A New Paradigm for the Sociology of Childhood? Provenance, Promise and Problems', in A. James and A. Prout (eds), *Constructing and Reconstructing Childhood: Contemporary Issues in the Sociological Study of Childhood* (2d edn) (London: Falmer).

Pyżalski, J. (2012), 'From Cyberbullying to Electronic Aggression: Typology of the Phenomenon', *Emotional and Behavioural Difficulties* 17(3–4): 305–17.

Qi, S. J., Starfelt, L. C. and White, K. M. (2016), 'Attributions of Responsibility, Blame and Justifiability to a Perpetrator and Victim in an Acquaintance Rape Scenario: The Influence of Marijuana Intoxication', *Journal of Sexual Aggression* 22(1): 20–35.

Quayle, E. (2008), 'The COPINE Project', *Irish Probation Journal* 5(9): 65–83.

Quayle, E., Lööf, L. and Palmer, T. (2008), *Child Pornography and Sexual Exploitation of Children Online* (Bangkok: ECPAT International).

Quayle, E. and Ribsil, K. (eds) (2012), *Understanding and Preventing Online Sexual Exploitation of Children* (Abingdon: Routledge).

Quayle, E. and Taylor, M. (2001), 'Child Seduction and Self-Representation on the Internet', *CyberPsychology and Behaviour* 4(5): 597–608.

Qvortrup, J., Bardy, M., Sgritta, G. and Wintersberger, H. (1994), *Childhood Matters: Social Theory, Practice and Politics* (Aldershot: Avebury Press).

Radbill, S. X. (1968), 'A History of Child Abuse and Infanticide', in R. E. Helfer and C. H. Kempe (eds), *The Battered Child* (Chicago: University of Chicgo Press).

Radford, L., Corral, S., Bradley, C., Fisher, H., Bassett, C., Howat, N. and Collishaw, S. (2011), *Child Abuse and Neglect in the UK Today* (London: NSPCC).

Rafferty, Y. (2007), 'Children for Sale: Child Trafficking in Southeast Asia', *Child Abuse Review* 16(6): 401–22.

Ramsay, P. (2010), 'Overcriminalization as Vulnerable Citizenship', *New Criminal Law Review*, 13(2): 262–85.

Reder, P., Duncan, S. and Gray, M. (1993), *Beyond Blame: Child Abuse Tragedies Revisited* (London: Routledge).

Regan, P. C. and Baker, S. J. (1998), 'The Impact of Child Witness Demeanor on Perceived Credibility and Trial Outcome in Sexual Abuse Cases', *Journal of Family Violence* 13(2): 187–95.

Reid, J. A. (2015), 'Sexual Victimization and the Disputed Victim', in T. N. Richards and C. D. Marcum (eds), *Sexual Victimization: Then and Now* (Thousand Oaks, CA: Sage Publications).

Renold, E. and Ringrose, J. (2011), 'Schizoid Subjectivities? Re-theorizing Teen Girls' Sexual Cultures in an Era of "Sexualization"', *Journal of Sociology* 47(4): 389–409.

(2013), 'Feminisms Re-figuring "Sexualisation", Sexuality and "the Girl"', *Feminist Theory* 14(3): 247–54.

Rich, P. (2011), *Understanding, Assessing and Rehabilitating Juvenile Sexual Offenders* (2d edn) (Hoboken, NJ: John Wiley & Sons).

Richardson, D. (2000), 'Constructing Sexual Citizenship: Theorizing Sexual Rights', *Critical Social Policy* 20(1): 105–35.

Righthand, S. and Welch, C. (2001), *Juveniles Who Have Sexually Offended* (Washington, DC: Office of Juvenile Justice & Delinquency Prevention).

Rind, B., Tromovitch, P. and Bauserman, R. (1998), 'A Meta-analytic Examination of Assumed Properties of Child Sexual Abuse Using College Samples', *Psychological Bulletin* 124(1): 22–53.

Ringrose, J. and Barajas, K. E. (2011), 'Gendered Risks and Opportunities? Exploring Teen Girls' Digitized Sexual Identities in Postfeminist Media Contexts', *International Journal of Media and Cultural Politics* 7(2): 121–38.

Ringrose, J., Gill, R., Livingstone, S. and Harvey, L. (2012), 'A Qualitative Study of Children, Young People and "Sexting"'. A Report Prepared for the NSPCC, www.nspcc.org.uk/preventing-abuse/research-and-resources/qualitative-study-sexting.

Ringrose, J., Harvey, L., Gill, R. and Livingstone, S. (2013), 'Teen Girls, Sexual Double Standards and "Sexting": Gendered Value in Digital Image Exchange', *Feminist Theory* 14(3): 305–23.

Ristroph, A. (2009), 'Respect and Resistance in Punishment Theory', *California Law Review* 97(2): 601–32.

Rivers, I. and Noret, N. (2010), '"I h8 u": Findings from a Five-year Study of Text and Email Bullying', *British Educational Research Journal* 36(4): 643–71.

Robinson, G. (2002), 'Exploring Risk Management in Probation Practice: Contemporary Developments in England and Wales', *Punishment and Society* 4(1): 5–25.

Robinson, J. (2009), 'The Social Construction of Deviant Identities: The Devil Wears a Hoodie', in D. Kassem, L. Murphy and E. Taylor (eds), *Key Issues in Childhood and Youth Studies* (London and New York: Routledge).

Robinson, K. H. (2005), 'Reinforcing Hegemonic Masculinities through Sexual Harassment: Issues of Identity, Power and Popularity in Secondary Schools', *Gender and Education* 17(1): 19–37.

(2013), *Innocence, Knowledge and the Construction of Childhood: The Contradictory Nature of Sexuality and Censorship in Children's Contemporary Lives* (London and New York: Routledge).

Robinson, P. H. (1975), 'A Theory of Justification: Societal Harm as a Prerequisite for Criminal Liability', *UCLA Law Review*, 23: 266–92.

(2008), *Distributive Principles of Criminal Law: Who Should Be Punished How Much?* (New York: Oxford University Press).

Rochdale Borough Safeguarding Children Board (RBSCB) (2012), 'Review of Multi-agency Responses to the Sexual Exploitation of Children', www.cdn.basw.co.uk/upload/basw_20640-8.pdf.

(2013a), 'The Overview Report of the Serious Case Review in Respect of Young People 1,2,3,4,5 & 6', www.rbscb.org/UserFiles/Docs/YP1-6%20SCR%20RBSCB%2020.12.13.pdf.

(2013b), 'The Overview Report of the Serious Case Review in respect of Young Person 7', www.rbscb.org/UserFiles/Docs/YP%207%20SCR%20RBSCB%2020.12.13.pdf.

Rock, P. (1998), 'Murderers, Victims and "Survivors"', *British Journal of Criminology* 38(2): 185–200.

Roesch-Marsh, A. (2014), 'Risk Assessment and Secure Accommodation Decision-Making in Scotland: Taking Account of Gender?' *Child Abuse Review* 23(3): 214–26.

Romano, E. and De Luca, R. V. (2001), 'Male Sexual Abuse: A Review of Effects, Abuse Characteristics, and Links with Later Psychological Functioning', *Aggression and Violent Behavior* 6(1): 55–78.

Rose, L. (1991), *The Erosion of Childhood: Child Oppression in Britain 1860–1918* (London: Routledge).

Rose, N. (2000), 'Government and Control', *British Journal of Criminology* 40 (2): 321–39.

Rosen, I. E. (2003), *Sexual Deviation* (3d edn) (Oxford: Oxford University Press).

Rostoks, T. (2010), 'Securitization and Insecure Societies', in Ž. Ozoliņa (ed.), *Rethinking Security* (Riga: Zinātne).

Rousseau, J. J. (1762), *Émile* (London: Dent).

Rush, F. (1980), *The Best Kept Secret: Sexual Abuse of Children* (Englewood Cliffs, NJ: Prentice Hall).

Russell, D. E. (1986), *The Secret Trauma: Incest in the Lives of Girls and Women* (New York: Basic Books).

(1998), *Dangerous Relationships: Pornography, Misogyny and Rape* (London: Sage).

Ryan, G., Miyoshi, T. J., Metzner, J. L., Krugman, R. D. and Fryer, G. E. (1996), 'Trends in a National Sample of Sexually Abusive Youths', *Journal of the American Academy of Child & Adolescent Psychiatry* 35(1): 17–25.

Ryan, G., Leversee, T. F and Lane, S. (2010), *Juvenile Sexual Offending: Causes, Consequences, and Correction* (3d edn) (Chichester: John Wiley & Sons).
Sable, M. R., Danis, F., Mauzy, D. L. and Gallagher, S. K. (2006), 'Barriers to Reporting Sexual Assault for Women and Men: Perspectives of College Students', *Journal of American College Health* 55(3): 157–62.
Sahlstrom, K. J. and Jeglic, E. L. (2008), 'Factors Affecting Attitudes Toward Juvenile Sex Offenders', *Journal of Child Sexual Abuse* 17(2): 180–96.
Saleh, F. M., Grudzinskas, A. and Judge, A. (eds) (2014), *Adolescent Sexual Behavior in the Digital Age: Considerations for Clinicians, Legal Professionals, and Educators* (New York: Oxford University Press).
Salerno, J. M., Najdowski, C. J., Stevenson, M. C., Wiley, T. R., Bottoms, B. L., Vaca, R. and Pimentel, P. S. (2010), 'Psychological Mechanisms Underlying Support for Juvenile Sex Offender Registry Laws: Prototypes, Moral Outrage, and Perceived Threat', *Behavioral Sciences & the Law* 28(1): 58–83.
Salter, A. (1995), *Transforming Trauma: A Guide to Understanding and Treating Adult Survivors of Child Sexual Abuse* (Newbury Park, CA: Sage).
(2003), *Predators, Pedophiles, Rapists, and Other Sex Offenders: Who They Are, How They Operate, and How We Can Protect Ourselves and Our Children* (New York: Basic Books).
Salter, M., Crofts, T. and Lee, M. (2013), 'Beyond Criminalisation and Responsibilisation: Sexting, Gender and Young People', *Current Issues in Criminal Justice* 24(3): 301–16.
Salter, M. and Dagistanli, S. (2015), 'Cultures of Abuse: "Sex Grooming", Organised Abuse and Race in Rochdale, UK', *International Journal for Crime, Justice & Social Democracy* 4(2): 50–64.
Sampson, A. (1994), *Acts of Abuse: Sex Offenders and the Criminal Justice System* (London: Routledge).
Sanders, R. (2004), *Sibling Relationships: Theory and Issues for Practice* (Basingstoke: Palgrave Macmillan).
Sanders, S. and Spraggs, G. (1989), 'Section 28 and Education', in C. Jones and P. Mahony (eds), *Learning Our Lines: Sexuality and Social Control in Education* (London: The Women's Press).
Saraga, E. (2001), 'Dangerous Places: The Family as a Site of Crime', in J. Muncie and E. McLaughlin (eds), *The Problem of Crime* (2d edn) (London: Sage).
Sas, L. D. and Cunningham, A. H. (1995), *Tipping the Balance to Tell the Secret: The Public Discovery of Child Sexual Abuse* (London and Ontario: London Family Court Clinic).
Savell, J. (2013), *Report into Operation Ornament* (Guildford: Surrey Police).
(2015), *Report into Operation Outreach* (Guildford: Surrey Police).
Schneier, B. (2011). *Secrets and Lies: Digital Security in a Networked World* (New York: John Wiley & Sons).

Schönbucher, V., Maier, T., Mohler-Kuo, M., Schnyder, U. and Landolt, M. A. (2012), 'Disclosure of Child Sexual Abuse by Adolescents: A Qualitative In-depth Study', *Journal of Interpersonal Violence* 27(17): 3486–513.

Schott, R. M. and Søndergaard, D. M. (eds) (2014), *School Bullying: New Theories in Context*. (Cambridge: Cambridge University Press).

Schulhofer, S. J. (1974), 'Harm and Punishment: A Critique of Emphasis on the Results of Conduct in the Criminal Law', *University of Pennsylvania Law Review* 122(6): 1497–607.

Schwartz, M. D., De Keseredy, W. S., Tait, D. and Alvi, S. (2001), 'Male Peer Support and a Feminist Routing Activities Theory: Understanding Sexual Assault on the College Campus', *Justice Quarterly* 18(3): 623–49.

Schwartz, M.D. and Nogrady, C. A. (1996), 'Fraternity Membership, Rape Myths, and Sexual Aggression on a College Campus', *Violence Against Women* 2(2): 148–62.

Scott, S. (2001), *The Politics and Experience of Ritual Abuse: Beyond Disbelief* (Buckingham: Open University Press).

Scott, S., Jackson, S. and Backett-Milburn, K. (1998), 'Swings and Roundabouts: Risk Anxiety and the Everyday Worlds of Children', *Sociology* 32(4): 689–705.

Scott, S. and Skidmore, P. (2006), *Reducing the Risk: Barnardo's Support for Sexually Exploited Young People: A Two Year Evaluation* (Essex: Barnardo's).

Scraton, P. (ed.) (1997a), *'Childhood' in 'Crisis'* (London: Routledge).

(1997b), 'Whose "Childhood"? What "Crisis"?' in P. Scraton (ed.), *'Childhood' in 'Crisis'* (London: Routledge).

Seddon, T. (2008), 'Dangerous Liaisons: Personality Disorder and the Politics of Risk', *Punishment and Society* 10(3): 301–17.

Sgori, S. M., Blick, L. C. and Porter, F. S. (1982), 'A Conceptual Framework for Child Sexual Abuse', in S. M. Sgori (ed.), *Handbook of Clinical Intervention in Child Sexual Abuse* (New York: The Free Press).

Shariff, S. (2008), *Cyber-bullying: Issues and Solutions for the School, the Classroom and the Home* (London: Routledge).

(2015), *Sexting and Cyberbullying Defining the Line for Digitally Empowered Kids* (Cambridge: Cambridge University Press).

Shaw, I. and Butler, I. (1998), 'Understanding Young People and Prostitution: A Foundation for Practice?' *British Journal of Social Work* 28(2): 177–96.

Shaw, T. (2007), *Historical Abuse Systemic Review: Residential Schools and Children's Homes in Scotland 1950–1995* (Edinburgh: The Scottish Government).

Sheldon, K. and Howitt, D. (2007), *Sex Offenders and the Internet* (Chichester: Wiley).

Shiner, M. and Newburn, T. (1997), 'Definitely, Maybe Not? The Normalisation of Recreational Drug Use Amongst Young People', *Sociology* 31(3): 511–29.

(1999), 'Taking Tea with Noel: The Place and Meaning of Drug Use in Everyday life', in N. South (ed.), *Drugs: Cultures, Controls and Everyday Life* (London: Sage Publications).

Shoor, M., Speed, M. H. and Bartelt, C. (1965), 'Syndrome of the Adolescent Child Molester', *American Journal of Psychiatry* 122(7): 738–89.

Short, J., Williams, E. and Christie, B. (1976), *The Social Psychology of Telecommunications* (Chichester: Wiley).

Shoveller, J. A. and Johnson, J. L. (2006), 'Risky Groups, Risky Behaviour, and Risky Persons: Dominating Discourses on Youth Sexual Health', *Critical Public Health* 16(1): 47–60.

Shoveller, J. A., Johnson, J. L., Langille, D. B. and Mitchell, T. (2004), 'Socio-cultural Influences on Young People's Sexual Development', *Social Science & Medicine* 59(3): 473–87.

Shuker, L. (2013), 'Constructs of Safety for Children in Care Affected by Sexual Exploitation', in M. Melrose and J. Pearce (eds), *Critical Perspectives on Child Sexual Exploitation and Related Trafficking* (Basingstoke: Palgrave Macmillan).

Shute, S. (2004), 'The Sexual Offences Act 2003: (4) New Civil Preventative Orders – Sexual Offences Prevention Orders; Foreign Travel Orders; Risk of Sexual Harm Orders', *Criminal Law Review* 417–40.

Sidebotham, P. (2013), 'Culpability, Vulnerability, Agency and Potential: Exploring Our Attitudes to Victims and Perpetrators of Abuse', *Child Abuse Review* 22(3): 151–54.

Silver, H. (1977), 'Ideology and the Factory Child: Attitudes to Half-Time Education', in P. McCann (ed.), *Popular Education and Socialization in the Nineteenth Century* (London: Methuen).

Silverman, J. and Wilson, D. (2002), *Innocence Betrayed: Paedophilia, the Media and Society* (Cambridge: Polity Press).

Simon, J. (1998), 'Managing the Monstrous: Sex Offenders and the New Penology', *Psychology, Public Policy and Law* 4(1–2): 452–67.

Simon, W. and Gagnon, J. H. (2003), 'Sexual Scripts: Origins, Influences and Changes', *Qualitative Sociology* 26(4): 491–97.

Simpson, A. E. (1988), 'Vulnerability and the Age of Female Consent: Legal Innovation and Its Effect on Prosecutions for Rape in Eighteenth-Century London', in G. S. Rousseau and R. Porter (eds), *Sexual Underworlds of the Enlightment* (Chapel Hill: University of North Carolina Press).

Simpson, B. (2013), 'Challenging Childhood, Challenging Children: Children's Rights and Sexting', *Sexualities* 16(5–6): 690–709.

Sinozich, S. and Langton, L. (2014), *Rape and Sexual Assault Victimization Among College-age Females, 1995–2013*. Report NCJ248471 (Washington, DC: US Department of Justice. Bureau of Justice Statistics).

Sköld, J. and Swain, S. (eds) (2015), *Apologies and the Legacy of Abuse of Children 'In Care': International Perspectives* (Basingstoke and New York: Palgrave Macmillan).

Skuse, D. H. (1985), 'Non-organic Failure to Thrive: A Re-appraisal', *Archives of Disease in Childhood* 60(2): 173–78.

Skuse, D., Bentovim, A., Hodges, J., Stevenson, J., Andreou, C., Lanyado, M., New, M., Williams, B. and McMillan, D. (1998), 'Risk Factors for Development of Sexually Abusive Behaviour in Sexually Victimised Adolescent Boys: Cross Sectional Study', *British Medical Journal* 317(7152): 175–79.

Slovic, P. (2000), 'Informing and Educating the Public About Risk', in P. Slovic (ed.), *The Perception of Risk* (London and Sterling, VA: Earthscan Publications).

Smallbone, S., Marshall, W. L. and Wortley, R. (2008), *Preventing Child Sexual Abuse: Evidence, Policy and Practice* (Cullompton, Devon: Willan Publishing).

Smallbone, S. W. and Wortley, R. K. (2000), *Child Sexual Abuse in Queensland: Offender Characteristics and Modus Operandi* (Brisbane: Queensland Crime Commission).

Smart, C. (1999), 'A History of Ambivalence and Conflict in the Discursive Construction of the "Child Victim" of Sexual Abuse', *Social & Legal Studies* 8(3): 391–409.

Smith, J. (2016), *The Independent Review into the BBC's Culture and Practices During the Jimmy Savile and Stuart Hall Years* (London: British Broadcasting Corporation (BBC)).

Smith, P. K., Del Barrio, C. and Tokunaga, R. S. (2013), 'Definitions of Bullying and Cyberbullying: How Useful Are the Terms?' in S. Bauman, D. Cross and J. Walker (eds), *Principles of Cyberbullying Research* (New York and Abinngdon Oxon: Routledge).

Smith, P. K. and Steffgen, G. (2013) (eds), *Cyberbullying Through the New Media: Findings from an International Network* (East Sussex and New York: Psychology Press).

Soothill, K. (2005), 'Strongly Suspected of Serious Sex Crime and Future Danger', *Journal of Forensic Psychiatry & Psychology* 16(2): 221–24.

Soothill, K., Francis, B., Sanderson, B. and Ackerley, E. (2000), 'Sex Offenders: Specialists, Generalists – or Both? A 32-year Criminological Study', *British Journal of Criminology* 40(1): 56–67.

Soothill, K., Harman, J., Francis, B. and Kirby, S. (2005), 'What Is the Future Repeat Danger from Sexual Offenders Against Children? Implications for Policing', *The Police Journal* 78(1): 37–45.

Soothill, K. and Walby, S. (1991), *Sex Crimes in the News* (London: Routledge).

Sorenson, T. and Snow, B. (1991), 'How Children Tell: The Process of Disclosure in Child Sexual Abuse', *Child Welfare* 70(1): 3–15.

Sparks, R. (2001), 'Degrees of Estrangement: The Cultural Theory of Risk and Comparative Penology', *Theoretical Criminology* 5(2): 159–76.

Spears, B., Costabile, A., Brighi, A., De Rey, R., Pörhölä, M., Sánchez, V., Speil, C. and Thompson, F. (2013), 'Positive Uses of New Technologies in Relationships in Educational Settings', in P. K. Smith and G. Steffgen (eds), *Cyberbullying Through the New Media: Findings from an International Network* (East Sussex and New York: Psychology Press).

Spencer, D. (2009), 'Sex Offender as Homo Sacer', *Punishment and Society* 11(2): 219–40.

Sperry, D. M. and Gilbert, B. O. (2005), 'Child Peer Sexual Abuse: Preliminary Data on Outcomes and Disclosure Experiences', *Child Abuse & Neglect* 29(8): 889–904.

Sproull, L. and Kiesler, S. (1986), 'Reducing Social Context Cues: Electronic Mail in Organizational Communication', *Management Science* 32(11): 1492–512.

Stainton Rogers, R. and Stainton Rogers, W. (1992), *Stories of Childhood: Shifting Agendas of Child Concern* (Toronto: University of Toronto Press).

Staksrud, E. (2013), *Children in the On-line World: Risk, Regulation, Rights* (Surrey: Ashgate).

Stanford, S. N. (2011), 'Constructing Moral Responses to Risk: A Framework for Hopeful Social Work Practice', *British Journal of Social Work* 41(8): 1514–31.

Stanko, E. (1985), *Intimate Intrusion: Women's Experience of Male Violence* (London: Routledge and Kegan Paul).

Stanko, E. A. and Lee, R. (2003), 'Introduction: Methodology Reflections', in R. Lee and E. Stanko (eds), *Researching Violence: Essays on Methodology and Measurement* (London: Routledge).

Steedman, C. (1995), *Strange Dislocations: Childhood and the Idea of Human Interiority, 1780–1930* (Cambridge, MA: Harvard University Press).

Steinberg, L. (1987), 'Single Parents, Stepparents, and the Susceptibility of Adolescents to Antisocial Peer Pressure', *Child Development* 58(1): 269–75.

(2007), 'Risk Taking in Adolescence: New Perspectives from Brain and Behavioral Science', *Current Directions in Psychological Science* 16(2): 55–59.

Stewart, M. W., Dobbin, S. A. and Gatowski, S. I. (1996), '"Real Rapes" and "Real Victims": The Shared Reliance on Common Cultural Definitions of Rape', *Feminist Legal Studies* 4(2): 159–77.

Stone, L. (1974), 'The Massacre of the Innocents', *New York Review of Books*, 14 November: 25–31.

Strasburger, V. C. (2005), 'Adolescents, Sex, and the Media: Ooooo, Baby, Baby – a Q & A', *Adolescent Medicine Clinics* 16(2): 269–88.

(2012), 'Adolescents, Sex, and the Media', *Adolescent Medicine – State of the Art Reviews* 23(1): 15–33.

Strasburger, V. C., Jordan, A. B. and Donnerstein, E. (2010), 'Health Effects of Media on Children and Adolescents', *Pediatrics* 125(4): 756–67.

Straus, M. A. (1974), 'Forward', in R. J. Gelles (ed.), *The Violent Home: A Study of Physical Violence Between Husbands and Wives* (Beverly Hills, CA: Sage Publications).

Strydom, P. (2002), *Risk, Environment, and Society: Ongoing Debates, Current Issues, and Future Prospects* (Buckingham: Open University Press).

Student Consent Research Collaboration (SCORE) (2017), 'Stand Together Report', http://nexusni.org/archives/3304.

Sullivan, J. and Beech, A. (2002), 'Professional Perpetrators', *Child Abuse Review* 11(3): 153–67.

(2004), 'A Comparative Study of Demographic Data Relating to Intra- and Extra-familial Child Sexual Abusers and Professional Perpetrators', *Journal of Sexual Aggression* 10(1): 39–50.

Sullivan, J., Beech, A. R., Craig, L. A. and Gannon, T. A. (2011), 'Comparing Intra-familial and Extra-familial Child Sexual Abusers with Professionals Who Have Sexually Abused Children With Whom They Work', *International Journal of Offender Therapy and Comparative Criminology* 55(1): 56–74.

Summit, R. C. (1988), 'Hidden Victims, Hidden Pain: Societal Avoidance of Child Sexual Abuse', in G. E. Wyatt and G.R. Powell (eds), *Lasting Effects of Child Sexual Abuse* (Thousand Oaks, CA: Sage Publications).

Sun, C., Bridges, A., Johnson, J. A. and Ezzell, M. B. (2016), 'Pornography and the Male Sexual Script: An Analysis of Consumption and Sexual Relations', *Archives of Sexual Behavior* 45(4): 983–94.

Sun, S., Yoke, H., Hian, C., Shobha, V. and Iccha, B. (2013), 'Managing Peer Relationships Online – Investigating the Use of Facebook by Juvenile Delinquents and Youths-At-Risk', *Computers in Human Behaviour* 29(1): 8–15.

Surette, R. (2015), 'Performance Crime and Justice', *Current Issues in Criminal Justice* 27(2): 195.

Sutherland, E. (2016), 'Raising the Minimum Age of Criminal Responsibility in Scotland: Law Reform at Last?' *Northern Ireland Legal Quarterly* 67(3): 387–406.

Swedish Agency for Youth and Civil Society (2009), 'Young People, Sex and the Internet', translate.google.co.uk/translate?hl=en&sl=sv&u=https://www.mucf.se/publikationer/se-mig&prev=search.

Tait, S. (2008), 'Pornographies of Violence? Internet Spectatorship on Body Horror', *Critical Studies in Media Communication* 25(1): 91–111.

Tardieu, A. (1867), Étude Médico-légale sur les attentats aux moeurs (Paris: J. B. Ballière).

Tate, T. (1990), *Child Pornography: An Investigation* (London: Methuen Publishing Ltd).

Taylor, J. F. (2003), 'Children and Young People Accused of Child Sexual Abuse: A Study Within a Community', *Journal of Sexual Aggression* 9(1): 57–70.

Taylor, M., Holland, G. and Quayle, E. (2001), 'Typology of Paedophile Picture Collections', *The Police Journal*, 74(2): 97–107.

Taylor, M. and Quayle, E. (2003), *Child Pornography: An Internet Crime* (Brighton: Routledge).

Taylor, T. L. (2009), *Play Between Worlds: Exploring Online Game Culture* (Cambridge, MA: MIT Press).

Taylor, Y., Hines, S. and Casey, M. (eds) (2010), *Theorizing Intersectionality and Sexuality* (Basingstoke: Palgrave Macmillan).

Temkin, J. and Krahé, B. (2008), *Sexual Assault and the Justice Gap: A Question of Attitude* (Oxford: Hart Publishing).

Templeton, M., Lohan, M., Kelly, C. and Lundy, L. (2016), 'A Systematic Review and Qualitative Synthesis of Adolescents' Views of Sexual Readiness', *Journal of Advanced Nursing*, early online version, DOI:10.1111/jan.13207.

Tewksbury, R. (2005), 'Collateral Consequences of Sex Offender Registration', *Journal of Contemporary Criminal Justice* 21(1): 67–81.

(2007), 'Effects of Sexual Assaults on Men: Physical, Mental, and Sexual Consequences', *International Journal of Men's Health* 6(1): 22–35.

Tewksbury, R. and Lees, M. (2006), 'Perceptions of Sex Offender Registration: Collateral Consequences and Community Experiences', *Sociological Spectrum* 26(3): 309–34.

Tewksbury, R. and Levenson, J. (2009), 'Stress Experiences of Family Members of Registered Sex Offenders', *Behavioral Sciences & the Law* 27(4): 611–26.

Thakker, J. (2012), 'Public Attitudes to Sex offenders in New Zealand', *Journal of Sexual Aggression* 18(2): 149–63.

Thomas, A. G. and Cauffman, E. (2014), 'Youth Sexting as Child Pornography? Developmental Science Supports Less Harsh Sanctions for Juvenile Sexters', *New Criminal Law Review* 17(4): 631–51.

Thomas, N. (2007), 'Towards a Theory of Children's Participation', *International Journal of Children's Rights* 15(2): 199–218.

Thompson, S. (2014), 'Sexting Prosecutions: Minors as a Protected Class from Child Pornography Charges', *University of Michigan Journal of Law Reform Caveat* 48(1): 11–19.

Thorne, B. (2002), 'From Silence to Voice: Bringing Children More Fully into Knowledge', *Childhood* 9(3): 251–54.

Thorne, B. L. and Luria, Z. (1986), 'Sexuality and Gender in Children's Daily Worlds', *Social Problems* 33(3): 176–90.

Thornton, D. (2003), 'The Machiavellian Sex Offender', in A. Matravers (ed.), *Sex Offenders in the Community: Managing and Reducing the Risks* (Cullompton, Devon: Willan Publishing, Cambridge Criminal Justice Series).

Tidefors, I., Arvidsson, H., Ingevaldson, S. and Larsson, M. (2010), 'Sibling Incest: A Literature Review and a Clinical Study', *Journal of Sexual Aggression* 16(3): 347–60.

Tilly, C. (2008), *Credit and Blame* (Princeton, NJ: Princeton University Press).

Tokunaga, R. S. (2010), 'Following You Home from School: A Critical Review and Synthesis of Research on Cyberbullying Victimization', *Computers in Human Behavior* 26(3): 277–87.

Tolman, D. L. and Diamond, L. M. (2001), 'Desegregating Sexuality Research: Cultural and Biological Perspectives on Gender and Desire', *Annual Review of Sex Research* 12(1): 33–74.

Tomaszewska, P. and Krahé, B. (2016), 'Attitudes Towards Sexual Coercion by Polish High Students: Links with Risky Sexual Scripts, Pornography Use, and Religiosity', *Journal of Sexual Aggression* 22(3): 291–307.

Turgoose, D. (2016), 'Coercive Control and On-line Space: 21st Century Technology, Social Media and the Hyper Regulation of the Everyday Routines of Women and Children', paper presented at the Coercion and Control in the Commission of Domestic Violence and Abuse Conference, De Monfort University Leicester, 11 November.

Turner, J. W. C. (ed.) (1952), *Kenny's Outlines of Criminal Law* (Cambridge: Cambridge University Press).

Tuzin, D. (1995), 'Discourse, Intercourse, and the Excluded Middle: Anthropology and the Problem of Sexual Experience', in P. R. Abrahmson and S. D. Pinkerton (eds), *Sexual Nature, Sexual Culture* (Chicago: University of Chicago Press).

Twill, S. E., Green, D. M., and Traylor, A. (2010), 'A Descriptive Study on Sexually Exploited Children in Residential Treatment', *Child & Youth Care Forum* 39(3): 187–99.

Twohig, M. P., Crosby, J. M. and Cox, J. M. (2009), 'Viewing Internet Pornography: For Whom Is It Problematic, How, and Why?' *Sexual Addiction & Compulsivity* 16(4): 253–66.

Tyson, D., Dobson, A., & Rasmussen, M. L. (2012), '"Sexting" Teens: Decriminalising Young People's Sexual Practices', *The Conversation*, 28 September.

Ungar, M. (2008), 'Resilience Across Cultures', *British Journal of Social Work* 38(2): 218–35.

Ungar, S. (2001), 'Moral Panic Versus the Risk Society: The Implications of the Changing Sites of Social Anxiety', *British Journal of Sociology* 52(2): 271–92.

Utting, W. (1997), *People Like Us: The Report of the Review of the Safeguards for Children Living Away From Home* (London: HMSO).

Vagg, J. (1998), 'Delinquency and Shame: Data from Hong Kong', *British Journal of Criminology* 38(2): 247–64.

Valentine, G. (1996), 'Angel and Devils: Moral Landscapes of Childhood', *Environment and Planning D: Society and Space* 14(5): 581–99.

Valentine, L. and Feinauer, L. L. (1993), 'Resilience Factors Associated with Female Survivors of Childhood Sexual Abuse', *American Journal of Family Therapy* 21(3): 216–24.

Valier, C. (2005), *Memorial Laws: Victims, Law and Justice* (London: Cavendish).

Valkenburg, P. M., Schouten, A. P. and Peter, J. (2005), 'Adolescents' Identity Experiments on the Internet', *New Media & Society* 7(3): 383–402.

Van Dam, C. (2001), *Identifying Child Abusers: Preventing Child Sexual Abuse by Recognizing the Patterns of Offenders* (New York: The Haworth Press).

Van den Burg, C., Biljeveld, C. and Hendriks, J. (2017), 'The Juvenile Sex Offender: Criminal Careers and Recidivism Risk', in T. Sanders (ed.), *The Oxford Handbook of Sex Offences and Sex Offenders* (New York: Oxford University Press).

Vanderburgh, R. (2009), 'Appropriate Therapeutic Care for Families with Pre-pubescent Transgender/Gender-Dissonant Children', *Child and Adolescent Social Work Journal* 26(2): 135–54.

Vandiver, D. M., Dial, K. C. and Worley, R. M. (2008), 'A Qualitative Assessment of Registered Female Sex Offenders Judicial Processing Experiences and Perceived Effects of a Public Registry', *Criminal Justice Review* 33(2): 177–98.

Vandiver, D. and Kercher, G. (2004), 'Offender and Victim Characteristics of Registered Female Sexual offenders in Texas: A Proposed Typology of Female Sexual Offenders', *Sexual Abuse: A Journal of Research and Treatment* 16(2): 121–37.

Vandiver, D. M. and Walker, J. T. (2002), 'Female Sex Offenders: An Overview and Analysis of 40 Cases', *Criminal Justice Review* 27(2): 284–300.

Vann, R. T. (1982), 'The Youth of Centuries of Childhood', *History and Theory* 21(2): 279–97.

Van Ness, D. W. and Strong, K. H. (2014), *Restoring Justice: An Introduction to Restorative Justice* (5th edn) (London: Routledge).

Van Vugt, E., Lancôt, N. and Lemieux, A. (2016), 'Can Institutionalized Adolescent Females with a Substantiated History of Sexual Abuse Benefit from Cognitive Behavioral Treatment Targeting Disruptive and Delinquent Behaviors?' *Criminal Justice and Behavior* 43(7): 937–50.

Vares, T., Jackson, S. and Gill, R. (2011), 'Preteen Girls Read "tween" Popular Culture: Diversity, Complexity and Contradiction', *International Journal of Media & Cultural Politics* 7(2): 139–54.

Veneziano, C. and Veneziano, L. (2002), 'Adolescent Sex Offenders: A Review of the Literature', *Trauma, Violence & Abuse* 3(4): 247–60.

Veneziano, C., Veneziano, L. and LeGrand, S. (2000), 'The Relationship Between Adolescent Sex Offender Behaviors and Victim Characteristics with Prior Victimization', *Journal of Interpersonal Violence* 15(4): 363–74.

Vizard, E., Hickey, N., French, L., and McCrory, E. (2007), 'Children and Adolescents Who Present with Sexually Abusive Behaviour: A UK Descriptive Study', *Journal of Forensic Psychology and Psychiatry*, 18(1): 59–73.

Vize, C. and Klinck, B. (2015), *Legacy Report – Further Investigation into the Association of Jimmy Savile with Stoke Mandeville Hospital: A Report for*

Buckinghamshire Healthcare NHS Trust (Amersham: Buckinghamshire Healthcare NHS Trust).
Völlink, T., Dehue, F. and Mc Guckin, C. (eds) (2016), *Cyberbullying: From Theory to Intervention*. Current Issues in Social Psychology Series (London and New York: Routledge).
Von Hentig, H. (1948), *The Criminal and His Victim* (New Haven, CT: Yale University Press).
Vygotsky, L. S. (1962), 'The Genetic Roots of Thought and Speech', in L. S. Vygotsky, E. L. Hanfmann, and G Vakar (eds), *Thought and Language: Studies in Communication* (Cambridge, MA: MIT Press).
(2004), 'Imagination and Creativity in Childhood', *Journal of Russian & East European Psychology* 42(1): 7–97.
Waddington, P. A. J. (1986), 'Mugging as a Moral Panic: A Question of Proportion', *British Journal of Sociology* 37(2): 245–59.
Waites, M. (2005), *The Age of Consent: Young People, Sexuality and Citizenship* (Basingstoke and New York: Palgrave Macmillan).
Walkerdine, V. (2000), 'Violent Boys and Precocious Girls: Regulating Childhood at the End of the Millennium', *Contemporary Issues in Early Childhood* 1(1): 3–23.
Walklate, S. (2007), *Imagining the Victim of Crime* (New York: McGraw-Hill).
Walkowitz, J. R. (1980), *Prostitution and Victorian Society: Women, Class and the State* (Cambridge: Cambridge University Press).
Waller, W. (1937), 'The Rating and Dating Complex', *American Sociological Review* 2(5): 727–34.
Wallerstein, S. (2009), '"A Drunken Consent Is Still Consent" – Or Is It? A Critical Analysis of the Law on a Drunken Consent to Sex Following Bree', *The Journal of Criminal Law* 73(4): 318–44.
Walling, W. H. (ed.) (1909), *Sexology* (Philadelphia: Puritan).
Walrath, C., Ybarra, M. and Holden, E. W. (2003), 'Children with Reported Histories of Sexual Abuse: Utilizing Multiple Perspectives to Understand Clinical and Psychosocial Profiles', *Child Abuse & Neglect* 27(5): 509–24.
Walsh, W., Wolak, J. and Finkelhor, D. (2013), *Sexting: When Are State Prosecutors Deciding to Prosecute? The Third National Juvenile Online Victimization Study (NJOV-3)* (Durham: University of New Hampshire, Crimes Against Children Research Center).
Walters, M. A. (2013), 'Why the Rochdale Gang Should Have Been Sentenced as "Hate Crime" Offenders', *Criminal Law Review* 131–44.
Walvin, J. (1982), *A Child's World: A Social History of English Childhood, 1800–1914* (Harmondsworth: Penguin Books).
Ward, T., Hudson, S. M. and Marshall, W. L. (1996), 'Attachment Style in Sex Offenders: A Preliminary Study', *Journal of Sex Research* 33(1): 17–26.
Wardle, C. (2007), 'Monsters and Angels: Visual Press Coverage of Child Murders in the USA and the UK, 1930–2000', *Journalism* 8(3): 263–84.
Warner, N. (1992), *Choosing With Care* (London: HMSO).

Warren, G. (2008), 'Interactive Online Services, Social Networking Sites and the Protection of Children', *Entertainment Law Review* 19(7): 165–68.

Waterhouse, R. (2000), *Lost In Care* (London: HMSO).

Watkins, B. and Bentovim, A. (1992), 'The Sexual Abuse of Male Children and Adolescents: A Review of Current Research', *Journal of Child Psychology and Psychiatry* 33(1): 197–48.

Wattam, C., Parton, N. and Thorpe, D. H. (1997), *Child Protection: Risk and the Moral Order* (Bastingstoke: Macmillan).

Webb, S. A. (2006), *Social Work in a Risk Society: Social and Political Perspectives* (Houndsmills: Palgrave Macmillan).

Webster, R. (1998), *The Great Children's Home Panic* (Oxford: Orwell Press).

Webster, S., Davidson, J., Bifulco, A., Gottschalk, P., Caretti, V., Pham, T., Grove-Hills, J., Turley, C., Tompkins, C., Ciulla, S., Milazzo, V., Schimmenti, A. and Craparo, G. (2012), 'European Online Grooming Project: Final Report', www.europeanonlinegroomingproject.com/media/2076/european-online-grooming-project-final-report.pdf.

Wells, M. and Mitchell, K. J. (2007), 'Youth Sexual Exploitation on the Internet: DSM-IV Diagnoses and Gender Differences in Co-occurring Mental Health Issues', *Child and Adolescent Social Work Journal* 24(3): 235–60.

West, C. M., Williams, L. M. and Siegel, J. A. (2000), 'Adult Sexual Revictimization Among Black Women Sexually Abused in Childhood: A Prospective Examination of Serious Consequences of Abuse', *Child Maltreatment* 5(1): 49–57.

West, C. and Zimmerman, D. H. (1987), 'Doing Gender', *Gender and Society* 1 (2): 125–51.

Whaley, R. B., Hayes-Smith, J. and Hayes-Smith, R. (2013), 'Gendered Pathways? Gender, Mediating Factors, and the Gap in Boys' and Girls' Substance Use', *Crime & Delinquency* 59(5), 651–59.

Whaley, R. B., Hayes, R. and Smith, J. M. (2016), 'Differential Reactions to School Bonds, Peers, and Victimization in the Case of Adolescent Substance Use: The Moderating Effect of Sex', *Crime & Delinquency* 62(10): 1263–85.

Wharton, J. (2017), *Something for the Weekend: Life in the Chemsex Underworld* (London: Biteback Publishing).

Wheeler, R. (2006), 'Gillick or Fraser? A Plea for Consistency over Competence in Children', *British Medical Journal* 332(7545): 807.

Whitty, M. T. and Joinson, A. N. (2009), *Truth, Lies and Trust on the Internet* (Hove and New York: Routledge).

Wiehe, V. R. (1997), *Sibling Abuse: Hidden Physical, Emotional, and Sexual Trauma* (2d edn) (Thousand Oaks, CA: Sage Publications).

Wilcox, D. T., Richards, F. and O'Keeffe, Z. C. (2004), 'Resilience and Risk Factors Associated with Experiencing Childhood Sexual Abuse', *Child Abuse Review* 13(5): 338–52.

Williams, G. L. (1957), *The Sanctity of Life and the Criminal Law* (New York: Knopf).

Williams, M. L. and Hudson, K. (2013), 'Public Perceptions of Internet, Familial and Localised Sexual Grooming: Predicting Perceived Prevalence and Safety', *Journal of Sexual Aggression* 19(2): 218–35.

Willis, G. M., Levenson, J. S. and Ward, T. (2010), 'Desistance and Attitudes Towards Sex Offenders: Facilitation or Hindrance?' *Journal of Family Violence* 25 (6): 545–56.

Wilson, A. (1980), 'The Infancy of the History of Childhood: An Appraisal of Philippe Ariès', *History and Theory* 19(2): 132–53.

Wilson, D. (2009), *A History of British Serial Killing* (London: Sphere).

Wilson, W. (1999), 'Doctrinal Rationality After *Woolin*', *The Modern Law Review* 62(3): 448–63.

Wolak, J. and Finkelhor, D. (2011), *Sexting: A Typology* (Durham: University of New Hampshire, Crimes Against Children Research Center).

Wolak, J., Finkelhor, D. and Mitchell, K. J. (2004), 'Internet-initiated Sex Crimes Against Minors: Implications for Prevention Based on Findings from a National Study', *Journal of Adolescent Health* 35(5): 424–33.

Wolfe, S. E., Marcum, C. D., Higgins, G. E. and Ricketts, M. L. (2016), 'Routine Cell Phone Activity and Exposure to Sext Messages Extending the Generality of Routine Activity Theory and Exploring the Etiology of a Risky Teenage Behavior', *Crime & Delinquency* 62(5): 614–44.

Wolfram, S. (1983), 'Eugenics and the Punishment of Incest Act 1908', *Criminal Law Review* 508–18.

Worling, J. R. (2001), 'Psychopathic Traits in Adolescent Sex Offenders: An Evaluation of Criminal History, Clinical and Psychological Correlates', *Sexual Abuse: A Journal of Research and Treatment* 13(3): 149–66.

Worling, J. R. and Långström, N. (2008), 'Risk of Sexual Recidivism in Adolescents Who Offend Sexually', in H. E. Barbaree and W. L. Marshall (eds), *The Juvenile Sex Offender* (New York: Guilford Press).

Wortley, R. and Smallbone, S. (eds) (2006), *Situational Prevention of Child Sexual Abuse*, Crime Prevention Studies, Vol. 19 (Monsey, NY: Criminal Justice Press, and Cullompton, Devon: Willan Publishing).

Wyatt, G. E. and Peters, S. D. (1986), 'Issues in the Definition of Child Sexual Abuse in Prevalence Research', *Child Abuse and Neglect* 10(2): 231–40.

Wykes, M. (2017), 'Social Media, Cyberspace and Sex Crime: Deviant and Democratizing Spaces', in T. Sanders (ed.), *The Oxford Handbook of Sex Offences and Sex Offending* (New York: Oxford University Press).

Wyre, R. (2000), 'Paedophile Characteristics and Patterns of Behaviour', in C. Itzin (ed.), *Home Truths About Sexual Abuse Influencing Policy and Practice: A Reader* (London: Routledge).

Wyre, R. and Tate, T. (1995), *The Murder of Childhood: Inside the Mind of One of Britain's Most Notorious Child Killers* (Harmondsworth: Penguin).

Yar, M. (2012), 'Crime, Media, and the Will-To-Representation: Reconsidering Relationships in the Social Media Age', *Crime Media Culture* 8(3): 245–60.

Yates, P., Allardyce, S. and MacQueen, S. (2012), 'Children Who Display Harmful Sexual Behaviour: Assessing the Risks of Boys Abusing at Home, in the Community or Across Both Settings', *Journal of Sexual Aggression* 18(1): 23–35.

Yoder, J. and Ruch, D. (2016), 'A Qualitative Investigation of Treatment Components for Families of Youth Who Have Sexually Offended', *Journal of Sexual Aggression* 22(2): 192–205.

Young, J. (2009), 'Moral Panic: Its Origins in Resistance, Ressentiment and the Translation of Fantasy into Reality', *British Journal of Criminology* 49(1): 4–16.

Young, T. and Hallsworth, S. (2011), 'Young People, Gangs and Street-Based Violence', in C. Barter and D. Berridge (eds), *Children Behaving Badly?: Peer Violence Between Children and Young People* (Chichester: John Wiley & Sons Ltd).

Zedner, L. (2002), 'Victims', in M. Maguire, R. Morgan and R. Reiner (eds), *The Oxford Handbook of Criminology* (3d edn) (Oxford: Oxford University Press).

(2005), 'Securing Liberty in the Face of Terror: Reflections from Criminal Justice', *Journal of Law and Society* 32(4): 507–33.

(2007), 'Pre-crime and Post-criminology?' *Theoretical Criminology* 11(2): 261–21.

(2009), 'Fixing the Future? The Pre-emptive Turn in Criminal Justice', in B. McSherry, A. Norrie and S. Bronitt (eds), *Regulating Deviance: The Redirection of Criminalisation and the Futures of Criminal Law* (Oxford: Hart Publishing).

Zehr, H. (2015), *The Little Book of Restorative Justice* (Revised and updated) (New York: Skyhorse Publishing, Inc.).

Zelizer, V. (1994), *Pricing the Priceless Child: The Changing Social Value of Children* (Princeton, NJ: Princeton University Press).

Zhang, S. X. (1995), 'Measuring Shame in an Ethnic Context', *British Journal of Criminology* 35(2): 248–62.

INDEX

CAMBRIDGE STUDIES IN LAW AND SOCIETY

Books in the Series

Diseases of the Will: Alcohol and the Dilemmas of Freedom
Mariana Valverde

The Politics of Truth and Reconciliation in South Africa: Legitimizing the Post-Apartheid State
Richard A. Wilson

Modernism and the Grounds of Law
Peter Fitzpatrick

Unemployment and Government: Genealogies of the Social
William Walters

Autonomy and Ethnicity: Negotiating Competing Claims in Multi-Ethnic States
Yash Ghai

Constituting Democracy: Law, Globalism and South Africa's Political Reconstruction
Heinz Klug

The Ritual of Rights in Japan: Law, Society, and Health Policy
Eric A. Feldman

Governing Morals: A Social History of Moral Regulation
Alan Hunt

The Colonies of Law: Colonialism, Zionism and Law in Early Mandate Palestine
Ronen Shamir

Law and Nature
David Delaney

Social Citizenship and Workfare in the United States and Western Europe: The Paradox of Inclusion
Joel F. Handler

Law, Anthropology, and the Constitution of the Social: Making Persons and Things
Edited by Alain Pottage and Martha Mundy

Judicial Review and Bureaucratic Impact: International and Interdisciplinary Perspectives
Edited by Marc Hertogh and Simon Halliday

Immigrants at the Margins: Law, Race, and Exclusion in Southern Europe

Kitty Calavita

Lawyers and Regulation: The Politics of the Administrative Process
Patrick Schmidt

Law and Globalization from Below: Toward a Cosmopolitan Legality
Edited by Boaventura de Sousa Santos and Cesar A. Rodriguez-Garavito

Public Accountability: Designs, Dilemmas and Experiences
Edited by Michael W. Dowdle

Law, Violence and Sovereignty Among West Bank Palestinians
Tobias Kelly

Legal Reform and Administrative Detention Powers in China
Sarah Biddulph

The Practice of Human Rights: Tracking Law Between the Global and the Local
Edited by Mark Goodale and Sally Engle Merry

Judges Beyond Politics in Democracy and Dictatorship: Lessons from Chile
Lisa Hilbink

Paths to International Justice: Social and Legal Perspectives
Edited by Marie-Bénédicte Dembour and Tobias Kelly

Law and Society in Vietnam: The Transition from Socialism in Comparative Perspective
Mark Sidel

Constitutionalizing Economic Globalization: Investment Rules and Democracy's Promise
David Schneiderman

The New World Trade Organization Knowledge Agreements: 2nd Edition
Christopher Arup

Justice and Reconciliation in Post-Apartheid South Africa
Edited by François du Bois and Antje du Bois-Pedain

Militarization and Violence Against Women in Conflict Zones in the Middle East: A Palestinian Case-Study
Nadera Shalhoub-Kevorkian

Child Pornography and Sexual Grooming: Legal and Societal Responses
Suzanne Ost

Darfur and the Crime of Genocide

John Hagan and Wenona Rymond-Richmond

Fictions of Justice: The International Criminal Court and the Challenge of Legal Pluralism in Sub-Saharan Africa
Kamari Maxine Clarke

Conducting Law and Society Research: Reflections on Methods and Practices
Simon Halliday and Patrick Schmidt

Planted Flags: Trees, Land, and Law in Israel/Palestine
Irus Braverman

Culture Under Cross-Examination: International Justice and the Special Court for Sierra Leone
Tim Kelsall

Cultures of Legality: Judicialization and Political Activism in Latin America
Javier Couso, Alexandra Huneeus, and Rachel Sieder

Courting Democracy in Bosnia and Herzegovina: The Hague Tribunal's Impact in a Postwar State
Lara J. Nettelfield

The Gacaca Courts, Post-Genocide Justice and Reconciliation in Rwanda: Justice Without Lawyers
Phil Clark

Law, Society, and History: Themes in the Legal Sociology and Legal History of Lawrence M. Friedman
Edited by Robert W. Gordon and Morton J. Horwitz

After Abu Ghraib: Exploring Human Rights in America and the Middle East
Shadi Mokhtari

Adjudication in Religious Family Laws: Cultural Accommodation, Legal Pluralism, and Gender Equality in India
Gopika Solanki

Water on Tap: Rights and Regulation in the Transnational Governance of Urban Water Services
Bronwen Morgan

Elements of Moral Cognition: Rawls' Linguistic Analogy and the Cognitive Science of Moral and Legal Judgment
John Mikhail

Mitigation and Aggravation at Sentencing
Edited by Julian V. Roberts

Institutional Inequality and the Mobilization of the Family and Medical Leave Act: Rights on Leave
Catherine R. Albiston

Authoritarian Rule of Law: Legislation, Discourse and Legitimacy in Singapore
Jothie Rajah

Law and Development and the Global Discourses of Legal Transfers
Edited by John Gillespie and Pip Nicholson

Law Against the State: Ethnographic Forays into Law's Transformations
Edited by Julia Eckert, Brian Donahoe, Christian Strümpell and Zerrin Özlem Biner

Transnational Legal Ordering and State Change
Edited by Gregory C. Shaffer

Legal Mobilization Under Authoritarianism: The Case of Post-Colonial Hong Kong
Waikeung Tam

Complementarity in the Line of Fire: The Catalysing Effect of the International Criminal Court in Uganda and Sudan
Sarah M. H. Nouwen

Political and Legal Transformations of an Indonesian Polity: The Nagari from Colonisation to Decentralisation
Franz von Benda-Beckmann and Keebet von Benda-Beckmann

Pakistan's Experience with Formal Law: An Alien Justice
Osama Siddique

Human Rights Under State-Enforced Religious Family Laws in Israel, Egypt, and India
Yüksel Sezgin

Why Prison?
Edited by David Scott

Law's Fragile State: Colonial, Authoritarian, and Humanitarian Legacies in Sudan
Mark Fathi Massoud

Rights for Others: The Slow Home-Coming of Human Rights in the Netherlands
Barbara Oomen

European States and Their Muslim Citizens: The Impact of Institutions on Perceptions and Boundaries

Edited by John R. Bowen, Christophe Bertossi, Jan Willem Duyvendak, and Mona Lena Krook

Environmental Litigation in China: A Study in Political Ambivalence
Rachel E. Stern

Indigeneity and Legal Pluralism in India: Claims, Histories, Meanings
Pooja Parmar

Paper Tiger: Law, Bureaucracy and the Developmental State in Himalayan India
Nayanika Mathur

Religion, Law and Society
Russell Sandberg

The Experiences of Face Veil Wearers in Europe and the Law
Edited by Eva Brems

The Contentious History of the International Bill of Human Rights
Christopher N. J. Roberts

Transnational Legal Orders
Edited by Terence C. Halliday and Gregory Shaffer

Lost in China? Law, Culture and Society in Post-1997 Hong Kong
Carol A. G. Jones

Security Theology, Surveillance and the Politics of Fear
Nadera Shalhoub-Kevorkian

Opposing the Rule of Law: How Myanmar's Courts Make Law and Order
Nick Cheesman

The Ironies of Colonial Governance: Law, Custom and Justice in Colonial India
James Jaffe

The Clinic and the Court: Law, Medicine and Anthropology
Edited by Ian Harper, Tobias Kelly, and Akshay Khanna

A World of Indicators: The Making of Government Knowledge through Quantification
Edited by Richard Rottenburg, Sally Engle Merry, Sung-Joon Park, and Johanna Mugler

Contesting Immigration Policy in Court: Legal Activism and Its Radiating Effects in the United States and France
Leila Kawar

The Quiet Power of Indicators: Measuring Governance, Corruption, and Rule of Law
Edited by Sally Engle Merry, Kevin Davis, and Benedict Kingsbury

Investing in Authoritarian Rule: Punishment and Patronage in Rwanda's Gacaca Courts for Genocide Crimes
Anuradha Chakravarty

Contractual Knowledge: One Hundred Years of Legal Experimentation in Global Markets
Edited by Grégoire Mallard and Jérôme Sgard

Iraq and the Crimes of Aggressive War: The Legal Cynicism of Criminal Militarism
John Hagan, Joshua Kaiser, and Anna Hanson

Culture in the Domains of Law
Edited by René Provost

China and Islam: The Prophet, the Party, and Law
Matthew S. Erie

Diversity in Practice: Race, Gender, and Class in Legal and Professional Careers
Edited by Spencer Headworth and Robert Nelson

A Sociology of Constitutions: Constitutions and State Legitimacy in Historical-Sociological Perspective
Chris Thornhill

A Sociology of Transnational Constitutions: Social Foundations of the Post-National Legal Structure
Chris Thornhill

Shifting Legal Visions: Judicial Change and Human Rights Trials in Latin America
Ezequiel A. González Ocantos

The Demographic Transformations of Citizenship
Heli Askola

Criminal Defense in China: The Politics of Lawyers at Work
Sida Liu and Terence C. Halliday

Contesting Economic and Social Rights in Ireland: Constitution, State and Society, 1848–2016
Thomas Murray

Buried in the Heart: Women, Complex Victimhood and the War in Northern Uganda
Erin Baines

Palaces of Hope: The Anthropology of Global Organizations
Edited by Ronald Niezen and Maria Sapignoli

The Politics of Bureaucratic Corruption in Post-Transitional Eastern Europe
Marina Zaloznaya

Revisiting the Law and Governance of Trafficking, Forced Labor and Modern Slavery
Edited by Prabha Kotiswaran

Incitement on Trial: Prosecuting International Speech Crimes
Richard Ashby Wilson

Criminalizing Children: Welfare and the State in Australia
David McCallum

Global Lawmakers: International Organizations in the Crafting of World Markets
Susan Block-Lieb and Terence C. Halliday

Duties to Care: Dementia, Relationality and Law
Rosie Harding

Insiders, Outsiders, Injuries, and Law: Revisiting 'The Oven Bird's Song'
Edited by Mary Nell Trautner

Hunting Justice: Displacement, Law, and Activism in the Kalahari
Maria Sapignoli

Injury and Injustice: The Cultural Politics of Harm and Redress
Edited by Anne Bloom, David M. Engel, and Michael McCann

Ruling Before the Law: The Politics of Legal Regimes in China and Indonesia
William Hurst

The Powers of Law: A Comparative Analysis of Sociopolitical Legal Studies
Mauricio García-Villegas

A Sociology of Justice in Russia
Edited by Marina Kurkchiyan and Agnieszka Kubal

Constituting Religion: Islam, Liberal Rights, and the Malaysian State
Tamir Moustafa

The Invention of the Passport: Surveillance, Citizenship and the State, Second Edition
John C. Torpey

Law's Trials: The Performance of Legal Institutions in the US 'War on Terror'
Richard L. Abel

Law's Wars: The Fate of the Rule of Law in the US 'War on Terror'
Richard L. Abel

Transforming Gender Citizenship: The Irresistible Rise of Gender Quotas in Europe
Edited by Eléonore Lépinard and Ruth Rubio-Marín

Muslim Women's Quest for Justice: Gender, Law and Activism in India
Mengia Hong Tschalaer

Children as 'Risk': Sexual Exploitation and Abuse by Children and Young People
Anne-Marie McAlinden